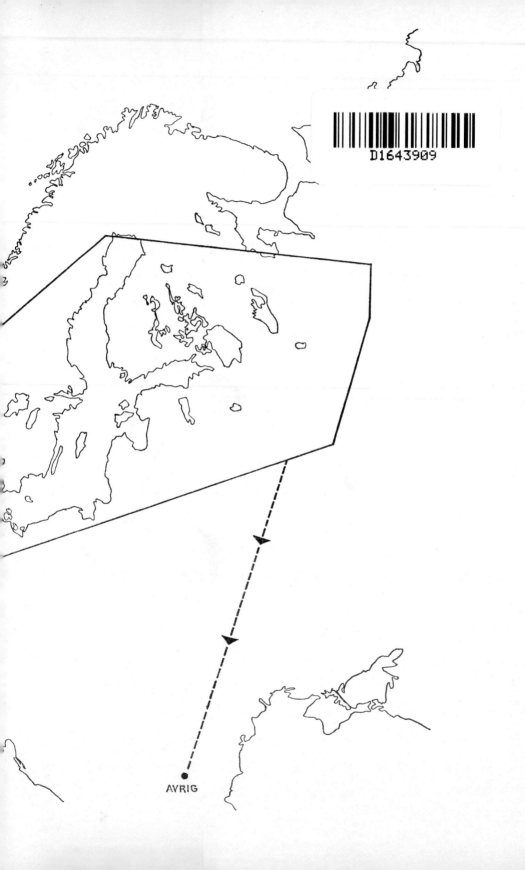

AVRIG

THE NEW WILDFOWLER
IN THE 1970's

Pinkfeet   (From a painting by Peter Sco

THE NEW WILDFOWLER

IN THE 1970's

Edited by
NOEL M. SEDGWICK, PETER WHITAKER
and
JEFFERY HARRISON

Foreword by
H.R.H. THE PRINCE PHILIP, Duke of Edinburgh, K.G., K.T.

Introduction by
THE RT. HON. THE EARL OF MANSFIELD

Preface by
PETER SCOTT, C.B.E.

BARRIE & JENKINS
LONDON
published under the auspices of
THE WILDFOWLERS' ASSOCIATION OF GREAT BRITAIN AND IRELAND

"The New Wildfowler"
First Published by Herbert Jenkins Ltd., 1961
Reprinted 1963
New edition revised and reset as
"The New Wildfowler in the 1970s"
Published by Barrie & Jenkins Ltd.
2 Clement's Inn, London W.C.2

© *The Wildfowlers' Association of Great Britain and Ireland 1970*

ISBN 0.257.65227.2

Printed in Great Britain by
Cox & Wyman Ltd., London, Fakenham and Reading

BUCKINGHAM PALACE.

I am delighted to know that the splendid book "The New Wildfowler" is to be followed by "The New Wildfowler in the 1970's" as one of WAGBI's contributions to European Conservation Year 1970. It contains virtually everything there is to be said about wildfowling in the present day, and together with the Introduction by Lord Mansfield and the Preface by Peter Scott there is very little I can add. Except perhaps this. The book is primarily about wildfowling but it is also about conservation and as such I hope it will be read by people who are interested in conservation but who are not necessarily wildfowlers.

The pressure on all forms of wildlife is so intense that the only hope is for all groups interested in any aspect of the conservation of wildlife and wild places to act in concert. Population, reclamation and pollution, whether intentional through herbicides and insecticides, or unintentional are together creating a situation where wild populations can no longer exist. It is much too late for any group to say "We're all right Jack", none of them are "all right Jack" and the more we all work and plan together to stop the rot the more likely we are to succeed.

Make no mistake, the pressure to squeeze the last drop of production from the last square inch of land is very great indeed. The demand for more and more water for industrial and domestic use is more likely to grow than to ease off. In the end everything will be justified for the short term aims of more food production and more water. This pressure is going to be very hard to resist. It is going to take courage to argue against more food production, it is going to be very unpopular to put forward alternative proposals for the supply of water at greater costs, but these things have got to be done if we are to insure that these islands continue to be worth living in.

For hundreds of generations the natural and man-made beauties of these islands have produced a love and affection unequalled anywhere else in the world, we cannot allow them to be destroyed under any pretext.

1970.

Philip

INTRODUCTION

by The Earl of Mansfield BA., F.Z.S. F.Z.S., (Scot.), M.B.O.U., J.P.

President, Wildfowlers' Association of Great Britain and Ireland; Trustee, The Wildfowl Trust; Member, Secretary of State for Scotland's Wild Bird Advisory Committee; Past President, British Trust for Ornithology.

WHEN, in 1960, I wrote the Foreword for *The New Wildfowler* I said that if, five years before, anyone had suggested that a new book on wildfowling would be published under the auspices of the Wildfowlers' Association, with a preface by the Director of the Wildfowl Trust and with contributions from the Director General of the Nature Conservancy and the Secretary of the Royal Society for the Protection of Birds, he would have been laughed to scorn and might well have been advised to have his head examined.

Publication of the book in 1961 provided an excellent example of the spirit of tolerance and compromise so often found in this country and, more important still, it was a promising augury for the future of wildfowl in Great Britain. Of course, we still have, as always, the "lunatic fringe" at each end—on the one hand the selfish gunner (I will not dignify him with the honoured name of wildfowler) who cares for nothing except his own bag, and who in getting it is prepared to sacrifice both the interests of all other fowlers and of the wildfowl themselves. At the other end we still have the anti-blood-sport fanatic and the "dear little dickie-bird" sentimentalist; but as long as we have this spirit of friendship and co-operation among all those who are seriously interested in geese and duck from the joint angles of sport and of natural history, we and the wildfowl ought to be able to look forward to a future much more rosy than we had good cause to fear would be the case in the middle 1950s.

Never before had such a full and comprehensive work on every aspect of wildfowling been presented to the public, nor had the increasingly important aspects of conservation been brought into one book on wildfowl and wildfowling.

That the first edition was so successful as to create a demand sufficient for it to go out of print a year ago is an indication that the sportsman and the naturalist, as well as the general public, really wanted to see and understand what might be termed the full wildfowl picture. Where, previously, conservation had been found worthy of mention, it had often been for the purpose of encouraging the reader to obtain the largest possible bags for shooting.

This new volume has enabled the editors to range more widely over what has certainly become a field of endeavour which our European friends now regard as something they themselves must establish and emulate in the future.

There is much in wildfowling which is unchanging. The gundog, for example, happily remains a gundog, and the wildfowler, despite all the modern aids, still needs to overcome the elements, to study and understand the habits of his quarry and, in the end, to develop the art of placing himself within range of the fowl at a time he hopes they will be moving from somewhere he thinks they are to somewhere he expects them to go.

At the same time there is much that has changed. The responsible wild-fowler has come to realize that he can no longer shoot at will or take more than can reasonably be taken from the harvestable surplus. He has discovered what, of course, many already realized, that there is far greater satisfaction in shooting if he is better informed on all matters concerning his quarry and is able to contribute in practical terms to its conservation.

It is for this reason that I again recommend to all those who have made or will make the opportunity of taking advantage of them, those sections of this book which deal with the setting up of local reserves, the rearing, ringing and release on to unshot waters of the sporting species of wild duck and geese, and the development wherever possible of improved or new wildfowl habitat, which is often much easier than is usually thought.

Whether a piece of secluded water, large or small, is shot two or three times a season or not, its value as a resting-place and as a sanctuary at all other times must be considerable. Any piece of water, however small, down to even a tenth of an acre, is of value if it offers shelter and quiet to wildfowl whether by day or by night. Throughout the country there are countless properties, farms, and pieces of land, large and small, which if taken in hand could provide such facilities often at very little cost, by damming, excavation, the use of explosives—often even just by removing overhanging trees or surplus vegetation.

Nine years ago in these pages I expressed the hope that *The New Wildfowler* would have the circulation it deserved among both wildfowlers and naturalists and that it would become, in the years ahead, the "bible" of all who were interested in both the shooting and the preservation of our wildfowl heritage. The first edition achieved everything I had hoped for it. Now, with the new volume brought up to date and extended, I would add my belief that, since we in Britain have now brought about the ideal in enlightened long-term thinking on matters concerning wildfowl, there will be a steady broadening of knowledge and an increase of constructive work as a result of the thought, effort and, indeed, dedication which has made this book a reality.

PREFACE

by Peter Scott, C.B.E., D.S.C., LLD.

Hon. Director, The Wildfowl Trust; Chairman, British Section World Wildlife Fund; Chairman, The Wildfowl Conservation Committee, Nature Conservancy; Chairman, Survival Service Commission, International Union for the Conservation of Nature.

IT was raining hard and blowing from the south-east as we topped the sea-wall in the darkness. A lark was lit momentarily by the torch as it jumped from the rough grass of the bank. We struck out across the salting along the old summer track of the samphire gatherers, and ahead of us twinkled the distant lights on the fairway buoys. It was going to be a wild morning for the goose flight and our hopes were high.

Ten minutes later it was time to douse the torch and to listen. The falling tide must have left the geese among the crab-grass at the salting's edge, and we did not want to walk into them. But the fresh wind into which the geese must fly, and which we hoped would keep them low, blew away all sounds in front of us.

The blackness of the overcast sky had turned to dark grey, and low above the horizon was a break in the clouds, but the rain still cut into our faces if we turned that way to look. Suddenly a goose called. The sound was half-heard, but it was away to our left. If the tide had floated the geese in to the west of us, during the night, then the flight inland would pass to the west of us. The call was repeated; and again. Certainly there were pinkfeet a quarter of a mile to our left. We moved across, jumping two narrow creeks, so as to place ourselves sixty yards apart in their expected line of flight, and we crouched progressively lower among the scanty cover as the day began to break.

Six mallard tore past us downwind on their way out from the potato fields. A single curlew flew along the marsh and almost spluttered its alarm whistle when it saw me. From time to time the geese called in front of us as we waited in the wholly delightful excitement of anticipation. There must surely be two thousand geese to come this morning, fighting their way against the wind only ten yards high; it was the chance we had been waiting for, the day of days. A dozen geese would be ours—no less. They were late moving this morning; on some mornings the flight would have been in full swing by now.

The rain had eased off by this time and the wind was not quite so strong. The patch of clear sky had grown into a wide, yellow crescent of light. Against it away on our right I could see a great skein of geese followed by another and another, their line of flight passing a mile to the east of us. A moment later I saw the geese in front of us rise up, two hundred strong. They headed in a gradually spreading skein towards us at first, so that I gripped my gun and crouched lower into my creek. This was going to be it. But then I saw the great birds were sliding away to the right on the wind. The very end of the skein passed only just out of shot, and joined the stream still pouring into their feeding grounds across the clear yellow of the eastern sky. The geese had beaten us again.

It is forty years since that morning flight and the geese no longer go to that particular marsh in any numbers, but I remember it especially because on that morning I first learned that enjoyment in wildfowling bore no relation at all to the bag. The anticipation had made it one of my best wildfowling memories, and the dozen geese were there for another day.

As an adventurous and exacting pursuit, the wildfowling that can still be enjoyed in Britain is worth some effort to retain. It remains for the most part a truly wild affair when practised on tidal waters at dawn or dusk or under the moon; and it should not be confused with the inferior kinds of shooting which are so often labelled with the same name. Wildfowling proper implies lying in wait at flight time in some remote place, on flood or reedy marsh or salting, or creeping among the mudflats of an estuary in a gunning-punt. But it does not in my view include the artificialities of a baited flight pool, nor the extensive use of decoys, both of which provide dull shooting, and often an excessive bag. Such practices, I hope, will soon fall into disfavour among shooting men; but so long as the wild places remain and there are abundant wildfowl to inhabit them, true wildfowling will continue to play a significant part in the sporting life of our country.

Yet these things are gravely threatened. The rapid growth of human population, the progressive drainage of marshland, the spread of industry, and the means and leisure for people to travel widely—all these are factors bearing heavily on the interests of wildfowl, not only in Britain, but through-out the European flyway. In the face of such pressures the continued existence of adequate stocks can no longer be taken for granted. If we want to have wildfowl in the future, now is the time for all those who are interested to band together and ensure that it shall be so. In such a campaign the wildfowler has strong allies among the bird-watchers, the photographers, the painters, and even the less specialized nature lovers, all of whom would like to see more rather than less duck.

The basic problem, from which all others stem, is not so much the shortage of duck, but the growing scarcity of habitat. In the old days, if a place was too much disturbed the birds may have been able to move elsewhere for a while, but there are fewer and fewer places for them to move to, and much greater care must be taken of those that remain. At the same time there is already scarcely enough room for everyone to go wildfowling just whenever and wherever he pleases. Many areas which could hold wildfowl have been so greatly disturbed that they now hold next to none; in the expressive American phrase they are "burnt out". Often the disturbance is caused by ignorant and thoughtless people, who know little of true wildfowling.

As a start, therefore, let us try to make sure that everyone who wants to shoot wildfowl really has the interests of his sport at heart. Already most genuine wildfowlers have realized that the privilege of free shooting on the foreshore is too precious a right to squander on hooligans who cannot be bothered to learn the manners and customs of their sport. People who do not know what they are shooting at, nor what is the effective range of their weapons, should not be allowed to endanger this ancient heritage (or, for that matter, their neighbours at flight time). With this book there is no longer any excuse for ignorance; the standards have been set and wildfowling must (and with the aid of WAGBI quite easily can) keep its house in order.

Secondly, let us husband every available acre of habitat and be sure that it is used to the best advantage. If we can increase the capacity of our country-side to accommodate breeding duck in summer, and migratory duck in winter, it will at least help to compensate for the places irrevocably lost to development. The key to the problem lies, of course, in food supplies; provided that these are adequate, even quite small roosts, so long as they are free from disturbance, will suffice for many thousands of birds. Research into the food of wildfowl is thus of paramount importance as a prelude to habitat improvement. Already WAGBI and The Wildfowl Trust have co-operated in the groundwork of discovering the food preferences of individual species; this has led on to the experimental planting of some of the more valuable foods; and eventually will open up a whole new field of marsh management.

In the meantime, however, there is still the urgent need to stop, wherever possible, the present wastage of prime habitat. In a hundred years much more than half the country's marshes and wildfowl have gone; yet even now there can be few places in Britain where one has to travel more than a dozen miles to find a duck, or more than fifty to see a wild goose, and this is surely as it should be. It would be small comfort to a Londoner to be told that the only remaining geese were in Scotland, or to an Aberdonian that he must go to Cheshire to see a pintail. Our task must, therefore, be to maintain our stocks of wildfowl not only in their present strength, but in their present distribution, as close to our doorsteps as possible. One way of achieving this, and I am sure the best, is to have a network of refuges at key-points throughout the country. The strongholds would then carry the nucleus of the local population, and the other resorts would carry the overflow. Any such plan must, of course, be based on a detailed knowledge of conditions in every part of the country, and to this end The Wildfowl Trust has undertaken a full survey of wildfowl and wildfowl habitat in Great Britain. Once again the help and advice of WAGBI have been sought and freely given at every stage.

With this agreed statement to work upon, WAGBI, The Nature Conservancy, and The Wildfowl Trust have come together to plan constructively for the future; and let us be clear about it, the main object of these refuges is to increase the stocks, thereby improving the wildfowler's sport rather than curtailing it. As a natural resource wildfowl should be regarded as a legitimate crop, and wildfowling is the traditional way of harvesting it. We must only be sure that the harvest is there to gather.

The first publication of this extremely comprehensive and authoritative book marked the beginning of a new era of mutual confidence and respect between WAGBI and the Wildfowl Trust. The chapters that follow show

how close the link now is, and how dependent we are, one upon the other. So long as these bonds of friendship and common interest remain, the future of wildfowl and wildfowling is, I believe, assured; and with the same excitement of anticipation on a windswept morning long hence our grandchildren will be able to watch the wild geese coming in from the shore.

Slimbridge.

EDITORS' NOTE TO THE NEW WILDFOWLER

WILDFOWLING did not begin with *The New Wildfowler*. The new wildfowler himself has evolved slowly and at times painfully over the past decade in the face of changing conditions and increased opposition to his sport. The bitter controversies aroused over the introduction of the *Wild Birds Protection Act 1954* are now a thing of the past, but in those days no one could even have expected such a book as this to appear in 1961, with representatives from all sides in those days contributing—and, furthermore, contributing free, for all royalties are to go to WAGBI.

We hope that we have produced the most comprehensive book on wildfowling in all its aspects that has ever been achieved in this country. Certainly this is the first time that the fields of conservation and research have been covered so widely. Possibly some might wish to criticize the book on account of its size, but we have felt that if we were to produce a book at all, then that book must be truly comprehensive, so that the wildfowler should have all his information between two covers.

It now remains our very pleasant task to thank most sincerely our many contributors who have so willingly and ably helped us and made our task of editing so pleasant and exciting. We have drawn our contributors from a wide circle and we are indeed honoured to have the President of the Wildfowlers' Association of Great Britain and Ireland, the Director-General of Nature Conservancy, the Director of the Wildfowl Trust, the Secretary of the Royal Society for the Protection of Birds and the Professor of Conservation at Cornell University contributing to our book, which also includes chapters by scientists, a game-keeper, a dog trainer, a housewife and not a few wildfowlers. That is as it should be and we are deeply grateful to them all.

EDITORS' NOTE TO THE NEW WILDFOWLER IN THE 1970's

WE live in a rapidly changing world. On the day of the last Editorial meeting before the publication of *The New Wildfowler*, 12th April, 1961, Yuri Gagarin made one orbit of the earth, the first man in outer space. Today, as these notes are being drafted, the Americans have just made the second manned landing on the moon.

While we salute these achievements, they should remind us that the more mundane task of ensuring a future for wildfowl and wildfowling becomes more and more complex and pressing. The romantic days of the "lone wolf" wildfowler are gone for ever. It is now more fashionable to be a rebel, a drop-out or a marsh cowboy—but this does our cause great harm.

It is now more imperative than ever that every true shooting man—or woman—should support WAGBI, so that the aims of sportsmen can be expressed with the utmost vigour. It is understandable that the "lone wolf" individualist objects to being organized; nevertheless, it is now essential that we all stand together.

It is to be hoped that this new volume, by comparison with the first, will show that it is not only in space travel that great strides have been made since that momentous day when Gagarin made his first flight. Much has changed in the wildfowl world, not all of it for the better, but by and large there are grounds for cautious optimism.

In Europe, widespread co-operation, which transcends all political bound-aries, has been built up through the International Wildfowl Research Bureau. At home, there is harmony between WAGBI and all the National naturalists' organizations. Readers of this book will find that our wildfowl population in Britain is in a flourishing state and they will see how much more has been learnt from ringing, as shown in the recovery maps, both of wild birds and of WAGBI hand-reared stock.

The success of the Association's Greylag Scheme, of its local reserves and of its duck rearing are all detailed in this book, which has been produced as one of WAGBI's contributions to European Conservation Year 1970.

We are deeply conscious of the great honour which has been accorded to the Association by our Patron, His Royal Highness Prince Philip, Duke of Edinburgh, who has graciously consented to write a special Foreword for *The New Wildfowler in the 1970's*.

Our grateful thanks are also due to Mr. Peter Scott who has so kindly painted a new Frontispiece for us.

Once again it is our great pleasure to thank all those who have contributed to the work and given so freely of their time and talent, and we would like to acknowledge our deep gratitude to Leslie Brockbank, who has acted as our co-ordinator throughout the production of this new volume, an undertaking which has lightened our work enormously.

In addition to the contributors, a number of other people have assisted in the production of this book. We are particularly indebted to Messrs. William Collins Sons and Co., Ltd, the publishers, and to the joint authors, Guy Mountford, Philip Hollom and Roger Peterson for permission to reproduce Peterson's wildfowl identification illustrations from their famous *Field Guide to the Birds of Britain and Europe*. The British Ornithologist's Club kindly allowed us to reproduce plate 55 and Messrs. Andre Deutsch Ltd, publishers of Jeffery Harrison's *A Wealth of Wildfowl*, generously granted the use of a colour plate from that book captioned Greylag geese taking off.

We are also most grateful to R. A. Richardson for his two drawings of wading birds, to J. G. Tatham for his plan of a duck trap, to B. H. Grimes and the map department of the Nature Conservancy for preparing the maps of the National Reserves, to A. W. Colling for revising the chapter on National Wildfowl Refuges, and to the Wildfowl Trust for allowing us to use the duck-count graphs. Peter Olney has drawn the sketches illustrating wildfowl foods, James Harrison those on taxidermy and hybrids, while those illustrating duck rearing were drawn by Alan Walker.

Our debt of gratitude to the Kent Sand and Ballast Company and its former managing director, George Wallis, for granting our Association and the Wildfowl Trust management facilities on the gravel pit in West Kent is indeed great. It has provided the basis for the chapter on Local Reserves. Since 1967, the reserve became a part of Redland Quarries, Ltd., which has continued to grant us the same facilities. We are deeply indebted to Leslie Smith and Pat Parnell-Smith, Directors of the Company and to Angus Meikle, the quarry manager, for all their help. Both John Carter and John Wickens are invaluable as honorary wardens.

Major R. Ruttledge, R. W. Milliken, B. Stronach, J. Temple-Lang, O. Merne and John Anderton were all kind enough to advise on the chapter dealing with wildfowl conservation in Ireland, as did Hugh Boyd for the North American chapter. Stanley Duncan Junior provided the material for his father's biography. Martin Goodsell prepared the maps and charts illustrating the movements of WAGBI mallard and the wildfowl migration maps, from the originals provided by the authors of those chapters and went to great trouble to render them suitable for publication. Miss Vanda Salmon has put in a great many hours' secretarial work on our behalf, Mrs. Rosa Worgan and Mrs. Violet Green have given much time to the WAGBI ringing scheme, and the excellent facilities provided by Mr. and Mrs. Leslie Morrison of the Red Lion, Pulborough, Sussex, have eased considerably the pressures of editorial conferences.

The original bibliography, prepared by the late Dr. Henry James has been fully revised by John Gow and Jeffery Harrison.

It is our hope that the book will win many new supporters for the Association and the great cause we represent.   NOEL M. SEDGWICK
                                                          PETER WHITAKER
                                                          JEFFERY HARRISON

POSTSCRIPT

"Tim" Sedgwick died at his Pulborough, Sussex, home on the 30th June 1970.
The son of a sporting parson who took him punt-gunning as a very small boy, his ambition was to become a farmer but, following the death of his father, he went to Sandhurst towards the end of the 1914–18 war after which he took up poultry and pig farming. Throughout a variety of jobs, including those of gamekeeper, rabbit catcher—and even barman—his knowledge of the countryside and country matters increased.

He began contributing to the Shooting Times *while still in his teens, making the most of his ability to write both as a sportsman and a naturalist and, after a spell as Assistant Editor, became Editor of the* Shooting Times *in 1932, a position he held for thirty-three years until ill-health brought about semi-retirement. He remained Editor-in-Chief until his death at which time he had, with his fellow Editors, already set the pattern for this book.*

Throughout his career, which inevitably was closely bound up with WAGBI, he was one of the Association's staunchest supporters and had for some years been one of its Vice-Presidents. His knowledge, wisdom, simplicity, courage and humour were a wonderful example to all who knew and worked with him. He typified what many people regard as the WAGBI spirit. "Tower-Bird" will long be missed not only for his writings but as a loyal and generous friend. With his passing we have lost one of the greatest countrymen of our times.

CONTENTS

LIST OF PLATES

Colour

Black and White

Photographs by Pamela Harrison, Honorary photographer to WAGBI

THE WILDFOWLERS' ASSOCIATION OF GREAT BRITAIN AND IRELAND

by John Anderton V.R.D.

Director, Wildfowlers' Association of Great Britain and Ireland; Past Chairman of Wildfowl Conservation Committee, Nature Conservancy and a Member of the Home Office Wild Birds Advisory Committee.

and Leslie Brockbank, M.B.O.U.

Vice-President, formerly Hon. Treasurer and now Assistant Director, Wild-fowlers' Association of Great Britain and Ireland.

THE Wildfowlers' Association of Great Britain and Ireland, now known almost universally as WAGBI, was formed in 1908 by the late Stanley Duncan of Hull. He was an engineer, a highly experienced wildfowler and naturalist, and well known for his knowledge of wildfowling and matters related thereto. His object in forming the Association was threefold. He wished to help the professional wildfowlers then eking out a meagre living on our coasts; he was becoming alarmed at the increasing drainage and subsequent development of much excellent wildfowl habitat, and he realized that as time went by it would be necessary to defend the sport of wildfowling against factors that were moving contrary to its interests, namely the growing enthusiasm of extremists bent on complete protection.

Today there are no longer any professional fowlers other than a few guides, there are fewer—though still dangerous—extremists, and the threats to wildfowling grow stronger—even more so than was then the case.

In 1908, having canvassed and obtained the support of a body of far-seeing and experienced sportsmen, our founder called an inaugural meeting in his wildfowling hut which, until destroyed by floods last autumn, stood at Patrington Haven, not many miles from Hull. Rules were adopted, Stanley Duncan became the Association's first Honorary Secretary, an office he held for forty years, and the famous wildfowler and sporting author, Sir Ralph Payne-Gallwey, Bt., was elected President. WAGBI, with the support of a small committee, built up a system whereby there would be, in every wild-fowling district, officials able to give advice and represent or support wild-fowling and associated interests whenever they became threatened.

Largely as a result of Stanley Duncan's tremendous enthusiasm, dedication and the high regard in which he was held by the sporting public through his writings, drawings, sporting achievements and knowledge, WAGBI became known within wildfowling circles and was accepted as the authoritative and representative body of such interests in this country.

The war of 1914–18 meant that the Association and its activities had to be placed virtually in cold storage, and its actions immediately after the war were on a modest scale, Stanley Duncan confining his activities to enrolling as members such persons as were interested, and dispensing advice whenever this was sought.

Between the wars he saw the sport subjected to increasing pressure from bodies of persons who wished to suppress or curtail the shooting of wildfowl, and in the years immediately prior to the outbreak of the Second World War the Association gave ground to pressure from the "anti" interest which resulted in legislation being passed that curtailed the season at both ends, and generally gave the protectionists the impression that the tide was running very much in their favour.

In those years, immediately prior to 1939, when the control of wildfowling lay substantially in the hands of the County Councils, there was a growing body of opinion in the country that the law relating to wildfowling should be put on to a national basis, and that decisions as to what birds could or could not be shot, and when, should be made at national level.

The war had an immediate effect on the amount of support wildfowlers in the country could give to the defence of their sport, mainly due to the fact that most young and active men interested in wildfowling were serving their country. With the cessation of hostilities wildfowlers returning from war service quickly realized that in their absence the protectionists, invariably part of an older generation, had not been idle, and the initiative had passed to their side. Clearly if wildfowling was to enjoy any future then WAGBI must be prepared to fight for the rights of its members.

In 1947 the call went out urging such members of WAGBI as had survived the war to attend a meeting at Hull, at which plans to revitalize the Association and prepare for the coming struggle were laid. At a further meeting held in Manchester shortly afterwards Stanley Duncan, now visibly ageing, resigned the office of Secretary and went into retirement, taking with him the sincere gratitude and deep respect of all wildfowlers. At this meeting new rules were adopted, a new committee was appointed and the foundation of the modern WAGBI was laid.

The long expected attack on wildfowling came when, in both Houses, legislation was proposed which the Association regarded as both unfair and unnecessary.

Although a strictly voluntary organization with no paid staff, a small group of public-spirited men gave considerably of their time, energy and private funds, determined to see that the interests of wildfowlers were given a fair hearing and their beliefs upheld. Many meetings were convened and thousands of letters written, whilst there was considerable lobbying of members of both Houses for, in the opinion of those serving the WAGBI cause, there had been very considerable misrepresentation of the true facts.

"In the events that followed"—as the lawyers say—the ultimate outcome was the *Protection of Birds Act 1954*, an Act which WAGBI finally accepted as something far removed from the original Bill but, on the whole, fair and reasonable. Even so there remained certain clauses that did not and still do not appeal to all wildfowlers although in 1970 such views are confined to a very small minority.

Having participated in the protracted and sometimes heated deliberations culminating with the 1954 Act, WAGBI has since done everything possible to ensure that sportsmen respect and, when necessary, enforce the provisions of the Act.

While acknowledging the tremendous contributions made by that handful of dedicated Association officials, it is equally important that full credit be given to the Editor and staff of the *Shooting Times*. It would be wrong to assume that the *Shooting Times* came to our aid only at that time, for that excellent weekly magazine has, in fact, acted for an unbroken period of sixty-two years as the Association's official organ, disseminating sound advice week by week and never shrinking from the truth, particularly in its down-to-earth editorials and correspondence columns. The page it devotes entirely to WAGBI is more than a mere noticeboard. WAGBI has at all times been granted great strength and support by its Editor-in-Chief, "Tim" Sedgwick and Editor, Philip Brown. We are confident that the remarkable bond of friendship, trust and confidence which exists between our two organizations will further prosper and continue far into the future, so providing a lasting marriage of ideas and beliefs.

The effect of the publicity and behaviour that preceded the 1954 Act was so profound that throughout the country there developed a determination that never again should genuine sportsmen find themselves in similar circumstances. All over the country those who valued their sporting heritage and its future began to seek membership and many of them, with WAGBI's help and advice, set about forming local clubs and associations thus bringing together many who, individually, could do little to safeguard that future, but collectively could and would—if it became necessary. This did not mean, however, that wildfowlers would cease to follow their sport singly or with a companion or two as they still do today.

In 1949 the Nature Conservancy, incorporated by Royal Charter and responsible to the Committee of the Privy Council for Nature Conservation, came into being. Subsequently it has become an integral part of the National Environment Research Council. The Conservancy's functions so far as wildfowlers are concerned are to provide advice on the conservation, control or protection of natural fauna and to establish, maintain and manage nature reserves in Great Britain, many of which embrace shooting zones jointly managed with WAGBI.

When the Conservancy was first formed it was felt that the cause of wildfowling had been ignored whilst the naturalists were well represented, and therefore decisions would be made and discussions would be held without reference to our opinions and rights. Ultimately a meeting was arranged with the two bodies at which there was very plain speaking which in turn led to the establishment of an informal wildfowl discussion group under the Conservancy's auspices and at which all shades of opinion were represented. It is to the great credit of the then Director General (E. Max Nicholson, c.b., now a WAGBI Vice-President) that he saw the real need for such a meeting.

This group, founded at a time when wildfowlers were full of bitterness and suspicion at what they considered to be the "scheming and unfair propaganda" that had taken place behind the scenes prior to the 1954 Act, became the recognized and fully established Wildfowl Conservation Committee in 1960.

It now constitutes a formal gathering of many interested bodies with a genuine interest in the future well-being of wildfowl and provides its members with regular opportunities of discussing every matter any way allied. From a beginning fraught with suspicion and mistrust has grown, among many things, complete accord and confidence, with the Chair alternating between the Wildfowl Trust and WAGBI. The Committee, and WAGBI, fully appreci-ate that "our" wildfowl are shared with other European countries. They are common to all and, unlike us foolish humans, they do not recognize political or national barriers, hence the development of our wildfowl refuges that are a part of a broad European pattern.

Since 1950 WAGBI, then having five affiliated organizations, namely Southport and District Wildfowlers' Association (1887), Morecambe Bay Wildfowlers' Association (1929), Blakeney and District Wildfowlers' Asso-ciation (1927), Frodsham and District Wildfowlers' Club (1938) and the Tay Valley Wildfowlers' Association (1949), has grown into a mammoth organiz-ation comprising no fewer than 228 such affiliated organizations, including one in the U.S.A. and another in Sweden, 17 Regional Joint Councils and in excess of 20,000 members.

The formation of local affiliated organizations, now covering all forms of sporting shooting and not merely wildfowling, with the support and backing of their parent body, WAGBI, has provided much-needed common meeting grounds. The Clubs are chiefly responsible for education of the newcomer, operating the WAGBI-recommended practical conservation schemes that embrace the rearing, ringing and release of various species of duck and geese, improving habitat and the leasing and subsequent management of sporting rights over fresh and salt water marshes, foreshore and agricultural land. Local associations also arrange social occasions including film shows, illus-trated talks and lectures, clay-bird shooting and organized pest control shoots which are of tremendous benefit to the farming community.

The Joint Councils co-ordinate and represent the interests of clubs within laid-down areas, encourage sporting competitions, maintain a watch on developments that are not in their best interests and generally relieve National Headquarters of certain responsibilities better dealt with on a regional basis by members with local knowledge.

National H.Q., responsible to a Management Committee which is appointed annually by the Association's members, is now full-time and professionally administered. It comprises the Director, Assistant Director, and Develop-ment Officer with a supporting staff currently numbering eight employees. Additionally the Association's Boarstall Decoy Conservation Centre is professionally managed by a full-time Warden Decoyman and his Assistant. However, the voluntary and honorary aspect happily remains well to the fore, consisting of specialist advisers covering the law, conservation, public relations, publications, films, etc., and, of course, every member of the Management Committee serves in an honorary capacity.

Among many recent achievements are the Authorities granted to the

Association by the Crown Estate and Duchy of Lancaster whereby a member whilst carrying a gun over land in their ownership and not already subject to a lease of shooting rights cannot be proceeded against as a Criminal Offender under the provisions of the *Firearms Act 1968*. Wherever possible, WAGBI has, for obvious reasons, encouraged local associations to lease the shooting rights, appoint wardens, and accept responsibility for the shooting conduct and conditions in these areas. Recognition by the Sports Council came in 1968 with subsequent financial grant aid.

The Association is represented on the Councils or Committees, or working most closely with: Nature Conservancy, Wildfowl Trust, Royal Society for the Protection of Birds, Council for Nature, The Game Conservancy, Game-keepers' Association of the United Kingdom, Gun Trade Association, Ltd., Clay Pigeon Shooting Association, Crown Estate, Duchy of Lancaster, Duchy of Cornwall, International Wildfowl Research Bureau, Advisory Committee on Oil Pollution of the Sea, National Trust, International Council for Bird Preservation, British Field Sports Society, Long Room Committee, Central Council of Physical Recreation, County Naturalists' Trusts, Water Recreation Sub-Committee of the Regional Sports Councils, National, Regional and Local Wildfowl Refuges, nature reserves, etc., County Council and Local Council Wildlife and Bird Committees, and the Conseil International de la Chasse (European Hunting Organization).

It might be wondered why the Association is working in the European field. As already intimated wildfowl are migratory in the main, and therefore common to and shared by many countries. This calls for joint responsibility. It is at European level that decisions in future will be made with regard to possible blanket laws concerning length of seasons, methods of taking fowl and, in fact, virtually every aspect of the sport. Obviously British sporting interests must be cared for and WAGBI is the one organization equipped to do so. It is worthy of mention that in the European mind the triumvirate comprising Nature Conservancy, Wildfowl Trust and WAGBI is regarded as being a blue print that is ten years ahead of Europe.

The foregoing represents only a brief account of The Wildfowlers' Association of Great Britain and Ireland whose current work, responsibilities and aspirations are complex and far reaching. Nevertheless it forms an essential background to a book which ably represents not only what has been and is being achieved, but covers virtually every aspect of what is undoubtedly an ancient and honourable sport that WAGBI is determined to maintain for the generations that follow. Although the Association is working for and representing all forms of shooting, other than stalking and clays, there can be no doubt that wildfowl are by far the most in need of care and long-term thinking since they are, in the main, migratory and, therefore, widely subjected to the risks of bad weather and "progress" which entails drainage, development, disturbance and a growing list of herbicides and insecticides.

Although the past has led to a better understanding of present needs for wildfowl and wildfowling, the future is shadowed by the unfortunate trend towards mass thinking based on urban rather than rural understanding.

The countryman, or the town-dweller who has a real appreciation of country life, is therefore in a minority and at a disadvantage in the face of emotionalism easily inspired by the mass media of press, radio and television.

While it is from this minority that WAGBI has gained its strength, a growing number of thinking naturalists have realized that only through practical conservation allied to a reasonable harvesting of the surplus can the future of wildfowl and wildfowling be assured.

Those who might once have been against the wildfowler, through ignorance or lack of understanding, are today supporting WAGBI in increasing numbers as the constructive policies it has inaugurated—and which are outlined in this book—bear fruit. This surely is the right attitude not only for today but for the future if we, as a nation, are to preserve our wildlife in an ever-decreasing countryside that more and more is being spoiled by man in his demand for progress

THE WILDFOWLERS' ASSOCIATION OF GREAT BRITAIN AND IRELAND
Grosvenor House
104 Watergate Street
Chester.

CHAPTER 1

WILDFOWLING AND THE LAW IN ENGLAND AND WALES

by Peter Turner, M.A.

Hon. Legal Adviser, Wildfowlers' Association of Great Britain and Ireland. Member, Wildfowl Conservation Committee, Nature Conservancy.

LEGAL technicalities are probably anathema to most wildfowlers. It is, however, an inescapable fact that the privilege, or right, to enjoy the pursuit of fowl in the splendid wilderness of the marshes depends for its continuance upon the law. By the same token the law imposes duties upon those who enjoy its privileges. To neglect these duties is to run a grave risk of ultimately losing their concomitant rights. The prudent wildfowler will therefore carry out meticulously the duties which the law and traditions of his sport impose. At a lower level a more than passing interest in the law is required of the wildfowler who wishes to avoid trouble for himself or to protect his shooting rights. Certainly no official of the great preponderance of WAGBI clubs which maintain a reserve can afford to be without a working knowledge of the law.

LICENCES AND CERTIFICATES

No wildfowler, or any other shooting man, may lawfully possess, purchase or acquire a shotgun without holding a shotgun certificate authorizing him to possess shotguns under the provisions of the *Firearms Act 1968*. For the purposes of the Act a shotgun is a smooth-bore gun with a barrel not less than twenty-four inches in length, not being an air-gun.

To obtain a shotgun certificate, application has to be made on a prescribed form (obtainable from police stations) to the chief officer of police for the area in which the applicant resides. The Act requires the chief officer of police to grant the application unless he has reason to believe that the applicant is prohibited by the Act from possessing a shotgun or cannot be permitted to possess a shotgun without danger to the public safety or to the peace. For most practical purposes a prohibited person is one who has been imprisoned for three years or more, or who applies for a shotgun certificate within five years of being released from a term of imprisonment for three months or more but less than three years.

An applicant who is aggrieved by the decision of the chief officer of police has a right of appeal to quarter sessions. On the determination of an appeal the court may make such order as it thinks fit as to payment of the costs of the appeal. It cannot be said with certainty that a successful appellant would obtain an order for costs against the chief officer of police; but it is possible. A great deal would depend upon the circumstances of the appeal.

Once granted, a shotgun certificate remains in force for three years but can be renewed. No conditions other than such as may be prescribed by the Secretary of State may be imposed on the grant of a shotgun certificate. The only conditions so far prescribed are that the certificate holder must report to the police any change in his address or the loss or theft of any shotgun in his possession.

There are exceptions which enable certain persons to use or have in their possession a shotgun without holding a certificate. Probably the two most important from the wildfowler's point of view are, first, that which enables a person to borrow a shotgun from the occupier of private premises and to *use* it on those premises in the occupier's presence and, secondly, that which enables a person who does not hold a shotgun certificate to *use* a shotgun at a time and place approved for shooting at artificial targets by the chief officer of police for the area in which that place is situated.

A police constable is entitled to demand the production of a shotgun certificate from any person whom he believes to be in possession of a shotgun. Failure to produce the certificate enables the constable to seize the gun and to require the person who has failed to produce the certificate to declare his name and address. It is prudent therefore to carry the certificate on all occasions when a gun is carried.

It is an offence to sell or transfer to any other person, other than a registered firearms dealer, any Section 1 firearm or a shotgun unless that other person produces a certificate authorizing him to purchase or acquire it. It is, therefore, essential when selling a gun to examine the purchaser's shotgun or firearm certificate. Similarly when taking a gun for repair the firearm or shotgun certificate must be produced to the repairer.

Possession of a shotgun without holding a certificate is punishable on conviction with a maximum fine of £200 and/or six months' imprisonment.

Since the use of rifled weapons for wildfowling is contrary to the spirit of the sport and against the rules of WAGBI it is probably only necessary to say that a firearm certificate is necessary to possess any rifled weapon or ammunition therefor (other than an air weapon) or to have a smooth bore gun with a barrel less than twenty-four inches in length. Similarly for most types of distress flare cartridges a certificate is required; even if they are fired from a shotgun.

The *Game Licences Act 1860* requires a person who shoots pheasants, partridges, grouse, blackgame, moorgame, hares, snipe, woodcock, rabbits or deer to hold a game licence. This licence is obtainable as of right at any main Post Office on payment of the duty, but it is only valid from the hour of issue. An annual licence costs £6 and runs from 1st August to 31st July next following. A licence from 1st August to 31st October costs £4. A licence from 1st November to 31st July costs the same. A licence for any continuous period of fourteen days costs £2.

Only the annual licence gives the holder the right to sell game, and then only to a licensed dealer. Nowadays game is defined in the *Game Act 1831* as pheasants, partridges, grouse, blackgame, moorgame and hares. No licence is needed to deal in wild duck, pigeon, snipe, woodcock or rabbits.

The law provides so many exceptions to the rule of having a game licence to shoot rabbits or deer that, in practice, the sportsman can almost always do without one. The *Game Licence Act 1860* itself provides that all those who kill rabbits or deer on any enclosed land whatever by permission or order of the tenant or owner need not hold a game licence. Similar provisions exempt a person lawfully exercising his rights under the *Ground Game Act 1880* and the *Hares Act 1848*.

The game licence of a person convicted of trespass in pursuit of game under Section 30 of the *Game Act 1831* is automatically invalidated. Pursuit of game without holding a game licence constitutes two offences. First under the *Game Act 1831* and secondly under the *Game Licences Act 1860*. Proceedings can be instituted under both Acts in respect of the same offence but only the local authority can prosecute under the latter Act, unless the appropriate procedure under Section 4 of the *Finance Act 1961* to enable the police to prosecute has been put into effect. Anyone can prosecute under the former Act. The penalties are cumulative and the maximum fine under the former is £5, under the latter £20. The offence under the *Game Act 1831* can only be committed in respect of game as therein defined.

An owner or occupier of land, or a police officer, or a person who himself holds a game licence can demand to see the licence of a person doing any act for which such a licence is necessary. Refusal to produce the licence and to give one's name and address on request constitutes another offence for which the maximum penalty is £20.

The *Dog Licences Act 1959* requires dog owners who use their dogs for sport to hold a dog licence. Failure to hold a licence gives rise to an offence for which the maximum penalty is £5. Refusal to produce the licence on request to a police or county council officer is a further offence attracting a similar maximum penalty. A separate licence is required for each dog more than six months old and may be obtained as of right from any main Post Office. A dog licence is valid for twelve months unless its holder is disqualified from keeping a dog.

In addition to taking out a dog licence the dog owner should take out an insurance policy to indemnify him against loss or damage caused by the dog. Chasing of sheep and poultry by dogs can lead to substantial claims for damages.

MINORS

The *Firearms Act 1968* has conveniently consolidated the law concerning possession and use of firearms by minors. Formerly the law on this topic was somewhat difficult to discover; being scattered amongst several different statutes.

The first point of importance is that it is an offence for a person under the age of seventeen to purchase or hire *any* firearm. Although this provision does not prevent the gift or loan of a firearm to such a person, a different section of the Act prohibits a gift or loan of any Section 1 firearm or ammunition therefore to persons under the age of fourteen. Section I applies to all firearms and ammunition, except a shotgun as previously defined, and air weapons not of a type declared by the Secretary of State to be specially dangerous, and normal ammunition for use in such weapons. A similar provision makes it an offence to part with the possession of such a firearm or ammunition to a person under fourteen years of age subject to limited exceptions of little importance to the wildfowler. Similar rules concerning the purchase and sale, hiring, and parting with possession apply to air weapons; but with fewer exceptions.

So far as shotguns are concerned it is an offence to make a gift of such a weapon or ammunition to a person under the age of fifteen. It should be noted that a loan is not prohibited and therefore a boy under the age of fifteen may be lent a shotgun and ammunition. If he has no shotgun certificate it can be used only in the circumstances mentioned earlier relating to exemptions from holding a shotgun certificate. If, however, a boy under fifteen years of age is the holder of a shotgun certificate he can be lent a shotgun and ammunition; subject to the proviso that it is an offence for a person under the age of fifteen to have an assembled shotgun with him except whilst under the supervision of a person aged twenty-one or over, or while the gun is so covered with a securely fastened gun cover that it cannot be fired. Shotgun certificates have been granted to boys under fifteen as there is nothing in the Act to prohibit such a step. The Act does not therefore prevent a father from educating his son in the use of a shotgun from whatever age he considers appropriate; provided that it is done under the supervision upon which any wise parent would insist.

Air weapons are treated differently from shotguns and Section I firearms. The basic rule is that it is an offence for a person under the age of fourteen to have an air weapon or ammunition for an air weapon with him. There is an exception to this rule permitting a person under the age of fourteen to have an air weapon with him while he is under the supervision of a person aged twenty-one or over; even so if the weapon is used to fire a missile beyond the premises on which it is being used an offence is committed both by the person who fires the missile and the person who is supervising the youngster concerned.

It is also an offence for a person under the age of seventeen to have an air weapon with him in a public place except an air-gun or an air-rifle so covered with a securely fastened gun cover that it cannot be fired. It should be noted that the exception does not extend to air-pistols.

GUNPOWDER AND CARTRIDGES

In order to purchase gunpowder for muzzle-loading weapons and loading black powder cartridges a permit, issued by a chief constable, is needed by virtue of Statutory Instrument No. 1598 of 1953 made under the *Emergency Powers Laws (Misc. Provs.) Act 1953*. No permit is needed for percussion caps. The holder of a stock of shotgun cartridges which is held for sale needs to have a permit for storage from his local council but if the cartridges are for the holder's own use no permit is required.

FORESHORE SHOOTING

The myth, at one time widely believed, that any member of the public has a right to shoot on the seaward side of sea walls has been finally exploded by the case of *Beckett v. Lyons* [1967] 1 AER 833. That there is no public right to shoot on the foreshore there is no doubt. Nor is there any doubt that such a right cannot be acquired by custom or usage by the general public. The only public rights over the foreshore are for purposes ancillary to navigation or fishing. As a consequence anybody on the foreshore is a trespasser unless he has permission from its owner or is exercising his right of navigation or fishing. The true significance of the principles so clearly enunciated in *Beckett v. Lyons* can only be appreciated when viewed against the background of the trespass provisions of the *Firearms Act 1968*. This Act makes it an offence for a person who has a firearm with him to enter or be on any land as a trespasser and without reasonable excuse (the proof whereof lies on him). For the purpose of this section "land" includes land covered with water. Thus, not only does the wildfowler trespassing on the foreshore render himself liable to a civil action for trespass but, he also renders himself liable to prosecution under the Act.

WAGBI, on behalf of its members, has negotiated a form of authority entitling its members to be on foreshore in the ownership of the Crown and the Duchy of Lancaster. Members of WAGBI having shotguns with them on foreshore so owned do so with the consent of the owners and, therefore, commit no offence under the section. The authority does not extend to foreshore owned by any other person or body or which has been let to any other person or body by either the Crown Estate Commissioners or the Duchy of Lancaster without reserving the sporting rights. In all other cases permission must be obtained in some form or another if the risk of prosecution or proceedings for trespass are to be avoided. In this connection it should be noted that there are substantial stretches of coast-line where the Crown, which in the absence of evidence to the contrary, is presumed to be the owner, has either granted the foreshore absolutely, or a lease of it, to a subject.

This authority is not adequate to make a wildfowler on the foreshore into an "authorized person" for the purposes of the *Protection of Birds Acts 1954 and 1967*. He can only shoot the duck, geese and waders listed in the Part II of Schedule I and in Schedule III to the 1954 Act. He must not shoot birds in Schedule II; such birds include pigeons, gulls, cormorants, etc.

Whilst considering the question of trespass in relation to the foreshore it is important that it should be properly defined. The Standard definition is that the foreshore is that part of the sea shore which is more often than not covered by the flux and reflux of the four ordinary tides occuring midway between springs and neaps. For most practical purposes this can be construed, so far as the landward limit of the foreshore is concerned, as the medium line of ordinary tides midway between springs and neaps.

This definition excludes most green marshes, saltings, or merses (call them what you will) which lie on the seaward side of the sea wall in many places. Hence the wildfowler must not shoot there unless he has permission.

Access to the foreshore can only be lawfully had over public rights of way.

There is not necessarily a public right of way along a sea wall. Even if there is a right of way along a sea wall or elsewhere such a right is exactly what it says and no more. Thus, although it may be lawful to carry an unloaded gun along a public right of way, the minute a person fires a gun whilst exercising this right of passage he becomes a trespasser as against the owner of the soil over which it passes.

Modern Ordnance Survey maps indicate public rights of way, where space is available, as shown on the Definitive Maps of such rights which local councils are now obliged to maintain. In the absence of any indication on the Ordnance map inquiry should be made of the local council in whose area any alleged public right of way is thought to exist.

TRESPASS—OTHER THAN ON THE FORESHORE

Anyone who enters on another person's land without permission or lawful authority is a trespasser and renders himself liable to a civil action for damages, or for an injunction to restrain a further trespass, or (if he has a gun with him) to the crimical proceedings, discussed in the section on foreshore shooting, under the *Firearms Act 1968*. In addition anybody who can be proved to have been trespassing in the daytime in pursuit of Game, Woodcock, Rabbits or Snipe can be prosecuted under Section 30 of the *Game Act 1831*

Under Section 24 of that Act it is also an offence to take out of the nest the eggs of any game bird, swan, wild duck, teal or wigeon unless one has the shooting rights or the permission of the owner of such rights. Under the *Protection of Birds Acts 1954 and 1967* it is an offence for anyone, even the occupier or shooting tenant, to take the eggs of a wild duck, goose, or swan except for the purpose of causing them to be hatched.

A trespasser who shoots pigeons or any of the other birds mentioned in Schedule II of the 1954 Act may be prosecuted under that Act; in addition to the other remedies against him. For, being a trespasser, he is not an authorized person, within the meaning of, and as required by, that statute. This does not apply in the case of wildfowl listed in Schedule III of the Act, nor does Section 30 of the *Game Act* apply to wild duck and geese.

Although no reasonable neighbour would stop a person from retrieving a dead bird which had fallen over the boundary he has a perfect right to do so and it is just as much trespass to enter on somebody else's land for this purpose as any other. The only proper thing to do is to be courteous and seek permission. Should this not be possible because the landowner concerned is not available, or for some other good reason, it is prudent to leave one's gun on one's own land. Failure to do so increases the risk of prosecution under the *Game Act* and makes it virtually certain under the *Firearms Act 1968*.

The *Game Laws (Amendment) Act 1960* has substantially increased the power of the courts and police in relation to trespassing and poaching offences. For example upon conviction for trespass in pursuit of game in the daytime a court can order the offender to pay a fine of up to £20 and confiscate his gun. The police are empowered to enter land without invitation if they have reasonable grounds to believe that a person on that land is committing an offence under Sections 1 or 9 of the *Night Poaching Act 1828* or Sections 30 or 33

SHELDUCK

RUDDY SHELDUCK

♂

MALLARD

PINTAIL

WIGEON

SHOVELER

GARGANEY

TEAL

♂ GADWALL

GOOSANDER

SMEW

RED-BREASTED MERGANSER

Plate 1

DUCKS IN FLIGHT

SHELDUCK
Black, white and rufous pattern, large white fore-wing patches.

RUDDY SHELDUCK
Pale cinnamon colour.

MALLARD
Dark head, two white borders on speculum, neck ring.

PINTAIL
Needle tail, one white border on speculum, neck stripe.

WIGEON
Large white shoulder-patches, grey back.

SHOVELER
Heavy spoon bill, large bluish shoulder-patches.

GADWALL
Largely white speculum.

GARGANEY
Small; large bluish shoulder-patches.

TEAL
Small, dark-winged; green speculum.

SMEW
White head and belly, white, fore-wing.

GOOSANDER
Merganser shape; white chest, large wing-patches.

RED-BREASTED MERGANSER
Merganser shape dark chest, large; wing-patches.

Plate 2

DUCKS IN FLIGHT

TUFTED DUCK
Black back, broad white wing-stripe.

SCAUP
Grey back, broad white stripe on rear edge of wing.

FERRUGINOUS DUCK
Mahogany colour; wing-stripe.

POCHARD
Grey back, broad grey wing-stripe.

RED-CRESTED POCHARD
Broad white patch extends nearly length of wing.

GOLDENEYE
Large white wing-squares, short neck, black head with white spot. Wings whistle in flight.

LONG-TAILED DUCK
Dark unpatterned wings, white on body.

HARLEQUIN
Stocky, dark; small bill, white marks.

KING EIDER
White fore-parts, black rear-parts.

EIDER
White back, white fore-wings, black belly.

VELVET SCOTER
Black body, white wing-patches.

SURF SCOTER
Black body, white head-patches.

COMMON SCOTER
All-black plumage.

TUFTED DUCK

SCAUP

FERRUGINOUS DUCK

♂

RED-CRESTED POCHARD

POCHARD

GOLDENEYE

LONG-TAILED DUCK

HARLEQUIN

KING EIDER ♂

EIDER

SURF SCOTER

VELVET SCOTER

COMMON SCOTER

of the *Game Act 1831*. Such a person can be arrested by the constable and searched. Any game or gun found in the course of the search may be seized.

The *Poaching Prevention Act 1862* as amended by the 1960 Act enables a police constable who has good cause to suspect a person of poaching game to stop and search him and any vehicle on any road or public place and seize any game, guns or ammunition which he finds. If the search discloses sufficient evidence the constable must bring the charge under the Act. Upon conviction the offender can be fined up to £50 and any game or guns found in the search may be confiscated. For the purpose of the 1862 Act game includes pheasants, partridges, grouse, blackgame, moorgame, their eggs, and hares, rabbits, woodcock and snipe.

The *Night Poaching Acts 1828–44* make it an offence unlawfully to take or destroy any game or rabbits by night on any land, open or enclosed, or on any road or path or in any gate or entrance-way on to a road or path, or unlawfully to enter by night on to any land with any gun, net, engine, or other instrument in order to take game. For the purpose of these Acts "game" means the same as in the *Game Act 1831*. Only the owners or occupiers of land or their gamekeepers and the police have powers of arrest for the purposes of this Act.

HIGHWAYS

Although there is no express rule to prohibit shooting on the highway it is (apart from the question of safety) a hazardous thing to do.

First, Section 19 of the *Firearms Act 1968* makes it an offence for a person without lawful authority or reasonable excuse (the proof whereof lies on him) to have with him in a public place a loaded shotgun or loaded air weapon or any other firearm (whether loaded or not) together with ammunition suitable for use in that firearm. Whilst possession of a shotgun certificate may well amount to lawful authority, and the fact that one has the sporting rights on the land on one or both sides of the highway concerned may constitute a reasonable excuse, these defences are, as yet, by no means certain. The prudent shooting man will therefore avoid having a loaded shotgun in a public place unless he wishes to become the subject of a leading case. Until the courts have given a ruling on the point the, not uncommon, practice of driving birds to guns standing on the highway is of doubtful legality.

Secondly the *Highways Act 1959* makes it an offence to discharge a gun without lawful authority or excuse within fifty feet of the centre of the highway which consists of or comprises a carriageway, and thereby to endanger, injure, or interrupt any person using the highway. To constitute the offence it is essential to show that someone using the highway was endangered, interrupted, or injured and unless this can be proved it is no offence under this Act to shoot birds from the highway. That this provision was not repealed by the *Firearms Act 1968* may be a useful point to make in a case concerning that Act in the circumstances described in the preceding paragraph.

B

The Protection of Birds Acts

The days when all legislation designed to protect birds was strongly opposed by sportsmen have long since gone. WAGBI, representing wild-fowler-conservationists is proud to have made positive suggestions for improved conservation which are incorporated in the *Protection of Birds Act 1967*.

The 1967 Act is, however, only an Act designed to strengthen and bring up to date the *Protection of Birds Act 1954*. This Act, whilst suffering from defects which must beset any statute, has proved both workable by, and accept-able to, all those concerned with either conservation or sport or, better still, both. It could perhaps, if suitably adapted, form a guide for other European nations currently concerned with the same problems which were apparent in the United Kingdom in the 1950s.

The Act is basically simple in that it makes it an offence to kill, injure, or take any wild bird. An attempt to do these things is also an offence. Similar protection is given to nests and eggs.

Having created overall protection the Act then creates some exceptions to this general protection by listing many species of birds in Schedules to the Act and making special provisions with regard to those birds. Except for Sections 5, 10 and 12 of the 1954 Act and Section 5 of the 1967 Act game birds are not given any protection beyond that given to them by the *Game Acts*.

Thus Schedule I lists birds which are rare, or which for some other reason need special protection. Birds listed in this Schedule are protected by a special penalty. This Schedule is itself divided into two parts. Part I contains a list of birds specially protected throughout the year. Those only so protected during the close season are listed in Part II of Schedule I. Birds listed in the Second Schedule (which includes such agricultural pests as pigeons and such enemies of the game preserver as the carrion crow) may be killed by author-ized persons at any time, except in Scotland on Sundays and Christmas Day, and in England and Wales in counties where Sunday shooting of Schedule II birds is prohibited. Authorized persons are the owners or occupiers of the land on which the killing, etc., takes place; the person having the sporting rights over the land; a person having the permission of such persons to shoot over the land; and persons having the written permission of the Local Authority and certain Statutory Bodies. A trespasser "only after a few pigeons" therefore commits an offence under the Act; as does a wildfowler shooting Schedule II birds on the foreshore unless it is owned by or let to his club.

Schedule III lists the wildfowler's legitimate quarry and includes the birds in Part II of Schedule I and the common species of duck and geese. The birds in this Schedule may be killed or taken outside the close season, and not only by authorized persons. Again shooting on Christmas Day and Sundays in Scotland and in certain counties in England and Wales on Sundays is pro-hibited.

The open seasons created by the Act are indicated in the table at the end of this chapter.

If it can be shown to have been necessary to prevent *serious* damage to crops, vegetables, fruit, growing timber or any other form of property, or to fisheries, the killing of birds in the close season or of birds enjoying the general pro-tection of the Act is lawful. This defence does not apply in the case of birds listed in Schedule I and the onus of proof is on the defendant. Those who indulge in August duck shooting on cornfields should be very sure, therefore, that they can discharge such onus.

The Secretary of State can vary the open season; but only to make it shorter. In this connection it should be noted that the 1967 Act contains a detailed procedure for preventing shooting of birds in Schedule III during severe weather for periods of up to fourteen days. There are adequate safe-guards in the procedure for the shooting man, but at the same time the fowl can be given protection speedily at a time when no responsible sportsman would wish to shoot them.

On the topic of wildfowl shooting between 1st and 20th February two important points must be mentioned. First, the area where this is permitted by no means coincides with the area previously defined as "foreshore" which is much more restricted. It certainly includes saltings which are flooded by ordinary spring tides. Secondly the extension does not apply to waders; only to duck and geese.

A final point on the general working of the Act is that the Secretary of State can add birds to or remove them from the Schedules. He may also declare certain areas as sanctuaries. This power is in addition to that contained in any other statutes. Before he makes any of the orders which the Act empowers him to make the Secretary of State must consult an advisory com-mittee, provide for the submission of objections and representations, and, if he thinks fit, hold a public inquiry.

The pattern of the Act is, therefore, of strict protection, whilst at the same time recognizing the legitimate right of the sportsman to take the harvestable surplus; coupled with a degree of flexibility to enable natural fluctuations in the bird population to be catered for.

Having assimilated the general nature of the Act the wildfowler should attempt to obtain a good working knowledge of the important detailed pro-visions which affect his sport.

Section 5 of the 1954 Act as amended by the 1967 Act prohibits certain means of taking or killing any wild birds, including game birds. It is illegal to use or set in position any spring, trap, gin, snare, hook and line, any electrical device designed to frighten birds, any poisoned, poisonous or stupefying substance, a floating container holding explosives or use any gas, net, baited board, bird lime or similar substance. Live decoy birds may not be used if they are tethered, blind or maimed. Shotguns (e.g. punt guns) having an internal diameter at the muzzle of more than one and three-quarter inches may not be used to kill wild birds. Except in order to find a wounded bird the use of an artificial light for killing or taking birds is unlawful; unless the birds concerned are listed in Schedule II.

The Secretary of State has power to forbid the use of decoys of any sort, and in any specified area. This power has been exercised in the statutory instru-ment which permits the killing or taking of barnacle geese in certain parts of Scotland for a short period each year.

The use of a mechanically propelled vehicle or boat, or an aircraft in immediate pursuit of any wild bird for the purpose of driving, taking or killing it is prohibited. There is no decided case on the point but it may well be that an offence is committed even though the engine in the vehicle or boat is not running. The prudent wildfowler will, therefore, dispense with an engine altogether.

The sale of dead wild geese is prohibited altogether by the 1967 Act and the sale of dead wild duck is only permitted between 1st September and the following 27th February.

Wildfowlers who ring birds must ensure that they are authorized persons (as previously defined) and must also confine their activities to wild geese, duck, pheasants, partridges, grouse, blackgame and ptarmigan. Similarly wildfowlers who collect eggs for rearing schemes must ensure that they are authorized persons and that they confine their activities to the eggs of wild geese, wild duck and swans.

The police have substantial powers under the Act and a constable can stop and search any person found committing an offence and any vehicle or boat which that person is using. He can also arrest the person if he fails to give his name and address to the constable's satisfaction. Wild birds, and any weapon or other article capable of taking a wild bird, may be seized. Upon conviction of an offender the court must confiscate any wild bird, egg, skin, or nest, and may forfeit any weapon, decoy bird, or other article by means of which the offence was committed. This is in addition to any fine or imprisonment which the court may order. Except in cases to which the special penalty applies, the court can order a fine of up to £5 per bird. The special penalty is up to £25 per bird and/or up to one month's imprisonment for a first offence and for subsequent offences a similar fine and/or up to three month's imprisonment.

INSURANCE

Whilst no sum of money can provide adequate compensation for a life lost or a body maimed, every shooting man should insure against third-party liability. The amount of the indemnity should be not less than £100,000.

CONCLUSION

This summary of the law is only sufficient to inform the wildfowler about the more common legal points which are likely to crop up in his shooting career. Those who wish to be better informed must study the statutes and cases for themselves. All should be scrupulous in their own observance of the law affecting the sport and vigilant to see that others do likewise. Failure in this respect can only damage the sport. The right to shoot is too precious to be lost as a result of the failure of a small number to honour their obligations.

Although changes in the law have made it necessary to re-write substantial parts of this chapter it follows the pattern set by the chapter on the same topic in the first edition of this book. That chapter was written by a former honorary legal adviser to WAGBI, Mr. J. C. Gow, to whom the present author is greatly obliged for assistance in the preparation of this chapter, and in other matters.

Counties in England and Wales in which there is No Sunday shooting of Schedule III birds

Anglesey
Brecknock
Caernarvon
Cardigan
Carmarthen
Cornwall
Denbigh
Devon
Doncaster—County Borough
Glamorgan

Great Yarmouth—County Borough
Isle of Ely
Leeds—County Borough
Merioneth
Montgomery
Norfolk
Pembroke
Somerset
Yorkshire—North Riding
Yorkshire—West Riding

N.B. (1) This list can, by Statutory Instrument, be altered from time to time.
   (2) "Game" cannot be shot on Sundays or on Christmas Day throughout England and Wales.

THE SCHEDULES TO THE PROTECTION OF BIRDS ACT 1954

THE FIRST SCHEDULE

WILD BIRDS AND THEIR EGGS PROTECTED BY SPECIAL PENALTIES

PART I

AT ALL TIMES

Avocet
Bee-eater, all species
Bittern, all species
Bluethroat
Brambling
Bunting, snow
Buzzard, honey
Chough
Corncrake (landrail)
Crake, spotted
Crossbill
Diver, all species
Dotterel
Eagle, all species
Fieldfare
Firecrest
Godwit, black-tailed
Goshawk

Grebe, black-necked
Grebe, Slavonian
Greenshank
Harrier, all species
Hobby
Hoopoe
Kingfisher
Kite
Merlin
Oriole, golden
Osprey
Owl, barn
Owl, snowy
Peregrine
Phalarope, red-necked
Plover, Kentish
Plover, little ringed
Quail, European

Redstart, black
Redwing
Ruff and reeve
Sandpiper, wood
Serin
Shrike, red-backed
Sparrow-hawk
Spoonbill
Stilt, black-winged
Stint, Temminck's
Stone curlew

Swan, whooper
Tern, black
Tern, little
Tern, roseate
Tit, bearded
Tit, crested
Warbler, Dartford
Warbler, marsh
Warbler, Savi's
Woodlark
Wryneck

PART II

DURING THE CLOSE SEASON

Whimbrel
Wild duck of the following species:
    Common scoter
    Garganey teal
    Goldeneye
    Long-tailed duck
    Scaup-duck
    Velvet scoter

N.B. The birds in the first part of this Schedule, all the year round, and those in the second part, during the close season, are protected by a special penalty under Section 12 (2) (a). This special penalty also applies to all offences under Sections 5 and 8, and can apply to offences in any area specified as a sanctuary under Section 3 of the Act, and to offences against Section 1 of the 1967 Act.

THE SECOND SCHEDULE

WILD BIRDS WHICH MAY BE KILLED OR TAKEN AT ANY TIME BY AUTHORIZED PERSONS

Bullfinch (only in certain areas)
Cormorant
Crow, carrion
Crow, hooded

Domestic pigeon gone feral
Gull, greater black-backed
Gull, lesser black-backed
Gull, herring

Jackdaw	Shag
Jay	Sparrow, house
Magpie	Starling
Oyster-catcher (only in certain areas)	Stock-dove
Rook	Wood-pigeon

N.B. From the standpoint of the wildfowler, the expression "authorized person" means—the owner or occupier of land, or person having the sporting rights over the land, or any person authorized by them to shoot over the land.

THIRD SCHEDULE

WILD BIRDS WHICH MAY BE KILLED OR TAKEN OUTSIDE THE CLOSE SEASON

Any wild bird included in Part II of Schedule 1 to this Act.
Capercaillie
Coot
Curlew (other than stone curlew)
Godwit, bar-tailed
Moorhen
Plover, golden
Plover, grey
Redshank, common
Snipe, common
Snipe, jack
Wild duck of the following species:
    Common pochard
    Gadwall
    Mallard
    Pintail
    Shoveler
    Teal
    Tufted duck
    Wigeon
Wild geese of the following species:
    Bean-goose
    Canada goose
Greylag goose
    Pink-footed goose
    White-fronted goose
Woodcock

N.B. The following wildfowl which may be encountered sometimes are protected at all times:

Brent goose, Egyptian goose, Eider duck, Herons, Snipe (great), Oxbird or Stint, Ruddy shelduck, Shelduck or Bargoose, Snow goose, Swans (mute).

Any wild bird other than a game bird, not in the 3rd Schedule or the 2nd is, protected at all times and must not be killed.

The Greylag goose is protected throughout the United Kingdom during the close season but may be shot in the open season.

OPEN SEASONS FOR GAME AND WILDFOWL
(All dates inclusive)

	Shooting	Importation (of dead birds) (i)	Sale (of dead birds)	Statute
Wild Ducks (ii). In Pt.2. of Sched. I & in Sched III P. of B. Act 1954.	Inland: 1st Sept.–31st Jan. next / Below High Water Mark of Ordinary Spring Tides 1st Sept.–20th Feb. next.	1st Sept.–31st Jan. next	1st Sept.–27th Feb. next.	Protection of Birds Act 1954.
Wild Geese (ii) of the following species: Bean, Canada, Greylag, Pinkfoot, and Whitefront.	Inland: 1st Sept.–31st Jan. next / Below High Water Mark of Ordinary Spring Tides 1st Sept.–20th Feb. next.	1st Sept.–31st Jan. next.	1st Sept.–27th Feb. next.	Protection of Birds Act 1954.
Woodcock	*In England and Wales*: 1st Oct.–31st Jan. next. *In Scotland*: 1st Sept.–31st Jan.	1st Sept.–31st Jan. next.	1st Sept.–27th Feb. next.	Protection of Birds Act 1954.
Snipe	12 Aug.–31st Jan. next.	1st Sept.–31st Jan. next.	1st Sept.–27th Feb. next.	Protection of Birds Act 1954.
Capercaillie	1st Oct.–31st Jan. next.	1st Sept.–31st Jan. next.	1st Sept.–27th Feb. next.	Protection of Birds Act 1954.
Curlew and other birds in Schedule III of the Prot. of Birds Act, 1954.	1st Sept.–31st Jan. next.	1st Sept.–31st Jan. next.	1st Sept.–27th Feb. next.	Protection of Birds Act 1954.
Ptarmigan	*In England*: At no time. *In Scotland*: 12th Aug.–10thDec.	At any time (iv). 12th Aug.–10th Dec.	At any time (iv). 12th Aug.–10th Dec.	Protection of Birds Act 1954. 13 Geo. III. C. 54. 1773.
Pheasants	1st Oct.–1st Feb. next.	No restriction under Game Acts.	1st Oct.–11th Feb. next. (Except foreign, imported dead.)	*England*: Game Act 1831. *Scotland*: 13 Geo. III. C. 54. 1773. (v) (sale) Game Licences Act 1860, and Game Act 1831.

OPEN SEASONS FOR GAME AND WILDFOWL—*continued*

	Shooting	Importation (of dead birds) (i)	Sale (of dead birds)	Statute
Partridges	1st Sept.–1st Feb. next.	No restriction under Game Acts.	1st Sept.–11th Feb. next. (Except foreign, imported dead.)	*England*: Game Act 1831. *Scotland*: 13. Geo. III. C. 54. 1773. (v) (sale) Game Licences Act 1860, and Game Act 1831.
Grouse	12th Aug.–10th Dec. next.	No restriction under Game Acts.	12th Aug.–20th Dec. next. (Except foreign, imported dead.)	*England*: Game Act 1831. *Scotland*: 13 Geo. III. C. 54. 1773. (v) (sale) Game Licences Act 1860, and Game Act 1831.
Blackgame (iii).	20th Aug.–10th Dec. next.	No restriction under Game Acts.	20th Aug.–29th Dec. next. (Except foreign, imported dead.)	*England*: Game Act 1831. *Scotland*: 13 Geo. III. C. 54. 1773. (v) (sale) Game Licences Act 1860, and Game Act 1831.
Pigeons	At any time.	At any time.	At any time.	Protection of Birds Act 1954.
Hares	At any time.	At any time.	*Foreign, imported dead.* At any time. *Killed in U.K.* 1st Aug.–28th Feb. next.	Hares Act 1892.
Rabbits	At any time.	At any time.	At any time.	

Notes:

(i) Subject to orders of Board of Trade and Ministry of Agriculture and Fisheries.

(ii) Other species of ducks and geese are protected, except barnacle geese which may be shot only in certain areas between 1st Dec.–31st Jan Stat. Inst. 1751 (S) 141 of 1955.

(iii) Open season for shooting in Devon, Somerset, and New Forest is 2nd Sept.–9th Dec.

(iv) Provided it has not been killed in contravention of the law.

(v) The Game Licences Act 1860 imported to Scotland the provisions of the Game Act 1831 as to dealing in game.

(vi) Birds listed in Schedule 2 of the Protection of Birds Act 1954 may be shot at any time by authorized persons and sold at any time. They may also be imported at an time.

(vii) The Game Act 1970 makes it possible for dealers and others to have dead game in their possession (but not to sell it) out of season.

N.B. Quail (Common) may not be shot in, or imported into or sold in, the U.K. Other varieties of quail bred in captivity here, and/or killed otherwise than in contravention of the 1954 Act may be sold here. In strict law "game" (other than foreign) may not be sold more than ten days after

CHAPTER 2

WILDFOWLING AND THE LAW IN SCOTLAND

by William Brotherston, B.L., N.P.

Hon. Legal Adviser (Scotland), Wildfowlers' Association of Great Britain and Ireland.

SCOTS law differs in many respects from English law including to some extent those branches of the law which affect the activities of wildfowlers. It is the purpose of this chapter to outline the most important aspects of the law which are of interest to wildfowlers, and particular attention will be paid to those rules which differ from the English ones.

The first important question is: where can wildfowling be done? Most obviously, one can shoot wildfowl on one's own land, or on land over which one has permission to shoot. The problem in law arises in relation to other land. Then it is important to consider the law of trespass. Trespass consists in temporary intrusion on to land or other heritable property, such as a private loch, without the owner's permission or other legal justification. A public or private right of way would constitute such justification to get to an area of land where shooting was permitted.

Trespass is dealt with both by the civil and the criminal law, but the civil law ways of dealing with it are cumbersome. The owner of the land over which the trespass is being committed is entitled to order or conduct the trespasser off his land but he is not entitled to use force to achieve this end, unless it is made necessary by the use of force on the part of the trespasser; and even then the landowner's force must be only as much as is reasonably necessary. The use of such preventive devices as man traps and spring guns is not permissible.

Unless actual damage is caused, the landowner cannot sue the trespasser for damages. He can, on the other hand, obtain from the courts an order of interdict, which prohibits the trespasser from trespassing again. The usefulness of interdict is, however, severely limited. It only prevents future trespass by the same trespasser. It will only be granted if repetition of the trespass is feared, and is in any event only granted in the discretion of the court.

More important, in practical terms, are the various statutory criminal offences relating to trespass. There are a number of old statutes dealing with trespass, and in particular trespass in pursuit of game. There is no general definition of game in Scots law, and it is necessary to look at the terms of particular statutes to determine their scope. For that reason, the only such statute which is of importance to wildfowlers is the *Game (Scotland) Act 1832* (otherwise known as the *Day Trespass Act*) which applies to trespass in search or pursuit of "game or of woodcocks, snipes, *wild duck* or conies" (but not wild geese). Such a trespass during the hours of daylight (i.e. from the last hour before sunrise to the first hour after sunset) is an offence. If a bird is shot from one's own land, but neither killed nor mortally wounded, it is an offence under the Act to pursue it on to neighbouring land. Only if the bird is killed, or rendered moribund, may it be recovered without contravention of the Act. The offence under the Act may also be committed by sending one's dog on to land in pursuit of game, even when the dog's owner does not himself trespass. This Act is notable in respect of two procedural anomalies. Private prosecutions, not normally allowed in Scotland, are specifically provided for in the Act, and conviction may proceed on the evidence of a single witness. (The *Night Poaching Act 1828*, which deals with the period of the day not covered by the Act of 1832, defines "game" in such a way as not to concern the wildfowler).

A more modern offence is that created by Section 20 of the *Firearms Act 1968*. Under that section it is an offence for any person, who has in his possession a firearm, to enter or be on any land as a trespasser and without reasonable excuse (which he must prove). It should be noted that this offence is committed whatever the purpose of the trespass may be. In terms of penalty, too, it is a much more serious offence.

There is one apparent exception to the law of trespass in Scotland which is of particular importance to wildfowlers. That exception relates to the foreshore. The basic rights in the foreshore, like other land, belong in feudal theory to the Crown. But the Crown's right in relation to the foreshore is different from that in respect of other land. Even where the foreshore is owned by private individuals there remains in the Crown certain rights which are held in trust for the public. The public is therefore entitled to resort to the foreshore for certain purposes including recreation. In this connection, recreation may be regarded as including wildfowling. It is therefore generally legitimate in Scotland (so far as questions of trespass are concerned) to engage in wildfowling on the foreshore. The foreshore in Scots law means that area lying between the high- and the low-water marks of ordinary spring tides. (The English definition of foreshore is slightly different.)

Some practical limits on that public right exist. It may be taken away by statute in particular cases, as it has been in relation to Nature Reserves. It also suffers from the practical limitation that it may be difficult to get to a stretch of foreshore overland without trespassing.

Open and close seasons are governed, so far as wildfowl are concerned by the same statute in Scotland as in England, viz: the *Protection of Birds Act 1954*. There is, however, one variation of the rules as they apply to Scotland. By virtue of a special limitation of Section 2 of the Act, it is not permissible to shoot wildfowl (or various other birds) in Scotland on Sundays, even in the open season, or on Christmas Day.

It is thought that the word "game" in the *Game Licences Act 1860* does not include wildfowl, and accordingly such a licence is not required by a wildfowler. Gun licences were abolished in 1966, but firearms are now dealt with by the *Firearms Act 1968*, which applies equally to Scotland and England.

CHAPTER 3

WILDFOWL AND WADER IDENTIFICATION AND DISTRIBUTION —HYBRIDIZATION OF WILDFOWL

by **James Harrison** D.S.C., M.B.O.U., F.Z.S. (Sci.), M.R.C.S., L.R.C.P.

Vice-President, Wildfowlers' Association of Great Britain and Ireland; Past Vice-President, British Ornithologists' Union; and Chairman, British Ornithologists' Club.

Plumage Sequences. Most species of duck have the following plumages and, although space does not permit any detailed description of these, the general scheme can be illustrated by those of the mallard:

(1) Downy young, i.e. the duckling.
(2) Juvenile plumage, the first covering of definitive feathers, i.e. the "flapper".
(3) First winter and summer plumages; these are the same.
(4) First eclipse plumage (both sexes).
(5) Adult winter and summer plumages; these are again the same.
(6) Second, or adult eclipse plumage (both sexes).
After this the alternation of (5) and (6) continues throughout life.

The acquisition of an "eclipse" plumage in duck is particularly to be noted. This dress is assumed during late summer in most species by both sexes, but most strikingly by the drakes when they closely resemble the duck.

Eclipse plumage is occasioned by the return to the resting phase of the sex glands at the end of the reproductive season, and subserves the important function of survival, the plumage becoming cryptic in eclipse. This is all the more important since, at this season, duck as well as geese are rendered flightless for a time, as all the flight feathers are moulted simultaneously. At this time duck remain in the thick cover of the reeds until the feathers are sufficiently grown to make flight possible. Shelduck undertake a moult migration to the Bight of Heligoland where they spend the period of flight-lessness; some, however, are known to remain in Bridgwater Bay, Somerset, for this purpose. It is important to note that geese do not have any eclipse plumage but they do, like duck, moult all flight feathers simultaneously, becoming flightless for a time. This is also the case with swans.

As a generalization, the first eclipse plumage can be recognized by the retention of some juvenile feathers. In those species which, when adult, have white shoulder patches such as the drake wigeon and both sexes of the goldeneye, recognition is easy for the retention of the drab wing-coverts establishes the first eclipse birds at once. In other species the retention of juvenile body feathers provides the answer. However, in most species these latter are not discernible in the field, except in the case of the drake pintail, which at this season has a striped breast and belly.

In the following species both sexes have an eclipse plumage: shelduck, mallard, teal, garganey, wigeon (first eclipse plumage recognizable), gadwall, shoveler (in both latter species the drakes assume the bill colour of the duck), pintail (first eclipse plumage recognizable), goldeneye and common eider.

In the following species the drakes only go into eclipse: common pochard (the duck is said to have a summer plumage), red-crested pochard, common scoter, velvet scoter, goosander, red-breasted merganser and smew.

Tufted duck and scaup acquire what is regarded as a summer plumage, while a distinctive summer plumage, quite unlike any phase of the duck is assumed by the drake long-tailed duck.

In the descriptions which follow no attempt has been made to describe the species other than when in full plumage, although in September and October many individuals in partial "eclipse" will be obtained. Neither has it been thought necessary to describe the different downy young. An exception is made in the cases of species in which a field distinction exists between the adults and first winter individuals and those species in which the adult and first eclipse plumages are recognizable.

Brief reference is made to plumage varieties. These are of much interest in the study of evolution of wildfowl, in that characters regular in one species may be found exceptionally in others. Thus the white neck ring is found regularly in mallard drakes, very occasionally in gadwall drakes and as a white neck spot in drake teal. As a transient variety it may be found for a short while in immature drake shovelers moulting into first winter plumage, when they may be seen with white neck rings as well marked as any mallard, until they merge with the developing white breast.

SPECIES' LIST

The Order and Nomenclature adopted is that of Scott's *A Coloured Key to the Wildfowl of the World* (1957), and includes not only those species which are legitimate quarry but also others which are fully protected, these latter being indicated by the latter "P". The following rare species are not included: red-breasted goose, snow goose, black duck, American wigeon, blue-winged teal, ring-necked duck, Steller's eider, harlequin duck, buffelhead, hooded merganser, but these feature in the illustrations. Eye colour is hazel-brown unless otherwise stated. For the fullest details of all species, readers should consult Jean Delacour's *The Waterfowl of the World*, which has been invaluable to me in the preparation of these notes.

SWANS

Swans are large birds, the adults being white, the immatures fawn-grey. Habitat, fresh and brackish waters, floods and tidal estuaries: less common on the actual coast. Fly in V formation with neck stretched out. Wing beats of the mute swan make a singing noise. Those of whooper and Bewick's swans are silent.

P. MUTE SWAN, *Cygnus olor* (Gmelin)

Adults: large white birds. Head and neck carried in graceful curves; on water, tail carried in slightly up-tilted position. **Bill orange-yellow, base black, and in cob with a large knob;** black extends to eye; nostrils, edges of bill and tip blackish. Legs and paddles dark grey. Posture both on water and on land, elbows raised and wing feathers fanned open.

Immatures: greyish-fawn; bill greyish-flesh, no knob, blackish at base, edges and tip. Legs and paddles as in adult.

Voice: a silent species but hissing and snorting frequently uttered, also less often a shrill note.

Distribution: British Isles, Denmark, central and southern Sweden, Germany, Poland, the Balkan States, Asia Minor and eastwards to Manchuria.

Varieties: the so-called "Polish Swan", in which the legs and paddles are pink, is recognized as a colour phase.

P. BEWICK'S SWAN, *Cygnus columbianus bewickii* Yarrell

Adults: large white birds, but smaller than mute swan. **Bill blackish-slate, base of upper mandible bright chrome-yellow to level of nostrils, not beyond.** Legs and paddles dark grey. On water, tail carried at water level. Head and neck held erect, wings not fanned.

Immatures: greyish-fawn; bill pale greyish-flesh on sides. Legs and paddles same as adults.

Voice: a gabble, somewhat similar to that of a goose; also a goose-like honking.

Distribution: northern Russia and Siberia, wintering in Scandinavia and British Isles (increasing), Europe and S.W. Asia.

P. JANKOWSKI'S SWAN, *C.c. jankowskii* Alpheraky

This, the eastern race of Bewick's swan resembles the latter in general characters, but it is said to have a somewhat larger bill in which the yellow is brighter.

Distribution: Eastern Siberia to Anadyr; winters in China, Japan and occasionally northern India. Possibly occurs in Britain.]

P. WHOOPER SWAN, *Cygnus cygnus cygnus* (Linnaeus)

Adults: large white birds, approximating size of mute swan. General characters much like Bewick's swan, but **yellow on sides of upper mandible extends well beyond nostrils.** Posture and carriage of tail on water same as Bewick's swan. Head and neck held erect, wings not fanned.

Immatures: greyish-fawn, bill greyish-slate at tip; sides, yellowish-flesh. Legs and paddles greyish-flesh pink.

Voice: a loud whooping "hoohoohoo".

Distribution: breeds southern tip of Greenland, Iceland, Scotland (sparingly), northern Scandinavia, eastwards across Asia to Anadyr. Winters in the British Isles (increasing), across Eurasia as far as Korea and Northern China in the east and south to Asia Minor and north Africa.

GEESE

The geese include species which are associated with the fresh marshes, the so-called "grey geese" and also the two marine geese, the brent and barnacle geese, and the Canada goose, an introduced parkland species, which is now established and feral in the British Isles. Geese, whether in skeins or gaggles, are noisy birds and their calls vary from the exciting gabble of the whitefronts, the notes of the lesser white-fronted goose being higher pitched, to the rather low-pitched "ung-unk" of the bean and pink-footed geese. The latter also produces a sharper "wink-wink" call. The note of the greylag goose is almost identical with that of the farmyard goose.

Brent have a rather soft, low-pitched and metallic call which nevertheless carries a long way. Barnacles seldom fly in formation and are as a rule, in a loose pack, and utter yapping calls similar to that of small dogs, while the Canada goose has been well named the "honker". The notes uttered by this species are loud and ringing: this has been syllabalized "ah honk" with the emphasis on the "honk", the pitch of which rises somewhat.

In flight all grey geese show white above the tail which is dark by contrast and has a thin white terminal band.

YELLOW-BILLED OR FOREST BEAN GOOSE, *Anser fabalis fabalis* (Latham)
Adults: brownish above, barred pale ash; head and neck dark chocolate-brown, a narrow white ring above base of bill. Breast ashy-grey, flanks barred and delineated by white. Rump, belly, upper and under tail-coverts white. **Bill blackish, orange-yellow on sides,** nail black; **legs and feet orange.**
Immatures: duller than adults and lack white at base of bill.
Distribution: winters in the British Isles, Europe to Mediterranean from its breeding grounds in northern Scandinavia and north Russia.

PINK-FOOTED GOOSE, *A.f. brachyrhynchus* Baillon
Adults: greyish-brown above, barred pale ash, head and neck chocolate-brown, darker than rest of the bird. Flanks barred brownish and delineated by white. Underparts paler, greyish-brown, indistinctly barred palest ash. Belly and tail-coverts white. **Bill blackish with variable amount of pink on sides and above nail.** Legs and feet pink.
Immatures: browner and duller.
Varieties: occasionally the adult shows traces of white on forehead at base of bill and minimal black on the breast. Leucistic examples are well known. Legs and feet are very rarely orange.
Distribution: winter visitor to Britain from breeding grounds in south-eastern Greenland and Iceland. Possibly occasionally from Spitzbergen, but

SWANS AND GEESE

BEWICK'S SWAN
Adult : Base of bill yellow.
Immature : Dingy; bill dull flesh to base.

WHOOPER SWAN
Adult : Yellow on bill more extensive, forming point.
Immature : Larger than Bewick's, longer neck.

MUTE SWAN
Adult : Bill orange, with knob.
Immature : Bill flesh, black at base.

SNOW GOOSE
Adult : White, with black wing tips.
Immature : Dingier; bill dark.

BARNACLE GOOSE
Black chest and neck, white face.

CANADA GOOSE
Black neck, light chest, white cheek-patch.

BRENT GOOSE
Black chest and neck, small white neck-spot. Immature birds lack the neck-spot.
Dark-bellied form : Dark under-parts. In Britain, mainly East and South coasts.
Pale-bellied form : Light under-parts. In Britain, mainly West, especially Ireland.

RED-BREASTED GOOSE
Chestnut breast, broad white flank-stripe, head pattern.

Juv Juv Juv
Adult Adult Adult
BEWICK'S WHOOPER MUTE

MUTE SWAN

WHOOPER SWAN
BEWICK'S SWAN

Adult

SNOW GOOSE

BARNACLE GOOSE

CANADA GOOSE

Light-bellied form
BRENT GOOSE
Dark-bellied form
RED-BREASTED GOOSE

GREY GEESE

Grey Geese with ORANGE Legs

WHITE-FRONTED GOOSE
Pink bill with white patch around base; black blotches on belly.

GREENLAND WHITE-FRONTED GOOSE
A subspecies; winters mostly in Ireland and western Scotland. Darker; bill yellow.

BEAN GOOSE
Bill yellow with black markings, but variable.

LESSER WHITE-FRONTED GOOSE
Smaller; stubby bill, *yellow ring* around eye. White more extensive on forehead. A distinct species.

Grey Geese with PINK legs

PINK-FOOTED GOOSE
Small; dark neck, bill black and pink.

GREYLAG GOOSE
Large and pale; bill has no black.

WESTERN GREYLAG
(The subspecies occurring in Britain.) Darker; orange-yellow bill.

EASTERN GREYLAG
Paler, with broad, light feather edges; pink bill.

Juv

Adult WHITE-FRONTED

Greenland form

LESSER WHITE-FRONTED

BEAN

Adult   Juv

WHITE-FRONTED GOOSE

GREENLAND WHITE-FRONTED GOOSE

BEAN GOOSE

LESSER WHITE-FRONTED GOOSE

Eastern form

Western form

PINK-FOOTED GOOSE

GREYLAG GOOSE

PINK-FOOTED

Western   Eastern

GREYLAG

♂ MALLARD ♀

♂ PINTAIL ♀

♂ GADWALL ♀

♂ WIGEON ♀

♂ SHOVELER ♂ MANDARIN ♀

♂ TEAL ♀

♂ GARGANEY ♀ MARBLED DUCK ♂

SURFACE-FEEDING DUCKS

MALLARD
Male: Green head, white neck-ring.
Female: Some orange on bill, whitish tail.

PINTAIL
Male: Needle tail, neck-stripe.
Female: Grey bill, slender pointed tail.

GADWALL
Male: Grey body, black rear.
Female: Yellowish bill, white speculum (in flight).

WIGEON
Male: Rufous head, creamy crown.
Female: Short blue-grey bill, light shoulders (not often visible when swimming).

SHOVELER
Male: Spoon-bill, dark chestnut sides.
Female: Spoon-like bill, blue shoulders (in flight).

MANDARIN
Male: Orange "side-whiskers", orange "sails".
Female: White mark around eye, white chin.

TEAL
Male: Small; grey with dark head, horizontal white stripe above wing.
Female: Small size, green speculum.

GARGANEY
Male: White stripe on head, bluish shoulder-patch.
Female: From Teal by greyer wings, obscure speculum.

MARBLED DUCK
Mediterranean. Dappled plumage. Dark smudge through eye, white tail.

DIVING DUCKS

GOLDENEYE
Male : Round white spot before eye.
Female : Grey body, brown head, white collar, white on wing visible when swimming.

BARROW'S GOLDENEYE
Iceland.
Male : White crescent on face; blacker above than Goldeneye.
Female : Very similar to Goldeneye.

FERRUGINOUS DUCK
Male : Deep mahogany; white under tail-coverts.
Female : Similar, but duller.

SCAUP
Male : Black foreparts, pale back, blue bill. "Black at both ends, white in middle."
Female : Sharply defined white patch at base of bill.

TUFTED DUCK
Male : Black foreparts, black back, drooping crest.
Female : From female Scaup by suggestion of crest. White at base of bill restricted or absent.

POCHARD
Male : Grey; black chest, rufous head.
Female : Buff mark around eye and base of bill, blue band on bill.

RED-CRESTED POCHARD
Male : From Pochard by red bill and white sides.
Female : White cheek, dark crown; from female Common Scoter by white wing-patch, red on bill.

GOLDENEYE

BARROW'S GOLDENEYE

FERRUGINOUS DUCK

SCAUP

TUFTED DUCK

POCHARD

RED-CRESTED POCHARD

this population winters in Denmark, Germany and Holland, less regularly in France.

TUNDRA BEAN GOOSE, *A.f. rossicus* Buturlin
Generally resembles the western bean goose but the body and neck are shorter, the head larger and the bill shorter with less yellow on it.
Distribution: breeds to the eastward of the western form, wintering in south of Europe as far west as Holland, Belgium and northern Germany. May easily occur in Britain.
Varieties: "Sushkin's Bean Goose"; this bird has pink legs and feet and is regarded by most authorities as a colour phase of the species.]

EUROPEAN WHITE-FRONTED GOOSE, *Anser albifrons albifrons* (Scopoli)
Adults: slightly smaller than the bean goose. Above greyish-brown, barred ash; head and neck darker; **around base of bill a white band but not however, as far back as the eyes** (cf. lesser white-fronted goose). Underparts ashy-white with irregularly disposed and in some individuals **heavy black barring.** Belly, rump and tail-coverts, white. Bill pink, nail whitish; legs and feet orange-yellow.
Immatures: lack the white facial mask and black bars; generally duller and underparts spotted brownish.
Distribution: Breeds on the Arctic tundras of Eurasia as far as the Kolyma river, possibly farther eastwards. Winter visitor to western and southern Europe to Mediterranean coasts.
Varieties: leucistic examples are recorded.

GREENLAND WHITE-FRONTED GOOSE, *A.a. flavirostris* Dalgety and Scott
Adults: general pattern as in the European bird but much darker and with **a yellow bill.**
Immatures: resemble those of the European form, but are also extremely dark.
Distribution: breeds in north-west Greenland, winters in Ireland, western Scotland and Wales, occasionally recorded England and eastern North America.

P. LESSER WHITE-FRONTED GOOSE, *Anser erythropus* (Linnaeus)
A relatively small goose.
Adults: closely resemble the European white-fronted goose, but **white facial mask extends on to the crown beyond level of eyes** (c.f. European white-fronted goose). **Eyelids orange-yellow.** Below rather darker than *A. albifrons.* Flanks barred and delineated white. Heavy barring on breast and underparts. Belly and tail-coverts white. Legs and feet orange.
Immatures: duller and lack the white facial mask and barring of underparts.
Distribution: breeds in the extreme north of Scandinavia and U.S.S.R., eastwards to the Behring Sea. Winters south through north-western Europe,

to the eastern Mediterranean and the delta of the Nile; south-eastwards to the mouth of the Ganges and in a wide circle north and east to Shanghai, Korea, Japan, Sakhalin and north to the Behring Sea: rare straggler to Britain, but recently proved to be almost annual.

WESTERN GREYLAG GOOSE, *Anser anser anser* (Linnaeus)

A large goose, overall lighter in colour than the preceding species; head and neck less dark and contrasting.

Adults: above brownish-grey, the feathers narrowly edged pale ash, giving a barred appearance. Below whitish-grey, lower breast and belly barred irregularly with black though never as heavily as in white-fronted goose. Flanks brownish, lightly barred pale ash, and delineated by white. In flight **pale bluish-grey "shoulders"** are diagnostic. **Bill orange, nail white;** legs and feet pinkish-flesh.

Immatures: duller than adults; have no black marking on underparts; legs and feet greyish-flesh and the bill greenish-grey.

Distribution: a few pairs breed in Scotland; main breeding grounds Iceland, Scandinavia, western U.S.S.R., central and eastern Europe, wintering in western Europe and North Africa.

Varieties: Albino examples have been recorded.

[EASTERN GREYLAG GOOSE, *A.a. rubrirostris* (Swinhoe)

Adults: much paler than the western form, the light barring of underparts and flanks much more pronounced, while **the bill is pink.**

Immatures: duller than the adults and lack the blackish markings on the underparts.

Distribution: breeds to the eastward of the river Volga, but intergrades with the western form where breeding areas meet. Northern limit latitude 60° N., southern limit roughly 40° N. Winters south to the Persian Gulf across northern India to China as far south as latitude 20° N.

Note: pink-billed greylag geese have been observed, but not yet taken in British Isles.]

ATLANTIC CANADA GOOSE, *Branta canadensis canadensis* (Linnaeus)

A large goose with very distinctive white "cut-throat" pattern of black head and neck.

Adults: rather dark greyish-brown above, barred pale ash. **Head and neck black; prominent white cut-throat marking** extending lower throat and upwards on either side of face to level of ear-coverts. Underparts whitish, faintly barred pale ash. Flanks brownish, barred ash. Belly and under tail-coverts pure white. Bill, legs and feet black.

Immatures: rather duller and somewhat smaller than adults. Pale edges to wing-coverts.

Distribution: an introduced species native to eastern Canada and U.S.A. now well established and feral in many localities in Britain and western Europe, also New Zealand.

Varieties: leucistic varieties are known.

P. BARNACLE GOOSE, *Branta leucopsis* (Bechstein)
A very distinctive goose, predominantly black, grey and white.
Adults: head, neck and upper breast black except for **face, which is creamy white. Upperparts a pure french grey, barred black and white.** Underparts pure white, flanks greyish. Bill, legs and feet black.
Immatures: duller and browner, less well marked.
Distribution: from its breeding grounds in north-eastern Greenland, Spitzbergen and southern Novaya Zemlya, spends the winter on the coasts of Europe; in the British Isles mostly in the north and west.

THE BRENTS
The brents are rather small predominantly grey and black geese, with a semi-collar of white markings on either side of the neck. They are of marine habitat and are seldom found on the fresh marsh. Two forms frequent the British Isles.

P. DARK-BELLIED BRENT GOOSE, *Branta bernicla bernicla* (Linnaeus)
Adults: head and neck black, **semi-collar of white markings on** either side of the neck. **Back and underparts dark grey,** vent and tail-coverts white. Bill, legs and feet blackish.
Immatures: duller and lack the white semi-collar and feathers of upperparts and wing-coverts margined whitish.
Distribution: breeds Arctic shores of U.S.S.R. Winters on coasts of British Isles and western Europe.

P. LIGHT-BELLIED BRENT GOOSE, *B.b.hrota* (O. F. Müller)
Adults: resemble the previous form but underparts much paler, in some almost white.
Immatures: resemble those of the dark-bellied form, but paler underneath.
Distribution: breeds on the Arctic shores of eastern Canada, northern Greenland, Spitzbergen, Franz Josef Land; winters on the coasts of north-west Europe and in the British Isles, mostly in Ireland, also Atlantic coast of North America.

DUCKS

Ducks may be conveniently divided into four main groups:
I. Shelducks: this group in many of its characters may be recognized as occupying an intermediate position between the geese and the ducks. The sexes are similar. They are mostly found on littoral habitat.
II. Dabbling Ducks: this group includes the species which were formerly referred to as the "surface-feeding" duck, an obvious misnomer when their up-ended feeding is remembered. They swim high in the water, tails raised. This group frequents both coastal areas and inland waters, not only at sea

level, but also at considerable altitude. The wing speculum is well developed and bright, often metallic.

III. Diving Ducks: these birds are very adaptable as to habitat and the various species include those which are purely marine, e.g. the scoters and others such as the tufted duck and common pochard, which are more at home on inland waters.

In structure this group is quite distinct from the "dabblers", the relatively large paddles and lobulated hind toe, small wings and an ungainly waddle when ashore being distinctive, as well as their "pattering" take-off from the water, compared with the clean spring of a dabbling duck. They swim low in the water, tails parallel with it.

IV. "Saw bills": these birds have become adapted to a specialized life. This is evident from the bill which is thin and is furnished with a series of sharp little "teeth", which enables them to secure the fish upon which they live. They swim very low in the water, tails on the surface.

P. COMMON SHELDUCK, *Tadorna tadorna* (Linnaeus)

A large duck, brightly coloured in **contrasting black, white and chestnut.**

Adult male: iridescent green head and neck, two broad parallel black markings on either side of the back extending towards tail. A broad chestnut band encircles the bird at the level of the shoulders; from the posterior edge of this, running backwards over the belly to the vent, there is a dusky-black band, while the under tail-coverts are dull chestnut mixed with dusky-black. The bill is bright carmine and in the drake is furnished with a knob, especially in the breeding season, of the same colour. Legs and feet flesh-pink.

Adult female: general appearance similar to drake but less bright, bill not so vivid and lacks the knob.

Immature: above ashy-grey mantle, below white and in front of face and eyes. Bill dull pinkish-grey. Legs and feet dull pinkish-flesh.

Voice: the duck has a short "quack", the drake a whistle.

Stance and flight: the former rather goose-like, walks and runs well; flight is strong and also rather similar to that of geese.

Distribution: a wide distribution from the British Isles, north-west Europe to the Caspian, south to about latitude 30° N., north to about latitude 60° and eastwards to Manchuria. Greatly increased as a British breeding bird during past fifty years.

P. RUDDY SHELDUCK, *Tadorna ferruginea* (Pallas)

About same size as common shelduck.

Adult drake: **yellowish cinnamon,** head somewhat whitish on face; chin and foreneck washed strong cinnamon: narrow black neck collar. Rump and tail black. Abdomen, including under tail-coverts, chestnut. In flight wings appear black and white. Bill slate, legs and feet dark slate.

Adult duck: much like adult drake but duller and lacks black collar and is whiter on face.

Immatures: much resemble the duck, but are greyish on scapulars.

Stance and flight: deportment somewhat anserine; strong flight.

Voice: noisy whooping call by drake and a strident harsh call "ka-ha-ha" uttered by duck.

Distribution: a wide breeding area. In Europe only in the south of the Iberian peninsula and in the Balkan peninsula. Extends eastwards across the whole of central Asia almost to the coasts of the Pacific Ocean. Winters in the valley of the Nile, and throughout India, Ceylon, Burma, northern Siam and Annam, the whole of China, Korea and the southern islands of Japan. Rare straggler to Britain.

PINTAIL, *Anas acuta acuta* (Linnaeus)

A large-sized, long-necked graceful duck.

Adult drake: **Head and neck chocolate brown, on front for about one-third of its length. On either side of the white breast and belly, a thin white line runs upwards to the level of, and behind, the ear-coverts.** Mantle and flanks pure pearl-grey. Long lance-shaped scapulars, black margined white, overhang the wings. Rump and upper tail-coverts black. Wing speculum bronze-green, becoming blackish posteriorly, bordered buff in front, white at back. **Central pair of tail feathers elongated into the "pin".** Under tail-coverts black, at vent fulvous. Bill greyish, on sides blue, black at base, nail blackish. Legs and feet greyish, webs dusky.

Adult duck: head and neck brown. Upper parts brown variegated by paler edges to feathers. **Long scapulars and tail feathers with markings reminiscent of hen pheasant.** Underparts from throat to belly paler. Bill, legs and feet greyish.

Immatures: similar to duck but duller, drake greyer, central tail feathers not markedly elongated.

Stance and flight: graceful poise, stands rather high; flight fast with rapid wing beats, which make a hissing sound and are sickle-shaped.

Voice: drake utters a low double whistle (display). Ordinary note described as "kruck"; when alarmed said to utter a "cheeping-peevish cry". Duck produces a low "quack" and a growl reminiscent of duck wigeon.

Varieties: Totally white individuals have been recorded and occasionally the drake in partial eclipse has a white neck ring.

Distribution: breeds in northern Eurasia, the British Isles (increasing) and North America. Winters in the Old World south to North Africa, Egypt, Abyssinia and across northern Asia to south China. In the New World south to the West Indies and Hawaiian Islands.

TEAL, *Anas crecca crecca* (Linnaeus)

A small duck; the drake brightly coloured.

Adult drake: **head and neck rich maroon; on either side a broad iridescent green marking from in front of eye to nape,** delineated in white from base of bill backwards. From base of bill and over crown somewhat brownish to dusky-blue on nape. In front a blackish chin spot. Above vermiculated greyish-white. **Scapulars jet black, edge white and cream: wing speculum green and black, bordered buff in front and thin white behind.** Breast fulvous and spotted blackish, belly white, flanks vermiculated greyish, posteriorly white and then black. Undertail coverts fulvous at sides black below. Bill dark slate, legs and feet usually greyish but variable, in some ochraceous.

Adult duck: sombre brown, sometimes greyish-brown, variegated lighter and darker from dark centres of feathers; underparts paler.

Immatures: resemble duck but duller.

Stance and flight: stands low on the ground, flight very rapid with frequent dipping and diving movements of flocks in perfect unison, but sometimes erratic.

Voice: the scientific name is apt for the drake's "crick crick" is one of the characteristic features of our marshes. The duck utters a rather harsh and high-pitched "quack".

Distribution: a wide distribution as a breeding bird extending across the whole of the northern hemisphere approximately to latitude 40° N.; winters as far south as Africa almost to the Equator, and in Arabia, Persia, India, Siam and southern China.

Varieties: the teal seems very prone to show variations which include the following in drakes: (1) general spotting of the undersides including belly; (2) a white loral spot of varying sizes; (3) a triangular white mark of variable size, at the root of the neck in front; (4) an accentuating of the feathers at the nape producing a tuft; (5) the "ghost" pattern of a character referred to as "bridling". Drakes of the *American race*, occasionally identified in Britain, have white crescent mark near the shoulder.

BAIKAL TEAL, *Anas formosa* Georgi

A small duck, slightly larger than teal.

Adult drake: very distinctive head markings, crown and ear-covert region green. **Face and front of neck buffy-yellow, cheeks "bimaculated" by a blackish bridle from around eyes to join black chin patch.** Posterior part of neck dusky green. Breast-shield buffy-brown, spotted dusky at sides. Rest of under-parts buffy-yellow. Under tail-coverts black. Flanks vermiculated grey bordered by white at shoulder region and in front of tail-coverts. Upper parts brownish: long sickle-shaped scapulars buffy-yellow and black. Wings sepia, speculum green. Rectrices sepia. Bill slate, legs and toes dull ochraceous, webs and nails dusky.

Adult duck: warm earth-brown, feathers edged paler giving markedly speckled appearance: head and neck darkish-brown, cheeks pale, marked pale superciliary stripe. **Very prominent white loral spot.** Pale cheeks in some females divided by a dusky "bridle". Bill, legs and feet slate coloured.

Immatures: resemble females but lack loral spot.

Stance and flight: resembles that of rest of genus *Anas*. Flight less fast than that of teal.

Voice: very distinctive, that of male a single or double cluck; female utters a harsh quack.

Distribution: breeds in northern Asia from longitude 80°, eastwards to Kamchatka but not on the coast of the Arctic Ocean; southwards to approximately latitude 55°N. Winters to just south of the Tropic of Cancer and eastwards to Japan.

As a British bird this duck, although not yet officially accepted, has occurred on a sufficient number of occasions to have a serious claim for inclusion as a genuine British immigrant of irregular and rare occurence.

MALLARD, *Anas platyrhynchos platyrhynchos* Linnaeus
A large-sized duck.

Adult drake: a distinctive bird; **Glossy green head and neck, separated from greyish-brown mantle and rich chestnut breast-shield by a white ring,** though in most individuals incomplete on back of neck. Back and scapulars vermiculated pale grey, flanks greyish, finely vermiculated. Upper tail-coverts black with the characteristic double curl, under tail-coverts black: tail feathers light, outermost whitish. Underparts pale grey. **Wing speculum violet-blue edged white on both borders. Bill pale chrome-yellow,** legs and feet orange.

Adult duck: predominantly brown, striated and spotted, pale eye stripe, throat and underparts of body paler, front of neck markedly striated. Tail feathers whitish; **speculum as in drake.** Bill dull sepia with greenish or dull chrome markings, legs and toes paler yellow, webs dusky.

Immatures: broadly resemble the duck, but duller, feathering less compact and soft parts duller.

Stance and flight: stands firmly, walks well, flight strong and moderately fast, wing beats rapid.

Voice: drake a soft slightly nasal note, the duck an oft-repeated and somewhat loud low "quack".

Distribution: breeds across the whole of the northern hemisphere to about latitude 40° N. Winters south to North Africa, northern India to the east coast of China.

Varieties: very prone to throw "sports". These include: (1) a spotted breast-shield, thus resembling the Greenland mallard, *A.p. conboschas;* (2) completely white individuals; (3) pied birds; (4) melanism; (5) erythrism; (6) the "cayuja" type, i.e. black with a white triangular marking at root of neck in front; (7) "pepper and salt" variety; (8) cinnamon coloured and others which integrate in one way or another with these main types. In size and weight, also, there is great variation and the above, to some extent, depend upon the admixture of birds which have been interbred with domestic or semi-domestic stock and which through circumstances have become inbred. Completeness of white collar variable. Drake occasionally has a blue beak.

GADWALL, *Anas strepera* Linnaeus
A medium-sized duck.

Adult drake: generally rather sombrely coloured. Head and neck brownish, rest of upper parts and flanks greyish; **chestnut and black on shoulders** (wing-coverts) usually hidden by flank feathers, some chestnut on scapulars.

Wing speculum white. Breast-shield barred blackish and white. Under tail-coverts black. Bill dark, at sides ochraceous in eclipse, legs and toes ochraceous, webs dusky.

Adult duck: variegated brownish, paler underneath. **Wing speculum white.**

Immatures: drake resembles adult drake in eclipse; duck similar to adults but wings duller.

Stance and flight: stands easily and walks well. Flight mallard-like, but wings more pointed.

Voice: duck has a mallard-like "quack" but softer and note tends to drop at end of series of quacks; drake utters a soft whistle and a grunt, but a more vocal and varied repertoire when displaying.

Distribution: a wide distribution across North America, Europe and Asia to Sea of Okhotsk. In British Isles somewhat local and mainly East Anglia: breeds sparingly. Increasing.

Varieties: drakes occasionally show an incomplete and, less often complete white neck ring.

WIGEON, *Anas penelope* (Linnaeus)

A medium-sized duck, smaller than mallard.

Adult drake: **pale yellow forehead and crown, rest of head and neck chestnut,** blackish chin spot. Upper parts grey finely vermiculated; white shoulders (1st eclipse drake drab shoulders), long lanceolate scapulars jet black and white; wing speculum green, bordered white, **breast vinaceous,** belly white. Upper and under tail-coverts black, central pair of tail feathers somewhat elongated. Bill blue, tip and nail blackish, legs and feet dark grey.

Adult duck: two phases, one predominantly brownish; the other, possibly as result of mature age, grey. In both, underparts white; speculum less bright than in drake—green merging into black. Soft parts as drake but duller.

Immatures: resemble duck but duller, particularly the speculum.

Stance and flight: stands easily and walks nimbly. Flight is rapid and powerful. Wings tend to be sickle-shaped.

Voice: drake utters the familiar "whee-oo", the last syllable being given some accentuation. Ducks produce a curious growling purr.

Distribution: breeds right across the whole of northern Eurasia, south to latitude 50° N. Winters south to north and west Africa almost to the Equator and eastwards to Persia, India, Siam and to the east coast of China. Breeds sparingly in the British Isles (increasing) and is abundant on all coasts in winter and more recently inland.

Varieties: spotting and barring of the upper breast occurs occasionally in drakes, also white collar (rare).

GARGANEY, *Anas querquedula* Linnaeus

Slightly larger than teal.

Adult drake: in summer plumage head and neck rich brown, on either side **a broad white crescentic marking from in front of eye to nape.**

Upperparts brown, lanceolate black and white scapulars overlay wings and pale blue shoulders. **Speculum green, broadly edged white, back and front.** Breast brown, closely barred darker brown. Flanks vermiculated pale grey and delineated black and white. Rump, upper and under tail-coverts brownish. Belly white. Bill slate; legs and toes greyish, webs dusky.

Adult duck: generally brown with whitish underparts; speculum less bright and less broadly bordered than in drake. Shoulders less pure grey.

Immatures: like duck but duller.

Stance and flight: stance typical of dabbling duck; flight fast, wing beats not quite so rapid as teal; looks somewhat larger, particularly head and bill.

Voice: drake makes a rather hard grating call, duck a soft, short "quack".

Distribution: a widely distributed species, breeding right across Eurasia between approximately 60° N. and 30° N. and as a rarity in Iceland. To the British Isles a summer visitor and double passage migrant. Winters south to central Africa, southern Asia, occasionally to Australia.

SHOVELER, *Anas clypeata* Linnaeus

A medium-sized duck.

Adult drake: glossy-green head and neck; upperparts mainly white and brown, but long scapulars black and white, outermost edged sky-blue, shoulders sky-blue. Upper and under tail-coverts black, tail whitish. **Breast white, belly and flanks rich chestnut,** white posteriorly. Speculum green, edged in front by broad and behind by narrow white. **Bill longer than head, narrow at base, spatulate at tip,** black. Iris bright yellow. Legs and toes orange-yellow, webs slightly dusky, nails dark.

Adult duck: lightish-brown, feather edges paler. Pale eye stripe and pale below eye. Iris brown. Bill pale fulvous-brown, nail darker. Legs and feet ochraceous, webs and nails slightly dusky.

Immatures: closely resemble duck but duller.

Stance and flight: former horizontal; walks somewhat awkwardly. Flight is rapid and wings make a distinct rattling sound. In flight blue shoulders show prominently and the head and beak look disproportionately large.

Voice: male's described as a guttural "took-took" and also a double "quack", that of duck similar to, though softer than that of mallard.

Varieties: the following transient characters have been recorded: (1) white neck ring; (2) pale crescent on face; (3) pale chin spot; (4) pale spot at base of bill; (5) barring and spotting of lower breast; (6) dark crescents on upper breast; (7) partial albinism.

Distribution: breeds across the whole of Eurasia except in the extreme north where it extends up to or just over the Arctic Circle, south to about 40° N. Increasing in Britain. In the New World breeds in the western interior from Alaska to the great lakes, south to 40° N. Winters south to north Africa, parts of east Africa, Asia Minor, eastwards through India, north Siam to the east coasts of China and to Japan.

P. Common Eider, *Somateria mollissima mollissima* (Linnaeus)
A large heavily built diving duck of marine habitat.
Adult drake: top of head black, **back of head pale green.** Breast white, slightly buffy. Belly and tail with its coverts black. **Flanks black with large white circular markings posteriorly,** face, neck and back white. Bill greenish-yellow, nail whitish, legs and feet pale ochraceous.
Adult duck: pale chestnut-brown, barred closely sepia, paler generally on head, neck and breast. Bill, legs and feet greyish.
Immatures: duller and more uniform as markings less contrasting. Bill, legs and feet dull greenish-grey.
Stance and flight: stands squarely and somewhat erect, walks and runs well considering heavy build. Flight strong. Swimming and diving superb.
Voice: call of drake a ringing "coo-ru-hu" and of duck a harsh "kor-r-r".
Distribution: northern Europe, Jan Mayen island, Iceland, northern U.S.S.R. east to Kola Peninsula; Scotland, northern England, Ireland, Brittany, Holland, shores of the Baltic. Winters south as far as the Mediterranean.
Varieties: drakes occasionally have black V on throat.

P. King-Eider, *Somateria spectabilis* (Linnaeus)
Slightly smaller than Eider.
Adult drake: **whole of crown pale French grey darker at nape: cheeks and face pale green,** a dusky patch below eyes on either side. A thin whitish line from above eyes to nape dividing cheeks from back of head. **Bill orange-red much swollen and giving a high forehead,** base outlined narrowly by black feathers, nostrils dusky, nail whitish. A pronounced V-shaped marking at throat, apex directed forwards. Neck and back white; breast buffy–pink; shoulders white, scapulars black, decurved into white circular patch on sides of rump. **Two characteristic "sail feathers" on mantle,** remaining regions black. Legs and feet yellowish, webs and nails slightly dusky.
Adult duck: rather rich reddish-brown variegated sepia, markings undulating rather than barred as in eider. **Shows truncated "sail feathers".** Bill greyish, not swollen at base; legs and toes greenish-yellow; webs, joints and nails slightly dusky. Iris yellow to brown.
Immatures: like those of Eider, but lighter below.
Immature drake: dusky head, ochraceous bill, dusky-white neck, breast and edges of mantle.
Stance and flight: similar to Eider.
Voice: resembles that of Eider, but less loud. Usually silent except during breeding season.
Distribution: a breeder on the shores and islands of the Arctic Ocean of Europe, Asia and America. A straggler to the British Isles in winter.

P. Red-crested Pochard, *Netta rufina* (Pallas)
A large-sized diving duck, but which feeds almost as much from the surface.

Adult drake: **head and upper part of neck, including throat, bright chestnut, feathering forming full rounded crest;** iris red. Nape and rest of neck, breast, belly, upper and under tail-coverts black. Shoulder region and flanks white, edged greyish-fawn, rest of upperparts greyish-fawn. Bill bright coral red, nail whitish, legs and feet fulvous flesh, webs and nails dusky.

Adult duck: crown and back of neck dark earth-brown, rest of upperparts earth-brown, barred paler earth-brown, sides of head, breast and flanks pale ash-brown; belly and under tail-coverts whitish-ash. Bill pale grey, legs and toes fulvous-brown, joints, webs and nails dusky.

Immatures: resemble females.

Stance and flight: stance slightly erect, flight easy action; **both sexes show much white on wings in flight,** both in primaries and secondaries.

Voice: drake usually silent except during the nesting season then utters a hard, wheezy note, also a low grunt; duck produces a grating "kaar" or "kurr".

Distribution: breeds in the Mediterranean region and in central Europe. Local in Germany, Switzerland and the Low Countries. Eastward from northern shores of the Black Sea, Caspian and Aral Seas as far as central China. In the British Isles increasing from introduced birds. Winters south to delta of the Nile, shores of the Red Sea, Asia Minor, Persia, northern India and Burma.

POCHARD, *Aythya ferina* (Linnaeus)

Smaller than preceding species.

Adult drake: head and neck rich chestnut, darker than preceding species; iris red; breast black, **upperparts and flanks palest grey,** but belly slightly darker; upper and under tail-coverts black, tail dark. Bill grey, a pale bluish-grey band between nostrils and dark slate tip. Legs and toes bluish-grey. Webs and nails dusky.

Adult duck: head and neck rather dark earth-brown, pale at base of bill, on throat and behind eye. Upperparts dark greyish-brown, tail-coverts sepia. Flanks greyish-brown and belly greyish-white. Bill slate, pale greyish band between nostril and dark tip. Legs and toes bluish-grey, web and nails dusky.

Immatures: closely resemble the duck.

Varieties: individuals of a pied nature have been recorded, also individuals showing the white chin spot.

Stance and flight: slightly erect, waddles, flight strong and fast.

Voice: drake has a low soft whistle, duck emits a low hard "kurr".

Distribution: breeds across the whole of Eurasia including Iceland, north to the Arctic Circle, eastwards to Kamchatka and Japan, south to approximately latitude 50° N. Increasing in Britain. Winters in western Europe south to Mediterranean countries, Morocco and Algeria, Nile Valley, Persian Gulf, India south to Mysore, Burma and the Philippines.

FERRUGINOUS DUCK, *Aythya nyroca* (Güldenstädt)

About size of tufted duck.

Adult drake: **head and neck, breast and flanks bright chestnut-brown; iris white;** back, rump and tail rich dark maroon-brown, mantle with greenish gloss. Vent dusky-brown, **under tail-coverts white,** wing speculum white; bill, legs and feet grey. Bill blue, dusky base, nail black.

Adult duck: similar to drake but duller and darker.

Immatures: like females but duller.

Stance and flight: similar to other members of the genus. Flight rapid, in distance looks like tufted duck but white of wings more extensive, and shows white under tail-coverts.

Voice: resembles that of pochard.

Distribution: central and southern Europe including Mediterranean islands; extends eastwards to central Asia. Winters in North Africa and along the west coast as far south as Cap Blanco; in the valley of the Nile, at the mouth of the Persian Gulf, in Palestine, Persia, northern Arabia, at the head of the Red Sea, eastwards to Burma, south in India as far as about Madras and Caldicot. Increasing in the British Isles, casual elsewhere in Europe.

TUFTED DUCK, *Aythya fuligula* (Linnaeus)

A small diving duck.

Adult drake: distinctive **black and white bird with long dependent crest,** entirely black, except for belly and flanks which are white. Iris bright yellow. Bill pale bluish-grey, tip dusky. Legs and toes greyish, joints, webs and nails dusky.

Adult duck: rich dark brown above, including head, neck, breast and tail-coverts. Iris dull yellow. Belly white, flanks striated lighter and darker brown. Wing speculum in both sexes white. The crest is short and truncated. Bill greyish-blue, tip dusky. Legs and toes greyish; joints, webs and nails dusky.

Immatures: resemble duck but duller.

Varieties: (1) white chin spot; (2) white under tail-coverts; (3) white facial mask; (4) heavy brown flecking of underparts.

Voice: usually silent; drake utters a double note "spur-spur" and duck a harsh "karr".

Distribution: nests roughly between latitudes 50° and 70° N. Greatly increased in Britain this century. In Scandinavia as far as the extreme north, sparingly in the Balkan peninsula. Winters south to Mediterranean and coasts of Morocco and Nile valley; east to Iraq, shores of the Indian Ocean as far south as Caldicot on the west and Pondicherry on the east, then east through northern Burma and Siam to the Pacific coastline as far as Pohai. Common and increasing in Britain as a breeding bird and winter visitor.

SCAUP, *Aythya marila marila* (Linnaeus)

A medium-sized diving duck.

Adult drake: distinctive black and white uncrested duck; head and neck dark glossy-green. Iris bright yellow; breast glossy-black; **upperparts pale grey, coarsely vermiculated.** Tail dark, rump, upper and under tail-coverts and vent black, rest of bird white. Bill grey, tip dusky. Legs and toes grey; joints, webs and nails dusky.

Adult duck: head, and breast dark brown, **broad white facial band,** iris dark yellow. Upperparts greyish-brown, belly whitish, vent and under tail-coverts brownish; flanks brownish, lightly barred. Bill grey, tip dusky; legs and toes grey, joints, webs and nails dusky. Wing speculum in both sexes white.

Immatures : resemble duck but duller.

Stance and flight : somewhat erect, fly strongly and noisily; ungainly walk.

Voice : normally silent; drake emits a soft crooning courtship note and the duck a guttural "kurr-kurr".

Distribution : breeds in Iceland and northern Eurasia to approximately latitude 70° N., and eastwards to longitude 120°; in the south to latitude 60° N. Winters on coasts of British Isles, north-western Europe, the Mediterranean countries, the Black and Caspian Seas and in south-eastern Europe and south-western Asia as far as the Gulf of Kutch.

COMMON SCOTER, *Melanitta nigra nigra* (Linnaeus)

A medium-sized marine diving duck.

Adult drake : **entirely glossy black. Bill black with a pronounced black knob at base: across middle of upper mandible an orange-yellow band.** Legs, toes and webs dark blackish-slate.

Adult duck : crown of head, back of neck and entire upperparts dark brown. Sides of face and throat greyish-white, breast, flanks and vent, dark brown, belly paler brown. Bill, legs and toes greyish-slate, webs and nails dusky.

Immatures : resemble duck but duller; drakes often appear pied when juvenile plumage fades and black first winter feathers start moulting through.

Stance and flight : somewhat erect, flight strong; ungainly gait.

Voice : of drake said to be varied and melodious, that of duck a harsh growl.

Distribution : widely distributed, breeding across northern Eurasia, north of latitude 60° N. including Iceland and Spitzbergen (rarely), but also in northern Scotland and in north of Ireland. Winters off coasts of British Isles and Eire, north-western Europe, the Baltic and Mediterranean basin, south to west Africa.

VELVET SCOTER, *Melanitta fusca fusca* (Linnaeus)

Slightly larger then common scoter, of marine habitat.

Adult drake : very distinctive **glossy-black bird; small white marking under and extending behind eyes and a white wing speculum.** Iris silvery white, bill at base and around nostrils slate, sides orange-yellow, nail white. **Legs and toes vivid crimson, joints, webs and nails dusky.**

Adult duck : predominantly warm earth-brown, on cheeks below eye two circular whitish markings. Underparts slightly paler and flecked whitish. Wing speculum white. Legs and feet as in drake but less bright.

Immatures : resemble duck but duller.

Stance and flight : somewhat erect, ungainly gait, strong flight.

Voice : drake produces a whistling "whur-er" and the duck a harsh growling note.

Distribution : breeds in Scandinavia, the Baltic coasts and across U.S.S.R.

north of latitude 55° N., eastwards to the Tamyr Peninsula. Winters south to coasts of the British Isles; western Europe to the Bay of Biscay and the Black, Caspian and Aral Seas.

P. SURF-SCOTER, *Melanitta perspicilata* (Linnaeus)

A medium-large marine diving duck.

Adult drake: **black with conspicuous white forehead and nape.** Bill white, nail slightly yellowish; above from nostrils to nail bright red, at base bluish, black patch on sides, outline of bill at feather margin yellowish-orange. Iris white; legs and toes ochraceous, nails, webs and joints dusky.

Adult duck: brown, pale brownish-white patches on lores behind eyes, **and on nape.** Iris dark, bill heavy pale bluish-grey, a darker shade on sides at base. Legs, feet, etc., as in male but duller.

Immatures: rather resemble duck, but paler and have whitish underparts.

Stance and flight: stands slightly erect, flies well and presents as a black duck with white markings on head, no white wing speculum and a yellowish bill.

Voice: silent except in the breeding season when the drake has a clear whistle syllabized as "puk-puk"; the duck utters a harsh croak.

Distribution: resident in North America west of Hudson Bay. Winters south to California and from Nova Scotia to South Carolina. Has occurred in Britain.

LONG-TAILED DUCK, *Clangula hyemalis* (Linnaeus)

A medium-small marine diving duck.

Adult drake: at once recognizable by its generally **black and white aspect and long pheasant-like tail.** Head and neck white, a large dusky spot behind and below eyes. Black of breast extends over both shoulder regions to rump and black central tail feathers; scapulars white, wings blackish, rest of underparts white. Bill, base dark slate, rest orange-yellow, nail slate. Legs, toes greyish, webs and nails dusky. In summer, head and neck black, white patch encircling eye. Scapulars sepia, edged light brown.

Adult duck: head and neck white, rest of underparts white, flanks white, edged brownish. At root of neck and on breast a dusky-band, upperparts and wings brownish. Bill, legs and toes greyish, web and nails dusky. In summer, black patch below and behind the eye and black on throat.

Immatures: resemble duck but duller.

Stance and flight: rather erect and walks with ease, flight strong, swinging from side to side and with wings held curved downwards, alighting on water breast first.

Voice: drakes utter a series of musical whistles and the ducks a low growl.

Distribution: breeding is wide and circumpolar in both the Old and the New Worlds. Range includes Greenland, Iceland, Bear Is., Spitzbergen, Norway to 71°, northern Sweden and Finland. Winters south to coasts of British Isles, north-western Europe, the Baltic countries, the Caspian Sea and central Asia, eastwards to northern Japan.

GOLDENEYE, *Bucephala clangula clangula* (Linnaeus)

A medium-sized diving duck.

Adult drake: predominantly black and white; **head glossy-green, fully crowned; circular white spot at base of bill.** Iris yellow. Neck, breast and flanks pure white, vent washed greyish. Above black scapulars, black and white; wing speculum white. Bill slate, tip dusky. Legs and toes ochraceous; joints, web and nails dusky.

Adult duck: head and neck warm earth-brown, iris yellow; white collar. greyish across breast extending to flanks, back and upper parts; tail dark grey, Belly white, vent greyish. Wing speculum and shoulders (wing-coverts) white; bill, base slate, rest dull ochraceous-yellow, tip dusky, legs and toes, ochraceous, joints, webs and nails dusky.

Immatures: resemble duck but lack the white shoulders and are duller.

Stance and flight: somewhat erect, gait ungainly. Flight strong and direct, producing loud rattle.

Voice: usually silent, drake produces a wheezy sound and the duck a grunting growl.

Distribution: breeds in Eurasia from approximately latitude 60°N. Winters south to British Isles through central Europe, northern shores of Black and Caspian Seas, east to western China and Japan, south to North Africa, the Nile Valley and northern Arabia.

P. SMEW, *Mergus albellus* Linnaeus

A small sawbill.

Adult drake: an immaculate little black and white duck. **Head and neck white, but from base of bill surrounding eye a black marking.** Crown feathers white form a truncated crest; at nape a triangular black marking. Iris red. Neck, breast, belly and under tail-coverts white. Extending forward from sides of neck on to breast **two fine black semi-circular markings;** mantle black, scapular regions white, rump, upper tail-coverts and tail feathers grey; flanks vermiculated pale grey. Wing speculum black. Bill pale grey, nail dusky. Legs and toes leaden-grey, webs and nails dusky.

Adult duck: throat and sides of neck white, at base of bill a dusky black patch. Crown to nape fox-red. Breast, flanks and back, rump, tail and tail-coverts grey, scapular areas and shoulders white. Speculum black. Belly, vent and under tail-coverts white. Iris dull red; bill, legs and toes dark grey, webs and nails dusky.

Immatures: closely resemble the duck, but lack the dusky black patch at base of bill and white on shoulders.

Stance and flight: stance slightly erect, walks well, flight strong and fast.

Voice: as a rule silent, but drake produces a hissing note during courtship and the duck a harsh "quack".

Distribution: breeds in wooded areas across northern Eurasia from about latitude 65° N. to beyond the Arctic Circle where suitable hollow trees are found. Winters south to the Mediterranean basin, though scarce in west; Black Sea, Asia Minor, Iraq, Persia, the Aral Sea, east through northern India and China to the Pacific coast. In Britain, mainly on reservoirs, except in hard weather.

RED-BREASTED MERGANSER, *Mergus serrator serrator* Linnaeus

A medium-sized sawbill.

Adult drake: head and upper part of neck glossy-green; **long feathers of crown form a double crest**; iris red, lower part of neck white, **breast pale chestnut with blackish longitudinal striations.** Mantle and shoulders black, the latter with **conspicuous white "window" markings.** Scapular region and speculum white. Flanks vermiculated grey; lower breast, belly and vent white washed with **pale rosy-pink.** Bill carmine, culmen and nail dusky, legs and feet orange.

Adult duck: head and neck pale brown, whitish in throat region. Upperparts grey as also breast and flanks. Underparts white. Scapular region white. Iris red, bill pale carmine, culmen dusky, legs and feet dull carmine.

Immatures: resemble duck but duller and crest shorter.

Stance and flight: stance somewhat erect, walks well, flies rapidly and not infrequently in V-formation.

Voice: apart from the courtship season both sexes silent; drake produces a double purring call, the duck a harsh quack.

Distribution: breeds in Scotland, Ireland, Iceland and throughout northern Eurasia and America. Winters south to the Mediterranean and coasts of North Africa; also in Asia Minor, the Aral and Caspian Seas, India, China, Japan, the Pacific coasts of America and on the Atlantic coast to the Gulf of Mexico.

GOOSANDER, *Mergus merganser merganser* Linnaeus

A large sawbill.

Adult drake: head and upper part of neck glossy-green, **full rounded crest**; iris red. Rest of neck, breast, belly and flanks white **washed pale salmon-yellow.** Tail, rump, vent and upper tail-coverts grey. Mantle black, scapular regions white, also shoulders and speculum. Bill carmine, legs and feet orange, nails dusky.

Adult duck: head and neck brown, throat white. Upperparts grey, wings sepia, speculum white. Iris red. Breasts, flanks and vent grey, belly white. Bill carmine, duller than in drake, legs and feet orange, nails dusky.

Immatures: resemble duck but duller.

Stance and flight: somewhat erect, walks easily, flies strongly, with a whistling sound.

Voice: as a rule quiet, but drake makes a croaking note and the duck a harsh "kurr".

Varieties: symmetrical white wings are recorded.

Distribution: breeds in northern Eurasia, including Iceland, Scotland and north England as far north as latitude 71°, south into Denmark, N.E. Germany, Austria, Switzerland, S.E. Europe, east through Turkestan, Mongolia

Plate 3. White-fronted geese jumping

Plate 4. Three sibling hybrid pintail × wigeon, showing
differing degrees of intersexuality

Plate 5. (*Left to right.*) Chiloe wigeon, hybrid × Chiloe, European wigeon, American widgeon, European wigeon

Plate 6. Northern Shoveler × Cinammon Teal hybrid resembling Australian Shoveler

Plate 7. Black-tailed godwits—a protected species. Note white on wings and trailing legs

Plate 8. Bar-tailed godwits—a quarry species. Note comparison with black-tailed godwits

to Kamchatka. Winters south to the Mediterranean, Black Sea, Caspian and Aral areas, Asia Minor, Persia and Iraq to western India.

REFERENCES

Jean Delacour (1954–9). *The Waterfowl of the World*. London. Vols. 1–3.
Peter Scott (1957). *A Coloured Key to the Wildfowl of the World*. The Wildfowl Trust.

WADER IDENTIFICATION

Wildfowlers are perforce made aware of the numerous shore-birds which share the habitat of the ducks and geese which are their primary interest. As it is essential that they should be familiar with the former, particularly as most are now protected by law, brief field identifications are given below.

In the list which follows the protected species are indicated by the prefix "P" as was done in the list of the ducks and geese, and it is believed that the majority of wildfowlers would not in any case regard the smaller species, such as dunlin, ringed plover, sanderling, stints, etc., as worthy quarry. However, a knowledge of the field characters of these species is well worth while and will add greatly to the fascination of wildfowling days spent on the tideways of estuaries and shores, as well as inland, to say nothing of those trips made to the fowling grounds during the close season, especially in the spring, late summer and autumn, when the knots, godwits and curlew-sandpipers can be seen on their way to and from their breeding grounds in the north, some at this latter season in the resplendent red nuptial dress, while other species, such as the grey plover, golden plover and dunlin, hurry on their respective migrations with the handsome jet-black throats and underparts in which their courtship is practised. Even the bizarre ruff may be seen in the spring carrying its full regalia of ruff, tippet and warty face, hardly two males coloured and patterned alike.

Where a strikingly different spring plumage is assumed, this is briefly mentioned in the list below. The competence to recognize the different shore-birds should be a matter of pride and is indeed now incumbent upon anyone using a gun under the *Protection of Wild Birds Act 1954*. Doubtless many are already familiar with the common species but, despite this, the emphasis placed on the salient field characters of the birds included in the list may help towards a quick identification.

For reasons of space, it is impossible to describe even briefly all the species of wader which have been included in the British list, and the object is rather to concentrate on those birds which are "fair game" and to include some which might well be shot in error and contrary to the law, and wildfowlers are urged to get a good book on bird identification and to become proficient as field naturalists and therefore better wildfowlers.

The order of the species in the list follows a natural grouping which should prove helpful in differentiation.

G

FIG. I. *Waders that may be shot in season.*

FIG. 2. *Some of the more common waders protected all the year round.*

P. OYSTERCATCHER: rather large, short-legged, general appearance a sharp contrast in black and white. Head and neck black, rump and proximal half of tail white, distal half black. In flight broad white wing-bars, rest of bird white. **Bill about twice as long as head, bright orange.** Iris red; legs and feet flesh-pink. Voice: a shrill "kleep", occasionally varied bisyllabic "kler-eep".

P. LAPWING: at once recognizable by its glossy green upperparts, black throat (summer only) and breast, white underparts and fulvous under tail-coverts. **Pronounced crest.** In flight rounded wingtips, proximal half of tail white, rest black. Voice: the familiar "kee-wi".

GREY PLOVER: a medium-sized wader, pale grey above, underparts white. In flight shows wing-bars and on under surface of wings **striking black patches.** In summer black throat and breast. Voice: a plaintive, "tlee-lu".

GOLDEN PLOVER: about same size as grey plover. Upperparts spangled sepia and gold, breast fulvous, faintly striated, rest of underparts white. In flight no wing-bars. In summer, throat and breast black. Voice: a clear piping whistle "tlui".

P. TURNSTONE: a small bird, bill shorter than head, slightly tilted, legs short, orange-yellow. Above, rather dark grey-brown, rump white; below throat white, prominent dark pectoral patches, rest of underparts white. In flight, wing shows double white markings, white rump, tail, first a black band, then white and terminal broad black band tipped white. Spring plumage, head almost white, a black bridled facial pattern, mantle handsomely variegated black and bright chestnut. Voice: rather sharp high-pitched "tuk-a-tuk" in quick time.

SNIPE: a slim, medium-sized wader, generally dark above with bright fulvous longitudinal stripes including centre of crown and above eyes; tail closely barred, neck and breast barred, flanks transversely barred; bill much longer than head, rest of underparts white. Erratic flight, tail barred and shows very little white; narrow white wing-bars. Voice: a rather nasal "schrape". "Drums" with outer tail feathers on breeding grounds.

P. GREAT SNIPE: considerably larger than preceding: general pattern similar to common species but flight is slower, less erratic and tail shows much white on outersides. Underparts heavily barred and wing-bars more marked. Voice: seldom vocal, occasionally utters a "croak".

JACK SNIPE: about half size of common snipe. Very dark above with contrasting fulvous stripes on back; narrow wing-bars and very little white in more or less uniform and rather pointed tail. Flight less erratic than common snipe. Voice: usually silent, a muffled drumming but only on breeding grounds.

WOODCOCK: rather large and heavily built wader, short-legged, long-billed; usual habitat woodland. Upperparts various shades of brown, fulvous and blackish-sepia. Crown and nape blackish-sepia transversely barred pale russet. Underparts ashy, closely barred ashy-brown. In flight, tail shows broad subterminal dusky band and terminal white tips. Voice: during display only, a soft purring note and sometimes a sharp "tsiwik".

P. GREENSHANK: a fairly large wader, from crown to mantle greyish (sometimes appears very dark), rump and upper tail-coverts white, underparts white. Tail white transversely barred pale grey, bill greenish-grey, long and **slightly up-turned at tip, legs and feet green.** In flight shows much white contrasting with blackish wings; no wing-bars. Voice: a loud "tu-tu-tu".

REDSHANK: smaller than the former species, above light brown, neck and breast striated, flanks barred; underparts white. Tail white barred greyish, rump white. In flight shows much white on wings. Bill straight about one- and-a-half times length of head, red at base, dusky at tip. Legs and feet orange-yellow. Voice: a vociferous species especially when alarmed, when vehement loud whistling "tu-hu-hu-hu" echoes over the saltings, on breeding ground a warbling whistle.

P. SPOTTED OR DUSKY REDSHANK: stands higher than foregoing species; above rather pale grey, white rump, tail white barred grey. Below white. Long, slender, dark bill; legs and feet red. In flight, posterior halves of wings appear grey, where in common redshank white; part of tarsi and whole of feet project beyond end of tail. Voice: a shrill penetrating "tschui-tschui" is usual alarm note. Summer plumage jet-black.

P. KNOT: a small stocky wader pale grey above, white below. Bill length of head. Summer plumage, rich maroon-red replaces white of winter. Voice: a low, pitched "nut" and also a sharp "twit-wit".

P. AVOCET: a fairly large contrasting black and white bird, above whole of top of head to nape black, tips of wings black. On mantle and on wings next to body broad black wedge-shaped markings directed backwards. **Bill long and fine, up-tilted from about its middle,** black. Legs long, feet partly webbed. colour pale grey, in flight project considerable distance beyond end of tail. Voice: loud modulated whistle "kleet-kleet, kleit-kluit".

WHIMBREL: about half size of curlew, above brown, striated. Head pattern, centre of crown buffy-yellow, above eyes blackish and then buffy-yellow; rump white, tail barred brown. Sides of face striated, throat whitish, neck, breast and flanks striated, belly white. No wing-bars. Bill long and strongly decurved, dark; legs and feet grey. Voice: a high-pitched rapidly uttered whistle repeated usually about seven times, hence "seven whistler". Also has bubbling song similar to that of curlew, and sometimes when alarmed utters the raucous "courli" of that species.

CURLEW: a large bird, general pattern very similar to that of whimbrel but lacks contrasting markings on head. Bill very long and strongly decurved, dark above, flesh at base. Voice: guttural loud alarm "courli-cr-wee-croo-ee" also has bubbling liquid song uttered all the year round.

P. BLACK-TAILED GODWIT: a graceful upstanding wader, above greyish-brown, below whitish, rump and upper half of tail white, rest of tail black, latter shows both in flight and when at rest. Bill flesh, about three times length of head, slightly upturned from about middle. Legs and feet greyish, in flight project well beyond end of tail; broad white wing-bars. Summer plumage; generally suffused maroon-red where in winter white, belly and under tail-coverts white, flanks strongly barred dark sepia. Voice: "reeta-reeta-reeta".

BAR-TAILED GODWIT: smaller than former and shorter legged, above pale greyish-brown, striated; neck faintly striated, underparts whitish, often suffused pale fulvous. Rump white, tail white barred brownish; no wing-bars, tips of wings dusky. Bill long, upturned at tip, flesh coloured. Legs and feet greyish, feet only just project beyond tail in flight. Summer plumage, rich chestnut-red replaces white of winter. Voice: rather quiet, utters occasional "krick-kirrick".

HYBRIDIZATION IN WILDFOWL

Hybridization in wildfowl is sufficiently common to make it desirable that the practical wildfowler should have some knowledge of the phenomena involved. It is not proposed in this brief survey to do other than indicate broadly the effects of this and only in the species dealt with in this book. The term "hybridization" is used here in the strict sense, i.e. the crossing of two species recognized as distinct, and it must be stressed that the results of such matings can be strikingly different and that such individuals are of paramount scientific value, in providing clues to the relationship of the various species and to their evolutionary descent, i.e. ancestry.

As a generalization it can be stated that the progeny of an interspecific cross may be in its characters (1) intermediate between its parents, or (2) unlike either parent but resembling another species. This latter phenomenon will be explained later and has been referred to by the writer as a reverse mutation. All such cases call for the closest study both as to their external characters and their internal anatomy, for there is often as much of interest within such a subject as without. This calls for special techniques in investigation to obtain the maximum results.

Wildfowl hybrids are so various, so numerous and at times so fantastic that in the space available it would be impossible to enumerate them all and it has therefore been considered best to list briefly some of those in which the species mentioned in this book are concerned. In illustration examples are shown of interspecific crosses in which the progeny is intermediate between the two parent species and where the progeny shows quite different characters.

It should be mentioned that although many of the hybrids have occurred in the wild state, others have been reared from captivity birds—all are of great value, those resulting from controlled breeding having, of course, the advantage of being of known parentage and age. Among the important issues are those affecting the fertility of the progeny and also the compatibility or otherwise of the parent species.

In the following list, vernacular names only are used, the conventional sign for hybridization, "X", indicating the actual crossing.

Mute swan ×
- Greylag goose
- Canada goose
- Whooper swan
- Bewick's swan

Bewick's swan ×
- Mute swan

Whooper swan ×
- Mute swan
- Greylag goose

Bean goose ×
- Greylag goose
- Brent goose
- Canada goose
- White-fronted goose
- Barnacle goose
- Pink-footed goose

Note: The Bean and Pink-footed goose are regarded as races of the same species and the cross is therefore not in the strict sense a hybrid but only an instance of intergradation.

White-fronted goose ×
- Lesser white-fronted goose
- Brent goose
- Canada goose
- Barnacle goose

Lesser white-fronted goose ×
- White-fronted goose
- Brent goose
- Barnacle goose

Greylag goose ×
- Mute swan
- Whooper swan
- Barnacle goose
- Shelduck

Canada goose ×
- Mute swan
- White-fronted goose
- Greylag goose

Barnacle goose ×
- White-fronted goose
- Greylag goose
- Lesser white-fronted goose
- Brent goose
- Canada goose
- Brent goose

Brent goose ×
- White-fronted goose
- Greylag goose
- Bean goose
- Lesser white-fronted goose
- Canada goose

Common shelduck ×
- Greylag goose
- Mallard
- Common pochard
- Goosander

Pintail ×
- Shoveler
- Teal
- Wigeon
- Mallard
- Garganey
- Gadwall
- Common pochard
- Tufted duck
- Red-crested pochard
- Common eider

Teal ×
- Pintail
- Shoveler
- Wigeon
- Mallard
- Garganey
- Common pochard

Mallard ×
- Pintail
- Shoveler
- Teal
- Wigeon
- Garganey
- Gadwall
- Common pochard
- Tufted duck
- Goosander
- Red-breasted merganser
- Red-crested pochard
- Common eider
- Common shelduck

Gadwall ×
- Pintail
- Shoveler
- Wigeon
- Mallard

Wigeon ×
- Pintail
- Teal
- Mallard
- Shoveler
- Garganey
- Gadwall
- Common scoter
- Tufted duck
- Red-crested pochard

Shoveler ×
- Pintail
- Teal
- Mallard
- Wigeon
- Garganey
- Gadwall

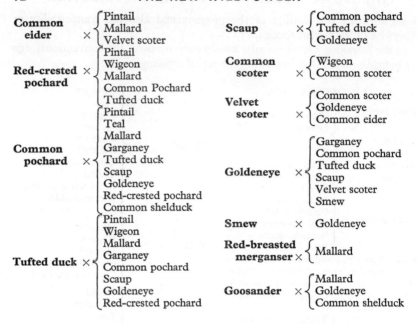

Common eider	×	Pintail Mallard Velvet scoter	Scaup	×	Common pochard Tufted duck Goldeneye
Red-crested pochard	×	Pintail Wigeon Mallard Common Pochard Tufted duck	Common scoter	×	Wigeon Common scoter
			Velvet scoter	×	Common scoter Goldeneye Common eider
Common pochard	×	Pintail Teal Mallard Garganey Tufted duck Scaup Goldeneye Red-crested pochard Common shelduck	Goldeneye	×	Garganey Common pochard Tufted duck Scaup Velvet scoter Smew
Tufted duck	×	Pintail Wigeon Mallard Garganey Common pochard Scaup Goldeneye Red-crested pochard	Smew	×	Goldeneye
			Red-breasted merganser	×	Mallard
			Goosander	×	Mallard Goldeneye Common shelduck

This list which by no means covers the full range of hybridization in wildfowl species is expressive of the very wide compatibility for crossing. Some examples of the different results may be quoted; thus, the interspecific cross between the mallard and pintail is intermediate in character and fertile, whereas that between the goldeneye and smew is intermediate, but sterile—an intersex. Examples of reverse mutation, in which a "bridled" facial pattern is exposed result from hybridization between the teal and shoveler and the teal and wigeon. In the drake hybrids, the face pattern is exactly similar to that of the Baikal teal. In fig. 3 is shown what is in all probability the genetic mechanism involved in which two individuals each carrying a recessive gene for "bridling" meet and mate, thus exposing this character, which is inherited from both parents and therefore becomes dominant. I consider that this indicates the importance of the baikal teal as an ancestral form. Other hybrids also show "bridling" or "bimaculation" and would seem to support this view. The specimen described many years ago from Essex as a new species, the "Bimaculated Duck", is now recognized to be a hybrid between the mallard and the teal, in which a similar face pattern has resulted to that shown on on plate 7. Other hybrids involving pintail and wigeon also reveal this pattern.

Since the above was written (for *The New Wildfowler*), a considerable addition to our knowledge of hybridization has accumulated, and the fact that a "ghost" bimaculated facial pattern has been demonstrated in otherwise normal individuals of the teal, in which there is no other evidence of hybridization, lends further considerable support to the hypothesis that this character is ancestral and archaic. Since it is a constant character in the drake Baikal teal,

Inheritance of a Specific Unit Character
"Bridling" or "Bimaculation"
Heterozygous Parents

♂ Teal   ♀ Shoveler

Homozygous Progeny
Hybrid Teal x Shoveler

- Gene for normal characters
- △ Gene (recessive) for aberrant characters
- ♂ male   ♀ female
- (Diagrammatic)

FIG. 3.

a character which incidentally also occurs occasionally in the female, this species must surely represent one of extreme antiquity in the evolution of the *Anatidae*.

This phenomenon in fact represents Darwinian atavism, the explanation for which must be sought for by a close study of the characters of all the individuals of the group for evolutionary "pointers"—specific unit characters.

Another important aspect in hybridization is the communal gene pool. This concept postulates that all the individuals of a species group carry all the genes of that group throughout its range, and that recombination of genes within the group can occasion the sort of anomalies we are discussing, as mutations. Of course the vast majority of species breed true to the species they represent, but hybridization is one of the mechanisms which can evoke such an anomaly. But this is not the only type of phenomenon which can occur, for it so happens that a hybrid is sometimes produced which closely resembles a different species. The most notable case of this kind was that of the supposed "lesser scaup" which masqueraded as a possible new British bird for a considerable time before it was demonstrated as a cross between a pochard and a tufted duck.

A recent instance of this kind of result of hybridization occurred in a cross between a Eurasian wigeon (*Anas penelope*) and chiloe wigeon, *A. sibilatrix*. Here, the result was an individual which could have deceived anyone in the field, so closely did it resemble the American wigeon, *A. americana*. (Plate 40.)

The same phenomenon can occur in geese, for a hybrid greylag X Canada goose bred on the WAGBI goose reserve in south Cumberland presented characters which strongly resembled those of the blue snow goose. These examples may well be termed the potentialities of the gene pool.

Hybridization is not necessarily limited to the crossing of two species, but is even known to involve multiple species during the generations through fertile hybrids. A wild-shot pintail x mallard x gadwall is on record.

In fact it is evident that diversified as the *Anatidae* are, they are obviously really genetically very close to each other. This also accounts for the extreme compatibility within the group, and emphasizes the rewards and fascination of research in the field of hybridization and variation.

It is perhaps appropriate at this stage to dispel some rather natural misconceptions, which were once accepted by orthodox ornithologists. The best example is provided by the bill of the familiar shoveler. This species was placed in its own genus, appropriately *Spatula* on its flat bill, spoon-shaped at the end. Moreover, the edges of the bill are provided with a series of little plates by which it is able to sift the water and retain the food elements.

This high degree of specialization in a structure was assessed as justification for creating a genus for the bird. Now, highest authority regards all this as recent specialization and in consequence the shoveler is reunited with the other "dabblers" in the genus *Anas*.

As in hybrids, genetic variants within the normal species may occur when two parents carrying the same recessive genes mate together and the recessive becomes dominant. This can account for many (but not all) anomalies of plumage.

The study of these variants is important, for they provide evidence of the evolutionary tree by which wildfowl, as we know them today, have developed. Interesting examples include the mallard-like white neck ring, which occurs as a variant in drake teal and gadwall. Another is the black V marking on the chin of the king eider and the Pacific eider, which is found occasionally in European eiders.

Another state to which the *Anatidae*, as well as other birds are prone, is that of intersexuality. This condition is usually in the direction of maleness in female birds and is familiar in the covert pheasant, when the bird is referred to as a "cocky-hen" or "mule bird". Intersexuality can result from ovarian disease and most examples are in individuals in which the ovary has wasted or has never developed, a condition known as ovarian agenesis.

Occasionally, the ovary which in most birds is situated in the left side, develops into a mixed gland, i.e. part ovary, part testis. Sometimes a right gonad (sex gland) may be of such a nature. A less common cause for male plumage in female birds results from disease of the adrenal glands resulting in a state of virilism.

Much more unusual is a change in the opposite direction, where for instance a drake mallard assumes the plumage of the duck. This can be due to a feminizing tumour of the testis; this is relatively very rare.

These are all pathological states which do not represent cases of true, functional sex reversal, although this has occurred, again as a rare event in the domestic fowl. This means that the individual has started as a female laying eggs, has undergone a *functional* sex reversal, and has then sired a brood of chicks.

Hybridization, variations and intersexuality are all loosely associated conditions and it is not always a simple problem to sort out the cause and effect. One brood of three pintail X wigeon siblings showed differing states of intersexuality from two almost female types in which the ovaries failed to develop, to a functional male type. (Plate 5.) The state of interseuxality has also been referred to as "sexual mosaicism" and Crew (1964) summarizes intersexuality by commenting:

"No one explanation can possibly accommodate all these instances of mosaicism in birds. In the finches and in some fowls, the cause appears to be due to the loss of an X chromosome."

REFERENCES

CREW, F. A. E. (1964). "Sex Determination", *Journ. Genetics*, 30: 48–49.

GREY, ANNIE P. (1958). *Bird Hybrids*, Commonwealth Agricultural Bureau.

HARRISON, JAMES M. (1943). "A wild cross between *Glaucionetta clangula* and *Mergus albellus*; some endocrine and anatomical features", *Ibis*, 86: 228–30.

HARRISON, JAMES M. (1964). "Plumage, Abnormal and Aberrant", *A New Dictionary of Birds*: 643–6.

HARRISON, JAMES M. (1964). "Plumage, Variant", *A New Dictionary of Birds*: 646–9.

HARRISON, JAMES M. (1967). "Three Wigeon × Pintail hybrid siblings: a study in intersexuality", *Bull. Brit. Orn. Club*, 87: 25–33.

HARRISON, JAMES M. (1968). "Examples of Intersexuality in the Mallard and Teal", *Bull. Brit. Orn. Club*, 88: 154–60.

HARRISON, JAMES M. and HARRISON, JEFFERY G. (1966). "Hybrid Greylag × Canada Goose suggesting influence of Giant Canada Goose in Britain", *British Birds*, 59: 547–50.

CHAPTER 4

THE MIGRATIONS OF BRITISH GEESE AND DUCKS

by Hugh Boyd

WAGBI Member; Research Supervisor, Migratory Birds, Canadian Wildlife Service.

MOST wildfowl found in Britain are migrants, spending the winter in this country or passing through it on their journeys between northern breeding places and wintering areas farther south and west. This chapter summarizes what is now known about the summer and winter distribution of the British visitors and the timing of some of the simple migrations. The distribution of birds is a dynamic process so that our knowledge is continuously changing and will probably always be obsolescent. Though it is relatively easy to see something new, it is harder to recognize that what was true five or ten years ago no longer holds.

Much of the information on migration is obtained from birds ringed in Britain or overseas which are picked up later. Few ducks dying from natural causes are ever found, so that wildfowlers provide the bulk of the reports from which the pictures can be drawn. Few individual recoveries are mentioned here and most of the maps are summaries of hundreds or thousands of records. Few countries permit the killing of birds in the summer, so that breeding distributions are harder to define than migration routes.

One of the most important but elusive characteristics of the wildfowl visiting Britain is that most of them come from only a part of the entire breeding range of the species. At all times of year they are partially or wholly segregated by their tendency to return to familiar haunts. Only the young are explorers, though the males of those ducks that form pairs in winter often have to follow the directions of their mates. Sometimes bad weather, such as strong cross winds at migration times or severe cold in midwinter, drives birds into strange places but, in general, they stick to the places they know, for the very good reason that this increases their chance of survival.

GEESE

Four species of grey geese winter regularly in the British Isles. The breeding of three are now well defined, but we still do not know for certain where the bean geese *Anser fabalis* breed. Formerly they wintered in thousands in Britain, now only a hundred or two occur and only three haunts are used regularly. Probably these geese come from Lapland or north-west Russia, rather than from farther east. They usually arrive in late December or January and have often left again by March. The cause of the decline of the bean goose in Britain is still largely mysterious. The only clue to their immigration is that one ringed in Friesland in February 1958 was shot near Holbeach, Lincs., in January 1962. In Holland their numbers have risen again in recent years after a marked decline but no corresponding increase has taken place here.

Over 15,000 pink-footed geese were ringed in Britain between 1950 and 1959 and a further 10,000 in Iceland in 1951 and 1953. Recoveries show that the pinkfeet wintering in Britain breed chiefly in central Iceland, with no more than 1,000 pairs in east Greenland, though the latter are joined by many Icelandic birds in later summer for the period of wing moult. Pinkfeet also breed in Spitzbergen, but that stock winters in north Germany and Holland, mixing only occasionally and accidentally with Icelandic birds. Pinkfeet arrive in Britain in the second half of September and October, the majority usually appearing in one or two waves associated with the movement of high-pressure systems producing tail winds. Return to Iceland in spring may begin as early as the end of March and may not end until the third week of May. During the last twenty years, while pinkfeet have increased from 30,000 to well over 60,000 in early autumn, they have been concentrating in Scotland and declining in all their former English strongholds except Lancashire. In autumn first arrivals appear at the major wintering places at nearly the same time. In spring the English haunts are deserted well before the return to Iceland and there are often concentrations in Easter Ross and elsewhere in northern Scotland where geese are scarce in autumn.

Two races of the white-fronted goose winter in Britain. The typical race, *Anser a. albifrons*, is the grey goose of southern England and Wales, while the Greenland race, *A. a. flavirostris*, occurs largely in Ireland and western Scotland, with small outlying flocks in Wales and north-west England. The typical race has a very extensive breeding range in Siberia, but ringing has shown that British visitors come only from the north-west, from the Kanin Peninsula and Kolguev Island east to Dikson Island (fig. 4). In autumn the main passage is along the south side of the White Sea, across Karelia and along the east side of the Baltic to east Germany. That journey is made in a few days, in late September or early October. A few geese come right through to England at that time but the great majority of our visitors linger until December or January with the much larger numbers that winter in west Germany and, increasingly, in Holland. In spring the English whitefronts leave in March and pause for only a short time, if at all, in Holland and Germany before moving nearly due east to the Tula and Ryazan districts of Russia, south of Moscow, where they stay until late April or early May. Then they move slowly north and north-east, reaching their breeding places at the end of May.

The migrations of the Greenland whitefronts are even more striking. They breed on the west side of Greenland and in autumn migrate across the vast and high central ice-cap for about 400 miles before crossing the Denmark Strait to Iceland. Many do not stop in Iceland but fly on across 1,400 miles or more of the Atlantic Ocean to Ireland and Scotland. In spring most of the whitefronts go straight from Ireland to Greenland but many then move up the west coast by easy stages instead of crossing the ice-cap.

The remnants of our native breeding stocks of greylag geese *Anser anser* (less than 2,000 birds in all) are confined to the Outer Hebrides and the north of Scotland and do not migrate. In autumn more than 50,000 greylags that breed in the lowlands of Iceland move to Scotland, a few also going to northern England and Ireland. They arrive in October and leave again in April. The Icelandic geese do not mix with the native Scottish birds, though

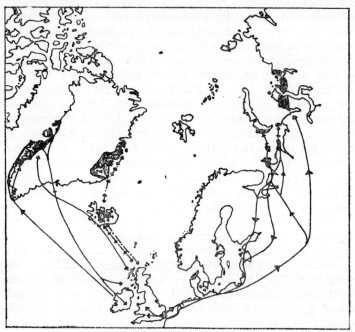

FIG. 4. *Breeding areas and migration routes of British grey geese. Breeding areas of white-fronted geese in solid black, of pink-footed geese dotted, of greylags in Iceland marked by small crosses.*

they do overlap with the feral stocks now flourishing in Galloway and north-west England. Greylags breeding in Scandinavia, Europe and Asia do not visit Britain regularly, though a few occur accidentally.

British Canada geese *Branta canadensis* are all from introduced stock. They now breed in many parts of the country, north to Perthshire. Several groups make short movements that are regular enough to be called migrations. Much the longest and most unexpected is a moult-migration of geese from colonies in Yorkshire. Each year 200–300 non-breeders go north to the Beauly Firth shortly before replacing their flight feathers and stay there for about two months before returning south.

The barnacle goose *Branta leucopsis* breeds in east Greenland, Spitzbergen and on the Siberian islands of southern Novaya Zemlya and Vaigach. Greenland breeders winter in the Hebrides and on the islands off north-west Ireland, from late October to late April. On passage most of them stop in

Iceland for several weeks. The barnacles wintering on the Solway Firth, which dwindled to only a few hundred by 1950 but have now recovered to over 4,000, come from Spitzbergen by way of islands off the Norwegian coast. Most of them arrive on the Solway in early October but an increasing proportion stay in Norway until quite late in the winter. The peak numbers occur in late February and March not long before the geese leave again in April. Siberian barnacles winter in Holland and Germany and appear only as stragglers in Britain, just as occasional Spitzbergen birds are found in east

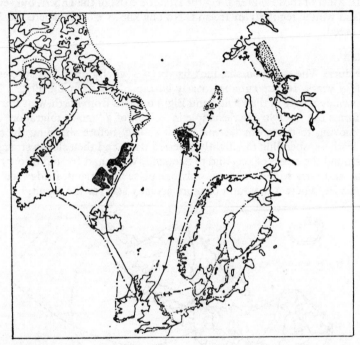

FIG. 5. *Breeding areas and migration routes of British black geese. Breeding areas of barnacle geese in black, of dark-bellied brent dotted, of light-bellied brent enclosed by dotted lines.*

Scotland or south-east Ireland and odd Greenland birds join the Solway flocks.

Two races of brent geese winter in the British Isles. The dark-bellied *B. b. bernicla* visit the east and south coasts of England, particularly the muddy estuaries of Essex. It breeds in northern Siberia, on the mainland of west Taimyr and on a few islands, and journeys more than 2,500 miles to reach England, along the routes shown in fig. 5. In autumn most brent travel overland across Karelia and Finland then through the Baltic to south-west Denmark. A minority go by way of the North Cape and off the Norwegian coast. From Denmark they move to Holland and England, where few arrive before late November. They are usually most numerous in January. In March they return gradually to Denmark, where they stay until mid-May before moving off through the Baltic to the north-east.

From Norfolk to Northumberland dark-bellied brent are mingled with light-bellied birds of the race *hrota*. The latter, whose occurrences are now brief and diminishing, also come to England from Denmark, mostly in January and February. Light-bellied birds on the east coast breed in Spitzbergen and perhaps also in Franz Josef Land, even farther north and east. Light-bellied brent also breed in north Greenland and the north Canadian islands. Most of those winter along the Atlantic coast of the U.S.A. but several thousand winter regularly in Ireland. No one knows exactly where the Irish birds breed.

Ducks

Shelduck. The common shelduck has been a wholly protected species for over fifty years. In late summer nearly all the adults from the British Isles join a vast assembly in the Heligoland Bight of birds from north-west Europe. This forms the most striking example in Britain of a "moult migration", the birds moving to the north German coast shortly before shedding their old flight feathers, spending the flightless period there and then slowly straggling back around the coasts of England to Scotland, Wales and Ireland through the autumn and early winter. There is only one place in England, Bridgwater Bay in Somerset, where a thousand or more actually stay for the moult.

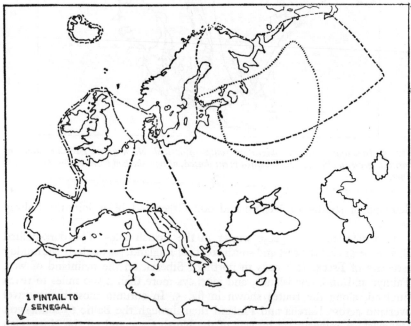

FIG. 6. *Summer and winter ranges of pintail and shoveler ringed in Britain. Summer range of pintail enclosed by broken line, of shoveler by dotted line. Winter range of pintail enclosed by line — — — — — —, of shoveler by line—— · —— · ——— -.*

Dabbling, or surface-feeding ducks. Seven species of the genus *Anas* occur regularly in Britain. In five—pintail, teal, mallard, wigeon and shoveler—the majority of our immigrants come from the countries around the Baltic, or farther east. The ranges shown in the maps (figs. 6 and 7) are based on recoveries of British-ringed ducks in the breeding season (roughly, April to

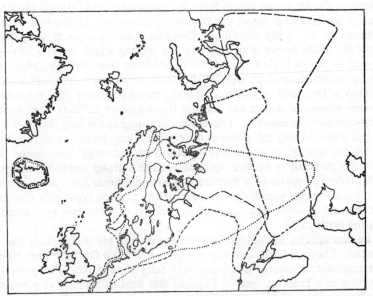

FIG. 7. *Summer range of mallard, teal and wigeon wintering in Britain. Range of mallard enclosed by dotted lines, of teal by broken lines, of wigeon by long-dashed lines.*

August). They do not represent the breeding range of the entire species but only that of those stocks which are known to visit Britain. All the species also breed in this country but, because of the small scale of the maps used here, the local distribution is not shown. Only in the case of the mallard does the British-breeding stock make up a substantial proportion of wintering birds.

The main features of the summer ranges shown in figs. 6 and 7 are these: all five species breed around the Baltic, especially in the great lake area of Russia, east of Leningrad; the mallard has the most westerly range, the wigeon the most easterly; the range of our wintering shoveler is relatively small and it alone does not reach the coasts of the Arctic Ocean. All the breeding areas are much larger than the British Isles.

Fig. 6 also shows the wintering areas used by pintails and shovelers visiting Britain; these areas being drawn to enclose recoveries in the months November to February. The recoveries used are not limited to those in the same season as the ducks were ringed, so that birds recovered in France have not necessarily passed through Britain in the winter of recovery. The wintering areas of British-ringed mallard, teal and wigeon, which are not mapped, are similar to those of pintails and shovelers. The only important differences between the species are that teal and shovelers are more often found in Spain and Portugal than the others, and that British mallards rarely go into southern France or the Iberian Peninsula. The recovery in January 1969 in Senegal (at 16·01° N. 16·30° W.) of a young pintail ringed in Suffolk in September 1968 was the first south of the Sahara for a British-ringed duck.

Because the migration routes from the north-east pass through the nearer parts of the breeding range, the migratory movements of the five common dabblers are not easily described. There is little evidence of long flights, except for ducks breeding in Iceland. The wigeon which travel 3,000 miles to reach us probably do so in a series of relatively short journeys, often with lengthy intermediate stops. Most of the ducks which come to Britain from the east stop in Denmark or Holland, or both, remaining there until the weather becomes severe, so that in late autumn the migratory influxes often become "hard-weather movements". The exodus in spring too is long drawn out. In any particular locality the patterns of migration may be clear and consistent, but for the country as a whole the pictures are far more complicated. The mallard is particularly baffling, since autumn and winter stocks in most parts of the country consist of a mixture of residents, birds from other parts of Britain and foreign immigrants, in proportions that are constantly changing. The mallard of south-east England treat the Low Countries as continuous with the British Isles.

The two species of dabblers not yet mentioned are the gadwall and the garganey. They are both relatively scarce and, because few have been ringed, their migratory movements are not very fully worked out. The gadwall is spreading as a breeding bird in England and Scotland, partly as a result of introductions but also naturally in a change affecting much of Europe, it being a southern species that moved northwards as the climate warmed. British immigrants are known to include birds from Poland and Germany and emigrants have been found in Holland, France and England. The garganey is an even more southerly species, breeding in southern England and wintering here very rarely. British-ringed garganey have been shot on passage or wintering in Germany, Belgium, France, Italy (especially), Bulgaria, Turkey and Algeria. The winter range of the species goes far south into Africa and east through Arabia, but it is not yet known how far our breeding birds go.

EIDERS

The greatest breeding concentration of common eiders in Britain are on the Farne Islands and the east coast of Scotland. Birds from the Farnes and another large colony at Newburgh, Aberdeenshire mix off Fife and the Lothians in autumn. One ringed bird from Northumberland and one from Newburgh have been recovered in Denmark where large numbers of eiders, mostly from the Baltic and White Sea, are shot each year, but it is unlikely that regular emigration or immigration occurs. Increasing numbers of eiders off the east and south of England a few years ago were associated with rapid growth of the Dutch population but that growth has ended and the spread of eiders in Britain has lost impetus too.

POCHARDS

The three species of *Aythya* numerous in Britain are the pochard, tufted duck and scaup. Most of the ringed scaup recovered in Britain have come from Iceland, but this is rather misleading because there has been much more ringing in Iceland than in other parts of the breeding range. Recent winter ringing in Aberdeenshire has led to two recoveries in Iceland but also to others in Finland and the Komi Republic (at 62·10° N., 50·40° E.) and a Finnish bird has been found on the Humber. Other British-ringed birds have been killed on passage in Denmark and Germany. The scaup is typically a mid-winter bird, arriving in November or December and departing in March.

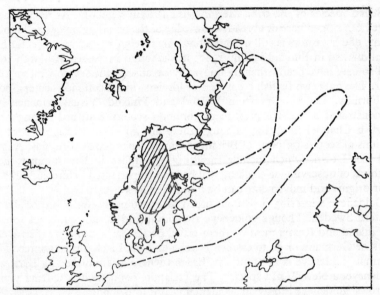

FIG. 8. *Summer ranges of tufted duck and pochard ringed in Britain and of ringed golden eye found in Britain. Tufted duck shown by broken lines, pochard by line of long and short dashes, goldeneye area hatched.*

The summer ranges of the tufted duck and pochard are shown in fig. 8. Several thousand tufted ducks breed in Britain. Few of them emigrate in winter though there are substantial movements within the British Isles, and two ringed as juveniles at Loch Leven in August 1966 were found in Finland in 1967. Winter visitors outnumber the residents. Those from Iceland occur mostly in Ireland and Scotland while those from Scandinavia, eastern Europe and Russia are more often found in eastern England. The cold winter of 1962–3 killed many tufted ducks and caused others to emigrate, producing two recoveries in Spain.

Comparatively few pochard breed in Britain. Until recently ringing has been on a small scale anywhere at any time of year but in the last ten years an unusual picture has begun to emerge. The pochard breeds over a large area in eastern Europe and the U.S.S.R., in a belt mostly between 50°—55° N. (farther south than most of the other ducks coming to Britain). Several pochards ringed when young in south Germany and Czechoslovakia have been found in England and Ireland. Winter visitors caught at Abberton, Essex, and Deeping Lake, Lincs. have been reported frequently in Russia as far as 70° E. and in September 1968 a Deeping bird was killed on the Sea of Okhotsk (at 59·38° N., 150·50° E.) some 4,500 miles away. Pochards are unusually erratic in their numbers in different parts of Britain and it will be difficult to work out a coherent account of their migrations.

SEA DUCKS AND SAWBILLS

Seven species of the tribe Mergini visit Britain regularly. As few of them have been ringed here or abroad, knowledge of the breeding ranges and movements of our visitors is still meagre. The only foreign-ringed velvet scoter had been marked in Finland in July 1961: it was found in Sussex in March 1963 and so may have been behaving unusually because of the severe weather that year. The only two British recoveries of foreign-ringed common scoters, both at Formby, Lancs, were from Iceland and Finland. Visual evidence has demonstrated a massive passage of common scoters eastward through the English Channel in spring. Though there are impressive offshore concentrations of scoters off parts of Britain as widely separated as Fife, East Anglia and Co. Down, which include moulting assemblies in late summer, new methods of observing or catching will have to be perfected before accounts of their origins and movements can be more than guesswork.

Goldeneye wintering in Britain breed in Scandinavia (fig. 8) especially in western Sweden. Though goldeneye are widespread in the coniferous forests of Finland and Russia most of them travel no farther south-west than Denmark or Germany or go to eastern Europe and the Black Sea in winter. The common goldeneye is not found in Iceland where it is replaced by Barrows' goldeneye, a New World species. The Icelandic population is sedentary and Barrows' goldeneye is only an accidental visitor to Britain.

Marking of red-breasted mergansers in Iceland has produced recoveries in Britain from October to January. Marking in Scandinavia has yet to produce a recovery in this country, though a Finnish bird has reached northern France. So far as is known our own breeding red-breasted mergansers, and goosanders, make only local movements. Ringing of wintering goosanders in the London area has shown them to come from Sweden, Finland and north-west Russia, by way of Germany and Holland. Goosanders ringed in Sweden have been found in Scotland in December and East Anglia in February. There is no information at all on where the long-tailed duck and smew that come to Britain breed.

FACTORS AFFECTING MIGRATORY MOVEMENTS

Little has so far been said about factors affecting the migration of wildfowl other than severe weather in winter. Comparatively little attention has in fact been paid to the behaviour of British ducks in this respect. Rather more is known about the geese. From observations in Scotland and Iceland it seems that, though movements may occur in almost any weather, in both autumn and spring large-scale overseas flights are most likely to occur in weather situations which provide following- rather than head-winds. What evidence geese use to appreciate this is not known. It is often supposed that migratory movements are particularly associated with the period of full moon, but statistical evidence gives surprisingly little support to that belief. This is presumably because geese migrate readily by day as well as night. From the meagre information that exists it is likely that the long ocean crossings made by geese are normally carried out in a single flight.

A British reader interested in the mechanism of duck migration is compelled to turn to a North American book, H. A. Hochbaum's *Travels and Traditions of Waterfowl* (Minneapolis, 1955), for a summary of present knowledge. That magnificent book is well worth hunting for. More recently two masterly papers by Frank Bellrose on the flight corridors of duck migrating in the United States of America have provided a model that should be emulated in Europe so as to enable us to put our insular impressions in a continental context.

CHAPTER 5

FOOD HABITS OF WILDFOWL IN BRITAIN

by Peter Olney, B.Sc., Dip.Ed., F.L.S.

Honorary Member, WAGBI. Curator of Birds, Zoological Society of London; Formerly Scientific Staff, The Wildfowl Trust, and Biologist, The Royal Society for the Protection of Birds.

IN order fully to understand a species' movements, habitat preferences, population size and density and its economic importance, it is essential to know the quality and quantity of food available to and consumed by that species. When that information is known, then conservation measures, if necessary, can be contemplated and put into practice.

In this country few such comprehensive studies have been made, even for our commonest bird species, and though the literature is extensive, it generally suffers from two faults. Either it records only the unusual or conspicuous food or feeding habit, or, and this is a common error, it is too vague. It is not enough to know that for a particular species "pondweeds" or "grass and grains" are part of the normal diet and to be of any real value, particularly with conservation measures in mind, identification of food items should be as precise as possible. Up to 1959 this has only been attempted by a few workers dealing with British wildfowl (Campbell, 1936, 1946 a and b, 1947; Höhn, 1948; Gilham, 1956; and Ranwell and Downing, 1959).

Most ornithological textbooks, often because of their now inherent need to précis the contents, contain only summarized food sections which are "handed down" from the standard works and this, often unaccompanied by a bibliography, makes the information meaningless and misleading. Occasionally there occurs a reference to a specific food being taken, as with Lynn-Allen's (1953) note on teal feeding on the seeds of sea aster (*Aster tripolium*) on the Minsmere Levels, or Cadman's (1953, 1956) identification of the roots of the common cotton-grass (*Eriophorum angustifolium*) and the shoots of the white beak sedge (*Rhynchospora alba*) as part of the winter diet of the Greenland whitefront on the peat bogs of Wales. However, notes of this sort can only be considered as parochial news and their value cannot be ascertained until a wider coverage is reached.

A review of the literature does show how ignorant we are as to the normal diet-sheets of British wildfowl, and before any form of management can be envisaged it is essential to have this fundamental information.

There are a number of different methods which can be used to determine the food and feeding habits of birds, most of them summarized by Lack (1954), Gibb and Hartley (1957) and Olney (1958, 1960). The methods employed will of necessity vary with the species of bird under study. Often it is only by careful analyses of the stomach contents, in conjunction with field observations that the food requirements of a species can be determined. Rarely, however, can *all* the important food being taken be identified accurately enough in the field, though often essential supplementary information can be obtained by careful and continual field observations.

A knowledge of how, when and where the food is taken, and to what extent the food supply is depleted are necessary facts which can only be obtained by field work. Knowledge of this sort may have an important bearing on the economic significance of a species. For instance, field observations on a flock of geese may show that the effect of trampling alone is a possible loss of potential crops, though this may be compensated by manuring and renewed leaf growth in the spring. Stomach analyses are really the only safe guide for ascertaining what is actually being eaten by a species under varying conditions and in differing habitats, but then only populations numerically large enough to withstand the loss of an adequate sample can be studied in this way.

In wildfowl there are few alternative methods apart from field observations. Faecal examination can produce useful information, though it is doubtful if it can ever provide the complete diet-sheet. Ranwell and Downing (1959) examined faeces from brent geese over a long period and were able to show a distinct seasonal pattern of feeding correlated with the main growth periods of the different food plants. Gilham (1956), working with mute swans, showed similar seasonal feeding behaviour, much of her work being based on field observations. It should be emphasized that, whatever the methods used are, there are going to be many limitations in reaching a complete picture and the final results can usually only be regarded as giving an approximate indication of the actual feeding habits. Numerous variations in the birds themselves, their environment, the methods used and the degree to which partial digestion has altered the original food proportions (Koersveld, 1950) make it unwise to view the data obtained as exact and infallible.

A scheme of work initiated by the Wildfowl Trust and grant-aided by the Nature Conservancy was started in 1957 in order to make a qualitative and quantitative survey of the food and feeding habits of various British wildfowl. The success of this scheme depended to a large extent on the close liason which was established between the Trust and wildfowlers. The viscera sent in to the Trust for food study were mainly supplied by members of clubs affiliated to the Wildfowlers' Association of Great Britain and Ireland.

Instructions as to the removal and preservation of the viscera, since described by Harrison (1960) and in an appendix at the end of this chapter, were sent to each collector or club. After removal of the viscera (oesophagus to rectum) a numbered tag was tied on and it was placed in a formo-saline solution for at least twenty-four hours. The number on the tag corresponded with a record of the species, the sex, date, time and locality of shooting. Any further information apropos feeding habits was welcomed. When the viscera were received at the Trust they were numbered in sequence by areas and their particulars noted on a record card. The contents of the oesophagus, proventriculus and gizzard were then removed into water or stored in 60 per cent alcohol. These were then sorted into organic and inorganic material and the latter into animal and plant items. Three measures were taken: the volume of each species found, the number of each species present and the frequency of each species. Where the numbers were very large only an estimate was a feasible measure. It is quite obvious that for different materials there are different rates of digestion (Koersveld, 1950; Pollard, 1967), depending on their ability to withstand chemical and mechanical decomposition. This has been taken into account in computing percentage ratios.

Though this survey has of necessity been confined to the shooting seasons, variations in diet and habits are distinguishable, not only from locality to locality, but from season to season and within the season. Thus, a sample of hand-reared mallard collected from a flight pond in Kent over two shooting seasons yielded very different results and showed the sort of variation found from year to year (Olney, 1962). In the 1958–9 shooting season, over 80 per cent of the total value of food consumed was found to be acorns (*Quercus robur*) and they occurred in 60 per cent of all the birds collected. The rest of the material taken was fairly representative of the seeds of the marginal vegetation found in the area with common bur-reed (*Sparganium erectum*) and hornbeam (*Carpinus betulus*) predominating. Barley and wheat formed only a small percentage of the food taken—3·2 per cent and 1 per cent of the total volume respectively.

In the 1959–60 season, mallard from the same area were found to be feeding mainly on barley which occurred in 25 per cent of the sample and occupied over 85 per cent of the total volume. Bur-reed and hornbeam seeds occurred in 37 per cent and 19 per cent of the stomachs respectively though the volume occupied was comparatively small. The total absence of acorns in the 1959–60 sample was a reflection of the almost complete failure of the acorn crop in that area during 1959. That oak is exceptionally erratic in its seed production is a well-known fact (Jones, 1959) and years of almost complete failure are frequent. Jones suggests that a uniformly heavy crop, as occurred in 1958 in this sample area, probably does not occur more frequently than once in six or seven years in the south of England. The interest of this particular flight pond, where artificial feeding is carried out, lies in the fact that in some years it is apparent that mallard prefer to feed on acorns rather than the barley or wheat put down for them. If there is a moral to this tale, it is that if a good acorn year is noted then much money can be saved by reducing the amount of artificial feeding.

Mallard from other inland areas showed variations in their feeding habits during the two shooting seasons of 1958–9 and 1959–60. A variety of localities was included in these samples ranging from lakes, reservoirs and pools to water-meadows, rivers and marshes. Cereal grain formed the highest volume of food taken, though, as to be expected, it was mainly consumed in September and October. Acorns occurred only in the 1959–60 sample (90 birds), again a reflection of the irregular local production of oak seed. A wide variety of materials was taken in both seasons, with plant seeds predominating. Common bur-reed, knotted persicaria (*Polygonum nodosum*) and broad-leaved pondweed (*Potamogeton natans*) were the most commonly occurring plant seeds in both

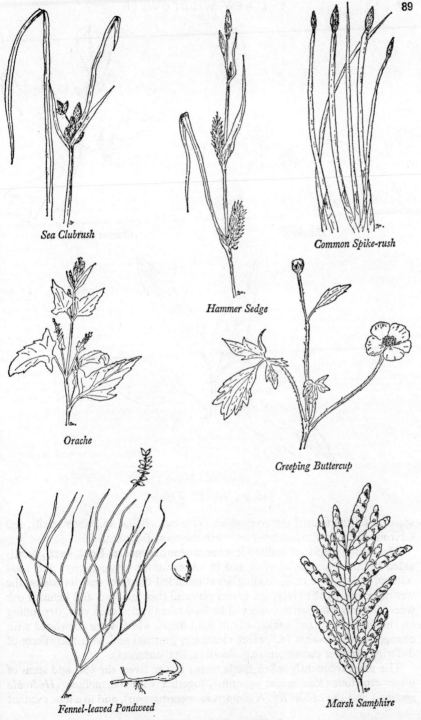

Sea Clubrush

Common Spike-rush

Hammer Sedge

Orache

Creeping Buttercup

Fennel-leaved Pondweed

Marsh Samphire

FIG. 9a. *Plant food of wildfowl.*

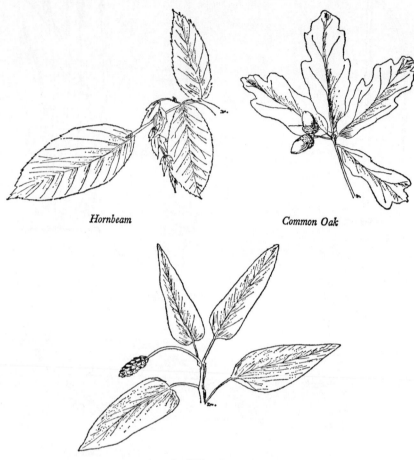

Hornbeam

Common Oak

Amphibious Bistort

FIG. 9b. Amphibious bistort.

seasons. Of the animal material which occurred, *Asellus* sp., water snails, and Chironomidae larvae (midge-flies) were the most frequent.

The feeding habits of mallard in an area near Sevenoaks, Kent, were investigated by 226 stomach analyses and by observations between 1957 and 1965 (Olney, 1967). The main feeding areas included the river and its banks, the wet meadows by the river, the gravel pits and their margins and beneath oak trees (*Quercus robur*) in the valley. The food taken varied each year, depending on the production and availability of food items, which were correlated with changes in the habitat (e.g. river clearance, grazing) and with the effects of differing weather conditions (e.g. flooding, dry summers).

The most frequently taken foods were: in the river, the leaf and stem of water crowfoot (*Ranunculus aquatilis*), together with the mollusc (*Hydrobia jenkinsi*) and the caddis fly (*Hydropsyche angustipennis*), and to a lesser extent

the seeds of flote-grass (*Glyceria fluitans*); from the river banks, the seeds of
bur-reed (*Sparganium erectum*) and water-pepper (*Polygonum hydropiper*);
from the wet meadows, the seeds of creeping buttercup (*Ranunculus repens*),
persicaria (*Polygonum persicaria*), hammer sedge (*Carex hirta*) and sharp dock
(*Rumex conglomeratus*); in and around the gravel pits a wide variety, mainly
the seeds of alder (*Alnus glutinosa*), various *Polygonum* species, *S. erectum* and
parts of horsetail (*Equisetum*), as well as Chironomidae and *Hydropsyche*
larvae.

Acorns were eaten in the years when oaks produced seed.

The largest sample of mallard feeding in saltmarsh and brackish water
habitats was collected from the Medway islands (Olney, 1964 a). Here they
were found to be feeding mainly on the seeds of sea clubrush (*Scirpus
maritimus*) and fennel-leaved pondweed (*Potamogeton pectinatus*) from the
adjoining brackish water marshes. There was comparatively little feeding on
the saltmarsh itself, though it was extensively used as a resting ground,
particularly within the tall cord-grass (*Spartina townsendii*).

Mallard collected from other saltmarsh and brackish water areas were found
to be feeding on similar plant seeds, though there appeared to be more actual
feeding on the saltmarsh itself. The seeds of common seablite (*Suaeda
maritima*), marsh samphire or glasswort (*Salicornia* sp.), and the oraches
(*Altriplex* sp.) were the main saltmarsh foods taken. Sea clubrush and fennel-
leaved pondweed seeds were the most important brackish water plants used.

Teal collected from over the same Medway islands showed a higher
frequency than mallard of actually feeding on the saltmarsh itself (Olney,
1963 a). The main foods taken were the small mollusc (*Sabanaea ulvae*), and
the seeds of marsh samphire, seablite and orache (*Atriplex hastata*). The main
brackish water plant seeds utilized were sea clubrush and tassel pondweed
(*Ruppia maritima*). A comparison of this sample with that from other teal
collected around the British coastline showed that it was fairly representative
of the general feeding pattern of this species in saltmarsh and brackish water
areas. The same plant and animal materials were taken, though in slightly
different proportions from area to area and from season to season. *Salicornia*
seeds were taken more often and in larger quantities than on the Medway
islands and it was the most important food item taken by teal during the three
seasons of 1957–60.

Teal feeding inland were collected from a variety of habitats and showed a
diverse diet sheet (Olney, 1963 a). Considering the rather wide locality range
and the comparative smallness of the sample (116 birds in two seasons), it was
particularly interesting to find the high frequency of the seeds of common
spike (*Eleocharis palustris*) and creeping buttercup (*Ranunculus repens*) and the
larvae of Chironomidae flies. Common spike rush and creeping buttercup seeds
occurred more often (28 per cent) than any other material, and they are probably the most important inland teal food during the shooting season months.

Analyses of the wigeon material and field observations have shown that the
main bulk of their feeding occurs around the coast, either on *Enteromorpha*
species, eel-grass (*Zostera* sp.) or on the saltmarsh grasses (mainly *Puccinellia*
sp.). Inland, they are again predominantly grazing birds feeding on such

grasses as the *Glyceria* sp., *Festuca rubra*, *Poa trivalis*, *Poa annua*, and *Agrostis stolonifera* var. *palustris*. They also take, though not often in large quantities, any of the duckweed species (*Lemna* sp.), the leaf and shoot of hornwort (*Ceratophyllum* sp.), Canadian pondweed (*Elodea canadensis*) and the water crowfoot species (*Ranunculus* sp. of the sub-genus *Batrachium*). They are almost entirely vegetarian, at least during the winter months, and any animal material taken is probably accidental, though in some areas molluscs may be taken in sufficient quantities to suggest a preference. Most of their feeding is by grazing, with leaf, shoot and root material forming the main bulk of the food.

Tufted duck collected from a gravel-pit near London between 1959 and 1961 had fed primarily on molluscs, and mainly on the zebra mussel (*Dreissena polymorpha*) (Olney, 1963 b). Tufted duck from other parts of the British Isles over the same period had a more variable diet, though again molluscs predominated but some crustaceans, insects and plant seeds were also taken. Other surveys (Olney, 1967) indicate there is considerable variation in diet from locality to locality.

Stomach analyses and a literature survey (Olney and Mills, 1963) showed that the goldeneye is predominantly an animal feeder. In estuarine and coastal areas small crustaceans and in particular the shore crab *Carcinus maenas* figured highly in the diet with some molluscs and small fish. In freshwater feeding birds insects predominated, particularly Trichoptea larvae, chironomid larvae and the adults of *Corixa* spp. Some crustaceans (*Asellus, Gammarus*) and small molluscs were taken and occasionally small fish. A small amount of plant material was taken in the form of seeds, mainly *Potamogeton* species. It was concluded that serious depredation of fish stocks is unlikely.

Pochard feeding inland were found to have fed mainly on *Chara* and *Nitella* species and to a lesser extent on *Potamogeton* and *Polygonum* species as well as on larvae of chironomidae. Pochard feeding in coastal areas, including brackish water situations are likely to have been feeding on *Ruppia* and *Zostera* species, and probably also on various molluscs (Olney, 1968).

In a sample of shelduck collected throughout the year under a special licence, the mollusc *Hydrobia ulvae* was found in all birds (Olney, 1965). It was obvious, and this was confirmed by the literature and by faecal analyses, that this mollusc was the most important food item during much of the year and in many different localities. Other species eaten included the bivalve *Macoma balthica*, the amphipod *Corophium volutator*, the ragworm *Nereis* sp., the alga *Enteromorpha*, and occasionally the seeds of various plants.

It was suggested that the distribution and numbers of *H. ulvae* may be an important factor in concentrating shelduck in certain areas at certain times of the year. However, with the increase in inland breeding shelduck in western Europe it may be that new food habits are being adopted and the apparent rigid adherence to one feeding niche and one food species will not be so noticeable or important in the future.

A useful survey of the foods of geese has been carried out by J. Kear (1966) based mainly on available literature. Only recently have intensive species studies been attempted and the results are likely to be published in the near

TEAL (Inland)

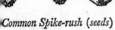

Common Spike-rush (seeds)   *Creeping Buttercup (seeds)*   *Chironomidae larvae*

TEAL (Saltmarsh and Brackish Water)

Marsh Samphire (seeds)   *Sabanaea ulvae*   *Tassel Pondweed (seeds)*

MALLARD (Inland)

Hairy Sedge (seeds)   *Water Pepper (seeds)*   *Redleg (seeds)*

MALLARD (Inland)

Broad-leaved Pondweed (seeds)   *Common Bur-reed (seeds)*   *Hydrobia jenkinsi*

MALLARD (Saltmarsh and Brackish Water)

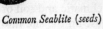

Common Seablite (seeds)   *Sea Clubrush (seeds)*   *Fennel-leaved Pondweed (seeds)*

FIG. 10. *Some common wildfowl foods (enlarged).*

future. A preliminary study of the feeding habits of the Greenland white-fronted geese in Cardiganshire, based mainly on faecal analyses techniques was published in 1968 (Pollard & Walter-Davies, 1968). They found that during much of the winter the preferred food plant species at Cors Tregaron was the white-beak sedge (*Rhynchospora alba*). Various grasses were also taken, especially during the spring.

Kear and Rodger (1963) have described the normal sequence of feeding behaviour for greylag and pink-footed geese in east Scotland, particularly in relation to agricultural interests. They showed that usually when the geese arrived in autumn they fed mainly on stubble fields from which they took grain and weed seeds. This behaviour would help to break cycles of cereal mildew infections. Potatoes may also be taken from harvested fields and this could help in the control of eelworm and disease. They found no evidence that winter wheat grain was dug up, though some grazing takes place. This can cause two shoots to grow out in the place of one which has been eaten. From mid-winter onwards grass becomes the favourite food and it is only in the spring that there may be direct competition with the farm stock for the available grass.

Kear (1965 a) has suggested that the increase in the numbers of pink-footed geese in Scotland in November can be correlated with the increase of acreage of barley.

The effects of grazing on young cereal crops has been studied by Kear (1965 b and c) using captive pink-footed and greylag geese. She found that there was no statistical difference between the yields of grain or straw on grazed and ungrazed controlled plots in December, March and April (winter oats and winter wheat), or in May (spring barley).

It is concluded that normally wild geese do not cause significant agricultural damage in this country (Kear, 1963).

Little work has been done for any of the swans, though a note on the spread of potato eating by the whooper swan was published in 1966 (Pilcher & Kear, 1966).

Once the food habits of a particular species are known and some idea of what foods are actually available in that locality, then conservation measures can be formulated. Propagation of plants of known food value can possibly help to retain in, or attract more wildfowl to, a particular area. A survey of this sort may also prove, of course, that the necessary food is plentifully available, and that the reasons why birds are not coming to that area are not connected with the food supply. A variety of factors may be affecting the environment causing the birds to move elsewhere, ranging from lack of available cover to too much shooting.

Very little information is available in this country on the propagation of plants which are used as food by wildfowl, and there is a considerable need for controlled experimental work in this field. It is essential to know the natural range of a particular species before attempting large-scale propagation work. The range of any plant species is dependent primarily on climatic and soil or water conditions and these may be quite different from those on the site into which the plant is to be introduced. Much time and money can be wasted by introducing plants into an area where they have little chance of survival. It is usually desirable to obtain plants from sources as near as possible to the situation in which the planting is to be made, or from areas having very similar climatic and environmental conditions. It is often only where the conditions have been artificially altered that new plants can successfully be established. Thus a slight rise in water level may drastically alter the spread and growth of a plant species, which may then enable a new plant of known food value to be introduced.

In Sevenoaks on the WAGBI-Wildfowl Trust Experimental Reserve a number of successful plant introductions were made in an area which, because of dredging operations, was comparatively bare of plants (Harrison & Harrison, 1965). By planting species of known food value in the area, before normal colonization had taken place, a larder of wildfowl food was established (Olney, 1964 b). It is an important fact which should not be forgotten in management schemes, that plants already in an area have predominated because the local conditions of water depth, turbidity, bottom type, temperature, acidity, alkalinity, climatic and other factors are optimum or at least favourable for their growth. That is, those plants are already there because they have survived in general competition and are best fitted to the local conditions. Thus, when establishing new plants of greater wildfowl food value, it is often essential to alter the existing growing conditions, to the detriment of the dominant species present and to the benefit of the introduced species. In some instances the eradication of a plant by chemical or mechanical methods may enable food plants to be introduced and become dominant.

To ensure the most successful results it is necessary to know what part of the plant is best suited to artificial propagation—whether it is the seed, or rootstock or other plant part. The actual material used will vary from species to species, and possibly with locality and time of year. The collection of material will again vary with the species involved and the situation in which it is growing. Information is also needed as to the means of storage and germination of propagating material.

APPENDIX

WILDFOWL VISCERA REMOVAL

The following procedure for removing wildfowl viscera is an abbreviated form of Dr. Jeffery Harrison's article published in the 11th Annual Report of the Wildfowl Trust in 1960, and of those instructions sent out to each collector by the Trust.

The procedure was designed to make the process as simple as possible and to ensure that the bird after its viscera had been removed was as edible as ever. The only essential instrument is a sharp-pointed knife.

a. Pluck underside from tail to breast-bone.
b. Push a wad of cotton wool on the end of a knitting needle down the throat until level with the shoulder-joints.

c. Cut across throat *above* the cotton-wool plug in order to sever food tract.

d. Cut open from vent to lower end of breast-bone without cutting into the intestines.

e. Feel for gizzard in gap made (hard object to bird's left, under the breast-bone). With thumb and forefinger feel above it for the proventriculus (upper part of stomach) and lower end of gullet, and free from surrounding tissue. The whole of the gullet, from the level where it was severed, can then be gently pulled downwards and out.

f. Tie the top end of the gullet above gizzard with tag, numbered in black Indian ink. Pencil tends to become illegible after long immersion in the preservative.

g. Cut across lower end of viscera just above vent and tie firmly.

h. Lift out complete viscera and place in a *formo-saline* solution for at *least* twenty-four hours.

i. For despatch, place in a polythene bag excluding as much air as possible, and post in a cardboard box or tin, including a list with the following details for each specimen:

(1) Number. (2) Species. (3) Sex. (4) Where shot. (5) Date shot. (6) Any other details or useful information. (7) Name and address.

Formo-saline solution is the preservative recommended and is made up as follows—commercial formalin diluted to eight times its volume in normal saline solution.

REFERENCES

CADMAN, W. A. (1953). "The winter food and ecological distribution of Greenland White-fronted Geese in Britain", *Brit. Birds*, 46: 374–5.

CADMAN, W. A. (1956). "The Wildfowler Naturalist", *Nature in Wales*, 2: 348–9.

CAMPBELL, J. W. (1936). "On the food of some British birds", *Brit. Birds*, 30: 209–18.

CAMPBELL, J. W. (1946a). "The food of the Wigeon and Brent Goose", *Brit. Birds*, 39: 194–200, 226–32.

CAMPBELL, J. W. (1946b). "Notes on the food of some British birds", *Brit. Birds*, 39: 371–3.

CAMPBELL, J. W. (1947). "The food of some British wildfowl", *Ibis*, 89: 429–32.

GIBB, J. and HARTLEY, P. H. T. (1957). "Bird foods and feeding-habits as subjects for amateur research", *Brit. Birds*, 50: 278–91.

GILHAM, M. E. (1956). "Feeding Habits and Seasonal Movements of Mute Swans on two South Devon Estuaries", *Bird Study*, 3: 205–12.

HARRISON, J. G. (1960). "A technique for removing wildfowl viscera for research", *Wildfowl Trust 11th Annual Report*: 135–6.

HARRISON, J. G. and HARRISON, J. M. (1965). "The management of a gravel-pit wildfowl reserve", *Trans. 6th Congress Int. Union Game Biol.*: 323–31.

HÖHN, E. O. (1948). *London Bird Report*, 12: 36–38.

JONES, E. W. (1959). "Biological flora of the British Isles: *Quercus* L", *J. Ecol.*, 47: 169–222.

KEAR, J. (1963). "Wildfowl and Agriculture", *Wildfowl in Great Britain*, 3: 315–28.

KEAR, J. (1965a) "Recent changes in Scottish barley acreages and the possible effect on wild geese", *Scottish Birds*, 3: 6: 288–2.

Plate 9. Three mallard

Plate 11. Putting out decoys

Plate 12. Never overface a young dog

Plate 13. A wildfowler's dog must be bold

KEAR, J. (1965b) "The Assessment of Goose Damage by Grazing Trials", *Trans. 6th Int. Union Game Biol.*: 333–9.

KEAR, J. (1965c). "The assessment by grazing trial of goose damage to grass", *Wildfowl Trust 16th Annual Report*: 46–47.

KEAR, J. (1966). "The food of geese", *Int. Zoo. Yb*, 6: 96–103.

KEAR, J. and RODGER, J. B. A. (1963). "Wild Geese in East Scotland", *Scottish Agriculture*, 43: 123–6.

KOERSVELD, E. V. (1950). "Difficulties in stomach analysis", *Proc. 10th Int. Orn. Congress*: 592–4.

LACK, D. (1954). *The Natural Regulation of Animal Numbers*, Oxford.

LYNN-ALLEN, E. (1953). "The ducks of Minsmere, 1946–1952", *Bird Notes*, 26: 11–16.

OLNEY, P. J. S. (1958). "Food and feeding habits of wildfowl", *Wildfowl Trust 9th Annual Report*: 47–51.

OLNEY, P. J. S. (1960). "Duck food research", *Bull. B.O.C.*, 80: 33–35.

OLNEY, P. J. S. (1962). "The food habits of a hand-reared Mallard population", *Wildfowl Trust 13th Ann. Rep.*: 119–25.

OLNEY, P. J. S. (1963a). "The food and feeding of habits Teal *Anas crecca crecca*", *Proc. Zool. Soc. London*, 140: 169–210.

OLNEY, P. J. S. (1963b). "The food and feeding habits of Tufted Duck *Aythya fuligula*", *Ibis*, 105: 55–62.

OLNEY, P. J. S. (1964a). "The food of Mallard *Anas p. platyrhynchos* collected from coastal and estuarine areas", *Proc. Zool. Soc. London*, 142: 397–418.

OLNEY, P. J S. (1964b). "Gravel pits as waterfowl reserves", *Proc. MAR Conf., I.U.C.N. Pub. No. 3*, Vol. 1: 414–20.

OLNEY, P. J. S. (1965). "The food and feeding habits of the Shelduck, *Tadorna tadorna*", *Ibis*, 107: 527–32.

OLNEY, P. J. S., (1967). "The WAGBI-Wildfowl Trust Experimental Reserve— Pt. II, The feeding ecology of local Mallard and other wildfowl", *Wildfowl Trust 18th Ann. Rep.*: 47–55.

OLNEY, P. J. S. (1968). "The food and feeding habits of the Pochard, *Aythya ferina*", *Biol. Cons.*, 1: 71–76.

OLNEY, P. J. S. and MILLS, D. H. (1963). "The food and feeding habits of Goldeneye *Bucephala clangula* in Great Britain", *Ibis*, 105: 293–300.

PILCHER, R. E. M. and KEAR, J. (1966). "The spread of potato-eating in Whooper Swans", *Brit. Birds*, 59: 160–61.

POLLARD, D. F. W. (1967). "Comparison of techniques for the analysis of wildfowl viscera", *Wildfowl Trust 18th Ann. Rep.*: 158–9.

POLLARD, D. F. W. and WALTER-DAVIES, P. (1968). "A preliminary study of the feeding of the Greenland White-fronted Goose *Anser albifrons flavirostris* in Cardiganshire", *Wildfowl*, 19: 108–16.

RANWELL, D. S. and DOWNING, B. M. (1959). "Brent Goose winter feeding pattern and Zostera resources at Scolt Head Island, Norfolk", *Animal Behaviour*, 7: 42–56.

CHAPTER 6

CLOTHES AND EQUIPMENT

by Peter Whitaker

Life Member, WAGBI. Editor, "Country Landowner".

SPORTING fashions have followed two distinct main lines over the centuries. On the one hand there are the colourful costumes of the chase, the purpose of which was to heighten the spectacle and make the huntsmen more easily identifiable, which gradually became increasingly like uniforms. On the other may be instanced the quieter clothes, subdued of hue, which were designed to enable the hunter to blend inconspicuously with the local scenery, hence the greys and greens which, since the hunter began to wear clothes, have always been so popular.

Wildfowling couture has always belonged to the second category for obvious —or rather not so obvious!—reasons. It has never aspired to the *haute classe*, partly because fowling was for centuries identified with the poor man's sport, but equally since the conditions under which the sport is practised hardly equate themselves with finery. At the same time, precisely because of these conditions, wildfowling clothing deserves a great deal more attention than it is sometimes given by those unaccustomed to the marsh in all its moods.

For many years now, a certain type of wildfowler seems to have become steeped in the masochistic idea that, to be a credit to his sport, he must endure all sorts of supreme discomforts and rate as a lively candidate for such unpleasantness as pneumonia, or at least the "screws" in later life, at the same time running the risk of drowning, or death from exposure each time he goes out. "It's rough; it's tough; it's rugged" is his proud theme song. And so it is, and it would not be wildfowling if it were not, but it is not half as bad as that—not nowadays, anyway, and a great deal of the discomfort and so-called unpleasantness is due entirely to lack of planning.

Nowadays, there is no excuse for a wildfowler going about his business inadequately clad. With nylon, terylene, Dacron, Gannex, polyester and similar man-made fibres, one can travel light and relatively cheaply, and still keep warm or cool, according to the climate.

In a consideration of basic requirements, the natural starting-point is boots. Leather boots may be "gear" in Carnaby Street, but on the marsh rubber thigh boots—not the knee length sort that let in the water as soon as you kneel down, as kneel down you must before long—are the modern answer. The more expensive kind have leather soles with metal studs, and the obvious advantage is that they can be re-soled. Disadvantages are that studs slip on icy surfaces and the "ledge" provided by the soles can make extrication from deep mud more difficult. Experience of these shows that the tops wear out before the bottoms. Don't expect your rubber boots to last more than two seasons. If they are well cleated to start with, they will wear longer and not slip. If the tops wear out first, cut these off and you have a pair of gum boots that will last you another year. Average cost of thigh waders is £5 a pair.

The life of a pair of thigh-boots depends largely on how they are kept when not in use. Always dry them when you take them off, by stuffing them with newspaper, or by leaving them overnight with a pair of electric boot-dryers working inside the foot. If they are dried in front of a fire, see that only the soles face the fire, but not too close. Never hang up the boots by the tops, which stretches and strains the rubber. Out of season suspend them in the dry from a cord looped round the foot.

Straps which secure the boot to belt or braces are a bore and uncomfortable. Get a pair of boots stiff enough to stand up without this aid. Carry a cycle puncture outfit in a pocket in case of a puncture. Clean the boots before hanging them up. Dirt encourages rot and cracking of the rubber.

Novice fowlers are sometimes advised when buying their first pair of thigh-boots, to choose a size larger than that of their normal shoes, on the principle that bigger boots can accommodate several pairs of socks. But this leads us to another mistake often made, the wearing of too many or too thick socks which defeat the foot-warming object because they impede circulation and, fitting tight between foot and boot, allow for no passage of insulating air. In a well-fitting—which does not mean tight—boot, a single pair of thin socks may be enough, especially if a "sock" is included between foot sole and boot.

Layers of newspaper cut to the shape of the foot make a primitive but effective moisture-absorbent sock of this kind, though perhaps better are those made of honey-combed sponge rubber.

Another combination is a thin silk or nylon sock topped by a pair of oiled wool seaman's stockings; it is worth securing the latter below the knee with a garter of some sort, for stockings that slip down round the ankle inside a long boot make walking uncomfortable and legs cold.

Best of all is a pair of thin wool socks and a pair of "Husky" thermo-insulated bootees. Made of polyester-filled, quilted nylon they are the answer to foot comfort in the coldest weather.

Some support round the ankle and heel is useful and indeed necessary when creek-crawling or stalking fowl out on the saltings. A length of strong cord tied round the instep, and above the heel, prevents boots pulling off in mud and also allows the boot to be withdrawn from it with a minimum of noisy, sucking sound.

So much, then, for boots and socks. From there we progress upwards to trousers.

These should be primarily windproof, and secondarily water-resistant. Here is to be found, usually, the most vulnerable gap in the fowler's defence against the elements. Impervious to rain and wind and the worst that the weather can do above and below, he is inclined to forget seating arrangements, only to be reminded of his oversight when the inevitable time comes to sit down in the damp.

Thin rubber over-trousers, which are the choice of many, are apt to tear, and overheat the nether regions.

The answer seems to be to choose a "pliable" pair of trousers of almost any material, so long as they are warm and windproof—breeches are hard to beat while a pair of dungarees deserve consideration—and to wear over them an additional pair of slacks which are waterproof. Recommended are those tough shorts in Maxproof or Barbour oiled cloth. Worn outside waders, they keep the posterior dry when at squat and at the same time allow enough freedom of movement for unimpeded creek jumping. Pyjama trousers worn next to the skin form a sound windproof base to any type of over-trousers.

Getting nearer the bone, what about underclothes? Remembering that the basis of all effective cold weather clothing is the provision of an insulating layer of air between flesh and the elements, there is little doubt that the string vest, and pants, proved in action and extreme conditions of wartime, are the best basis on which to build. There is one proviso here, for best results. The shirt topping this base must be of good, close-weft material which will do its share of keeping out the wind.

On top of this and beneath the outermost garment a seaman's jersey is the favourite winter choice. A point to be made here is that any gap at the neck-line is to be avoided, and it matters not whether a tie or scarf is worn so long as something, not too tight, is included at this level to keep out the draught. It is surprising what a lot of warmth there is in a tie. The simple addition or removal of this item is an additional advantage when a long, wearing walk to the marsh is involved. By leaving it off on the way there, one can move more freely, and clothing is allowed to breathe. Once in position, the donning of a tie or scarf contains the warm air layer, and when the time comes for a strenuous retreat it can be removed.

Clothing restrictions of any sort are to be avoided; bulk under the topmost garment leads to overheating and subsequent chilling of the body. Priority protection from the cold is advisable in the region of the lower back and kidneys, and one of the best ways of ensuring this is to wear a waistcoat, the back of which is made of flannel, or some similarly thick material. If the waistcoat is equipped with four pockets—with flaps—in front, so much the better. Waistcoats have the advantage of no sleeves or tightness about the shoulders that impede gun-handling when several layers of clothing are worn. The choice of additional sweaters, etc., is purely a personal one. Such dodges as wearing layers of newspapers to protect the back are now outmoded by modern clothing and here again "Husky" provide a perfect answer with their thermo-insulated shooting waistcoat.

In the matter of the outermost, overall garment, the choice is fairly wide, and all manner of coats and jackets are seen on the marsh. Selection is governed by weather conditions, availability and price. On fine and balmy days a sweater or battle-dress blouse may be sufficient. Ordinary jackets that droop below the waist are not recommended because their bottoms get wet as soon as the forgetful fowler stoops or bends down in water, and so do the cartridges carried in the side pockets.

The ideal fowling coat must be wind and waterproof, light and of a neutral colour to blend with the marsh, and long enough to cover the tops of thigh-boots. Smocks are still a favourite choice, and double-texture parkas, many of them surplus American army equipment, remain useful, especially since they are reversible, the outer side being coloured green and the inner white, an asset in snow. The parkas are extremely wind-resistant, but they are by no means waterproof, and even if the fowler does not have to contend with much heavy rain in a season, hiding and lying about in wet places soon leads to uncomfortable saturation.

First choice is one of the various Barbour or Maxproof oiled cloth coats. The lined type are warmer than the unlined. Get one big enough to cover sweaters, etc., and long enough to sit on, on the mud. A belt adds to its warmth and stops it dragging on the shoulders.

Whether a fowling coat is better for a zip or buttoned front, is a moot point. Buttons, even if they do come off from time to time, are more easily replaced than a zip, but the latter makes for easier access to binoculars. Button-fronted coats have an overlapping flap at the join, and appear to keep out the wet as well as a zip. The latter does not simplify access to inner pockets, waistcoat, etc.

Two areas worthy of protection remain to be considered; head and hands. Headgear is wide in variety. Something light and waterproof is the choice and a peak fore and aft is not adopted for affectation but to shield face from birds and neck from rain. Hats or hoods that act as ear plugs are not recommended. The fowler relies very largely on his hearing for warning of bird movement. A balaclava knitted helmet is an asset in cold weather and can be rolled up to form an adequate hat. But it is useless and most uncomfortable in rain. A face mask is not affectation. It hides the most noticeable feature of the gunner and helps to keep off the wind.

If anyone can shoot properly in gloves, he is welcome to wear them. They soon get wet and filthy on the marsh, however, and foul up gun and everything else one touches. A better proposition are wristlets—those with leather, fleeced-lined extensions to cover the back of the hands are warm and wear well. Hands will become acclimatized and stay warm longer if they are dipped in the water early on and allowed to dry naturally. This may be hard to believe, but it's true. Remember too, that fitness and food make for a good circulation and warmth. No amount of extra clothing will warm an unfit hungry body.

Given a gun, some cartridges and an adequate costume, the game shooter—and even his rougher, inland counterpart—can acquit and enjoy himself with a minimum of trouble. If it rains, he goes home; if he gets caught in the rain, he sends for his waterproof; if his cartridges swell in the damp atmosphere he sends for dry ones from his car; he stops for lunch at a convenient half-way halt when he is hungry or thirsty; if he finds himself or his gun or his dog in some trouble, there is someone close at hand to help him out. But if he is fowling, the chances are that he will have none of these things or people to help him out of a hole; he must depend in the main on himself and, if he is ill-prepared, he may well find himself not only short of sport, but indeed short of breath as well; in fact at his last salty gasp.

There is still a tendency, just as there always has been, to talk about wild-fowling in terms of extreme danger. Some writers have been inclined in their glamourization of the sport to make it sound so risky that it should not be undertaken by anyone short of superman. This, while it is undoubtedly wrong, is an error on the right side, for there are today a larger number of enthusiasts who have been driven to the shore-line for want of any other opportunity so cheap and easily accessible, without appreciating the impli-cations, and they are the ones who inspire the frightening pictures sometimes painted.

Many sports are dangerous if the participant goes in for them without thinking or making the necessary preparation. But wildfowling is no more— and indeed a great deal less—risky than such pastimes as rock climbing and motor racing. A field sport only becomes hazardous when something extra-ordinary, with fatal or frightening consequences, occurs, and the following suggestions are made with a view to preventing this sort of thing, as well as to simplify what is, of necessity, among the more awkward and uncomfortable sports.

The most formidable basic dangers that confront the shoreshooter are few and elementary. They comprise tide, fog (and snow in that it can be almost equally blinding), and mud. All can be defeated by a pocketful of gadgets.

Tides are treacherous, and their time of rising and falling may, and should, be determined from a Tide Table obtainable from any local ship's chandler. Flight times as well as the gunner's safety depend on tide tables, so they are a double necessity. See that you consult a current edition. More than one fowler has got wet by failing to look at the date of his borrowed and dog-eared copy. Do not trust in these tables implicitly. Study them in con-junction with a note of the wind. A strong onshore wind can advance a tide as much as an hour or more and pile it up higher. Similarly vice versa.

Used in conjunction, a reliable watch is an obvious necessity; best of all one that is waterproof. Unless the timepiece is 100 per cent waterproof, unbreak-able and impervious to mud, choose a pocket, as opposed to a wrist, model.

Here we must include the all-important torch, which is vital in all sorts of situations from signalling to one's fellows to spotlighting obstacles on the way off the marsh. Most serviceable are the rubber-cased models. Carry a spare bulb Sellotaped inside the reflector. A spare pocket torch of the pencil type is a double insurance.

First line of defence against invisibility, which may be caused by mist, snow, fog, or just plain nightfall, is a compass, and the ability to read it. Learn how to take a forward and back bearing from any Boy Scout's manual, or if this is too much bother, at least know the four main points and the one which spells safety and the sea-wall. Creeks running directly to and from the wall are good guides off and on to the marsh, and a compass bearing of the extremity of one of these, out on the mud, will set the wandering fowler on the right track. But let him note on which side of the creek he went out to sea, and head for home on the same side.

Compasses come in all sizes, and those incorporated in whistles, pocket knives, etc., are better than nothing. But the bigger the instrument, the more reliable, and although there is no need for an unwieldy large compass, let it be of proportions commensurate with accuracy. One large enough to fit into the eye-piece cover of a pair of field-glasses is sufficient, and this is a good place to carry it. No properly-equipped fowler sets forth without field-glasses or binoculars, and this fitting ensures a vital "double take". Don't despise the monocular by the way. It is less bulky, cheaper and highly effective.

There is no easily portable mud extricator within the meaning of the word, but a strong, sharp knife can be used for cutting off boots in an extreme emergency.

The lone fowler who gets into difficulty still has no recognized distress signal on which he can rely to summon help. Discussions continue in high places on the subject of distress signals, and one day members of wildfowling clubs may be able to obtain a 12-bore signal cartridge, or some similar means of attracting attention which is known to and recognized by all coast guards, police, lifeboat crews and fellow fowlers. But no distress signal will ever be an absolute guarantee of rescue, and the best way of avoiding trouble remains a sound knowledge of tides, weather and marsh, not going out alone, or at least leaving word of one's whereabouts before setting out.

Any gun becomes heavy quickly where a march of some distance to the shooting ground is entailed. When the going is as heavy as it usually is hard by or below the sea-wall, and the gun on the weighty side, as many fowling pieces are, it is an advantage to be able to rely on some other means of support other than one hand, which would be welcome to preserve balance or break the stumbling fowler's fall, if unencumbered. The answer, which Continental shooters of all sorts have been trying to teach us for years, and which we are so slow to learn, is a sling, whereby the weapon may be suspended from the shoulder or across the back, and there are many shooting occasions far from the wildfowler's world, on which such an appendage proves a boon, as any pigeon shooter will confirm.

Slings and sling fittings need not necessarily spoil the appearance of any gun, a main objection in the eyes of many, for the sling swivel is easily removable from its screw hole in the stock, and the same applies to the fitting screwed into the bottom rib, when the gun is to be used where a sling might be a nuisance. If these minor alterations are still considered undesirable, it is possible to buy a sling which loops over the small of the stock and the barrels. The disadvantages here, however, are that one never feels too certain about the forward fixture which is liable to slip off unless the barrels are of good length if the fowler is pretty boneless in the shoulder, and also that when the gun is mounted, the line of sight is interrupted by a thickish band across the barrel(s).

The ideal sling fittings would seem to be those that neither mark the gun nor interrupt the sight plane. Mechanically-minded fowlers may like to experiment with a forward sling fitting in the form of an eye affixed to a section of a slip-on handguard, with the backward loop slipped round the small, or grip of the stock. Ingenious improvisers can work out something on these lines for themselves.

Sooner or later out on the mud the gunner is bound to slip or fall in a creek and block his gun barrels with mud or some similar obstruction. All the old books advise the fowler to carry a pull-through in his pocket with which to dislodge such foreign bodies from his tubes. Anyone who has driven his barrels into a soft creekside will realize how useless a pull-through is for this purpose. If you object to the idea of swilling out the gun barrels in the nearest creek, take with you instead a sectionalized cleaning rod, or better still one of those metal rods with a cord running through the centre on the "Helvetic" pattern. Such a slender, short-lengthed tool is no trouble to tuck away in pack or bag, and will clear barrel obstructions, or poke out swollen cartridge cases (if a cartridge extractor has been forgotten) with speed and absolute efficiency. Which reminds us that a cartridge extractor should not be forgotten, for shooting in wet places leads sooner or later to swollen cartridge cases that are awkward to remove unless plastic case cartridges are being used exclusively. Whatever the type of cartridge extractor chosen—the pliers type has the advantage of being adaptable to any bore—make it a fixture, not to be forgotten, by securing it to cartridge belt or jacket lapel with a length of nylon cord.

Cartridges, except the plastic-cased type, deserve special protection from the elements, but at the same time they should be easily accessible. A favourite way of carrying cartridges on the marsh is in a belt, with a few tucked away in reserve in inside pockets. Nine times out of ten this allows for a more than sufficient supply. On the tenth occasion, few fowlers want to shoot more than this number, anyway.

Only one type of cartridge belt is worth considering and this is the one with closed loops. Two-and-a-half-inch cartridges will keep snug and dry in a belt of this sort, and the longer cases also, for they have the extra protection afforded by the deeper brass. A belt like this can be worn with confidence outside one's clothing if necessary, although it is better girt beneath the outer layer. It pays to keep any cartridge belt supple and waterproof by treating it from time to time with saddle soap.

Before adding further to the wildfowler's burden let us now consider how he is going to carry the bulkier items of his paraphernalia which refuse to fit comfortably or safely into pockets.

On the backs of most fowlers one can see what has come to be known somewhat romantically as a "goose bag", which may be of any material and dimensions—the larger, within reason, the better—the object of which is essentially to contain and carry home the successful hunter's bag. The object remains, but its fulfilment has long been relegated to the realms of wishful thinking in the minds of most fowlers, who carry such a bag just in case, on the one hand, but otherwise for the major reason that into it may be packed a lot of useful oddments on the outward trip, and as Dalgety in his *Wildfowling* excused its part in the scene: "It is useful to sit upon."

Game bags, goose bags, bags of any sort which suspend from one's shoulder and flap about against the fowler's rump, eventually working round to the front, unless restricted by diverse cords and straps, are nothing short of an awkward nuisance. Much to be preferred is a pack or haversack of some sort, which fits fairly and squarely on both shoulders, leaves both hands free, and cannot slip out of place when its wearer comes to jump a creek or slither in the mud. If you have to buy one, the Army style big pack is obtainable at very little cost from most surplus stores. Empty, it will take three pinkfeet easily, and more duck than result from the average flight. The unexpected big bag is never too hard to carry off the marsh, and a roll of string will cope with this and other emergencies.

Half a dozen thin rubber collapsible duck decoys take up next to no room in a big pack. Wear a duck or goose call round the neck, but *only* take one if you know precisely how and when to blow it. Being fairly water resistant, such a pack will also do duty as a seat or cushion in damp places. Other items it may be required to accommodate from time to time include a flask of soup, for long vigils, especially under the moon, a bite to eat, a piece of camouflage netting to drape over the dog and a coal shovel for trimming out a seat or hide in a gutter.

Any type of shooting stool makes a pack in which to carry it essential. Individual gunners may develop their own ideas of other equipment they want to take on the marsh, but it is a sound rule to reduce one's burden to the minimum and travel as light as possible. Those fowlers who take a thumbstick on their forays use it not so much to support their burden as to test water depths in gutters and to help progress over rough going. It is also a very useful support for a camouflage net.

CHAPTER 7

GUNS AND CARTRIDGES

by Gough Thomas (G. T. Garwood)

WAGBI Member; Gun Editor, "Shooting Times".

IN this chapter, I will try to describe the best kinds of guns and loads for wildfowl shooting, and the most important considerations affecting the sportsman's choice; but since experienced and successful wildfowlers are usually individualists with clear ideas on what they need for their particular sport, what I have to say will be addressed mainly to beginners and others who feel in need of guidance.

BASIC FACTS

Wildfowlers, more than any other shooters, need to recognize certain fundamental facts and limitations concerning shotgun performance. They may be summarized as follows:

(1) The shotgun is essentially and inescapably a short-range weapon. This arises from the fact that the shot charge in flight suffers a two-fold loss of killing power—first, because it is split up into numerous pellets, whereby it encounters a far greater air resistance than it would if it took the form of a solid bullet; and secondly, because the progressive dispersal of the pellets quickly reduces the number that can be brought to bear on a given target.

(2) The maximum effective range of a gun is determined by the weight of the charge and the degree of choke, as duly reflected in the density of the pattern. Assuming a normal size of shot, it is little affected by any other factors.

(3) The minimum charge (and therefore the weight of the gun) required to make a pattern of given density and pellet energy goes up in fantastic disproportion to range—actually, it increases according to a cube law. The operation of this law is masked over moderate ranges by the existence of several reserves, but as we press for longer and longer reach, it bears down with inexorable force, so that even a punt gun, weighing perhaps 100 pounds and firing over a pound of shot, is good for little beyond 100 yards.

(4) Guns firing heavier loads than those for which they were designed are almost certain to shoot low, so that the dense centre of full-choke patterns may pass completely below the point of aim.

(5) Guns and loads giving exceptional range are useless without exceptional marksmanship. This is because, up to about forty yards, crossing birds require a lead that is proportional to the range—that is to say, they need a constant angle of lead, with which the average shooter is familiar. But at extended ranges, this is not enough. For example, a duck crossing at sixty yards

requires considerably more than twice the lead of one crossing at half that distance. Few can achieve these abnormal leads without regular practice.

(6) The best degree of choke for filling the game bag is always the *least* degree consistent with the requirements of the class of sport concerned. The fact that certain kinds of wildfowl shooting may require the tightest possible choke does not affect this proposition in the least.

"WILDFOWLING" TOO VAGUE

There is no short answer to the question as to the best gun and load for wildfowling. The term covers several different kinds of sport, even though they are nearly all concerned with the shooting of duck and geese with shoulder guns. There is accordingly no single prescription for the best equipment, for the sort of gun and load indispensable for reasonable success in one kind of wildfowling could be quite unsuited to another.

For all that, there are certain basic requirements. The rifleman knows that the first thing needed for successful hunting is a *bullet*, which, when correctly placed, is capable of penetrating to a vital part of his quarry. Nothing less will serve. So with the wildfowler; but since he shoots with a shotgun, and cannot aim individual pellets, he must contrive to hit his target with a sufficient number of them to make it reasonably certain that one or more will reach a vital spot, or that the shock and damage they jointly inflict will bring the bird down and quickly prove fatal.

To satisfy these requirements, the wildfowler must have:

(*a*) pellets large enough, and travelling with sufficient speed, to ensure adequate penetration; and

(*b*) a pattern dense and regular enough to make it reasonably certain that a fairly aimed shot will score a sufficient number of hits.

It does not matter a rap what kind or bore of gun fires the charge, provided that these requirements are met. They can be met by a small-bore firing a light charge at close range; by an ordinary game gun or a small-bore magnum firing a medium charge at medium range; or by a big-bore firing a maximum charge at maximum range. So the basic question confronting the wildfowler in his choice of armament is, what is the range bracket within which he needs to be most successful if he is to make the best of his chances?

The question must be pressed, because until it is fairly faced and answered, no proper and satisfactory choice can be made. It is no good for the shooter to say, "Need you ask? I want a gun that will kill at the farthest possible distance, of course," because the gun that will do that will not be most successful for shooting at more moderate distances. The farthest-killing gun for present purposes may be taken to be a fully choked 8-bore, for that is the largest gun for which ammunition is currently being manufactured in this country. But if the sport in prospect is chiefly tapping in to inland streams and pools, or flight-pond shooting, or shooting over decoys, yielding shots which fall mostly within, say, twenty-five to thirty-five yards, such a gun, weighing perhaps fourteen pounds, would be a ridiculous burden, requiring costly ammunition, and one, moreover, that would throw too tight a pattern, making many misses at the shorter distances a reasonable certainty in the hands of an average man, and filling birds bagged so full of lead as to render them inedible. And if this is true of the 8-bore, it applies with something approaching the same force to a fully-choked 3-inch 12-bore, heavy enough to fire the Eley 1⅝ oz. Magnum cartridge. In a word, such guns, in average hands, and for the kind of sport considered, would actually lighten the game bag.

But when we come to consider shooting high-flying fowl at the sea-wall or the like—birds that barely come within the maximum range of a shotgun, unless beating their way out to sea against half a gale of wind—then we have a different story. For success at this sort of work, we may need the heaviest charges and the tightest patterns that guns can be made to throw, *as well as more skill than the average man possesses.*

So, the young or inexperienced shooter who rates his prospects of success in all branches of wildfowling in terms of the bore of his gun or the weight of lead he can throw into the sky, or the degree of choke in his barrels, or the big shot he uses, may often find himself in the position of a man who has nothing better than a sledge hammer for driving tacks. Besides, there is a great deal to be said for a *familiar* gun, and if a shooter is thoroughly used to a certain game gun, it nearly always pays him handsomely to use it for all purposes to which it is reasonably well adapted. A well-known landowner and Member of Parliament, who had a wonderful duck shoot on the lower reaches of the Hampshire Avon, and who probably shot more duck in a season than the average shooter shoots in a lifetime, used his ordinary game guns and No. 7 shot. His undeniable success lay in his recognizing the moderate range-bracket within which most of his birds could be taken and the close pattern made by his small shot within that bracket, whereby it was possible for him to make pretty sure of hitting them in the head and neck. Also, he possessed the judgment and self-control required to avoid long shots, which were unnecessary for the making of a good bag, and for which his equipment was manifestly unsuitable.

Again, an American friend of mine, a wildfowler of much experience, and a keen and expert judge of a gun, may be quoted to similar effect. In a recent letter he says, "When we shoot duck, we always try to put three stakes about forty-five yards from the blind or boat (one out to the front and one on each side), or, if the water is too deep, three decoys; and we don't shoot at duck beyond these markers unless it is a cripple. I have never found that a 12-bore gun, patterning well at around 55–60 per cent, and loaded with 3¼ drams equivalent and 1¼ oz. of No. 7½ (English No. 7) shot is in any way inadequate for our largest duck in these circumstances—if, of course, properly held. Geese can also be killed stone dead. I shoot the load mentioned in a Purdey gun of 7 lb. 2 oz., which, in my opinion, is completely adequate to make a bag of waterfowl anywhere *if they are to be gotten at all.*"

The three striking things in these observations are the moderate degree of choke favoured (i.e. quarter to half); the relatively small shot, as in the previous case quoted; and the concluding phrase, which I have italicized, and which may be taken as recognizing the limits imposed among other things by the skill, or lack of skill, of the shooter, who, given a gun adapted to kill at extreme range, could not necessarily make good use of it.

Having said so much to dispose of the all-too-prevalent conception that the best gun for wildfowling is necessarily the one best suited for long-distance work, we are in a position to examine more closely the needs of the various kinds of shooting lumped together under this broad heading.

This brings us back to the question of the patterns and pellet energies needed for successful duck and goose shooting, and the effective range of various guns and loads.

Many investigations have been carried out on the killing and wounding power of different kinds of projectiles, including shotgun pellets, and in some cases the results have been reduced to mathematical formulae. From these it ought to be possible to say with some degree of assurance what shot sizes and patterns are required to deal effectively with particular birds, and what would be the effective range of any gun of known performance when firing a specified load.

But conclusions based on such investigations tend to underrate what generations of practical and experienced shooters have come to regard as the proven capacity of their loads and weapons. The reason for this, I have little doubt, is that such shooters are reasonably satisfied with their performance at ranges somewhat in excess of what might theoretically be considered as the limit for consistent results. A good shot who bagged 70 duck with 100 cartridges in particular circumstances might well be pleased both with himself and his equipment. Yet it could be true that if he had confined himself strictly to birds within the range theoretically determined as being his effective limit, he might have bagged 60 duck with 75 cartridges—that is to say, an 80 per cent performance instead of 70 per cent, but a smaller bag.

There is in fact no specific limit to the range of a shotgun. This is because the number of pellets striking a bird big enough to intercept, say, a twentieth of the area covered by a pattern will not necessarily receive a twentieth of the pellets every time. On the contrary, the possibilities vary widely. In *Gough Thomas's Gun Book* (p. 160) I describe a practical experiment in which a mallard-sized target, caught in a normally good pattern dense enough to ensure an *average* of six hits, actually received anything from one to twelve pellets, according to its precise position within the pattern circle.

Even if we were sure that a given bird at a given range would always be struck by the same number of pellets, their effect would obviously vary according to the location of the various hits.

From all this it would seem that the only way to define shotgun performance in a manner acceptable to experienced shooters is to adjust our calculations of effective range, based on patterns and pellet energies, to a scale determined by the consensus of competent opinion. This is what I have done below.

We can start by laying down certain requirements as having been fairly determined by practical experience.

(1) Duck and geese require four or five hits to make reasonably sure of a kill. This implies minimum patterns of 80 and 70 respectively. (N.B. These are the patterns in a 30-inch circle at the range at which the bird is taken.)

(2) Pellet energies should be not less than $1\frac{1}{2}$ foot-pounds for duck, 2 for the smaller geese (e.g. whitefronts) and 3 for the largest (i.e. Canadas).

I should say that, in the light of accumulating evidence, these requirements are rather more exacting than I have previously considered necessary.

We can apply an immediate practical check to these figures. Experience gained over several generations has established the $2\frac{1}{2}$-inch 12-bore, if well bored and loaded with the old standard load of $1\frac{1}{8}$ oz. of suitable shot, as having an effective range against game and wildfowl of forty yards if bored improved cylinder, and fifty yards if full choke. Let us see what performance lies behind this reputation.

Assuming the popular No. 4 shot for duck and No. 3 for geese, and the nominal or textbook performance of the two borings, we get the following results:

Duck (No. 4)	Pattern		Striking Energy	
	40 yds	50 yds	40 yds	50 yds
Imp. Cyl.	95	—	2·7	—
Full choke	—	93	—	2·0
Geese (No. 3)				
Imp. Cyl.	78	—	3·4	—
Full choke	—	77	—	2·6

These figures show sufficient margins above the stipulated figures to suggest that for all duck and goose shooting (except possibly Canadas) the traditional range limits of forty and fifty yards stated are reasonably conservative.

But it is necessary to *be* conservative. The number of pellet strikes in practice is often below the average, as the experiment described above clearly indicated, and the striking energies shown are true only for those pellets that are fully up to size and perfectly round. Actual pellets, if somewhat undersized, and especially if they are badly deformed, may have as little as half their nominal energy.

The following chart has been worked out with due regard for these considerations. It shows the maximum effective range of various wildfowling guns and charges, and is substantially the same as the one I first published in *Shotguns and Cartridges*, except that it is slightly down-scaled.

The chart is best construed, not as a statement of specific maximum ranges, but rather as a broad composite picture of the effectiveness and limitations of variously bored and loaded guns. Owing to the rapid deterioration of patterns at extreme distances I have not felt competent to legislate for any ranges above sixty yards.

It should be noted that the maximum effective range indicated is defined as the greatest range at which it is *reasonably* certain that a clean kill will be made by a truly aimed shot. Note that word "reasonably"—it must stand to cover all the difference between theory and practice; between average and individual results; and between the expectations of a crack shot and his actual performance.

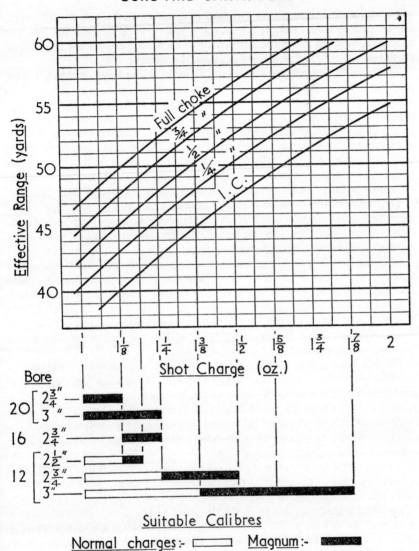

FIG. 11. *Effective ranges against wildfowl of various loads, borings and calibres (assuming No. 4 shot for duck, No. 3 for geese, or No. 1 for heaviest goose loads).*

LOADS AND SHOT SIZE

I have already emphasized sufficiently the fact that the long-range gun and the long-range load are not necessarily the best guarantors of success in wildfowl shooting, and that the combination for making the biggest bag in given circumstances is the one best adapted to the range-bracket within which most chances fall.

For the shorter ranges, the standard proprietary cartridges, or the corresponding home-loads, and the popular shot sizes (No. 4 for duck and No. 3 or 1 for geese) give us all we need: it is only when we come to the loads for maximum reach that we need to consider special measures.

The secret of success for long-range shooting is the balanced load. This is the load in which pattern and pellet energy are balanced so as to give the best prospect of a clean kill from a truly aimed shot. It excludes, on the one hand, the extra-dense patterns made by unduly small shot, which depend for success on the shooter having sufficient skill (like my M.P. quoted above) to be sure of hitting his birds in the head and neck; and, on the other hand, the use of extra large shot, whereby kills may occasionally be made by fluke at extreme distances, though at the risk of sending off many birds pricked or wounded, with perhaps only a single pellet in some non-vulnerable part of their anatomy.

There is admittedly scope here for difference of opinion, and experienced individual shooters may be able to justify exchanging pattern density for pellet energy within considerable limits; but the majority can best work to the patterns and pellet energies previously suggested.

The diagram opposite provides a key to well-balanced duck and goose loads on this basis. It is adapted from the one given on page 215 of *Gough Thomas's Gun Book*, and, for simplicity, assumes a common minimum pattern of 80. The right-hand half of the diagram shows the ranges to which a fully choked gun may be expected to throw various charges and shot sizes to give this minimum pattern. For example, $1\frac{1}{4}$ oz. of No. 3 would be good for about fifty-two yards, as indicated by the dotted line.

The left-hand half of the diagram shows the striking energies of the corresponding pellets at the ranges thus determined. Following the dotted line round, shows that a pellet of No. 3 at the last-mentioned range of fifty-two yards would have an energy of nearly $2\frac{1}{2}$ foot-pounds. This would accordingly make a well-balanced fifty-yard goose load for anything short of Canadas. At this range there would indeed be some energy in hand, *as there always should be when pattern is stretched to the limit.* With shot of normal or larger size, fired at normal or higher velocity, pattern fails before energy, and it is accordingly to his patterns that the wildfowler must look for successful performance at extreme range.

To take another example from the diagram, $1\frac{1}{4}$ oz. of No. 4 would make a pattern of 80 at nearly fifty-seven yards, at which range the corresponding pellet energy would be $1\frac{1}{2}$ foot-pounds. This is below the minimum given for geese and has no reserve for duck, though it would make a good duck load at somewhat shorter range (see fig. 11).

As a final example, consider $1\frac{1}{2}$ oz. of BB. In this case the required minimum pattern would not be attained beyond thirty-eight yards, at which distance the pellet energy would be 8 foot-pounds—an excessive value, probably sufficient to drive right through a goose, but not giving an adequate pattern at the extended ranges at which energy would still be ample. By no stretch of imagination could this be considered a balanced load, though even Canadas would be killed stone dead at moderate distances, and now and then, by fluke, at really long range. These occasions would warm the sportsman's heart, and

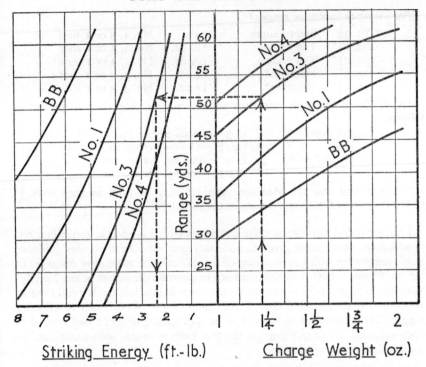

FIG. 12. *Key to balanced long-range loads. The right-hand diagram shows the ranges to which a fully choked gun will throw various charges of Nos. 4, 3, 1 and BB to make a minimum pattern of 80 in a 30-inch circle. The left-hand diagram shows the striking energy of corresponding pellets at the given ranges. Normal velocities assumed.*

might well give him a false impression of the merit of this size of shot for general use against geese. But it really needs 4-bore or punt-gun loads to develop the potential of these large pellets.

CARTRIDGES AND LOADS

The following cartridges from the Eley range are representative of suitable loads for duck and geese:

For use within moderate or game-shooting range :

12g. 2½″	Grand Prix	1₁⁄₁₆ oz.	No. 4 or 3 shot
12g. 2½″	Grand Prix (H.V.)	1⅛oz.	No. 4 or 3 shot

(In automatic weapons, the latter should be used)

16g. 2½″	Maximum	1₁⁄₁₆ oz.	No. 4 shot
16g. 2¾″	Alphamax	1⅛ oz.	No. 4 shot

For use up to more extended range :

12g. 2½″	Maximum	1₃⁄₁₆ oz.	No. 4, 3 or 1 shot
12g. 2¾″	Alphamax	1¼ oz.	No. 4, 3 or 1 shot

For use up to maximum range :

8g. 3¼″	Eight Gauge	2 oz.	No. 4, 3 or 1 shot
10g. 2⅞″	Ten Gauge	$1\frac{7}{16}$ oz.	No. 4, 3 or 1 shot
10g. 2⅝″	Ten Gauge	$1\frac{5}{16}$ oz.	No. 4, 3 or 1 shot
12g. 3″	Magnum*	1⅝ oz.	No. 4, 3 or 1 shot
12g. 2¾″	Magnum*	1½ oz.	No. 4, 3 or 1 shot

*N.B. These Magnum cartridges should only be used in guns proved as follows:

English proof	$\begin{cases} 12/3″\text{—4 tons per sq. in.} \\ 12/2\frac{3}{4}″\text{—}3\frac{1}{2}\text{ tons per sq. in.} \end{cases}$
Continental proof	$\begin{cases} 12/3″\text{—1000 kg. per sq. cm.} \\ 12/2\frac{3}{4}″\text{—900 kg. per sq. cm.} \end{cases}$

But note that the 2¾″ Magnum cartridge may be used in guns with 3″ chambers proved for 3½ tons/sq. in. or the earlier "Nitro Proof—1⅜ oz."

I have avoided associating these cartridges with any specific range bracket, to which the chart above gives all necessary guidance. Even so, this guidance needs tempering with a recognition of the difficulty of estimating distances in the air. Shooters have a strong tendency to overrate the power of any heavily-loaded cartridges, and it is well for them to bear in mind that every eighth of an ounce added to a normal charge adds only two or three yards to effective range. This is too small an amount to be appreciated against a background of open sky, and failure to recognize the fact leads to much "gun-stretching"— the cardinal sin of wildfowlers.

HOME LOADS

I give below a selection of loads recommended by IMI using their powders. Those marked "L.R." are special long-range loads taking advantage of the principle that large pellets lose velocity in flight more slowly than do small ones. They can accordingly be used in heavier charges, thus preserving pattern density and striking energy at extended ranges, even when fired at the somewhat reduced muzzle velocity necessary for the avoidance of any increase in recoil.

GUNS

In coming to guns last, I am not, as might appear, out of logical order, because any gun suitable for handling the charges discussed and capable of throwing fair patterns of the density required will kill wildfowl.

The effective range chart (fig. 11) gave a complete guide to the gauges and chamber lengths suited to the various loads, and at the risk of disappointing younger readers, I am not attempting to list and illustrate the different kinds and makes of gun conforming to these particulars.

Despite the wonderful accounts published of the performance of individual small-bore magnums (chiefly in American magazines), the uncommitted shooter would be wise not to look for some special magic in these guns. The balance of evidence is against them. The calibre traditionally associated with a particular load is still the one most likely to throw it to advantage. The only

TABLE OF LOADS

Gauge and Chamber Length	Powder Type N.G.S.P.	Powder Charge grs.	Shot Charge ozs.	Over-powder card, ins.	Kleena ins.	Under-shot card, ins.
20–2½	No. 62	21	$\frac{3}{4}$	$\frac{1}{8}$	$2\times\frac{3}{8}$	—
20–2½ L.R.	No. 62	17	$\frac{7}{8}$	$\frac{1}{8}$	$\frac{1}{2}$	—
20–2¾	No. 62	22	$\frac{7}{8}$	$\frac{1}{8}$	$2\times\frac{3}{8}$	—
20–2¾ L.R.	No. 62	18	1	$\frac{1}{8}$	$\frac{1}{2}$	$\frac{1}{8}$
16–2½	No. 60	20	$\frac{7}{8}$	$\frac{1}{8}$	$\frac{1}{2}$	$\frac{1}{8}$
16–2½	No. 62	24	$\frac{15}{16}$	$\frac{1}{8}$	$\frac{1}{2}$	$\frac{1}{11}$
16–2½ L.R.	No. 62	22	$1\frac{1}{16}$	$\frac{1}{8}$	$\frac{1}{2}$	—
16–2¾	No. 62	25	1	$\frac{1}{8}$	$2\times\frac{3}{8}$	—
16–2¾ L.R.	No. 62	21	$1\frac{3}{16}$	$\frac{1}{8}$	$\frac{1}{2}$	$\frac{1}{8}$
12–2½	No. 60	26	$1\frac{1}{16}$	$\frac{1}{8}$	$2\times\frac{3}{8}$	—
12–2½	No. 62	29	$1\frac{1}{8}$	$\frac{1}{8}$	$2\times\frac{3}{8}$	—
12–2½ L.R.	No. 62	27	$1\frac{1}{4}$	$\frac{1}{8}$	$\frac{1}{2}$	—
12–2½ L. R.	No. 62	25	$1\frac{3}{8}$	$\frac{1}{8}$	$\frac{1}{2}$	—
12–2¾	No. 62	31	$1\frac{1}{4}$	$\frac{1}{8}$	$2\times\frac{3}{8}$	—
12–2¾ L.R.	No. 62	27	$1\frac{3}{8}$	$\frac{1}{8}$	$\frac{1}{2}$	$\frac{1}{8}$
12–2¾ L.R.	No. 62	25	$1\frac{1}{2}$	$\frac{1}{8}$	$\frac{1}{2}$	$\frac{1}{8}$
12–3	No. 62	32	$1\frac{3}{8}$	$\frac{1}{11}$	$2\times\frac{1}{2}$	—
12–3 L.R.	No. 62	28	$1\frac{1}{2}$	$\frac{1}{8}$	$2\times\frac{3}{8}$	$\frac{1}{8}$
12–3 L.R.	No. 62	26	$1\frac{5}{8}$	$\frac{1}{8}$	$2\times\frac{3}{8}$	$\frac{1}{11}$
10–2⅝	No. 62	32	$1\frac{5}{16}$	$\frac{1}{11}$	$2\times\frac{3}{8}$	$\frac{1}{11}$
10–2⅝ L.R.	No. 62	29	$1\frac{1}{2}$	$\frac{1}{8}$	$\frac{1}{2}$	$\frac{1}{8}$
10–2⅞	No. 62	38	$1\frac{7}{16}$	$\frac{1}{11}$	$2\times\frac{3}{8}$	$\frac{1}{11}$
10–2⅞ L.R.	No. 62	33	$1\frac{5}{8}$	$\frac{1}{8}$	$2\times\frac{3}{8}$	—
8–3¼	No. 62	47	2	$\frac{1}{11}$	$2\times\frac{3}{8}$	$\frac{1}{11}$
8–3¼ L.R.	No. 62	38	$2\frac{1}{4}$	$\frac{1}{8}$	$2\times\frac{3}{8}$	—

N.G.S.P.—Nobel-Glasgow Sporting Powder.

L.R.—Long Range.

The shot size for the L.R. loads should never be smaller than No. 1 for the 8-gauge and 10-gauge cartridges and No. 4 for the remainder.

A $\frac{1}{16}$-in. card should be placed over the shot charge and $\frac{9}{32}$-in. tube should be available for the rolled turnover.

proviso I would make is that, for best results, the gun chosen should be suited as well as possible, not only to the duty required, but also to the shooter. It is a mistake to underrate the handicaps of excessive weight, clumsiness, bad fit, bad balance and bad trigger pulls in a duck or goose gun, for these things can be as prejudicial to success in wildfowling as they can in most other kinds of shooting.

When considering fit, allowance should be made for winter clothing; and sufferers from cold fingers, whether or not they shoot in gloves, should note that a single trigger, which I usually regard as disadvantageous in a double gun with open and choke barrels, may turn out to be a boon in really cold weather.

For wildfowling inland there are no special considerations affecting the gun that would not arise on any other kind of shooting calling for the same charges and patterns. For shore shooting, however, or work afloat, where the gun is subjected to salt water and mud, and where conditions are really unfavourable, there are good grounds for choosing the simplest, most reliable and most easily cleaned weapon to be had, and one that is not so precious as to be a source of anxiety. There is much to be said for a hammer gun for this sort of work; and for flighting, where bad balance or excessive forward weight is least objectionable, there is also much to be said for the pump gun. Incidentally, this kind of gun, which can be carried with a full magazine but an empty chamber, makes an admirable cripple-stopper for use with a punt-gunning outfit. WAGBI policy now discourages the use of such guns for wildfowling if loaded with more than three cartridges, because of the increased kick of long shots resulting in wounded birds.

Many wildfowlers are tempted by the desire for maximum reach, and by the few cartridges they fire, to use the maximum possible loads for which the guns are proved. There is no objection to this provided, as I have already indicated, that the gun does not shoot under the mark with such loads. It is only too likely to do so. No wildfowler who tries for the utmost reach should fail to test his gun for pattern and centering of the charge at the range at which he believes it to be effective, and to ask himself whether or not he is working with an efficient weapon and within sportsmanlike limits.

As for the preservation of guns subject to salt contamination, I have always found the best first line of defence to be hot water, which instantly dissolves and removes salt. Only when all traces of salt have been thus removed, and when the gun is dry and still warm, should it be oiled.

CHAPTER 8

THE WILDFOWLER'S DOG

by Peter Moxon

Kennel Editor, "Shooting Times".

WILDFOWLING more than any other form of shooting calls for the services of a good and efficient dog; one which faces water, mud and ooze boldly and retrieves smartly. A dog, furthermore, which will sit or lie quietly in a hide or in the open, enduring wet and cold without complaint. Indeed, the wildfowler's dog must be the canine counterpart of his master and must be, in some respects, more highly trained than a dog used for ordinary rough shooting.

It is impossible to treat the vast subject of training, feeding and general management within the confines of one short chapter except in a very sketchy manner. Indeed, many fowlers will know more about this specialized subject than I do, but I hope to give enough general advice to put the embryo wildfowler, or hitherto dogless creek crawler, on the right lines so far as his canine companion is concerned.

The first consideration is choice of breed. Bearing in mind the specialized work which the fowler will expect from his dog, the chief essentials are that it shall be a good and natural retriever and keen on water work. Hardiness is also important, but this is largely a matter of correct diet and management. It may also be that the dog will be required as a "maid-of-all-work" for general rough shooting as well as fowling pure and simple, in which case you will need to consider the question of questing for unshot game.

My best and wildest wildfowling days were soon after the war, and my dog was a big, strong liver-and-white springer bitch. As wild as a hawk but fearless in water and mud, a wonderful marker and with great perseverance, she taught herself, after many fruitless runs-in to shot, to watch the birds and to streak off as soon as one turned over in the air or, more often still, if the bird carried on after being hit. Susan was never wrong, and many a bird came to hand which I thought I had missed completely. She could also be used for general rough shooting, though was apt to range too far when hunting up.

However, for the man whose *main* sport is wildfowling or duck shooting, there is little doubt in my mind that a good labrador is the best dog. It can, when necessary, be used for more general work although a retriever never makes such an efficient quester (particularly of rough cover) as a springer. Apart from this, the labrador by temperament is a more sober and patient dog and will better adapt itself to long periods waiting in a hide or behind a hedge than the spaniel. To many spaniels long periods of inactivity are sheer physical agony, and nothing is more irritating (or disturbing to the flight) than a restless dog in a hide.

On the other hand, if more than half the dog's work is likely to be on a general rough shoot, then a reasonably placid springer, preferably with more colour than white for obvious reasons, should be seriously considered. Whatever you decide upon—and this is most important—obtain one *of working strain* and of a breed that you like. Show stock is often well-nigh useless for work, and any man has greater success with something of the "make" he fancies—be it a car, gun, typewriter or dog!

Labradors and springers are not the only breeds to consider, of course. There are golden retrievers—excellent water dogs with first-rate noses—flatcoats and curlies, few and far between but one or two kennels still specialize in them. Also the Irish water spaniel, a unique water dog and a true specialist but, quite frankly, not temperamentally suited to the first efforts of a novice trainer. German shorthaired pointers and even Weimaraners—the so-called "new" German breeds—are fast establishing themselves as all-rounders and will operate satisfactorily in water.

Back to the labrador, however, here we have a dog which has the ideal temperament and coat, is easily obtainable and comes in a "range of colours", from jet black through dark red and pale yellow to chocolate. Good working specimens, trained, part-trained or puppies, and of pure working stock, are available in every district throughout the country—indeed, all over the world.

Having selected the breed, the next consideration is the sex of the animal. I prefer bitches every time—they are easier and quicker to train and handle, seldom fight or roam, devote themselves to their masters and, most important of all, seem to keep their mind on their work and are not constantly sniffing about after other dogs. True, a bitch comes into season twice a year and may easily do so in the middle of the wildfowling season. This is a nuisance, admittedly, but if you shoot alone or without other canine company she can still be used and, in any case, I still believe that the advantages of the bitch outweigh the disadvantages. If you are never likely to wish to breed from her you can have her spayed and so do away with the one snag, but many men afterwards regret doing this because, sooner or later, they want to obtain a puppy from their idol to carry on when she is "past it".

For the purposes of this chapter I shall assume that you are going to buy a puppy and train it yourself, although, of course, many men prefer to obtain a started youngster or even a fully trained worker. However, the average wild-fowler is an individualist and requires his dog to be one, too, so better to start off with a dog young enough to get into your ways and learn together.

No puppy should leave its dam until it is about eight weeks of age. At nine weeks it is a good idea to innoculate it against distemper, hard-pad and hepatitis (a single shot will do all three) and, a little later, against *leptospirosos canicola*, a deadly form of jaundice which is carried by rats and which may infect any dog worked around dykes, ditches and rivers or any place where rats are likely to be encountered.

Feeding is most important, and there is nothing to beat a good natural diet of *raw* meat and bones, supplemented by milk in the early days, in which some form of cereal or biscuit meal can be soaked. Cereal feed and meat feed should be given separately, never mixed, and cod-liver oil and yeast tablets can be given as supplements to encourage growth and maintain health. A puppy of eight weeks or so will require three or four meals per day, reducing to two at four or five months and to one at ten or twelve months. Some dogs never seem to do well on a single meal, so watch condition and feed accordingly.

Serious obedience training—the king-pin of all training—should not commence too early, or the puppy will become frustrated and "sticky", losing drive and initiative. However, you cannot start retrieving practice too early and I like to get all my pups carrying a tiny dummy by the time they are nine or ten weeks old. In a gundog of working strain (apart from pointers and setters) retrieving is a natural instinct, which only needs encouraging and amplifying. Teach the puppy its name and to come when called or whistled, and get it used to a lead fairly early. A leather "slip" or choke lead is best, tactfully used. Dog collars are an abomination and not only do dogs look silly in them, in my opinion, but they are positively dangerous if worn when the dog is working, either on land or in water. I have known several tragedies caused by dogs becoming hooked up on wire or submerged branches.

At six or seven months intensive obedience work can commence, when the dog must be taught to sit to command or whistle and signal, remain on the drop until called, to wait for orders before retrieving, and to work to hand signal. All these training items must be taught in the right order and in short lessons of from ten to twenty minutes (twice daily if you like) rather than in long periods. According to the aptitude of the pupil, the weather, your own time and ability—and luck, this will take four or five months, perhaps a little longer, and I advise you to obtain a textbook on the subject if you wish to succeed. My own book *Gundogs: Training and Field Trials* (Popular Dogs Ltd.,) treats every aspect of gundog work likely to be required by the wildfowler.

Having thus so easily disposed of general training, I intend to devote the rest of this chapter to the specialized requirements of the fowler's dog as I see them, dealing with early retrieving lessons and water work, skipping general discipline and going on to working to directions at a distance on land or over water. One of the most important tasks of the wildfowling dog is, in my opinion, to be capable of crossing water and retrieving from the far bank of a river or stream, taking directions from its owner for any bird it has not had the opportunity to mark down. It should also be capable of working to signals on open water.

Early retrieving work can be taught with a small dummy—which may be anything soft from an old, rolled-up glove to a sock stuffed with rags or woodwool. A car radiator hose is useful and can be used plain or covered, the length being from eight to twelve inches according to the size of the puppy. It is a good idea to make a string loop and attach it to one end of the dummy, by which it can be thrown a good distance. To start with, throw the dummy a few feet and let the puppy run-in immediately to retrieve, calling and whistling as soon as its head goes down to pick-up, clapping your hands and running away, if necessary, to encourage it to retrieve to hand. Take the dummy very gently and praise the pupil, repeating the lesson two or three times—but beware of overdoing it.

Gradually the distance which the dummy is thrown will be increased and also you will throw it into cover of varying degrees of thickness and roughness, until your puppy will retrieve smartly anything which is thrown. After this stage is reached steps will be taken to steady the pupil to throw and it must wait for orders before going out to retrieve. I refer the reader again to his textbook.

By the time the puppy is five or six months old, and if the weather is suitable, the all-important water work can be commenced. For this you will obviously require a dummy which will float, and unless you block the ends your radiator hose will sink. I suggest a special water dummy (to which the puppy must first be accustomed on land), which can be an old sock stuffed with kapok or wood-wool, cork shavings or anything that will float. Some trainers use a small canvas boat-fender, cork or kapok-stuffed, which is most useful and hard-wearing.

Introduction to water work should take place at a pond or stream with gently shelving sides so that the pupil does not suddenly get out of his depth. Throw the dummy in a few feet and give the retrieving command at once—in other words, allow the puppy to run-in. If all goes well, repeat the process, gradually getting the dummy farther and farther out, until the pup has to swim to reach it.

Most gundog puppies, if bred right from working strains, will quickly take to water and little or no difficulty is experienced. The warmer the weather the better, for the pupil will be all the keener to splash about and enjoy himself. If reluctance to enter water is displayed, try throwing in a few pieces of biscuit or bread to encourage the pupil; or ask a friend to bring his keen water-loving dog along to give the pupil confidence. Indeed, success in water work is all a matter of building up the pupil's confidence and getting him swimming and enjoying work in the element. A very shy puppy may have to be encouraged by the example of its handler paddling in the shallows or (if the latter likes!) swimming, but this is seldom necessary.

Having got the pupil watering keenly, re-introduce the steadiness to thrown dummy and do not allow him to retrieve until ordered to do so. Always use the same command to retrieve, and make it clear and decisive. Once the puppy will enter water willingly on command, ring the changes by planting out on the water two or three dummies, unsighted by the dog, bring him to the bank and give the command to "get in". This is a useful command for cover or water work when you want the dog to investigate either element for an unsighted retrieve.

Working to command and signal, especially on unsighted and distant retrieves, is even more desirable for water work than on land, but it must be taught on land in the first instance. American duck "hunters" bring their dogs to a very high standard on this, but it is always taught on land first. Your textbook will give you a lot of information about it, but I suggest that there is no better method of teaching working to signal than what the Americans call the "baseball diamond" system.

Broadly speaking, this consists of leaving the dog on the drop and throwing out a dummy to the right. The handler then retreats a few paces behind the dog, gives a decisive hand and arm signal to the right and the command to retrieve. Having seen the dummy go out the dog retrieves immediately. Next, the dummy is thrown out to the left and the same process repeated, and all the time the idea of following your signal is being implanted.

As progress is made you can walk farther and farther out before throwing the dummy, and when you are satisfied that the pupil has "cottoned on" you can throw out two dummies, one to the right and one to the left, giving the pupil the signals to right and left in a mixed order until the time comes when he will go in either direction by signal and order alone. At this stage a third dummy can be introduced and thrown straight ahead, another clear signal being given, together with the command to "go back", so that with practice you should be able to send your dog to right, left or straight ahead by command and signal, stop it by whistle or command and *insist* that it follows your orders.

After a few weeks, or even a few days, on this type of work you should find that your puppy will work to signal even when he has not seen anything thrown. Leave him at home, go out into a field and throw out dummies right, left and straight ahead. Fetch the pupil, seat him at the correct spot and work him on them by signal. By degrees you can practise this in cover of varying thickness, but it is better to *start* on *bare grass* or anywhere that he can see the dummies plainly. The whole object is to build up the idea of following your arm signal and to work in the direction indicated, and this can only be done if you are consistent and give very plain and clear signals and commands.

As soon as you are reasonably satisfied with your dog's progress in this respect, practise the same things on large stretches of water. It is always more difficult to direct dogs on water, as they tend to swim round in circles looking for a retrieve. Especial attention must be paid to obedience to the stop whistle on water and the retrieves should be made very easy to start with. Use conspicuous and big dummies to help matters, and be sure to give only short lessons and make them interesting so that the pupil actually enjoys what it is doing.

The type of training indicated will be valuable when shooting on lakes or other large stretches of water, but it must be extended to the point where you can get the dog to cross a river or stream and work the far bank by signal for a bird which it has not had the opportunity to mark down. To this end you must start by teaching the pupil to cross narrow streams and retrieve from the far bank. I use the command "get over" for this, and it is simply taught by tossing the dummy over to remain in clear view on the opposite bank. When the dog has got the idea, throw the dummy well out and stop the pupil by whistle or command when it reaches the other side, giving the order "go back" and the clear signal. Then practise your right and left dummy throws, following on with hidden dummies out on the far side to right, left and straight ahead, just as you did in the early stages.

When you are satisfied about all this, try to gain access to wider streams and rivers and carry out the same sort of work, until ultimately you can take your pupil to a river bank, command "get over", and then direct it by signal, whistle and/or command when on the far side. The great things to remember are to make your dog *stop* and look at you when you blow the stop whistle, and to give a clear signal and order to indicate the direction of the search. I suggest for "get back" you use a signal as though you were throwing a ball overarm. For the left or right search a signal made by flinging the hand out from above the shoulder, at the same time giving the command "get out", saving the retrieve command until the dog is obviously within reasonable scenting distance of the dummy or bird.

Before this advanced work is finished you will require to test your dog on the real thing. Do this on land to start with, and again I refer you to your text-book. After success here, use dead birds on water in the same way as you have been accustomed to doing with your dummies. As your puppy will be required to tackle live birds as well as dead (unless you are such a good shot that you never have any cripples), simulate movement by attaching a dead bird to a long string and twitching it when the dog goes to retrieve it. The same practice can be conducted on water, and when the dog has proved its soft-mouthed ability, final practice with a tame, live duck may be given as illustrated in plates 12 and 13.

I do not pretend to have given you all the information. I could not hope to do this within the confines of a single chapter, but I do hope and believe that I have written sufficient to put you on the right track, enough to ensure that you enjoy training your dog and find it useful when the wildfowling season opens.

CHAPTER 9

SHORE SHOOTING

by Arthur Cadman

WAGBI Member; formerly Deputy Surveyor, The New Forest.

DESCRIPTION OF SHORE

The shore-line round Britain varies considerably. At one extreme there is the rocky shore, usually underlying a cliff-face. Much of the west coast is of this type. It is the least productive from a fowling point of view, although no coastal area should be written off entirely; at any rate, until a very thorough survey has been made. At the other end of the scale there are the vast expanses of saltmarsh, which tail off into thousands of acres of mudflats or sands, covered twice in every twenty-four hours by the tide. It is on such areas that the fowler has the widest possible scope.

In between these extremes the shore may consist of no more than pebbly shingle, flat sands devoid of vegetation, bare mud, or mud or sand colonized by marine vegetation. In many places the shore-line is an artificial bank, or sea-wall. In some places the shore-line is formed by a series of sand-dunes caused by wind-blown sand, derived from the open shore at low tide.

A wildfowler need not be a botanist, but it is a great help if he understands a little about the vegetation on the shore. Success depends much on his ability to observe; more so, perhaps, than on any other factor.

The highest levels of a saltmarsh are those which are only just reached by high water at the highest spring tides. Here the vegetation is the most stable. In some areas it will be good grazing grass. In others it will consist of the more shrubby species of saltmarsh plants and, often, rushes. The marsh vegetation extends down the shore and usually begins to fade out at about the point reached by high water at neap tides. Below this level in certain areas, usually those exposed only by low water of spring tides on muddy, rather than sandy shores, occurs the *zostera* grass, "sea wrack", or "wigeon grass". It is the main food of brent geese and a principal food of wigeon. It is, therefore, a very important plant from a wildfowler's point of view. It may be recognized by its ribbon-like appearance. Unfortunately, *zostera* has died out from many of its former haunts, probably due to a viral disease. However, in recent years it has recolonized some areas from which it had disappeared.

In many other areas of soft mud the main vegetation is spartina grass, a species which has colonized many thousands of acres. In places it has taken the place of *zostera*, as in Poole Harbour.

Where spartina has colonized a former *zostera* area, this grass raises the higher parts of the mud flats, by trapping silt in its foliage. This results in a more rapid run off between the higher parts, with the consequent formation of creeks and channels. The area is then unsuitable for *zostera*, which is a plant requiring fairly level mud with a relatively slow tidal run off. In places there has been a die-back of spartina, possibly caused by oil being trapped in its foliage. Die-back of spartina results in tidal erosion of the mounds of mud and a filling of the deeper channels and creeks, so that a habitat suitable for *zostera* may return. When this happens, a green algae seaweed, *enteromopha* frequently colonizes the mud first. This is a favourite food of brent geese.

From these very brief descriptions it will be realized that different levels of the saltmarshes are covered by sea water for very different lengths of time. the lowest zones for long periods; the highest zones for short periods. The highest of all are visited only by a few tides, usually twice a year, around the equinoxes. This is the main factor which determines the types of vegetation. In many parts of the shore, changes take place very frequently. Here, wind-driven waves and tidal currents are eroding the shore-line, cliff, sand-dune or even the saltmarsh edge; there, waterborne sand or silt is being deposited and colonized by vegetation, to increase the area of the marsh. Below the line of vegetation massive changes may take place. A whole sand-bank may move on one tide. The course of tidal creeks and run-offs may alter very considerably with each spring tide; these are matters which need to be observed closely, because they may affect the habits of the fowl. They may also provide cover or, often, hazards for the fowler.

The first essential for any wildfowler on any shore-line is to get to know the whole area well. Time spent in the close season getting to know every creek, every bend of every creek, every extra soft place, every hard bottom and crossing place, every bank, post, tussock or hollow which may provide cover, every flash which floods in the spring tides, in fact every portion of the salt-marsh, is time very well spent. When the geese are using the area the following winter, it is not good enough to go out for the morning flight and hope to find a convenient hiding place. It is necessary to know exactly where one is going to go (e.g. to a certain corner of a certain creek, where the cover is slightly better, perhaps by only four inches, than elsewhere). It is necessary to find this exact spot in the dark, without the use of a torch and without shouting, talking, or generally clattering about. If fog comes down when the spring tide is running, it is essential to know precisely how to get back again to the sea-wall. A compass is useful even for the old hand. (Once or twice I have regarded my compass with some surprise: but it is not worth arguing with it!) In areas where there is soft mud very great care must be taken. *Zostera* often grows on dangerous mud. It is unwise to venture on to soft mud without wearing mud pattens.

TIDE AND WEATHER

Any person who goes shoreshooting without knowing exactly what is the state of the tide is not worthy of the name wildfowler. For, one day, he may float in on the tide, feet first, whilst the shelduck laugh out on the mud, and the black-backs wheel and croak. At least he will achieve a brief moment of notoriety in the local press.

Tide Tables can be obtained from most newsagents or direct from James Munro of Glasgow. They cost but a trifle.

Always, the tide needs treating with the greatest respect. It is stupid to take any risk. How often the wind freshens with the incoming spring tide. What was a rustling trickle becomes a racing torrent. Little waves become big seas, pounding along the shore-line. Creeks fill and spill over and suddenly the whole marsh is sea. No one minds getting wet once in a while, but it is a different matter trying to swim in full wildfowling kit. Besides, a corpse causes so much inconvenience to so many people.

The simple basic facts, which are given only for the beginner, are these. At the time of the new moon and at the full moon the tides are known as spring tides; that is, the flood tide covers the greatest amount of the saltings, to the highest levels, whilst the ebb tide recedes farther on the mudflats, uncovering ground which is only uncovered at the time of the springs. After the peak, the tides fall daily until the period of the first and last quarters of the moon phases, when the tides are neap, that is, tides of the least range. During neap tides the higher parts of the saltings, and often the higher sands and mud-banks, remain uncovered.

In all forms of shoreshooting the tide is a most important factor to take into consideration. It affects the movement and habits of all fowl. The second factor, sometimes having an importance equal to, or even greater than, the tide is the weather. The third factor is the state of the moon. The fourth factor is the location of the feeding grounds and also the resting grounds of the fowl. On the shore these are nearly always influenced by the tide and the weather. But one must also take into account the inland feeding and resting grounds to which fowl will flight from the shore. In many places sport will be obtained by intercepting the fowl as they flight over the sea-wall, passing to and from their feeding and resting grounds. In many areas in recent years a fifth factor has to be taken into account—the habits of fellow "fowlers". These then are the main items which must be carefully considered before a plan is made for the day's outing.

What is it that draws a fowler out of his warm and comfortable bed on a dark, cold, wild, wet winter's morning? He may not be aware that he has assessed all these factors: but in his mind's eye he hears the wind whipping the waves as the spring tide rushes over the mudflats: he sees flight after flight of wigeon battling against the gale and he has a "hunch" that this is going to be *the* Great Flight at his favourite stand. He *has* to get up and go out, drawn as by a magnet. If his hunch is right, he will be well satisfied. If it proves wrong, he will still be better satisfied than if he had stayed in bed, imagining that he was missing the chance of a lifetime. Also, almost certainly, he will have gained useful knowledge for tomorrow. For one of the principal pleasures of wildfowling is anticipation—after assessing all the relevant factors. In short, the planning of a flight or a day's shoreshooting is often just as rewarding as the resulting bag. The things which the fowler will take back with him into his grey humdrum everyday life are the clean smell of the saltings, the cry of a curlew, the sight of a skein of geese cutting across the sunset: these things he will remember long after he has forgotten what he shot.

Knowledge therefore of the whole coastline; knowledge of the set of the tide; knowledge of the effects of the weather, especially of the wind, and, of course, a working knowledge of the habits and normal movements of the fowl —these are the main requisites. With a little mobility it is then possible to go to that part of the shore where the conditions are most favourable. There is really no short cut to this knowledge through the pages of a book. A few basic facts can be gleaned here and there, but all the words that have ever been written will never equal the knowledge which is gained by an observant pair of eyes, aided by a good pair of field-glasses away out on the saltings.

For what should we look? First of all, always, the state of the tide. The Tide Table will tell you what is the state at Liverpool and at various other places round the coast, but you must calculate your own additions and subtractions for your own area and for different points in your area. The first thing to check is the efficiency of your calculations. If there is a strong onshore wind the tide will be making ahead of schedule. You may have scarcely enough time to get to the point where you intend to go, but with an offshore wind you will have plenty of time; perhaps all the time in the world because, maybe, the tide will never reach the point to which you were going. So the tide and the wind and the general weather conditions must be closely observed. Then, every movement of fowl must be carefully watched. From where have they come? To what place are they flighting? Why have they moved? And, of course, what are they? Oystercatchers can sometimes look like wigeon. Green plover, half a mile away, can look surprisingly like geese twice as far. Perspective is difficult on the open shore. Even a mosquito, taking you by surprise, a few inches from your nose, can look for a moment like a curlew eighty yards away!

Part of the fascination of wildfowling lies in the fact that conditions are never constant for very long: as they change, so do the movements of the wildfowl, but tomorrow the conditions will be slightly different and you must be one step ahead to hit it off right. Yet providence is often kind, sometimes bountifully kind, so that when conditions seem hopeless, some damn-fool bird will fly on some damn-fool flight line over some damn-fool fowler, who is standing bolt upright, looking in the wrong direction, and at the last moment he will wake up, fling up his gun and bring down the only duck to be shot on the whole marsh that morning.

I was once waiting under the sea-wall close to the tide-line. There was a strong wind and I expected one big skein of geese to come out somewhere within a hundred yards of me. I had almost given up hope when a youth, wearing old flannel trousers, black shoes and a nondescript macintosh, sauntered along with a single-barrelled gun under his arm. By all normal rules he was too late, but at that precise moment the geese came. He put up his gun and two fell, stone dead. "Do you often come here?" I asked him. "Well, no," he replied; "as a matter of fact, this is the first time I have ever been on the shore and I've never used this gun before." He had the wit not to ask "What are they?" as he collected his two pinks. I am quite sure that he did not know.

WADERS

The bad old days of "What's hit is history and what's missed is mystery" are gone. Today, it is necessary for a fowler to identify his quarry before he raises his gun. The list of what may be shot legitimately is not a long one, but it is adequate.

The main sport on the shore in September will concern waders. There may be some teal and there will be the home-bred mallard which are pretty "green" up to about 8 a.m. on the morning of 1st September. But the great packs of wigeon and the weaving skeins of geese will not be there.

Waders, many of which are on passage at this time of year, are less wary than they are during the winter months. There is a greater turnover of individual birds as each wave of migration passes through at this time. Maybe it is not until a relatively stable local winter population has settled down in the area, that they have time to study the habits of wildfowlers!

The habits of waders vary considerably. Some species spend the greater part of their time on the mudflats where they feed and sleep. When the tide flows, they move in front of it, flying up and down the tide-line, or running across the mud. Eventually, when the flats are covered, they prefer to wheel, sometimes in enormous clouds, back and forth over the water, rather than fly to dry ground inland. They live by the tide and therefore their knowledge of the tide is greater than that of any other birds, not excluding duck and geese. They know precisely where they will find the best uncovered sand-bank. They know that by flying a mile or more along the coast they will be able to beat the tide, using their knowledge of the tide schedules and judging it to perfection. Watch them carefully, for nothing gives a better indication of the sequence with which the tide advances. You may find that you can do a tide flight in one place and, after being washed off, drive ten miles or so along the coast to do a second tide flight on the same tide elsewhere. This is possible in several places, although very few fowlers seem to realize it.

When the tide is making and the fowler is anxiously watching the water creeping up his thigh-boots, maybe he will throw many a match into the creek beside him. He will be hoping to see the match pause in its mad career upstream, and then, after aimlessly swirling back and forth, begin ever so slowly to slide downstream. So he will know that the tide has turned and he need not move from his place. Let him save his matches. Whilst he is looking down in worried concentration, it is a certainty that some bird will take him by surprise and slip past before he can lift his gun. It is better for him to keep his eyes on the distant tide-way, watching the restless oystercatchers, listening to their piping and twittering. Suddenly he will realize that they are silent. No longer do they run up and down. As if by some unseen command, every bird has tucked his head under his wing, or sunk it between his shoulders. The tide has turned. There is no more certain sign.

The main species which live almost entirely on the mudflats and open shore, as opposed to the saltings and marshes are the knot, the dunlin, the oystercatcher, the bar-tailed godwit and grey plover. Of these, only the last two may be shot: also whimbrel and (in certain areas) the oystercatcher. The redshank, though it may often be found on the mudflats, is really a bird of the salt-ings. Curlew divide the daytime between the mudflats, the saltings and the inland fields and pastures. But they return to the mudflats at night. Golden plover, too, may be found on mudflat, field, or salting. They are very fond of shingle-banks where their protective colouring makes them almost invisible, even to a person using powerful field-glasses. But golden plover usually roost in fields, or on pasture land. Snipe will be found only in the saltings, or fresh-water marshes. They are not birds of the mudflats. Last of all the woodcock; this is not a bird of the shore at all. But when it has been migrating across the North Sea in the face of an adverse gale, then it will flop down exhausted in any cover which there may be. The fowler, coming back from the morning flight, will be surprised to kick one up from some clump of sea-lavender. At such a time, every whin and gorse bush along the shoreline may hold a woodcock; even the marram grass in the dunes will shelter them. However, these places are above the high-tide mark and therefore outside the scope of this chapter.

One of the most exciting and productive ways to shoot waders is to intercept them as the tide moves them off the mudflats. It is surprising how effectively they learn the range of a gun. When shooting over water, birds often appear to be in range when they are not. Very often they flight fifty yards or so from the water's edge. It is obvious, therefore, that if one can select a point pro-jecting into the tide, then that gives one a good advantage. Such a point may be provided by a shingle-bank, sand-bank, outlying spur of the saltings, mussel-bed, or, sometimes, a breakwater. It then becomes a matter of con-cealment. Waders will take less notice of a hide than do other wildfowl. Nevertheless, a hide erected on an otherwise flat shore is a very obvious object. Whenever possible, it is more rewarding to shoot from a lying position, either in a pit or behind a small ridge, etc. If one covers oneself with a cam-ouflaged net, or other suitable material, then success is fairly certain. But, of course, as the tide advances, so one has to retreat. The best chances always come just as one is being washed off!

Many different waders will decoy to a few curlew silhouettes, but it is very questionable whether it is worth the trouble of putting them out. The tide will reach the decoys before it reaches the fowler. He must therefore rush out of concealment to collect the decoys. The few precious moments that he wastes doing this might well have resulted in several good chances had he remained concealed.

It is better to practise imitation of the various wader call notes. He who can make the right calls, which are not altogether difficult, will come home with the largest bag. Single birds always decoy best to a whistle.

When pursuing this sort of shooting on the tide's edge, it is very desirable to observe the set of the currents. Many birds will fall into the tide. When wader shooting, even a good dog may not be able to collect all that is shot. Anyway, it causes less disturbance if one can be certain that they will wash up along a stretch of sand where they can be collected when convenient. There are some conditions of tide and wind when anything shot is whisked away on an ever-receding current. If it is impossible to collect one's bag under such

Plate 14. Retrieving a wigeon

Plate 15. That soaking feeling!

Plate 16. *Colonel Hawker's celebrated double punt gun.*
Bore $1\frac{1}{2}''$; length of barrels $8'$ $3\frac{1}{2}''$; weight 193 lb.; weight of charge 2 lb. (1 lb. each barrel). Muzzle loading.
The barrels were set parallel, so that the patterns were displaced laterally, and only overlapped in the middle. Ignition was (*right*) flint and (*left*) percussion, and the difference in ignition times reduced the recoil "to a mere nothing in comparison".

Photo: John Tarlton

Plate 17. Hard weather on the Avon estuary

Plate 18. Brent off Leigh-on-Sea

Plate 19. Russian brent

conditions, it is stupid, wanton folly to shoot at anything which will fall into the water. Under modern conditions, wildfowl have enough hazards with which to contend. They should at least be spared the ignominy of having their lives wasted.

This tide shooting can provide a most fascinating time. There is usually a prolonged wait before the tide has moved the fowl sufficiently to pass within shot. But if one is provided with a pair of good glasses, there is never a dull moment. The whole pageant of the shore unfolds before one's eyes. Towards the end, just before the first few ripples reach one's place, one may have the delight of watching dunlin running about within a few feet. All the time, there is the chance of a very mixed bag—anything from a goose to a bar-tailed godwit.

One must be careful of two things; to keep one's powder and one's bottom dry. The first can be achieved by putting one's cartridges into a sponge bag, or a polythene bag. The second needs the aid of waterproof trousers. Even so, there are some people who always get wet and emerge with everything up to their ears including their guns, covered with mud. It is, of course, an age-old tip to cover hands and face with mud before the battle starts, but it is considerably easier to use a face mask and gloves.

CURLEW

Although the curlew will often be shot during a tide flight, the best chance to make a bag is at evening flight. Curlew flight on to the saltings and inland into fields at dawn, usually moving when it is broad daylight, after the duck flight is over. In the morning they tend to move singly, or in twos and threes on rather a wide front. In the evening, usually half an hour or so before duck-flighting time, they flight back in small "herds" or flocks. On a narrow estuary this flight line may be quite narrow and it is not difficult to place oneself in the right place and intercept them.

One has often heard an inland sportsman exclaim with surprise, "Shoot curlew? I will never shoot a curlew!" Many a beginner, standing on a small heap of empty cartridges on a curlew flight line is forced to the same conclusion. In truth, the curlew is a worthy mark. It is a strong bird and flies fast. Because it is keen-sighted it is not easy to fool. At the least movement it will swerve very quickly. Therein lies the main difficulty in shooting one. The secret of success is to take up a position from which one can get the gun up before the bird sees one: that means that one needs to be well concealed and yet have plenty of room to swing. It is much easier to put the suggestion on paper than to carry it out in practice, and that is why so many curlew are missed handsomely.

Although one associates curlew with mudflats and saltings, they are very widespread and occur even on the rocky west coasts. Off the west coast of Wales there is a low cliff below which the low tide leaves bare a wide area of rocks, boulders and large pebbles. Here vast numbers of curlew collect every evening, together with oystercatchers and, sometimes, golden plover. It is difficult ground to walk over with a gun, but a fowler lying amongst the rocks has some very interesting shooting. The curlew come out of the north, flying

E

at ground level, and they have to be taken well out in front like driven grouse. Normally, it pays the shoreshooter to allow his quarry to come as close as possible, within reason. A bird which is just within range can veer off so quickly. But if one leaves these low-flying Welsh curlew too late, they are upon one before one can manœuvre.

Curlew cannot be regarded as a great delicacy on a dish. But let he who hesitates to shoot on this account try making them into potted meat. Treated thus, they are excellent.

Curlew frequent nearly all saltmarshes, especially where the soil is mud or silt, rather than sand. Daytime creek-crawling, especially during the early part of the season, will often be rewarded by a shot or two at curlew. But *the* bird of such saltings is the redshank. Ever watchful, noisy and tantalizingly clever at keeping just out of range, he is an annoying bird. The life of many a duck or goose has been saved by the explosive alarm note of a redshank which has spotted the fowler stalking down a creek.

September is the great month for redshank shooting. There will be no geese or wigeon to occupy the fowler's time and therefore he can concentrate on redshank and other shootable waders. The redshank will always be the main quarry of the creek-crawling fowler. A party of two or more guns should split up, one gun stalking down the creeks and the others taking up strategic positions some distance away. There is no better way of getting to know an area than by creek-crawling: there are few better ways of obtaining a maximum amount of exercise! It is necessary to move slowly and as quietly as the mud and water in the creek bottom will allow. Field-glasses should be used frequently, especially before emerging out of a creek on to the level salting. Let no one decry this form of sport. The crack clay-pigeon shot will find, to his surprise, that there is a lot of spare space around a redshank, as he flits past shrieking abuse. No footwork is possible when one's feet are held in the mud. One must swing from the hips and fire quickly.

He who can use the call notes of redshank to decoy them will always do well in the saltings. Another trick which will sometimes work in September is to wave a piece of brown paper above the level of the marsh, the fowler remaining concealed at the time. This works quite well with curlew.

When creek-crawling, the odd mallard and teal are sometimes encountered, especially during frosty weather. The creek-crawler, stalking a known quarry such as a bunch of teal, will often be faced with the problem of whether or not to shoot at some lesser quarry—a snipe or a redshank, for instance. The lone fowler, who knows his ground, will be half expecting such an event and will have made up his mind what to do before it happens. "A bird in the hand . . ." is quite a sound maxim. Under such circumstances, the one thing not to do is to hesitate and then shoot; a miss is usually scored. But if the fowler is one of a party, his first consideration should be how his shot will affect the sport of the other guns.

There is room for a little more consideration of the other fellow's sport on the shore. I have seen shots fired with the express purpose of spoiling the other fellow's chances. I have known so-called fowlers fire a shot in order to spoil the chance of a punt-gunner, setting to fowl. Few actions can brand a man more certainly as ignorant of the finest sport in Britain and selfish in the extreme. How much better that he should take out his glasses and watch the progress of the stalk.

Snipe may be encountered in the saltings, especially during hard frosts. As with their inland haunts they have their favourite places. When these are known, a detour after morning flight will often provide a shot or two. Jack snipe are even more local than full snipe. On some saltings there is a carex, or sedge, which turns brown in winter. Such patches often harbour jack snipe.

Golden plover often fly in large flocks, or "stands", in a rather purposeless manner when full daylight has come. Again, during the day, they will frequently fly from the fields to the open shore, if the tide is out. Sometimes they fly low and give a good chance to the fowler under the sea-wall. Sometimes they fly at a great height. If a shot is fired when they are approaching at height, they will dive downwards and may give a good chance for the second barrel. Sometimes two or three golden plover will fly with a flock of green plover and it is always worth while to keep an eye open for such an event. At evening flight golden plover almost always fly singly, very low, when they present the most difficult shot of all.

DUCK

As every fowler knows, duck feed at night and rest during the day. For their day resting places they need freedom from disturbance and some degree of shelter from rough winds. Thus they will use large sheets of water and in calm weather the open sea. In rough weather duck using the open shore will seek what shelter is available in the lee of a sand-bank or sheltered bays in large creeks, rivers, etc. When the tide flows, if the weather is calm, they will ride out the tide. But if it is rough, then they are forced to move when the big waves reach them, in order to seek out more sheltered conditions.

They normally move between their resting and feeding grounds at dawn and dusk. This vast movement, which takes place twice daily all over the country at approximately the same time, provides the fowler with his best sport—duck flighting. All species of duck may flight at this time, but the most regular movements are made by the surface feeders—mallard, wigeon, teal, shoveler, gadwall, and pintail. The diving duck, pochard, tufted and goldeneye are not quite so regular and the sea duck, shelduck, long-tailed duck, scoter, and scaup least regular of all, because their movements are governed more by the tide than by the time of day. The surface feeders are the main quarry of the shore shooter.

When the tide is flowing just before evening flight time, duck will float in with the tide. They will then be lower when crossing the sea-wall than they are when they have started the flight from out on the mudflats.

In order to hit off the flight lines, it is very desirable to have some knowledge of their main resting and feeding grounds in the locality. For instance, if there is a large lake not far inland, there will be an inward movement at dawn and also as the tide moves them off the shore during the day: and an outward movement at dusk.

Flighting duck frequently follow major watercourses and rivers, large creeks, etc. Where the river has many turns and bends, duck generally follow a more or less direct line, cutting the corners, which make obvious flighting stands. But diving duck tend to follow the exact course of the water more faithfully.

A flooded freshwater marsh inside the sea-wall will draw many duck from the shore. They will flight in at dusk and out at dawn and may be intercepted as they cross the sea-wall, or as they cross the saltings, or near their day settling ground on the open shore.

In September, the main flight of mallard will be to stubble fields, barley and wheat being preferred to oats. A field that has been "laid" by the wind will be preferred to other fields, even after it has been harvested. Mallard which have fed on a stubble for an hour or so flight during the night to the nearest fresh water in order to drink.

In October mallard will be flighting to wet places—floodwater, flashes, ponds, etc. If there is a crop of acorns, they will flight to the edge of oak woods and often to single oak trees, or to small streams and ditches down which acorns may wash. In November, after frost has started to break down potatoes left on the surface, they will flight to potato fields.

In severe frost they will flight to any water which remains open; the creeks running through the saltings will attract mallard then, especially if an outfall drain connected to the creek at the sea-wall has passed through potato fields. On rocky shores mallard will often be found amongst sea-weed, especially in hard weather. These ducks are not so good to eat. Mallard will also flight to mussel- and cockle-beds in hard weather. A knowledge of the local feeding grounds will help a fowler to intercept duck as they flight. Teal do not flight to stubbles or to potato fields, unless they are flooded. They will come into smaller pieces of water and smaller ponds more readily than mallard. Shovelers always flight to shallow waters.

The duck of the shore is the wigeon. They begin to arrive in September, but a wigeon in the bag in September is always noteworthy. By mid-October, large numbers will be in the estuaries and along the shore. The next big influx comes when the Baltic begins to freeze. Watch the shipping reports for the Baltic. They will enable you to assess the arrival of large numbers of wigeon and mallard.

The main food of wigeon used to be *zostera*. It still is where it still grows. It is often necessary to wear mud pattens to get out to the *zos.* beds and it is a good thing to carry out an empty Snowcem tin, or something similar to sit upon. Good flighting may be had under the moon as well as at evening light.

With the decrease of *zostera*, wigeon changed their habits. Grass is their main food today. They like to feed when the grass is just awash, a habit which no doubt has its origin in the ancient *zostera* beds. They therefore often swim all along the edge of the tide, where they are very difficult to get at. The main evening flight is to shallow flashes and flood-water. On grassy river banks, wigeon will crop dry grass, as geese do; when they do this they may feed by day, like geese. This they do most frequently during the last quarter of the moon.

After the high spring tides in many salt marshes, pans and flashes of salt-water remain for a few days. Provided that the pressure of shooting and disturbance is not too great, wigeon will flight to these places. They should be carefully examined. Wigeon droppings are green, exactly like miniature goose droppings. If droppings are present you may get a good flight: but it is by no means certain, because they may only have been feeding as the tide covered the ground. If there are feathers and droppings, the chances are good. If there are feathers, droppings and many pieces of pulled-up grass, then the prospects are excellent—unless there are empty cartridge cases, too. Incidentally, it is a fallacy to assume that because some fellow has fired a whole heap of cartridges in a certain place, that is the place to choose—usually it is the place to avoid.

The three most exciting things which any fowler can achieve are first, a successful punt shot; second, a good flight at geese; third, a good wigeon flight. There are many who would put the wigeon first.

Very good sport may be had with wigeon under the moon. The ideal conditions are a fleecy sky (it is nearly impossible to see duck—or even geese—well against a starlit sky) a stiff wind and a rising tide.

Straight shooting depends very much on the precise position chosen. A few yards either way may make all the difference between a good bag, a series of inexplicable misses or no shooting at all. For evening flight the ideal is an oval-shaped flash about forty yards wide and sixty yards long with the long axis running north and south, a southerly wind and a small dry creek for cover about half-way along the east side. The wigeon will be dropping into the wind, giving a crossing shot outlined against the evening light. Of course, conditions are never arranged so conveniently. One must try to fit in as many of these desirable points as possible. It is most important to be comfortable. Few people can crouch for long periods and shoot well. One's body needs to be relaxed. If one sits on flat ground, so that one's heels and bottom are on the same level, the strain of sitting upright for long is too great. It is better to lie flat.

If one sits, one's feet must be at a lower level. Here again a Snowcem tin comes in useful. For soft mud, a sack filled with straw, bracken or rushes is ideal. It is useful to be concealed, but wigeon often flight late. If one remains motionless and wears a face mask and fairly light clothing, one will not be seen. At evening flight it is best to let your dog pick each duck as it falls. If you leave them all until the end, you will not collect many runners, and if the tide is running you may lose half the bag.

Teal will often be found in the saltings and sometimes they may be stalked with success. Cockle- and mussel-beds are always worth a flight, especially in hard weather. Here scaup may be found.

But, year in, year out, more shots will be fired from the sea-wall than from anywhere else. In normal weather the empty cases often tell a sad story of hopeless and impossible shots. The good chances rarely come without a wind. But in a gale, with the salt spray flying, ducks will come beating up into the wind hanging apparently motionless. They are then (as are geese) very easy to miss. One pokes at them. The only cure is to try to miss them in front.

The top of the sea-wall is flat and easy to walk along. The side is often steep and treacherous. The base may be strewn with debris from the tide. Therefore, it is common to see a procession of fowlers trailing, one after the other, along the top of the sea-wall. It is an excellent method for those who would add their bit to wildfowl conservation!

The correct way is to proceed along the foot of the wall, however tedious and inconvenient this may be. If there is a party of fowlers, they should be spaced about sixty yards apart. Every so often the leader should stop and peep very cautiously over the top. Then he should make a full survey with field-glasses. The other members of the party should not huddle together, talking, but remain spaced out, awaiting any signals which the leader may give as a result of his survey.

One still afternoon the following brief conversation was overheard from a creek in the saltings. Two armed youths, marching along the top of the wall, suddenly stopped, the second cannoning into the first: "Look at them b——geese, Ted. If we'd knowed they was there we cud of stalked 'em." As a matter of fact, they could not have stalked them. They could not have stalked a jack snipe. But they could have had the excitement of trying to stalk them, and they might have got within about one hundred and twenty yards and then had the pleasure of watching them through field-glasses.

Rivers, wide channels and big creeks will often hold duck, especially in cold or rough weather. Diving duck may be encountered there. If there are two guns, it always pays to split up and approach from opposite directions, the seaward end being the best position for a hiding gun.

Goldeneye, when they are feeding, dive for a minute or more. They can be stalked on the principle of "grandmother's steps". All movement must cease when the duck is due to reappear. The last twenty yards to the edge of the water can be covered at a run in readiness for the final emergence. Even then, the odds are on the duck.

Shoreshooting is very much a "lone wolf" hobby. If two or more fowlers join forces, they should know each other well, especially if they are going out for a whole day. This does not mean that they should huddle together on every possible occasion. On the open shore there is a good deal of wide open space. The fact that one often sees two and even three fowlers take up a stand side by side, even shoulder to shoulder, is quite incomprehensible. There is nothing to be gained. It is hard enough for one person to be concealed, twice as hard for two, usually impossible for three. The same three people, spaced out at eighty or one hundred yard intervals will cover a vastly greater area. Also, if a duck or goose sees one of the party, the chances are that it will veer off over one of the others.

GEESE

As both brent and barnacle geese (the latter with the exception of the Western Isles) are protected under the *Protection of Birds Act 1954*, only a brief note about them is needed. Brent have never been a major species with shoulder-gunners, because they are birds of the lower estuary and they usually fly over water. But there are certain sand-banks over which they flight when the tide is flowing, and ebbing. Their main food is *zostera*. An important food plant is the green algal seaweed *enteromorpha*. In many areas where *zostera* used to grow this plant is now the more common of the two. On the west coast of Eire they may be found feeding on sea-weed. Barnacle geese are birds of the saltmarsh grasses, and of the windswept turf of the islands of the west coast. They are common on Solway and on the north-west seaboard.

The movements of both species are governed by the tides.

The grey geese are *the* geese of the shoreshooter—pinkfeet, greylag, whitefronts and bean. Bean geese are so rare that they may be regarded as accidental. Lesser whitefronts are even more accidental. They occur, usually singly, amongst flocks of bean or amongst European whitefronts. Greenland whitefronts are geese of the peat bogs and western hill country, preferring to roost on moutain lochs. At times, particularly during hard weather, they may use the nearest estuary, but they are not primarily geese of the shore. When they do use the shore, their habits are similar to those of the other grey geese.

Therefore only pinkfeet, greylag and whitefronts need be considered here. Any sportsman, seeking to outwit any quarry in any part of the world must first study its habits. It is, therefore, necessary to set out the "basic facts" in relation to these three species.

Pinkfeet start to arrive in September, but the main mass, probably in the region of 40,000 or more, arrive towards the end of the first week of October.

Greylags begin to arrive about the same time, but the large concentrations usually turn up much later. Large bags are not usually made before November, although home-bred birds are present all the year round.

European whitefronts start to arrive in September, but the main build-up comes at the end of November, or more usually in the first week of December. They usually reach a peak in February and depart in March, whereas pinkfeet and greylags remain until May.

The broad habits of all the grey geese fall within a standard pattern. They rest at night, either far out on the shore, or on some inland water—lake, loch or reservoir. At dawn they flight to their feeding grounds. Where shooting pressure is high, they do not usually flight until it is quite light. Elsewhere, they move much earlier. At dusk they return to their roosting grounds, often flighting when it is almost dark.

If there is a bright moon, all three species will flight back to feeding grounds near the roosting site. Pinkfeet and whitefronts are rather more certain to move than greylags, although they, too, move freely under the moon. They will start to move three-and-a-half to four hours after dusk (i.e. when they begin to get hungry again), or, in rough weather, when the tide moves them. If the moon is overcast, they will not flight. When geese have been feeding under the moon their normal flight times become erratic. They may remain on the fields at morning flight time. If so, they often flight out to the shore early in the afternoon. Others will flight to the shore at morning flight time, whilst there are usually a few that flight normally.

Pinkfeet prefer stubbles when they first arrive. As the stubbles are ploughed, they turn to pastures, always having their favourite fields to which they return year after year. In November, they feed on potato fields, but not until frost has started to break down the small potatoes which remain ungathered. They are fond of reseeded grass fields and also winter wheat. They often feed on the saltings (except when disturbance is too great) especially in hard weather and in the spring.

Greylags' habits are somewhat similar, except that they are not very fond of potato fields. They also roost on inland waters more frequently than pink-feet. They are fond of rushy fields. In hard frost the numbers using the estuaries will be at a maximum.

Whitefronts are geese of the freshwater marshes and cattle pastures. They do not often frequent stubbles and potato fields. At several of the main centres for whitefronts, the geese roost locally and do not flight to the shore, although in hard weather they will be forced to do so.

These, then, are the main facts. However, it is most unwise to be too dogmatic. The man who says geese never do this, or always do that, usually has a surprise one day.

Nevertheless, there are one or two widely accepted theories which are bunkum. Geese are not possessed of great cunning. They are wary and exceptionally keen-sighted (how often, when watching geese through strong glasses, one gets the impression that they can see one equally well, without glasses!). They are powerful birds with a magnificent mastery of the air; therefore, they tend to fly high even when not persecuted. A keen-sighted, wary bird is exceptionally well placed to observe danger when flying at a fair height, but they are not possessed of great cunning. In some ways they are remarkably foolish. Certainly no mallard would accept the daily fusillade which takes place in some goose areas—they would move elsewhere much sooner than geese do.

Geese do not send scouts to spy out the land and make sure that all is safe. When this appears to happen, it is usually the case that a family party has been split up and the various members are flying round seeking each other. Similarly, many of the single birds which fly up and down the shore, alone, are not necessarily "pricked", or wounded birds. Very often it is one of a pair looking for its mate, or a young one looking for its family group.

Geese do not post sentries when feeding. Every goose in the flock is a potential sentry and each will throw up its head and spy out danger from time to time.

Another picturesque, but quite erroneous theory is that each skein is led by an old gander, the chieftain of the tribe, so to speak. Geese of either sex and varying ages may lead the skein. Young birds of the year often appear markedly smaller and the wise fowler will pick them out. They carry less shot and they are much more acceptable on a dish.

Geese are very robust birds with tremendous vitality. A wounded goose will fly a great distance. A winged goose will run quite as fast as a cock pheasant, and he is more clever at hiding than most fowl.

Apart from luck, which plays such a large part in all fowling forays, it is necessary to know the habits of the local geese. They have two great weaknesses. First, geese are very regular in their flight lines. One can almost set one's watch by them. Secondly, the wonderful wild clamour which they make gives them away, very readily. If they always flew silently, far fewer would be shot. To outwit them one must observe their movements carefully and relate their movements to the state of the tide, the weather and their known feeding grounds.

Let us take a few examples. Calm weather and low tide at evening flight: the chance of getting a goose is almost non-existent. They will come out sky-high and plane down, or wiffle, to their roost, a mile or more out on the sands. All you can do is to note, roughly, where they settle. Before morning flight the tide will have been in and out again. If there is no wind and only a slack tide, they will probably flight back approximately on the same line. The chances are that they will be too high for a fair shot when they reach the saltings. But if there is a big tide and a stiff wind, tide and wind will have drifted them some distance. Experience and local knowledge will enable one to get under them, on a flight line very considerably different from the line of the previous evening. Now, if there is a strong gale and big tide during the night, almost certainly they will not be anywhere near where they settled the previous evening. They will have taken wing and moved, perhaps to a more sheltered area, or even to the very edge of the saltings. Conditions are favourable for a good shot in the morning—if one can hit off the line. In some areas—the Solway is one such area—the geese will normally move once during the night and sometimes once again just before flight time. This last move is usually a washing and drinking move.

If the tide is high at evening flight time and there is a stiff wind, geese will often drop short of their fine-weather roost. In any case, they will nearly always fly lower when they reach the tide line. Similarly in the morning, if the tide is high at flight time, then conditions are favourable. They will tend to be nearer the shore-line. Even if they are not, they will usually fly lower over the water and only rise as they approach the edge of the saltings or landfall.

It is usually a good maxim to get as close to the geese as possible at morning flight; that is, as close as there is reasonable cover which may be reached without disturbing them. But in a real gale there is no need to go beyond the sea-wall. In fact, there is a great advantage in flighting from the sea-wall, because one is more mobile and it is possible to move in order to get under the flight line. A strong crosswind will, of course, cause the geese to drift sideways. It is a good policy to move beyond the place (i.e. downwind) where the first skein crossed. Incidentally, under such conditions it is no use swinging from tail to beak when one shoots. A clean miss will result. One must allow for the drift by swinging diagonally across the body of the goose, i.e. from the angle formed by the tail and the under wing to the angle formed by the neck and leading edge of the other wing.

Single geese and small skeins can be called quite readily, provided the fowler can imitate the right notes. A gander's call-note is higher pitched than the goose's. One other point: it is often the case that an odd skein or gaggle may behave quite differently from the larger battalions. This little lot may flight along the shore, rather than directly inland and they may well fly lower than the big lots. In calm weather, it is often preferable to go for the small lot, such as this, than to get under the main flight, none of which will be within reach of even a punt-gun.

Last of all, there is the question of digging in, or "sand-crawling", as some call it. Briefly this consists of going out on to the sands or mudflats, either at evening or morning flight, and taking up a position much nearer to the geese than is possible from the saltings. Let us be quite clear about this. On a small estuary where the geese are likely to be disturbed on their roost, or on any shore where the roosting site is very localized, then this practice will lead to the geese moving elsewhere. On any estuary a fowler who is not properly concealed may make the geese fly higher, or swing off their line, thus possibly spoiling the sport of others who are in the saltings. These are two very strong reasons for not doing it at all under such conditions.

On the other hand, there are conditions when it is permissible. When this is so, it is the most exciting and the most satisfying method of shooting geese. The conditions where it is reasonable to dig-in are: where the roost is adequately protected as a nature reserve, no shooting being allowed within the reserve; or where the roost is naturally protected by channels, etc., which cannot be crossed; or where the area available for roosting is so great that disturbance is impossible. In such cases, when the tides are low at flight time and when the weather is calm, the only way to get a fair shot at geese is to put oneself where they will be low enough. To occupy the saltings or gorse bushes at such a time is bad strategy.

Whereas to hit off the exact flight line on the vast, wide-open sands, to conceal oneself adequately on sand as level as a billiard table and to shoot straight from a prone position—these are things that test a wildfowler's skill and ability more than anything else. He will be rewarded first by a much greater understanding of geese and their local ways, because he will be able to observe them at much closer quarters. He will experience the greatest thrill of all—the sight of perhaps six hundred geese skimming the sands like driven grouse, towards him, and he should have the satisfaction of bagging a goose under conditions which otherwise would be impossible. After all, the good wildfowler is he who can get off his two barrels at geese at a range of no more than thirty yards.

However, digging-in must not be done thoughtlessly or without due consideration, first in the interest of the geese and secondly of other fowlers. In many areas, the local wildfowling club forbids this practice.

Whenever one goes for the morning flight there is one golden rule. Do not leave your place too soon. On a misty morning, particularly, geese may be very late in flighting. Very often they can be seen through field-glasses still standing out on the sands. In thick fog geese become confused and often fly up and down the saltings, settling in the first green fields they find.

In October, or in hard weather, the use of decoys on the shore may be quite rewarding. The chief disadvantage, under present-day conditions, is that few parts of the shore are sufficiently isolated from other gunners to ensure the freedom from disturbance which is essential. The setting up of decoys requiressome practice. The more decoys one has, the more effective they will be. They should be placed so that most of them face roughly up-wind. But they should not be symmetrically sited with every head exactly the same way. It is a good idea to arrange a large group, with several resting decoys, in one place and then to place a few "walking" decoys to one side of the main group to give the appearance of a family party joining the main group.

Flighting under the moon may provide good sport, although it may be most disappointing. If it is a good bright full moon, geese may start to move from 7 p.m. onwards, although often there is little movement before 8 p.m. If the wind is strong, they will move as the tide reaches them. Under the moon they flight in small gaggles and they do not usually fly so high as they do by day. As the moon wanes—moonrise is later each night—the geese start "talking" as soon as the moon is clear of the horizon. They will flight soon after it is well above it. Sometimes they fly quite silently and it is necessary to be very alert.

CONCEALMENT AND CAMOUFLAGE ON THE SHORE

The art of concealing himself effectively is one which every fowler must learn. The following are the main principles to bear in mind.

1. Wear sensible clothing. (For instance, if you must wear a black oilskin when there is a foot of snow on the ground, borrow a surplice to wear over it and a napkin to cover your hat.)

2. There is no other colour in the countryside the same as the human face and hands: they show up at a great distance. Five minutes' careful survey of any marsh with field-glasses will usually reveal ninety per cent of those fowlers who are not wearing face-masks.

3. The slightest movement will attract attention. When fowl are some way off, one may be able to move a short distance once. This must be done quickly. Do not make any second movement after that. Geese will spot the slightest movement even such as that of the left hand sliding up the barrel, or the turning of the head, or the movement of one's dog's head. The tilting of gun barrels may cause a glint. (It is a fact that fallow deer are much easier to see during summer, when the leaf is out and the cover most thick, simply because during the fly season their tails, which are only nine inches long, are constantly flicking.)

4. Background is more important than cover. It is far better to sit still in front of a good background (especially if it is in dark shadow) than to crouch behind a bush that is outlined against the skyline. Skyline is so very important on the flat shore because, to a low-flying bird, the slightest projection against the sky shows up. It is the low-flying bird which fills the bag—if it does not see you first.

5. If there is no natural cover one must improvise. The following are the main measures to take:

(a) PERMANENT BUTTS. Very good permanent butts can be made from old bedsteads. Three ends, wired together, staked and covered with gorse, rushes, reeds, etc., will withstand the tide and depredations of cattle. Sunken tubs, also make excellent permanent butts. They are very useful for *zostera* beds. A bucket must be firmly attached for baling-out before use.

(b) PORTABLE HIDES. It is possible to make a hide from many different materials. A man is an awkward shape to hide and geese know this shape whether it is standing, crawling, or lying. But, on the open shore, too large a hide will be very obvious. It is, therefore, important to try to match the surroundings. Wire-netting supported by light stakes interlaced with rushes can be rolled up and carried easily. Sacking attached to light stakes and painted to match the surroundings is another good type. Do not forget the empty tin to sit upon —no one can crouch for a long time and shoot well.

(c) PITS. Where it is possible to dig without the hole filling with water, it is easy to dig a pit. There are two types—a sitting pit and a lying pit. In either case it is important to know from what direction the fowl will approach. A lying pit is very comfortable to use, but needs a certain amount of skill to construct. It is not easy to shoot at birds which are outside the arc between 9 o'clock and 2 o'clock, the easiest shot being one coming from 12 o'clock (i.e. straight up one's legs). But one is only fully concealed from 9 o'clock. Before digging the pit, mark an arrow showing the direction of the flight. Call this 10 o'clock and then orientate the pit with the long axis at 12 o'clock, making a straight line 6½ ft. long. The spoil is placed outside the straight line to a distance of some three feet, so that the raised slope facing the flight line is not steep. This will be on one's left side as one lies in the pit, and it must be smoothed very carefully and then covered with ripple marks made with one's knuckles. It is essential that the inner edge of the pit shall be cut straight and perpendicular so that one's left side is lying under a miniature cliff. A head rest is desirable.

A light spade is a very useful tool to carry in the saltings. By cutting the natural slope of a creek to a perpendicular straight edge one can improve one's degree of concealment greatly.

(d) CAMOUFLAGE. One can lie on the open shore and cover one's self with driftwood, flotsam, etc., or one can use a camouflage net or other material suitably painted to match the surroundings. If covered with a net or cloth, this is drawn over the whole body right up to the eyes. The gun lies down the right side of the body, also covered. The left hand, placed near the face, holds the corner of the net, ready to fling it to one side as one sits up to take the shot. It is much easier than it sounds.

When using any sort of lying pit, or, for that matter, when crouching in a muddy creek, it is most important to be very careful not to get sand or mud up the barrels. Look through them frequently and keep a jointed rod handy.

During hard weather, ice forms on the tideway. Each tide piles up this ice into a line at the highest point which the tide reaches. During falling neap tides, one gets a series of such lines all across the shore. It is a very simple matter to lie covered with a white sheet amongst these ice flows. The whole aspect of the shore has changed so much that fowl do not spot danger so readily, and a vast new area of good cover is opened up to the fowler, where in normal open weather no cover exists at all.

THE USE OF DECOYS

Geese. It is of little use trying to decoy either geese or ducks to an area where they have not been accustomed to settle. If geese have been feeding on a part of a field where there is no cover, then decoys can be used to draw them within range of a well-concealed fowler in another part of the field, provided that it is natural ground for them to visit (i.e. not under trees, power lines, etc.). In such a case a handkerchief on a stick will tend to prevent them from settling in the undesirable part. Often geese can be decoyed into a field next to the one they have been using. But it is a waste of time to put out decoys where they do not feed normally, even if directly under a regular flight line.

It is all too easy to make a very large bag of geese over decoys. Therefore every true sportsman should restrict himself to a limit. No more than ten should be shot by anyone.

Greenland whitefronts decoy less readily than the other species, perhaps because they tend to feed in smaller, family groups. (The more intense the flock instinct, the more readily do individual members of the species decoy. On the other hand very large flocks do not decoy well to small numbers of decoys. When decoying any species, the best bags will be obtained from small parties.)

Duck. Decoys at evening flight time are of limited value, because it is only the early birds which will see the decoys. It is often a nuisance picking up the decoys in the dark after the flight, and it causes disturbance after shooting has finished.

On the other hand the use of decoys at morning flight on a loch, or inlet, or flash, or bay will prove to be well worth while, always provided that duck are accustomed to using the area anyway. As with geese, it is useless to put out decoys under a passage flight line.

The best use for duck decoys is when tide and wind are moving the duck. In rough weather, with a rising tide, they will be forced to move in order to seek shelter. A sheltered bay, a lagoon in the saltings, flashes on the marsh inside the sea-wall, or a lake within easy flighting distance of the sea will prove to be very favourable positions for floating decoys. The decoys should be anchored on the sheltered shore, which is the natural settling area. Also in such a position the decoys will "play" in the wind. If they are anchored on the downwind shore they will tend to become tangled or driven against the bank.

A very favourable position on the tideway is in the lee of an island, the fowler being concealed on the island or on a point which will cover duck dropping into the wind to join the decoys.

The relative positions of the decoys and the fowler will depend on several factors, chief of which are concealment, wind direction, and the direction from which the duck will come. For a lone fowler, the most effective position is at right angles to the wind direction and somewhat downwind of the decoys.

With two, or three, guns it is necessary to be sited across the wind, either in front of the decoys, when all shots will be taken well out in front of the guns and behind the decoys: or else the line should be behind the decoys. The disadvantage of this position, with three guns, is that approaching duck will have their attention diverted from the decoys by the slightest movement of the central gun: they are therefore much more easily put off. Also, although most birds should come in upwind, it often happens that some birds come in from the side and do a tight turn over the decoys. This means that the central gun may have to take shots both in front and behind him, which necessitates still more movement (and detracts from accurate shooting). In fact, when shooting over decoys, there are few situations where three guns are more effective than two.

In setting out decoys a frequent mistake is to bunch them too closely. It is better to have them spread over wide than too close. Also regular spacing must be avoided. Having put out the set, it is essential to go fifty yards downwind to have a "duck's eye" look at them. Any unnatural decoys must be reset.

All birds decoy best on a dull day. With bright sunlight there is a risk of a reflection even from the softest matt paint.

Decoys should be rather larger than life and the painting should be as natural as possible. Floating decoys should have the anchor string attached slightly outside the centre line. They will "swim" in the wind much more naturally. They must have flat bottoms rather than keels. A decoy with a keel rolls in a most unnatural manner.

CHAPTER 10

PUNT-GUNNING

by J. A. Field

Life Member, WAGBI; farmer and punt-gunner.

At 4.30 p.m. on Thursday, 30th March, 1967, a phone call from London started an eleven-week battle to save punt-gunning from a political death. This exhilarating exercise proved WAGBI's effectiveness after a respite of thirteen years from real trouble. Equally it proved not only who were our real friends, but how many friends we had without previously realizing it.

Unquestionably the honours go to John Farr, M.P., Chairman of WAGBI'S Parliamentary Lobby, and those many experienced punt-gunners, the chief contributors being Frank Stabler and Rex Irwin, neither of whom, regrettably, is with us today.

WAGBI H.Q., was the nerve centre of the battle but John Anderton could not have done what he did without the remarkable and enthusiastic support of so many active and participating punt-gunners, the majority of whom were not in fact WAGBI members at the outset.

If nothing else the "saga" proved that WAGBI will always fight for a minority interest within the sport of shooting so long as the cause is just and reasonable— as is punt-gunning. WAGBI, moreover, would never enter an arena thinking in any other terms than those of winning.

PUNT-gunning is essentially a stalking sport. A good day afloat is one on which a single satisfactory shot is fired after the fowler has deliberately allowed lesser opportunities to pass.

Unlike other forms of wildfowling with their thrill of killing fast-flying birds on the wing, the question of "marksmanship" occupies but a small place in the technique. Naturally, a well-placed shot is the culmination of a stalk, and all the classic authorities have been at pains to point out that it is only too easy to miss with a punt-gun. Which is a most soul-destroying thing when it happens. But the major sporting qualities are concerned with everything that precedes the shot—the grand strategy that sends the fowler to a particular point on the coast on a particular day, and the tactics of approach, stealthy yet sharply-timed, as the flowing tide changes the landscape from minute to minute.

Wildfowl, by their nature, congregate in greatest numbers on the wide, exposed spaces of floods, levels, coastal flats, tidal estuaries and the sea. Fowl in these places are unapproachable either on foot, or by boat. The shore-shooter in ambush can only wait for them to come to him; but the punt-gunner on the other hand can go to them. Not on account of his bigger gun, but because he possesses in his punt something that gives him the power of approach on open waters.

Perhaps the most widespread of all the popular fallacies about punting is the belief that punts operate by suddenly coming round corners in creeks, by laying-up in reed-beds, or by carrying piles of brushwood or stuffed swans on their bows. Once in a while, such stratagems may work, but to quote them as a part of general practice is bunkum.

Punts accomplish the seeming miracle of invisibility in the open because they are propelled by a man lying full-length in the cock-pit with his movements hidden by the breadth of the boat amidships, while a head-on course—to use Payne-Gallwey's phrase—gives an illusion of "imperceptible approach". It is, as a matter of fact, a moot point whether a successful stalk is one where the fowl are completely unaware of the boat's presence till it is too late, or whether they clearly see an approaching object, but do not realize that it is drawing in range.

Especially where there is some advantage from the light—i.e. before sunrise or after sunset, or at some other favourable moment—small parties of fowl in the open can often be approached within 12-bore range. Most fowlers usually bring off a few small shots with their cripple-stoppers in the course of a season. It has been said that nobody should be allowed a punt-gun till he has learned to use the punt itself so skilfully that he can shoot birds from it with a shoulder-gun; for once that apprenticeship is over there is no need to fire long shots with the big gun.

An early function of this chapter must be to define recent changes in the circumstances of fowling afloat. There is no doubt whatever that the most significant period in the history of punting from the very early times described in Folkard down to the present day was the ten years between 1929 and the outbreak of war in 1939.

By about 1931 most estuaries in the British Isles were affected by the disease of *zostera* which began two years earlier to sweep the entire world. At first, the fowl did not greatly change their habits. They clung obstinately to their old feeding-grounds and often by the end of winter had stripped bare those few banks which had shown faintly green in autumn. Gradually, however, a period of adaptation to freshwater feeding set in. Wigeon tended more and more to winter in flooded river valleys. In other districts—and this is a point that must be fully appreciated by the modern fowler—the estuaries were used mainly as resting places by day while the birds flighted regularly to freshwater at night.

Also, quite logically, the effects of hard weather were changed. In bouts of bitter east wind and below-zero temperatures birds tended to desert estuaries where there was exposure without feeding and to spend their time in dry or frozen marshes where they picked up the best living they could by grazing.

Simultaneously, another change was taking place. Those ten years were the sunset decade of the professional fowler. Farm wages in the 1930s were 36/- a week while wigeon sold readily for 1/3 to 1/6 and mallard for half a crown. Today, the ratio is: farm wages 263/-; wigeon 3/6 (if you can sell them at all);

mallard 5/- to 7/6. Nobody can sustain a reasonable standard of living from professional fowling today.

These two interacting developments have so altered the punt-gunning picture that it may be better to tabulate the points of difference.

1. Night shooting of the duck tribe is virtually over, except in those rare corners on the coast where a little feeding has come back. Compare Abel Chapman's recurring theme that after November the "game ducks", as he called wigeon, mallard, and teal, could only be shot at night except in conditions of severe weather, no self-respecting bird daring to linger inside any estuary after dawn.

2. For much the same reasons dawn shots themselves—the most killing of all fowling manœuvres—are of far less importance than formerly. This is counter-balanced by the greater opportunities for after sunset shots. Birds that have ridden out the day in an open estuary can often be shot in the failing light between sunset and flight-time.

3. The decline of professional fowling has decreased competition for the amateur. Disturbance, too, is lessened and fowl are not forced to spend the day at sea as in Victorian times.

4. Shots in broad daylight are more often to be attempted with greater opportunities for the man who is physically strong enough to handle his boat successfully in windy weather.

The Punt

At this stage it is proposed to deal with a number of technical points under separate headings. Expert advice on boat-building is sometimes offered, but the novice can hardly make the best use of his equipment unless he understands the principles underlying its design.

Duck-punts were originally un-decked, flat-bottomed boats, and this type lingered until recently on the Wash. Anybody who has been out in really rough weather in a *decked* punt with a choppy sea slapping down on top of it must realize the advantages of the Payne-Gallwey design. This design established in the 1880s a basic standard for a really seaworthy decked punt from which there have derived a large number of later modifications. (In *Shooting, Moor and Marsh* Sir Ralph Payne-Gallwey gives a number of specifications for both double and single punts.)

The curved and sloping fore-deck serves two further purposes beyond seaworthiness, first making possible the use of a "gunstick", which is the simplest form of elevating gear, and in the second place contriving that a head-on duck's-eye view of the hull is shaded off into the surrounding water.

A minimum length of 16 to 17 feet is related to obvious considerations of draught and buoyancy, but also, with equal importance, to steerage.

When setting to fowl, the fowler has choice of three instruments.

1. The single scull. This is worked from a rowlock situated near the after-end of the cockpit and is chiefly used for crossing deep-water channels in circumstances where hand-paddles would not give sufficient power. Its use is a difficult art to acquire and it is not easy to keep the working hand low enough to hide its movement from the birds. The beginner, however, should

learn to scull if he can. There might come a day when this instrument alone could put him in the way of a shot.

2. The setting-pole. In water of the right depth and especially with a firm bottom, this method gives the fastest and most controlled approach. It takes several seasons to learn to pole a boat really well, and the beginner may feel he is beginning to make progress when a special small muscle begins to show up at the top of his forearm near the elbow.

The fowler, of course, is lying as far aft as he can get with his feet stuffed tightly in the cavity under the after-deck, his upper-arm resting on the side-deck at a point where a detachable section of the coaming can be removed. To turn the boat, he must thrust at an angle to his line of progress. This will have the effect of pivoting the boat amidships, so that while the stern for instance swivels to port, the bows turn to starboard. This is where the length of the boat comes in. If too short, these sideway thrusts will merely push her sideways—they will not give steerage.

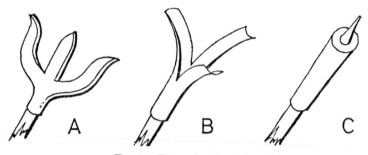

FIG. 13. *Types of setting poles.*

A   *Neptune's Trident type for very soft mud. A blacksmith's job.*
B   *Home-made general purpose style. The end of a section of 1-in. bore water pipe is slit with a hacksaw and the flukes bent outwards.*
C   *Lead-shod pole with short spike for soundless poling on a gravel bottom.*
Note : For all types 1-in. round ash should be used and all poles must be adequately weighted.

In single-handed punting, where the gun is aimed by aiming the boat, a great degree of skill is needed by the fowler. A cross wind may be exerting relentless pressure to turn the boat, and to hold accurately on aim as he approaches may be hard work indeed. The best control is obtained when poling dead against wind and tide.

3. The hand paddle. This is probably the easiest instrument to use. It is also independent of the depth of water. Its disadvantage is lack of power in which it falls far behind the setting-pole. Sometimes one can use it to cross a channel and then change to a pole as shallower water is reached. It *can* give better control than either pole or scull when travelling with the tide against a slight breeze.

The colour of a punt is important. There is an exact shade of very light grey which blends with the colour of the water on a dull day, or on a bright day after sunset or before sunrise.

Between stalks, punts are propelled either by rowing or sailing. The use of sail is a topic full of interest and it is possible that modern improvements in small-boat sailing might do something to extend the performance of punts.

THE GUN

The *Protection of Birds Act 1954* banned the use of punt-guns over $1\frac{3}{4}$-in. bore without, I feel, causing any great loss of freedom to the fowling fraternity. The extra range and power of such guns are more than counterbalanced by their excessive weight.

At present, the most popular size of punt-gun is the $1\frac{1}{2}$-in. bore which normally fires 1 lb. of shot. Heavily-built models can increase the charge to 20 oz.

It is worth considering the fire-power of a "1 lb" gun in terms of 12-bore performance. If 12-bore cartridges contain a game load of $1\frac{1}{8}$ oz. shot, a discharge of both barrels throws $2\frac{1}{4}$ oz. This is a fraction under one seventh of 1 lb. load. However, another factor affects the issue. As the size of punt-guns increases from the small 6 oz. to 8 oz. models, performance inversely decreases. In other words, the heavier the load, the smaller the percentage of pellets reaching the target. This effect is attributed to distortion of the outside of the charge by friction against the bore.

Allowing for this side-effect, one might estimate the striking power of a "1 lb." gun as five to six times that of a "double-barrel" from a 12-bore. In terms of range, the ratio is only 7 to 4. The big gun does not kill reliably beyond 70 yards and should not be fired at greater ranges in the hope of what it *might* do; 70 yards in this context compares with the 12-bore's maximum range of 40 yards.

It is believed that no firm is now making punt-guns, and one would imagine that the cost of a new gun made to order would be prohibitively high. Many good second-hand breechloaders come on the market from time to time with an amazing variety of breech systems. In some instances the locking device at the breech and the mechanism for firing and extracting the cartridge case are very poorly designed, although the metal of the gun may be sound enough.

Through sheer old age the number of serviceable muzzle-loaders is now steadily declining. Since the war, a number of adaptations of muzzle-loaders to an improved type of ignition have been carried out. The conversion consists first in removing or plugging the nipple and priming screw, and then in boring the breech-plug so that a cut-down pistol or rifle screws into it for the purpose of firing a blank cartridge directly into the powder charge. Misfires are practically ruled out, and loading is greatly speeded up. The powder charge—so easily contaminated from a fouled barrel, unless a thorough swabbing is given after every shot—can be rammed down accurately measured in a linen bag. The powerful flash burns through this covering.

The possible objection to this method is the risk that the screwed-in pistol barrel might strip its threads to cause a blow-back of gases. It is, however, quite widely used, and so far I have only heard of one—not serious—accident.

AIMING A PUNT-GUN

When any other kind of weapon is aimed, it is a truism to say that there is only one correct aim—the dead accurate one. In laying a punt-gun, however, a curious technical point is involved. As far as can be discovered, the only sporting writer to deal with it was Stanley Duncan, with a casual reference to the fact that a punt-gun mounted in a rowing-boat never achieves full efficiency because the height of the muzzle above water-level has the effect of "plunging the shot". The inference to be drawn here is that a charge fired from a punt with the muzzle no more than 9 in. to 12 in. above water-level deflects from the surface with very little loss of energy. The target is struck by a convergence of pellets, some flying direct from the muzzle of the gun, others deflecting from the surface of the water to carry on as ricochets.

In practice, there seems to be a good deal of difference in the individual laying of guns, and probably two basic methods are involved. In the first, the standard 6-foot killing circle is, so to speak, stood on its lower edge on the water at 70 yards so as to cover a flock of springing fowl. In the second method making use of the principle described above, part of the charge strikes the water short of the target.

OBJECTIVES

Before going on to discuss strategy, it may be as well to include some notes on the possible objectives the fowler has in mind. The first point may be illustrated as follows: Imagine one of the smaller estuaries—a place, say, three miles long by one and a half wide—containing a population of a thousand wigeon. In the course of one set of tides, three or four, or even one or two punt-gun shots will be enough to show the punt to the majority of the birds. Afterwards, they will be much wilder—perhaps unapproachable, except in a half-light. Is it not much more sensible to ensure than any shots fired are good ones?

Compare, for instance, four bad shots to kill a total of thirty birds, as against two good shots to kill fifty. The two good shots, which were, of course, harder to get, killed more fowl with less disturbance.

This is a part-answer to the question most frequently fired at the punt-gunner: "Why do you want to kill so many birds with one shot?"

But good—or shall we say heavy shots?—have another justification. They reflect greater skill and restraint. Apart from those rare opportunities when the veriest beginner can hardly go wrong, good shots are the result of skill; very good shots of very great skill.

Such questions now arise as: "What is a good shot?" "What is the smallest justifiable shot?" Answers depend, of course, on the size of the bore and the number of birds present, but taking the "1 lb." gun as par, here for what it is worth, is a rough, personal estimate of what a fowler's standards might be.

Wigeon are the most numerous of our winter duck, and they make up three-quarters of the total bag of all species made by British punt-gunners. Their close-sitting habits at certain stages of the tide lend themselves to good shots, and it seems to me that anything under ten wigeon is a very bad shot indeed.

Shots of up to about thirty-five wigeon are not uncommon at ranges of about seventy yards, but it seems that in order to shoot more than thirty-odd with 1 lb. of shot, the range must be considerably reduced. I know of three fowlers alive today who have killed over seventy wigeon in a shot.

Teal being about half the size of wigeon, suggest a minimum of about fifteen.

Mallard, on the other hand, rarely offer a respectable shot, although fifty years ago fowlers seemed to get goodish shots at them which are rarely paralleled today. If half a dozen mallard can be seen in a lump, they may well be snapped up.

After the wigeon, the brent goose, temporarily protected, forms the second of the two classic quarries of the punt. Brent geese dislike flying over land, and very few are killed by flight shooters. To the puntsman, their pursuit represents all that is most alive and exacting in his sport. Their traditional strongholds are the great East Coast fowling grounds of the Wash, the Blackwater, Foulness, and the Dengie Flats, where the navigation thrills and risks of fowling are at their height. Except during hard weather, brent are hard to approach in broad daylight, and the best chances are at dusk and dawn or at night. They are small birds, easily killed, and give opportunities for heavy shots.

The best account I know of shooting grey geese with a punt-gun is given in that excellent little book *Wildfowling*, by C. T. Dalgety, published in 1939 and quickly rendered out of print by the war. Shooting on the Scottish firths, Dalgety successfully obtained a number of shots at grey geese by day, usually just before or after sunrise. Grey geese can also be shot at night on their roosting grounds—a rather controversial subject.

STRATEGY

At the head of one estuary shot over is a mile-long stretch of mud intersected by the main channel (here about 150 yards wide at low water) and usually holding a fairish flock of wigeon. These mud-flats are not only unusually level, but oddly low-lying in relation to the other banks in the estuary. After two hours' flood, if not before, they will be under water and any fowl floated off and not worth considering.

In order to try for a daylight shot here, the following time-table had to be followed. Leave moorings on last hour of ebb, to reach main channel at dead-low water; begin pulling upstream for two miles as first of flood begins to run; reach head of estuary not later than one hour's flood; if fowl are seated on edge of channel, set to them without delay; if way back on mud, lay off not too far away to take the first chance of floating up a rill or gut the moment the flats begin to cover.

After operations are over the next problem is how to get home against a strong tide. A fair wind to make sailing possible is the best answer, but if the wind is contrary, the only solution is to wait for the ebb, or tie up and walk home. On one day a fortnight only these tactics are possible after sunset, for the favourable tide falls at the neaps, when the tide-table falls back over an hour a day.

This rather long instance of an actual fowling gambit is quoted to show the tangle of factors which go to make up strategy. Desperate exertions and long hours are quite useless without wise planning. But when things are right, wind, tide, the light and the clock being in a favourable conjunction, success can sometimes appear easy.

The fowler's task is to apply his experience and knowledge of general principles to the topography of a particular estuary. There may be all kinds of local snags and hazards he has not met before. The birds, too, may have habits quite different from what might have been expected. There is no universal norm of bird behaviour.

Knots of fowl seen in the distance through a telescope are not semi-permanent fixtures. There is always a steady flux of movement going on. Birds may doze far back on a bar or mud-bank for an hour or two, then wake up and come down to the water's edge for a wash and paddle. When the tide is beginning to flow, they may make off upstream to some other feeding ground before it reaches them. Or, they may stay obstinately dibbling till the last moment and then float about in the fairway in scattered formation. And there always comes a moment on the ebb when the uncovering corner of some sheltered bay suddenly draws off long, black necklaces of swimming fowl.

CRIPPLES

Yes!—this is one of the big controversial questions which should be answered with full candour. But first let us distinguish between the true cripple, the bird which falls to a shot with a broken wing, but retaining the full use of its legs, and the "pricked" bird which, although hit, continues in flight and is never gathered.

Every time a punt-gun goes off, one or more birds are likely to be crippled. At a very rough estimate, a well-placed shot that brings down anything between fifteen and thirty wigeon is liable to include 25 per cent of cripples. After the smoke has cleared, every one of these cripples is in full view of the fowler, with no cover in sight for hundreds of yards. The task is to overtake and shoot them without delay. They dive, of course, when they see the punt hard on their heels, and surface again with beaks only showing just above the water-line. Cripple-stopping is quite an art in itself, and some birds may take more than one cartridge but there is no reason why every bird should not be picked up. When cripples escape, they all do the same thing—go ashore, and a search of the sea-wall or saltings with a good dog will often account for any birds which escaped through some mischance.

When a shot is fired in relatively calm water, or in a channel not more than 100 yards wide, cripple-stopping is at its easiest. In other circumstances, say on wide open water with strong wind and a fierce tide running, it can be more difficult. On some occasions, no fowler worth his salt will fire and risk losing wounded birds too quickly scattered by wind and tide. The gunner usually has to turn away from such shots more than once every season; he has only once to know the shame of losing a number of cripples through firing a silly shot to be resolved never to take the same risk again.

An experienced punt-gunner definitely loses less wounded birds than the flight shooter who goes out without a dog, and no more than the man with a good dog who is forced to shoot near thick cover.

Cripple-stopping is what you make it. Be sure to make it easy.

And now about pricked birds. These fall into two sub-divisions—"droppers", birds which, like a towering game-bird, fly off but drop dead within a short distance, and those that carry on with non-fatal injuries.

Again and again critics say that the wide spread of a punt-gun distributed amongst a large flock of birds must prick many individuals. On the face of it, this appears a likely proposition, but it is quite untrue in fact. After a daylight shot, one can watch the departing flock quite clearly and the appearance of any lagging or sick birds would be only too obvious. But again and again the bird that "looks hit"—and it is common enough out pigeon- or flight-shooting—is just not a member of the twittering flock now rushing headlong out to sea. Why?

First of all, the shot fired from a punt-gun is of large size, ranging from No. 1 upwards. The gun itself is only used well inside its full range. The pellets therefore have high velocities and ample striking power. Two No. 1s from a punt-gun striking a bird at under 70 yards probably approximate to five No. 4s at 40 yards from a 12-bore—statistically a killing concentration. In practice, two No. 1s might not kill—they could produce a typically pricked bird, and the same could be said of a single No. 1 or BB pellet. But observation of a large number of punt-gun shots must convince the punter that a strong mathematical pattern, a framework of velocity, pattern, and the siting of vital parts, makes the seriously pricked bird far less common than where shoulder-gun shooting is concerned—in fact, a rare occurrence.

To summarize these remarks, a punt-gun used with discretion at reasonable ranges will involve fewer losses as compared to birds gathered than is the case with any other form of shooting.

DISTURBANCE

This vexed question, too, should be tackled. It is really very simple. Coastal wildfowl—and how well they know it—always have the option of complete safety during the daylight hours. Beyond the estuary, there is always the sea, and if the sea is too rough for comfort, the estuary will be too rough for fowling. Birds can easily be driven out to sea by day as the result of over-shooting, either ashore or afloat, but as long as there is safety at sea, they will not forsake a locality.

Night shooting in feeding grounds, either with punt- or shoulder-gun, is a much more disrupting factor. If birds *are* obliged to spend the day at sea they may use new flight lines, but will be more punctually on their way at dusk.

THE FUTURE

During the past thirty years bird life round our coastline as we have seen, has passed through a revolutionary period. Wigeon-grass has gone and so have the professional fowlers. But the punt-gunner's chief quarry, the wigeon, is more than holding its own. His second string, the brent goose, though protected at the moment, is still using its old haunts and its decline is said to be halted. Some estuaries and harbours have been ruined by that dreadful scourge—sometimes used for reclamation purposes—rice-grass or spartina. Others have surrendered their fowl to the competition of reservoirs and sanctuaries. Still others, badly sited for alternative freshwater feeding, will not be the same again until the *zostera* truly revives. But on many more places one can now see goodly numbers of fowl which no longer need to rush seawards at the first streaks of dawn.

The amateur, in fact, has never had such good prospects before him. All the same, I am afraid for the future of punt-gunning. What I fear is the dire force of badly informed public opinion directed against a tiny minority of enthusiasts who, apart from the paternal administration of WAGBI, are so widely scattered around the coast as to have no corporate voice whatever.

When I was invited to contribute this chapter, I seized the opportunity to state the facts about this branch of sport as clearly and dispassionately as possible. In so doing I have avoided controversial statements about sporting ethics. Arguments about what is and what is not sport are apt to be fruitless when people start from different premisses. At the same time I would like before this chapter closes, to give my personal views on this aspect of the subject.

First and foremost, wildfowling afloat seems to me the most truly adventurous wild sport left in Britain today. It is adventurous not from any qualities connected with the use of a special boat for stalking wildfowl—I'd as soon shoot clay-pigeons as use my punt on a Norwegian fjord or an Egyptian lagoon—but from the romantic mysterious, dangerous and ever-changing nature of the British coast-line itself. Get out a map and see what I mean. Starting at Poole Harbour, where Hawker shot, go anti-clockwise round the coast and visit in imagination or retrospect the classic haunts of wildfowl—the Solent, Chichester Harbour, Foulness, the Blackwater, the Orwell, the Stour, the Wash, the Humber; go north to Scotland and consider the goose-haunted Scottish firths. Cross the Irish channel to Strangford Lough and travel in fancy down the coast of Eire, where the east-coast estuaries snake their way through the soft green pastures of Dublin and Meath round the southernmost tip of Eire, past Cork and Waterford to the thunderous west coast tideways of the Shannon and Dingle Bay.

It is quite amazing in the midst of the twentieth century to find this heritage of maritime sport, unmatched in any other country in the world.

For the oddest thing of all about it is the fact that it is quite free. You cannot own, rent or buy a British estuary. The millionaire who wants to go punt-gunning stands the same chance as the local fowler who lives in a cottage near the sea-wall. And yet the sport is not overcrowded or overdone. It is protected by its own special difficulties, and risks, and its integrity has been very much strengthened by the "mechanical propulsion" clauses in the last *Bird Protection Act.*

CHAPTER 11

INLAND MARSH SHOOTING

by the late Noel M. Sedgwick

*Former Vice-President, Wildfowlers' Association of Great Britain and Ireland;
Editor-in-Chief, "Shooting Times" (Tower Bird).*

An inland marsh, for the purpose of this chapter, is any low-lying, boggy land, liable to flood, or to part-flood in late summer, autumn or winter, be it well drained or otherwise, and which lies on the other side of the sea-wall to the beach, saltmarsh, or muds. It may start directly at the foot of the sea-wall itself, when it will not, in fact, be a proper freshwater marsh, but a brackish one, with perhaps a long, narrow channel of water formed by the digging of those builders, lookers, and menders who erected, or keep the wall in repair. This channel, of course, runs parallel to the wall and lies almost under its shadow.

Nearer the centre of these brackish grazings are often flashes of shallow water to which a number of wildfowl come, frequently resting on them by day when the sea is particularly rough, or using them as temporary sheltered lay-bys when the wind drives off the sea at near-gale force. There are times when a hide may be built in the open and left unused until the fowl become accustomed to it. Then, one morning, when the sea is lashed to fury by the wind, the gunner, with his decoys out on the water in front, may enjoy some shooting. The decoys will probably be best set out a hundred yards in front, if this is possible, since any duck flying in from the sea will pass over the flash at a good height (especially if they have been much shot at from behind the sea-wall) and, after passing it and the ambushed gunner, will turn back into the wind and drop towards the decoys.

If there is any reed-cover on these brackish acres, no hide may be necessary. The water is brackish since, in some cases, waves splash hard against the sea-wall and spume is blown high and over it; sometimes, too, there are leaks under the wall, and it is not altogether rare to see spurting fountains of salt water at high tide rising from the floor up to twenty-five yards and more from the wall itself, where rabbits have had their burrows and a ferreting tide has found the weakness.

Thus, while such marshes may be used by duck and wading birds when a full tide has drowned the saltings and a certain amount of flighting and even decoying can be enjoyed then, the usual lack of cover and often the disturbance of people walking along the sea-walls keeps the birds very wide awake or scares them off; certainly much shooting does the reverse of encouraging them to use places of this kind.

But brackish marshes, though wigeon and other duck and waders may be flighted well on occasions, as at high water, both by day and when there is a full moon with plenty of cloud background, it is the true freshwater marshes where bags can be made, and these marshes may lie a mile or so from the sea, to a few miles inland.

Farther inland still we get those isolated grazing marshes and water-meadows where sport may be good in hard weather, and where some duck flighting can be had with more or less local birds. On these small, far-inland bits of boggy ground, where there is probably one good channel to take off the water, with a number of narrow runnels emptying themselves into it, sport is almost as local as are the birds, although there are times when extreme climatic conditions will bring southward-migrating duck and snipe, and even, perhaps, a small party of geese to them, adding spice to the more usual odd mallard or few couple of snipe shot by one or more walking guns. Most of these small places are included in the surrounding shooting rights so that only under an exceptional influx of birds, driven out of their usual haunts by frozen ground and water, are they shot with any seriousness. Most of the season they are kept quiet, unless the party shooting the surrounding ground decides to walk them for the odd covey or the few pheasants.

Perhaps some enthusiast among local sporting talent is allowed to walk the marsh land only for duck and snipe, when, if he is a fair shot and knows how to go about his job, he may shoot from a few to ten and more couple of snipe in a morning, walk-up a few mallard in their favourite sheltered lay-bys, or flight duck going out of, or coming into, the marsh at dusk, from surrounding lakes and ponds, after the stubbles have been ploughed under and there is less feed out on the farms.

What will be said later about making inland marshes more attractive to fowl and how best to shoot them under certain conditions, applies, on a smaller scale, to these little damp spots reaching right into the centre of the country.

Each marsh, of course, like each ballast-pit, stretch of river, lake, or pond has to be considered individually up to a point, for none is alike, but the general method of coming to terms with wildfowl forms a pattern on which lesser patterns can be worked out. Mallard and teal, for instance, behave very much alike the country through, and, though they may favour certain marshes and certain portions only of those, their main behaviour and characteristics should be studied, so that it becomes possible to know how to improve the attractions of a marsh to them, and then apply those methods of shooting them to good effect are carried out, on a larger scale, on more extensive marshes to which far more birds come.

In short, what advice follows in this chapter regarding larger duck marshes can apply to a great extent to smaller far-inland places, always provided that the rule of thumb is not too strictly followed, but an intimate assessment is made of local conditions, and such conditions may vary considerably in detail the country through. Even the larger fresh marshes close to the coast, or within easy goose- and duck-flighting distance of it may differ a great deal. One may be the daytime grazing place each winter of a large, or small population of pink-footed or white-fronted geese; another may seldom see a goose, but be well known for its fair-sized wigeon flock, and for a good scattering of pintail, mallard, and teal.

There are many good inland marshes which form part of the acreage of private estates, and where wildfowl are seldom, and sometimes never, shot. Such places are the true sanctuaries of the country, for, whether the estate itself is shot over privately or by a syndicate, it is the game which is the main concern, and, though the guns may enjoy an occasional duck flight in winter, such flights are carried out with due thought to preserve the flight lines and sanctuary of the fowl. Moreover, the keepers who look after the game and see that no shooting or poaching is done by outsiders, aid the stock of mallard by keeping down the crows and other corvines which would otherwise take countless duck eggs.

The locals, who may envy and even say hard words about the landowner, when they see hundreds of wigeon flying backwards and forwards over this private marsh, and sheltering there the day through, or watch mallard, pintail, shoveler, tufted, pochard, teal, and other duck afloat on its patches of flood-water, should realize that such unofficial sanctuaries are good for both the fowl and for themselves, for neither geese, feeding on the marsh by day, nor the duck resting there in peace, and sheltered from bitter winds, will remain on those few sacred acres. The geese will fly out at dusk and probably make for the coast and the sandy roosts beyond, to return at dawn, while the duck, becoming restless and noisy at dusk, will start to flight as the dusk deepens— flight out over the boundaries to their nocturnal feeding grounds which, in late summer and early autumn will be the cornfields and barley stubbles. But soon after September, their flight lines will become more settled, as they make for other low-lying ground and lakes and ponds, and generally flying round at night, joined by other duck which have spent the day resting on large waters such as lakes, reservoirs and smaller private marshes.

At dawn, when the geese are thinking of lifting and making inland, the duck of our private marsh will be returning along their flight lines, coming over high with the wind (especially if they have been much shot at), or battling low against it if it is blowing off the marsh. Any gunner, be he local or not quite so local, will watch and study the movements of these fowl, discover their lines of flight, and then seek permission somewhere along them to enjoy a little evening flighting, with perhaps odd morning flights when opportunity allows during the week-ends.

Time should never be wasted on attempting to decoy duck flying in or out at dusk or dawn for they have a set purpose then: to get out to their feeding grounds, and to return to their resting ground, and only on rare occasions will they alter course or altitude on seeing decoys set out. There are, nevertheless, exceptions which prove the rule, and occasionally during a morning flight duck will come down to decoys, but this is usually either early on in the season before the birds have formed fixed habits and many of them are still young, or when 'foreign' birds arrive, from stress of weather, which do not belong to local populations. They seem temporarily lost and may drop down to decoys even at flight time. About the countryside, within easy flighting distance to salt water, are disused gravel- and ballast-pits on which sometimes really large rafts of duck may be seen resting by day. Some of these pits are rented, for reserves, by local wildfowling clubs; some are "reserved" by bird-watching societies; others are retained by their owners, or the shooting let to small syndicates; today even a few winter sailing clubs attempt to rent them. These pits are sanctuaries in their own right, except when shot occasionally by any shooting syndicate renting them or when disturbed by fishermen; even then little damage is done to the birds which quickly learn the lesson. The wise coastal gunner, or his brother-in-arms on the other side of the sea-wall, should welcome them, for, as in the case of inland marshes, the duck cannot stay on such places, but must flight off at dusk and return at dawn; and there is always the chance of their being disturbed during the day by workmen or chance ramblers, when the gun on the saltings may suddenly see a couple of hundred mallard, or a sprinkling of various kinds of duck, swinging round his field of vision, and perhaps coming within range. Or they may fly inland to marsh or water-meadow and offer sport to any gunner there.

The foregoing is all by the way. It gives a very sketchy picture of the general habits of wildfowl movement inland, and, though it does not dismiss the smaller marshes as insignificant spots on the map, rather, it pin-points them as miniature marshes—scale-models of those larger ones well known for their winter wildfowl populations. And it emphasizes that what applies to the latter may apply, in lesser scale, to the former. Therefore, let us consider how best to improve and shoot a good duck marsh of several hundred acres.

Obviously, by its very size and the opportunity the fowl have of flying to one corner of it when their own corner is disturbed, and because the fowl can change their "corner" when the winds change, and so enjoy the shelter that resting duck need, a large marsh has a great advantage over a smaller one. On the other hand, there are large marshes (and many of them) with a problem: bits of the marsh may be kept quiet and shot very reasonably by their owners or shooting tenants; other bits may be always disturbed by locals who have obtained permission to shoot duck there: and there are other localized problems which need not arise here, but which nevertheless exist, often to the exasperation of the gunner who knows his job.

Long before 1st September, the duck which bred on the marsh have mainly departed to the lakes, reservoirs and rivers, chiefly because the marsh itself has either been grazed bare of cover, or a hot summer has caused a near-drought. The dykes, channels, drains, and runnels are low or empty of water, and filled with weed or slime. Disturbed by men cutting grass, and by cattle and sheep dogs, by hikers off target, and possibly harassed by swans and rats, the old duck have led their now strong-on-wing young away to the safe moorings of wide waters.

Every evening as dusk gathers and deepens the birds, noisy now and fully awake, rise and, joined by others from different waters, speed out to the stubble fields on the hills, or the surrounding flat-lands. For an hour or two they feed, then spend the remainder of the night flying round marsh and countryside, gaining strength of wing, and getting to know those marshes and ponds where, for instance, oak trees grow that will presently drop their acorns into the water. For duck are great feeders on acorns, and will flight straight to a pond holding fallen ones, or to oaks in parkland or open country where acorns litter the ground.

As soon as the shooting season opens, the duck shooter who has either been keepering a marsh, or simply watching points, comes into action. His thoughts are not on wigeon (unless there happens to be a few home-bred ones in his area), but on corn-feeding mallard and any early teal flocks, or family parties of those little birds which chance to be using the waters he shoots.

Naturally enough, local conditions vary extensively. A dozen or a score of mallard using a farm for feeding may be almost the only duck in the immediate neighbourhood. On the other hand, literally hundreds, or even thousands of mallard can be stubbling in areas where their numbers cause no surprise, and may not all be using the same patches of laid corn, or open stubbles.

At this time of the year, marsh shooting should not be taken too seriously, it being wise to leave such places reasonably quiet so that the duck are not badly disturbed. There may be no harm on the larger places in shooting a few mallard by walking-up the drains and ponds, and there may well be good flighting spots where a gunner can stand at dusk and shoot at birds coming down from the upland feeding for a drink, or when disturbed by shooting on the stubble, without actually disturbing the marsh itself. Indeed, if a pond, or other marshy spot has been fed—with corn, rabbit-guts, chap potatoes, rotting apples, acorns, etc.—and is discovered by duck also using the stubble fields and which fly down to it at night to have a wash and brush up and to take in a little more feed there is no reason why it should not be well shot at least once a week while the birds are enjoying their stubbling season.

A few greedy so-called sportsmen heavily feed flight ponds or marsh spots and make very heavy bags of duck at this time. Such men, in the general interests of wildfowl conservation and shooting stand condemned, for in early September it is obvious that a very great many of the duck of the year have not obtained full strength of wing and are inexperienced. Moreover, they cannot be hung for more than a day (particularly in hot or muggy weather) and are therefore best left to mature and so make better sport later on. A heavily-fed flight pond may draw not only local wild-bred birds, but the hand-reared ones brought up at some cost of time and expense by syndicate game shoots and by local wildfowling clubs doing their best to sow that they may reap and to put into the air more duck than they take out of it.

The sportsman, on the other hand, may enjoy some good flighting to a fed pond or marsh, or to pond or marsh not fed at all, but kept reasonably quiet and shot with consideration for both present and future. Duck come to any pond attractive to them (natural, or artificially made) at deep dusk, often when the very last patches of light to the west are in danger of vanishing. Or they may flight a little earlier. But whether the flighting place is only a small pond shot by one man, with perhaps a friend, or a larger water shot by several guns, great care should always be taken to smother greed and never to go on shooting till the flight is over. Always leave the place with duck still coming in, so that those which then arrive unshot at will assure a continuance of a flight line on other occasions.

Rarely are such spots worth a shot at dawn. One shot then may kill a duck, but the rest will leave hurriedly and may even desert the place on the following evenings.

The small pond or marshy-bit (unless it lies, like a patch of floodwater in the open, devoid of cover) may require no artificial hide, the gunner standing *quite still* among natural cover, or even in the open. But should he feel too "naked", a strip of camouflaged netting hung between two cut sticks (bamboo canes show up too much, unless stained) will hide him and the dog; or he can string up some rushes, or make a sandwich of them laid between bits of wire-netting.

On larger waters, or on completely bare ones, permanent, or semi-permanent hides should be built in advance of the shooting season, so that the duck get used to them, and should be sighted with care. Duck will often flight in against the wind, and although, if coming direct from a certain locality each evening, they may arrive with the wind, they will fly on and turn back into it before pitching. They may even give a false run-in or two in acknowledgement of the seasonal baptism of fire.

If the prevailing wind blows from the south-west, hides should face in that direction so that, even if birds flash downwind from the west, they will turn back to settle, and, in doing so, show up for an instant against the rapidly-fading patch of light. Therefore, when hide-building, likely wind-direction, western sky, and touching-down strip should be studied in conjunction with each other, and with any other strictly local points, such as the dark background of trees, a boundary fence, etc.

Whether or not decoys are used, or are necessary depends on the ideas of the individual gunner, some of whom seem to like to complicate what need only be a simple situation. To wade out and anchor a dozen decoys, and to have to retrieve them during the tail-end of a flight, just for the sake of using decoys, is simple foolishness.

On the arable feeding grounds, only the tyro can bungle matters, once he has found the stubble being used and has sought permission to shoot there. Duck can be shot on laid corn just as pigeon are shot, and wooden, or rubber decoys will bring them down quicker, if the birds prove a little wild and suspicious after having been shot at a few times. Similarly on the stubbles, decoys, though seemingly used only by the more enterprising gunners, can be of considerable advantage.

Once the actual feeding ground has been located, the only thing left to do (apart from setting out decoys) is to make a rough hide of rakings, after studying wind-direction and light. An open circle of rakings forms a good hide, the sides being added to where greater concealment of movement is necessary, such as the gunner slowly preparing to rise to his feet for steadier shooting. An armful of rakings can help to camouflage him if it is spread over his legs, and the same applies to hiding the dog. He should, of course, sit back to the wind, and, if his dog is facing him, he will see by the movement of its head and eyes if duck are approaching from the rear.

Back now along the shores of firths, lakes, reservoirs, rivers, and flashes, gunners are in hiding, keen to taste the fruits of a new season. Many flight lines, from resting waters to feeding grounds may be well defined, but where there is a trend towards fresh birds arriving from other places in the north, or from overseas, there may be quite a number of duck flying about in search of feeding or resting grounds, and for some time their flight lines will be erratic, and it is then worth putting out a raft of decoys, or just a spattering of them.

The duck which lie out on big waters will almost certainly have steady flight lines to their feeding grounds, and, though these may differ a little according to change of feeding areas, disturbance, or wind-direction, the observant local fowlers will know what to do, and where to go.

If there is no natural cover, or artificial hide, along a good line of flight a portable hide of camouflage netting with four light stakes (or even sticks) tied into it so that the hide has four walls each a yard wide is easily rolled up and carried, and may even make a good "wading-stick" if there is any doubt about the depth of water.

On many preserved shoots, where the guns like to enjoy some early duck shooting, no doubt the keeper has erected comfortable butts, or hides. On some river-banks, edged by swampy ground, semi-permanent hides are built at intervals, with every modern convenience, including pegs to hang bags on, duck-boards to stand on, shelves for cartridges and odd objects, and a "window" offering a perfect view.

Duck shot are retrieved by pickers-up, or, in a few cases, caught in nets strung across the water downstream. Guns take up their positions quietly before growing dawn, and either wait for morning flight or, in daylight, for birds driven off the river, or the surrounding water-meadows.

While duck are shot on the stubbles and on other inland feeding, in England at least the shooting and decoying of geese on their feeding grounds is frowned upon by fowlers out for sport, and most farmers will not allow geese grazing on their pastures, or feeding on the stubble or potato fields to be killed. Nor is it considered sporting to dig in or stalk them on their roosting grounds out on the sands, though there are two camps of thought about this. The recognized method of shooting geese for sport is as they flight in towards the land at dawn, or fly out to their roosts at dusk; preferably the former.

In Scotland, especially when large concentrations of geese are doing some damage, farmers will allow visitors to lie-up and shoot the big birds over decoys. This method has sometimes been made much of by "romantic" writers, but, while stalking feeding alert geese may well prove an arduous undertaking, shooting them over decoys, by daylight, or when they feed under a bright moon is quite *infra dig*. Far better a few geese shot battling against a wind, after several disappointing gooseless days, then making a big bag over decoys.

As with the coastal fowler, the inland-marsh shooter does not really consider that his season is beginning to blossom until he hears the first welcome voices high overhead of the first wigeon to arrive. The coastal gunner may first hear the *wheeoo-wheeoo* of cock wigeon riding out on the estuary and the purring or growling note of the hens. But inland, the flight shooter suddenly hears one evening twittering voices far above him—*widget-widget!*—and sees, perhaps one or more companies seemingly spying out the land below, searching for signs of flooding. If conditions are satisfactory, the birds may come down to feed. On the other hand, they commonly clear off and may not be seen again for as much as weeks. They have discovered no special attraction on the inland marshes, and for a spell may spend their daylight hours in rafts on an estuary, or on reservoirs and lochs or lakes, or out on a calm sea. Then the inland gunner sighs, and continues to flight his mallard in the evening, and fills in his spare time by day walking up the few snipe which bred locally, and welcoming any early influx that may come to his area.

Above the waist-line of the Midlands, however, where the grey geese—the greylags, pinkfeet, and whitefront (the bean goose need not be mentioned here, or the rare lesser whitefront)—gather, flighting from coast or big inland waters to inland marsh, the gunners will be out at dawn in their ever-increasing numbers, hugging the sea-wall, or intercepting the flight from gorse bush, hedge, and even artificial hides. After the early baptism of fire, the birds will grow more and more wary, beating in from their roosts, and lifting high over the recognized danger points. Then every fowler is praying for a strong wind blowing out to sea against which the skeins or mobs must fight, and, in doing so, keep closer to the ground and well in range of game guns, not to mention the heavier artillery.

This is no place to give the story, migratory or otherwise, of geese; it will be found elsewhere in this book. It should be said in passing, however, that the geese with which the inland gunner is concerned do not include the black geese, the barnacles and the brent, although there are certain washes and marshes close to the coast to which some of the latter come at times.

The Canada goose (rare in Ireland) does not leave the British Isles, to which it was introduced some three hundred years ago, but its widespread flocks move about the country during the winter, and several wildfowling clubs have introduced the bird into their districts.

Some greylags still nest in Scotland and the bird is present therefore all the year round mainly in north Scotland, Tay and Forth areas. Elsewhere it can be described as a passage migrant in comparatively small numbers (probably some family parties) reaching the marshes of the south coast.

The pinkfoot is located mainly on the east side of Britain, from Dornoch Firth to Norfolk and Lincolnshire; the Severn, north-west England, and Inner Hebrides. It is less common in north Scotland and in Ireland.

The whitefront occurs chiefly on the Severn and other widely-distributed coast and inland marsh areas, those coming from the east landing in the south; the Greenland birds dropping into Ireland and northern Scotland.

With the arrival of the geese and the wigeon usually comes a "cold-war"— the waiting for harder, wilder weather when the migrants will arrive in full force and the fowling season will at last come into its own. Meanwhile, the inland gunner still goes out on his marshes. There have been morning frosts and temporary flooding. There are more snipe about than was the case during September and early October; and more teal are turning up at their favourite spots and feeding from the seeds already spilling from rush and reed and other vegetation.

While mallard and teal remain perhaps the chief target of many minor forays—with the odd shoveler, pintail, or goldeneye drawn in —those days at

Plate 20. Keep moving and keep your barrels up

Plate 21. The first WAGBI meeting hut at Patrington Haven, East Yorkshire

Plate 22. The curlew—most deceptive in flight

Plate 23. Flighting teal

Plate 24. Canada geese can become wary and provide sporting shooting

Plate 25. Flightless Canada geese being rounded up for redistribution

Plate 26. Greylag—believe it or not!

early snipe, when the elms and willows and birches are yellowing and the marsh grasses form a painter's palate behind a wide fringe of tasselled great reeds with their pennants still green, and a breeze is blowing across the soggy ground of marsh and water-meadow, are happy ones for the snipe shot. If the long-bills have been feeding well under a bright moon they usually retire to their sleeping quarters in well-favoured patches of reed-tussocks, or sometimes to "seats" in a reed-bed, to sleep the sleep of the just. Soon they have digested their food, are rested, and while they may not necessarily be quick off the mark, they are at least alert. If, on the other hand, the night has been dark and wild, or the ground slightly hardened by frost, and the birds started only to feed well as the elements quietened just before dawn, they may seek to probe for food long after daylight, being very much alert, though they will be sluggish for the rest of the morning and sit tight.

There are two schools of thought about how snipe should be walked-up. The first prefers to walk the ground downwind, for birds flushed rise into the wind and so offer easy going-away shot. The second likes to walk upwind, believing that their approach across splash-splosh ground is less likely to be heard by resting snipe. A small third school will talk about walking across-wind. The answer is, of course, to know your sport and to know your quarry and your ground, when it will become obvious that no hard and fast rule can be right, but that the snipe shooter must be something of an opportunist, guessing (rather than theorizing) how birds are likely to behave after a quiet moonlit, or a wild, wet night. Experience of local conditions, as in all shooting, should be the indication of how to set about matters rather than reliance on the written word of authors forced to generalize.

Alert snipe, walked downwind on sploshy ground on a windy day, will obviously hear the approach of human feet, as well as the cart-horse-like ones of a four-legged labrador, or hairy-footed spaniel. If a shooter prefers to walk downwind, then let him leave his dog at sit before he comes within hearing range of snipe lying in a patch of reeds. Whether his dog remains seated, or runs-in once his masters has got off both barrels, does not seriously matter, so far as this kind of stalking is concerned, though he should be sufficiently obedient not to race out too far ahead.

Snipe should be walked-up carefully and slowly, and whether you snap at rising birds or take your time in pressing the trigger is strictly a matter for the individual.

Driven snipe, put up by beaters, or by half a team of guns walking and half standing can provide excellent sport. Even only two experienced guns can enjoy it in lesser degree, if there are plenty of snipe lying out in a chain of water-meadows, and one goes forward and stands behind a bush over which flushed birds are known generally to fly; the other zigzagging noisily toward him.

If usually well-populated snipe ground suddenly begins to offer poor sport, it may be that a sparrow-hawk or merlin is sharing the ground with the shooter, but it may also mean that short-eared owls are feeding there. A walk round isolated trees and particularly thorn-bushes may reveal the culprits, or they may be lying out in seats in the rushes. Whether or not they succeed

F

in killing a number of snipe is a moot point, but their presence in numbers can scare almost every snipe off a small marsh. The solution to the problem is to walk round and scare every owl off—by flushing them and firing old cartridges in their direction, but *not* at a bird rightly protected by law.

Suddenly the fowling season proper is upon us—rain, flooding, frosts, the fall of the leaf, migrant fowl! The whitefronts, the pinks, and the greys have become "educated" as the season advanced, and, with every gunner's barrels against them, they are as wild as ever they will get. The main populations may be still in the vicinity of their earlier haunts, or some may have moved farther south.

As winter arrives and really hard weather sets in, the whitefronts that came south to the banks of the Severn in Gloucestershire may remain in force, but some of them, perhaps three or four hundred, may make an appearance along the south coast, paying a visit, as they do, to certain good duck marshes. Small wandering parties of greylag and even a few pinks may drop down on to the quieter inland marshes or pastures adjoining them, to feed, sometimes staying out on the floods at night, more often flying out to sanctuary on coastal sand-bars.

The wise and wily duck shooter, plodding to his evening flighting stand in the afternoon, may put the geese on wing, and, if they use the marsh fairly regularly, he will note their line of flight when disturbed, or when flying to roost, and make arrangements accordingly.

By this time, a fair-sized marsh may hold many surprises, and flooding will reveal, through the glasses, a great assortment of fowl resting by day. Gulls and plover scold and wail as they fly over the wide wings of water, but a sweep with the glasses shows massed companies of wigeon sheltering under a woodland slope, a tall hedge, or a steep bank. With them, though on their own, are scattered mallard and pintail, pochard, tufted, teal, even the odd smew, perhaps, and a couple of cormorants sitting on submerged gate-posts.

Suddenly the duck are up and flashing low across the marsh. Up and down they race, the teal flocks, like a coastal phalanx of mixed waders, rushing here and there. A peregrine, chasing a pigeon, has caused panic.

But how to come to terms with this great assortment of duck? Much of the marsh is flooded, but odd islands of grass are not yet awash, though recently covered by floodwater. Observation will have shown the duck-shooter to which (if any) accessible (by boat or wading) patches the wigeon are coming at dusk to feed on—accompanied by small parties of other species. Probably the twittering flocks—following a few bolder spirits—decide to drop down, their wings set, on to a strip of grass right out on the open flood, with the nearest drowned gate-post standing up eighty yards from their chosen feeding ground. If it is possible, which it seldom is, to wade out to it, and to set a few decoys near the edge of the island (with perhaps a stuffed wigeon on the grass itself) well and good. But if the floods are not sinking too rapidly, thereby exposing a great deal more marsh within twelve hours, a hide should be built next morning on the strip, being well camouflaged to sink into the surroundings, and plans thought out for the following evening, when the wigeon will return to feed, having left the island soon after dawn.

Before mid-afternoon the gunner should be in his hide, with, perhaps, a couple of mallard decoys, or two pairs, well out on the water, and either mallard, or wigeon decoys placed as life-like as possible round the edge of the island. If it is necessary to take out a boat, or rubber dinghy, this should form the base of the hide, the latter being tipped-up and propped up, and draped with camouflage netting, with further netting surrounding the gunner, though, under some circumstances, a back door may be left wide open.

It is folly now to shoot at circling, twittering flocks as they pass over or near at extreme range. They should be allowed to come down, if they are showing signs of so doing, and even a few allowed to settle. After a double shot, neither man nor dog should move, for, although the birds will depart, probably out of sight, it is almost ten to one that they will soon return to make another attempt to get down to feed and are sure to be watching the spot.

After a shot or two have eventually been fired and the wigeon seem to have vanished for good, the gunner will glue his eyes on darkening sky for other duck, and presently he will hear once more those thin wigeon whistles far up against where first one and then another star is beginning to twinkle. For some time the companies, now suspicious, will fly round, and may even clear off for a further period, especially if mallard or teal are shot at, and they may not return until it is too dark to see them, or the moonlit sky is cloudless with no background to show up flying duck. If, however, the night is a good shooting one, with a bright, full moon hiding behind a very thin veil of mist, so that the heavens look like an inverted gold-fish bowl, or if a bright moon comes and goes behind sailing masses of cloud, the gunner may well find himself enjoying one of those exceptional, bag-filling occasions when wind, moon, cloud, flood and all else seem to have combined for his benefit.

Thus, when the marshes are in various stages of flooding, observation must be kept to watch where wigeon are feeding as the water rises or recedes, and, in a somewhat lesser sense, the same applies to other duck, and even to teal which love certain drains or areas of seed-providing marsh and will flight there as soon as these favourite places become uncovered. They also hunt vanishing pools of floodwater for food, and, when they are seen using such pools or flashes, or overfull drains, let the gunner, if possible sit facing such water when the very last light is draining from the sky (though shooting sitting is not a good plan for overhead flighting), and he will hear the *zip-zip* of teal flighting in behind him like bullets, missing his head by yards or inches, and get a glimpse of them momentarily against the shine of the water. This sport requires very good eyesight, quick reactions, and snap-shooting *par excellence*.

Meanwhile, any gunner, salt- or fresh-water, knows how he feels about shooting from a sitting position. In fact, he will get far more misses than if he rose to his feet and swung on to his target. That is learned by experience. But to be able to sit on a dry seat, and to be able to swivel, so that one can, without undue effort, keep a look-out fore and aft is a great advantage, and every shooting man, except the strictly conventional one, should have made for himself the swivel stool. The prototype was invented by "Johnnie" (Judge) Johnson, sometime Chairman of WAGBI, but was later "re-invented" by one who used four-ply instead of thick, heavy board. The diagram on this page shows how to make this most invaluable seat (which can be used for pigeon shooting among the reeds, or right out on open floods).

The diagram shows an adjustable stool, but one can also be made without adjustable seat and requires short and long main tubes, so that one can take out the seat most suitable for the occasions—short tubes for grass; medium

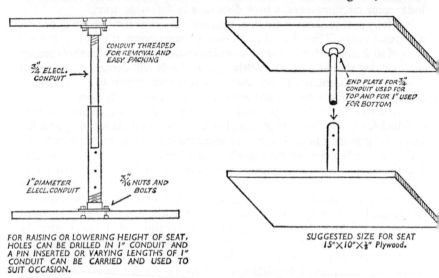

CONDUIT THREADED FOR REMOVAL AND EASY PACKING

¾" ELECL. CONDUIT →

1" DIAMETER ELECL. CONDUIT

⁵⁄₁₆" NUTS AND BOLTS

END PLATE FOR ¾" CONDUIT USED FOR TOP AND FOR 1" USED FOR BOTTOM

FOR RAISING OR LOWERING HEIGHT OF SEAT, HOLES CAN BE DRILLED IN 1" CONDUIT AND A PIN INSERTED OR VARYING LENGTHS OF 1" CONDUIT CAN BE CARRIED AND USED TO SUIT OCCASION.

SUGGESTED SIZE FOR SEAT 15"×10"×½" Plywood.

FIG. 14. *A swivel stool.*

for such cover as spartina grass; long tubes for floodwater sitting. These seats, or stools, allow one to hide behind a minimum of cover, and to swivel round without effort to keep a watching brief in the rear. It is felt that one can get good shooting from them at flight, but the "seater" should, if he wants to make a bag, wait until the birds are coming within good range and then slowly rise from his stool and very gently raise the barrels of his gun.

The stool is of even greater value in mud-gutter or for saltings, for the gunner can sit in the centre of a muddy channel down which water is trickling and remain dry, clean, comfortable, and out of sight.

No apology is needed for emphasizing that every marsh, or swamp, or chain of water-meadows has its own individual "peculiarities", and what form of shooting applies well to one may not altogether suit another, but it is, of course, quite impossible in a chapter of this kind to cover all and every eventuality throughout the country. There are some marshes to which wigeon seldom if ever come; there are others on which wigeon are regarded as the main objective. There are marshes known for their excellent snipe shooting; there are others which seldom hold a snipe. This chapter, then, applies perhaps more to the general kind of marsh, more often within flight of the coast, to which duck come in considerable quantities when cold weather sends them southwards and floodwater encourages them to settle and to remain for weeks on end, particularly if at least some parts of the marsh, or some neighbouring preserves, form daytime sanctuary and shelter.

All manner of problems arise on narrow strips of marsh, or water-meadows bordering small rivers and brooks. To give but one instance, while it is not difficult to walk-up mallard and teal on some twisting brook or stream, simply by coming on them round the bends, or by walking out into the meadow and then stalking back towards the bank at a spot where birds have been seen, such a place may not lend itself easily for snipe shooting. If patches of rushes or reed-tussocks lie near the river's bank and are more favoured by snipe than cover farther from the water, the birds, when flushed, will fly out over the water (especially against a prevailing wind) and if the current is very fast it may be difficult to recover them in numbers, even with a good dog. This is just a minor point, but one of many with which local conditions can face the rough shooter.

Another problem which not infrequently arises is when a flight pond has been fed and a flight line induced, and not over-scrupulous neighbours take advantage of it by shooting duck flighting to and from it over their ground.

The real problem of inland marsh shooting, however, is getting upon terms with the fowl there, when others have the same idea, for many marshes are split up so that they are owned or farmed by several men, each of whom may give leave to shoot to one or more of his friends. It is galling to hear a shot suddenly go off close by in the dusk just as a company of wigeon, or a big flock of teal are coming down to your decoys. On the other hand, it is equally galling to see quantities of duck flying about and settling at the far end of a marsh where there is no one to put them on wing. Therefore, "company" can be a two-edged sword, and, the "best bet" of all is when the gunners get to know each other and can come to some mutual understanding, however elastic it may be.

Some marsh shooters who operate only on Saturday afternoons have an understanding about matters and will even phone each other at a given time to make arrangements for that week, so that each knows the time when the other will be on the marsh, and other details, such as the using of decoys, etc. The extreme limit to such understanding is surely the case of a business man whose friend phones him when he sees the geese flighting in the direction of his home a mile or two away, giving the former the chance to pick up his gun, run upstairs to the flat roof of his place, and there get a shot in as the skein passes over.

But whether the gunners who "share" the shooting of a large marsh are friendly or "distant" with each other, they will usually combine against outsiders who unlawfully encroach on "their" ground, or who may go so far, say, as to bring a gunning-punt down to a flooded fresh marsh and use, perhaps, a swivel 4-bore against the resting duck by day, or under the moon, and floating over ground on which they have no business to be.

From Christmas till the finish of the duck- and geese-shooting season (which is 31st January except on the foreshore) is the best part of the inland shooter's year, for any prolonged spell of hard weather is likely to send more and more duck southwards; in any case, there is a natural movement south during the colder months, even if winter does not actually harden the land and seal up the water.

"Going afloat" on inland marshes usually implies taking a boat out to a good flighting point, or sometimes attempting to "punt" up to some geese or duck in a camouflaged boat, but with ordinary shoulder guns—a practice that is not really common and which is frowned upon on many marshes.

At the season's end the gunner's heart often bleeds, for the marsh is flooded and "black with duck". The wigeon sit out in great rafts and are flighting at dusk to perfection. Everything seems to have got into full swing—when the gong goes!

The duck shooter who is also a keen ornithologist may lay aside the gun with perhaps less regret than the gunner who shoots for sport and the pot. The more fortunate ones find their way down to the foreshore for the twenty extra days' shooting allowed there. But soon those days, too, have passed, and the marsh gunner is back on his old ground with a strange sense of loss and gain, to start his gunless rounds, perhaps, or carrying a gun to kill vermin.

There is a chapter in this book devoted to vermin destruction on the marsh, but there are also many unconventional and routine methods of dealing with pests. Often enough, as he sits in his hide near the water's edge in the fading light of a winter's evening, the gunner will hear the hoarse voice of a homing crow and see that villain pass like a shadow in the gathering gloom. He will most surely take advantage of the situation to down one of his worst enemies. More, should he be aware that homing crows (or even hunting crows during the day) are likely to come near, he will find that a dead duck, placed on its back on the edge of the flood, with a few scattered feathers round it, will bring a crow close in to investigate, and he may, in his patience, even wait for it to call its mate to the feast.

During the season, he will have shot any rat on sight, but now, with the close season on him, he will spend more time, particularly as spring approaches, walking round the channels, drains and ditches, letting his dog hunt out and bolt rats, and either shooting the swimming creatures with a shotgun, rifle, or even with a catapult. It is surprising how many rats can be killed like this, even on a short walk round on a Sunday morning.

Now, as he stands with very mixed feelings indeed, watching a thousand wigeon on a pool of receding floodwater, already gay in their courting plumage, and so busy about their affairs that they allow him to get fairly close and stand and watch them; when he hears the first redshank, back from the coast to nest once more in the fresh marsh; as he listens to the rooks talking and sees them building in the wood over the river—he begins to think along the lines of keepering and improving his marsh. Plank bridges have gone afloat in the floods. These can be found and replaced, this time with greater care and attention. To those likely spots for mallard to nest—those rushy, swampy corners—he may well carry a whitethorn branch or two, placing it where the reeds and rushes and grass can grow up round and through it, so that it will make a thorny retreat from vermin. Perhaps he can get permission to wire round similar odd corners of good nesting cover, to save them from trampling cattle, and so encourage duck to nest there.

The wigeon may still be there in March, and even April when mallard are sitting hard on eggs, or, in a mild season, have already hatched off an early brood or two, but now that restlessness which so assailed him throughout the shooting season is laid. He watches the mating duck with no thought of "murder" in his heart, but only a fresh awakening to his small duties towards improving his marshland acres.

Then one morning the last drop of surface water has left the marsh and the wigeon have gone. Their lovely piping and whistling are no longer heard; only the noisy gossiping of rooks in the rookery and the belling of a pair of red-shank as they race up and down their nesting territory, with perhaps the quacking of an agitated mallard duck as she sees the farmer's dog approaching her nursery.

Plover are wailing and weeping and casting themselves this way and that above where the first milkmaids and moon-daisies are showing pink and white heads above the lush grazing. A pair of snipe rise from the dampness of a patch of yellow kingcups, one circling to drum, wings and stiff outer tail feathers held rigid as the bird tip-tilts in a shallow-dive, its bleating heard at a great distance. Before very long, the first family of young mallard will be on wing at dusk, and thoughts will flash ahead to those first September evenings, when the duck will be flighting once more to the barley fields.

SETTING OUT DECOYS

Some mention of decoys has already been made, but the use and setting out of decoys, especially on inland marshes and flooded water-meadows deserves more than a few passing remarks. Indeed decoys can, not infrequently, ensure better and surer sport and reasonably larger bags. One of the main functions of decoys is to bring the duck into reasonable range and thus to obviate the temptation to take long shots. In this country the use of excessive numbers of decoys is not looked upon with favour and, when conditions are ideal, one should never be tempted to overshoot. During the last three months of the year, by which time wigeon have arrived in considerable numbers and mallard and teal have become educated to the ways of the man with a gun, thoughts about using decoys during evening flight will have turned to active measures. Later in the season, when most of the overseas wigeon have arrived, these active measures will assume far more serious and more frequently organized use of decoys. In, say, October and November, the gunner will probably be satisfied to set out perhaps half a dozen mallard decoys, either to attract passing duck during the day, or, more likely, as duck begin to flight as dusk deepens and they scout around for the evening safety of their fellows, having now more or less finished their gleanings on the arables, where already most of the stubble has been turned under.

In this chapter there is space only to generalize in the reasons for and the practice of using decoys. One well-known writer on wildfowling stated that the art is to get within range of the birds (it certainly *is* with punt-gunning), but another argues, and with good sense, that the art of the fowler should be to persuade his quarry to come within range of his gun. In this latter respect, it is obvious that decoying and/or calling must prove the attraction, and very fruitful they can be at times. A would-be user of decoys may learn the element-ary facts of decoying from others, but only his own experiences and initiative will make him proficient to deal with varying conditions of fowling grounds, weather, feeding places and so on. It is useless, as has been pointed out, to float decoys haphazard on a splash pool, wide ditch or dyke, where duck are returning to their daily lay-bys at dawn. On the other hand, decoys set out realistically on and about, say, the edges of a splash of floodwater much used as a landing place by wigeon favouring the lush grazing surrounding it, should attract the twittering companies during the evening at very deepest dusk. The enterprising gunner may even find satisfaction and somewhat better results if he has made for himself life-like wigeon decoys (always matt finished to prevent daylight or moonlight from showing them up for what they are), a few "swimming"; a few "standing at ease" on the edge of the pool; a few "asleep" or "resting" in obvious security.

Your writer of affairs sporting frequently states that all decoys should be pegged out facing the wind, but watch a party of mallard swimming and feeding and it will be seen that they do not conform to this conventional idea, for they do not swim and peck about in a straight line, do not keep a pattern, and odd numbers may leave the main group and be seen feeding away at the edge of the water, or even landing to waddle about, or to rest. Decoys should, therefore, always be made to look as natural and to "behave" as naturally as possible. The same applies when decoys are used on flight-ponds, or close to the banks of reservoirs and lakes.

Wigeon coming down to feed at their accustomed time and place may drop in to any decoys, although the more natural the better. They will fly around and down to a few mallard decoys, or even to a zigzag string of self-inflated decoys. The objects of decoying may be said to be threefold:

1. To bring the birds down to feed on water within range of the gunner lying in ambush.
2. To bring hard-shot wary duck down more quickly than they would come if no decoys were present.
3. To bring flighting or passing duck flying round within shot.

As to calling, this is a difficult study of its own and should never be attemp-ted until the gunner has learned for himself by careful study which note and inflection of a note is likely to attract a passing bird, and which will issue a warning to it. All too often tyro gunners can be heard "quacking like mad" on their newly-acquired calls—only to scare away every fowl within hearing, if not to risk getting peppered in the growing darkness by an even less experi-enced tyro learning duck shooting the hard way!

CHAPTER 12

ETIQUETTE AND SAFETY ON THE MARSH

by Bill Powell

WAGBI Member. Past Chairman, Solway Wildfowlers' Association (Dumfries Branch).

> ETIQUETTE. The formalities or usages required by the customs of polite society. (*Standard Dictionary of the English Language.*)

WHEREVER you are or whatever you are doing, the observation of common conventional courtesies and consideration makes the marsh a more agreeable place. However, wildfowling etiquette is more concerned with the observation of an unwritten code of laws and behaviour evolved down the years by experience—sometimes bitter—with a view to making the marshes happier and safer for *everybody* who uses them. The code is simply a combination of common sense, good manners and consideration for others.

A fowler who deliberately breaks the written laws runs a calculated risk of forfeiting his money, his gun, or even his liberty, but the wilful and habitual offender against the unwritten laws knows that he runs little risk to his own skin and, provided that the scorn and contempt of all true sportsmen mean nothing to him, usually goes unpunished until something drastic happens.

Because much wildfowling takes place in the dark or in a poor light, the dangers of a gun are greater than ever and safety precautions *must* be observed at all times. It is obvious that if a gun was *never* pointed at anyone there would be no accidents. This seems a simple rule, easy to observe, and yet hardly a week goes by without a shooting accident being reported in the Press. Most of us know the old jingle beginning

> Never, never let your gun
> pointed be at any one . . .

This seems, whether we realize it or not, to have sunk into our subconscious minds, because relatively few accidents happen while actually shooting. It is in the house, or in the car, or when crossing some obstacle, or in those more relaxed moments when we pause to tie a lace, or to take breath after wading through mud, or perhaps put our gun down to use binoculars, that danger lurks.

We must make it a cardinal rule to unload every time a gun is put down, and to keep it unloaded until it is actually at the ready for a likely shot. A gun may look safe enough leaning against a fence with its barrels pointed skywards, but it is not. A prowling dog, a startled sheep or even a clumsy man can knock it over with the barrels pointing in a different direction, and someone or something may be injured.

When crossing a gutter, jumping a ditch or climbing a fence, it is *not* sufficient to rely upon the safety-catch, or even to "break" your gun. The cartridges *must* be removed. At no time is a gun with a cartridge in the chamber entirely safe, and it cannot be stressed too often that the only possible way to render a gun harmless is to unload it.

Loaded guns have no place in boats, any more than they have in a motor-car, or on a tractor. And when they are being ferried, unloaded, they want special protection and stowage in case they are knocked about and dented—or at worst dropped overboard during an unsteady passage.

Many accidents in the field could be avoided if a shot was never taken "blind". A man who shoots at a bush because he sees movement there is nothing short of a criminal lunatic. Never shoot down the line or low in the half-light at flight, or at anything running if a dog is close behind. You may have your own ideas on the value of such a dog, but you can be certain that *someone* loves it.

Finally, on the subject of gun safety, if you see anyone, friend or stranger, behaving dangerously with a gun, it is your duty to tell him so emphatically, without pulling punches. He may be a very nice fellow but he is also a potential manslaughterer.

All fowlers should apply to join their wildfowling club at home, and if contemplating a shooting holiday should get in touch with the secretary of the local club, if any. He will tell you of local restrictions. He will advise where to get a tide-table, warn you of danger spots and tell where you can and cannot shoot. But do not expect him to tell you all about the best flight-lines as he is not going to run the risk of finding you comfortably installed in his favourite hide.

When making a reconnaisance of new grounds, always ask the farmer where you may park your car and, when parking it in the small hours of the morning, bear in mind that if *you* had given a stranger permission to park outside your house, you would not be amused if disturbed by car-door slamming, hearty conversation and dogs being called to heel. Unless your dog is perfectly trained it should be kept on a lead when crossing private ground.

Never go on to mudflats without learning the time and height of the tides. Brave men have lost their lives trying to rescue wildfowlers from difficulties that would never have arisen had these elementary precautions been taken. Know your marshes thoroughly in all their moods.

On public foreshore and club shooting-grounds especially, you should always be in good time for flights. There are few things more infuriating than having a flight ruined by late arrivals after you have been in your hide well before dawn. Also do use discretion over what you wear on the marsh. Remember that to be unseen is all-important. Gay sweaters and that snazzy hat with the coloured pom-poms that will attract the girls on the ski-slopes of St. Moritz will *not* attract the duck on the flight-lines of any estuary.

On morning flight get out to your hide as quietly as possible. If you chatter, it is difficult to hear and locate birds that may be roosting close inshore. You will also probably scare them away, thereby spoiling your own chances as well as those of other people. Reduce the use of your flashlight to a minimum, and if there is any chance of your dog leaving your hide when the shooting starts, keep it on a lead.

Never without permission, settle down within at least seventy-five yards of a gun already in position, and *never take long shots*. Some gunners seem to find it difficult to restrain themselves from shooting at wildfowl that are well out of range. A good method of learning whether a bird is within shot is to hang up a goose and/or a curlew with wings outstretched as in flying position and then from thirty-five yards away look at them down the barrels of a gun. Close one eye and take note of how much or how little of the bird's span is obscured by the barrels until you are thoroughly accustomed to their appearance at this distance, and withhold your fire if live birds pass at greater range.

Remember, there are two, and only two reasons for failing to kill your quarry. Either you have missed it, which is poor shooting, or else the bird is out of range, which is poor sportsmanship. So the next time you stand with smoking barrels watching a skein of geese fly on unscathed ask yourself: "Am I a poor sport, or just a rotten shot?" The remedy lies with you. Either you must mend your ways, or perhaps you need a little practice with the clays.

A lone fowler should always let someone know roughly where he is going. Accidents do unfortunately sometimes happen, and it is a great help to a search-party to have some idea of the area in which to start the search. Again, when out on the marshes with a party, should you become bored, cold or for some other reason wish to go home early, do not do so without letting a member of your party know of your departure. Your friends will not be pleased if after a protracted search in darkness or fog, they eventually locate you with a glass of hot toddy seated before a roaring fire at the local.

You should *not* shoot wild geese on their roosting grounds. Some old-fashioned books on wildfowling give instructions, sometimes with illustrations, upon how to dig in on the mudflats, but in the days in which those books were written wildfowlers were few and far between, and an occasional skilfully carried-out foray out on the flats was permissible and did little harm.

Now that wildfowling has become so popular, this form of shooting should be banned. Wild geese only frequent those areas where extensive mudflats provide them with security by night, and it has been proved that if subjected to persistent sand-crawling, they will leave a district altogether to seek sanctuary elsewhere.

If you observe a breach of wildfowling etiquette, do please point it out to the offender. Most mistakes are due to ignorance or perhaps thoughtlessness. A courteous approach when pointing out the error is more likely to be effective than an abusive one, the object being not only to make the marshes and wildfowling safer, but also more enjoyable. As pointed out at the beginning of this chapter, this code is simply a combination of common sense, good manners and consideration for others. If you are not already blessed with these qualities, or cannot acquire them, I beseech you to abandon wildfowling and leave it to genuine wildfowlers.

Finally, remember that you are not the only pebble on the beach. In your coastal wanderings you will meet all sorts of people on the marsh; fishermen, bird-watchers, naturalists, holiday-makers, beach-combers, and winkle-pickers.

To all of them be tolerant, helpful and good mannered. Don't forget that they will probably base their opinion of wildfowling on what they think of you.

CHAPTER 13

THE WILDFOWLER IN EIRE

by John Wardell, M.B.O.U.

Chairman, Wildfowlers' Association of Great Britain and Ireland, 1967–70;
Member, Wildfowl Conservation Committee, Nature Conservancy.

LESS than ten years ago it was possible to write of Ireland as the wildfowler's Mecca of the West, where the climate, and geography, shared by a human population of under four million, combined to support an abundant wildfowl population. Alas, today the twentieth century has caught up with the Emerald Isle and large-scale drainage schemes, coupled with the over-shooting of a population decimated by the hard winter of 1962–3, has meant that the days when "free" shooting could be had for the asking have gone for ever.

Fortunately all is not lost. Pressure from Gun Clubs and conservationists alike, together with the realization by the authorities of the value of sporting shooting as a tourist attraction, has resulted in energetic measures to halt indiscriminate exploitation and to improve both the shooting and hotel facilities available to visitors.

It is perhaps too late to save the partridge and the grouse, but pheasant rearing is on the increase, and it is possible for visitors to acquire first-class pheasant shooting by the day if they are prepared to pay for it. Most hotels in the west and south-west of Ireland have their own shooting, or can arrange it for visitors although, needless to say, it is prudent to inquire in advance.

In Eire, the Land Commission has acquired many thousands of acres of marshland, on which it leases the shooting rights at very reasonable rents.

At the moment, the shooting season for wildfowl opens in Eire on September 1st and continues until 12th February. On the protected list are brent geese, hen pheasants, quail and landrail. As, however, the shooting dates and protected species can be varied from year to year (partridges were fully protected for some seasons a few years ago and can now be shot during the month of November only), those who intend to shoot in Eire are advised to contact the Field Sports Officer, Irish Tourist Board, Dublin, for up-to-date information.

Wildfowling in Ireland falls into two fairly distinct categories. For a country of its size it has a long coastline and the west coast, in particular, has many estuaries, inlets, and harbours where the shoreshooter can find thousands of acres of salt marsh which are relatively little shot over. The coastal shooting is very good indeed, but the problems associated with it are similar to those met elsewhere in the British Isles, so I do not propose to consider Ireland in detail from the shoreshooter's point of view. For Ireland differs from the rest of the British Isles as far as the wildfowler is concerned in that almost any-where in the country you are likely to find wildfowling literally on your doorstep.

The inland shooter has two types of ground to consider, the bogs—known as red bogs which remain more or less waterlogged all the year round. They have little value to agriculture and provide large areas where wildfowl are seldom disturbed. Most bogs are predominantly acid and dissolved salts in the bog-water result in freezing-point depression, so that with the onset of hard weather they may remain open for some time after other types of marsh and swamp have frozen up.

Apart from the bogs, the great inland loughs, such as Corrib and Mask, with their attendant drainage systems, and also the rivers of the central plain and elsewhere, provide thousands of acres of marshland which remain moist enough to support a large breeding population of wildfowl, and which flood and remain flooded throughout a normal winter.

Access to many of these marshes can be difficult, as a traditional Irish method of bridging streams and ditches, which are often too deep to wade and too wide to jump, is a tree-trunk, circular and none too straight, surmounted by a strand or two of loosely-stretched barbed wire. Paradoxically, the stability of a bridge of this sort increases with the amount of floodwater covering it—if you can find it. Even so, the Irish wildfowler, unless he really knows his ground, is likely to suffer more frequent immersions than his colleagues elsewhere.

Turning to the wildfowl themselves, swans have the pride of place solely on account of their size, as they are of little practical interest to the wildfowler. Bewick's are more widespread than in England, and are sometimes abundant in the western half of the country: whoopers are less common. The barnacle is the most common of the black geese (the name according to one theory was originally bernicle from Hibernicle or Irish goose) and visits the northern and western coasts in large numbers. Brent geese are predominantly the pale-breasted form. As elsewhere, it is rare to find either of these species inland.

Pinkfeet are rare in Ireland, and the bean goose is uncommon; by contrast, greylags winter in the west of Ireland and in Counties Down and Wexford but in decreasing numbers. The shooting on the Wexford slobs or marshes is in private hands and carefully controlled; as a result, the goose shooting on the slobs probably surpasses anything else of its kind in the British Isles. Some winters odd specimens of snow geese turn up with the whitefronts on the Wexford slobs.

The whitefront is by far the most important goose, so far as the average Irish wildfowler is concerned, as this species winters in considerable numbers all over the country. The whitefronts wintering in Eire breed in Greenland, and in this respect differ from those that come to England via the Baltic migration route, being darker and with yellow bills. They arrive in Ireland early in October, remaining until March, and family parties establish them-selves on the red bogs all over the country. Except where these are in the vicinity of the coast they rarely flight out to sea. Their staple diet is cotton-grass, which is prolific on the bogs, but they are also as fond of freshly-flooded grassland, as are most other wildfowl, and it is when flighting on to flooded land from the bogs that they provide the wildfowler with his best opportunity.

Unlike mallard or teal, which will normally be found feeding on any one of a dozen flooded fields in a particular area, whitefronts show a preference for a much smaller number of feeding grounds, and will return to the same ones year after year. Normally diurnal feeders, except for a short period either side of full moon, whitefronts soon change to night feeding when they are much disturbed or shot and the gunner is more often successful at evening flight than in the morning

At the onset of hard weather, the geese spread out from the bogs and one may come across them in the most unlikely places for a few days before they move off farther south and west.

All those species of dabbling duck one is accustomed to find in England are present in Ireland, with the exception of the garganey which is rare. Both shoveler and pintail are possibly relatively more numerous than elsewhere in the British Isles.

As far as inland shooting is concerned mallard and teal are the most likely species to find in a wildfowler's bag during the shooting season. These will be found wherever there are water and cover, spending the day on loughs, ponds, and floodwater, and flighting in to feed in the evening much as they do elsewhere. Inland there are no well-defined flight lines and shooting consists of walking them up in the daytime where there is sufficient cover and waiting for them on their feeding grounds at evening flight. Wigeon winter on the inland loughs as well as around the coast; as on the Cambridgeshire Washes they have the faculty of turning up overnight whenever there are extensive floods.

Three species of diving duck, tufted, common pochard, and common scoter breed on Irish loughs; in addition, eiders breed on islands off the Donegal coast. In the shooting season, tufted, common pochard, and, to a lesser extent, goldeneye, are the species in this group of interest to the inland wildfowler; tufted in particular are sometimes found in enormous numbers. These diving duck winter on the loughs and when disturbed on large sheets of water they tend to fly or swim out to the middle rather than leave the area, so that the fowler will not often come to terms with them under these conditions. They will however, flight up the rivers, and on to floodwater and ponds, and, as they normally feed in daytime, may be found on the move at any time of day, as well as at morning and evening flight. In the winter common and velvet scoter, eider duck, and scaup are common round the coasts of Ireland, but it is rare to find them inland.

Of the sawbills, the red-breasted merganser breeds in considerable numbers in the west of Ireland, and to some extent elsewhere; during the summer months they become very tame and family parties can be approached to within fifteen yards or so without any attempt at concealment. Anyone who has shot and attempted to eat a merganser will not repeat the experiment, but anyone having seen them fishing on salmon and trout streams in the west must feel that there are some grounds for shooting them as vermin.

Ireland is justly famous for its snipe shooting. Snipe are found all over the country wherever there is cover and the ground is wet. A large breeding population is augmented by foreigners at the onset of winter, and it follows from the east–west migratory movement that the cream of the snipe shooting is mostly near the west and south-west coasts. Under normal conditions snipe are to be found on the red bogs as well as on other marshy ground, where they either spend the day on their feeding grounds, if there is sufficient cover, or flight on to more open floodwater to feed at dusk. Although the snipe population is very large indeed, it varies from marsh to marsh day by day, and for some reason more snipe are often found on the red bogs around about full moon—possibly birds resting on migration.

At the onset of hard weather snipe move on to the red bogs, but if the frost continues will then disperse all over the countryside to wherever there is running water. Very good shooting can be had under these conditions by walking up ditches and streams—there is usually thick cover and the birds sit tight.

Snipe are shot either by walking-up or driving, or by a combination of both methods. The difficulty with walking-up is that although on some days they will sit tight, on as many others they will not, so much so, that fifty or more may be put up in a marshy field without getting a reasonable shot. They are always sensitive to the sound of the human voice, but will usually sit quite close to gun shot, although occasionally the first shot will put up every snipe on the marsh.

All in all, chances are increased by walking snipe upwind, if other considerations allow this, but they are extremely difficult to hit if the shooter is walking into the sun. Driving is a much more satisfactory way of dealing with the smaller type of marsh that can be covered with, say, two guns heading it, and two or three others walking-up. Needless to say, you need to be sure of your guns when doing this. Driving has the double advantage of ensuring that one has chances at a far higher proportion of the snipe on the marsh, and also enables one to come to terms with whatever duck there are as well; most of the duck will rise when the first shot is fired.

Snipe shooting can be a difficult and fascinating sport offering a wide variety of shots, and comparatively few English shooters have sufficient practice at it to become really proficient. The really good Irish snipe shot is well worth watching in action. Walking-up he fires quickly before the bird starts to jink, and very rarely misses.

If you drive along the Irish roads in winter, you will see green plover feeding on almost every suitable field you pass; if you stop and put them up, you will probably pick out a few golden plover amongst them, and these will quickly climb to a considerable height and fly off out of shot.

The green plover winter population of Ireland must be immense, but these birds are now protected.

Golden plover arrive in quantity early in October; they tend to remain in flocks at first, later splitting up into smaller parties, but flocking again in hard weather. The most successful form of plover shooting, as elsewhere, is to find two or three favoured fields in the area you are shooting and to place one or more guns on each, so as to keep them moving. In the Boyne valley, and no doubt elsewhere, a very large flight of golden plover move upstream about an

Plate 27. Jim Worgan observing the pool through his peephole while his "piper" dog waits beside him.

Plate 28. Jim Worgan, WAGBI's warden-decoyman, working his dog "Nell" at Boarstall

Plate 29. A good catch of teal

Plate 30. Decoyed teal being held for release in the spring

Plate 31. One of the Wainwright traps at Abberton

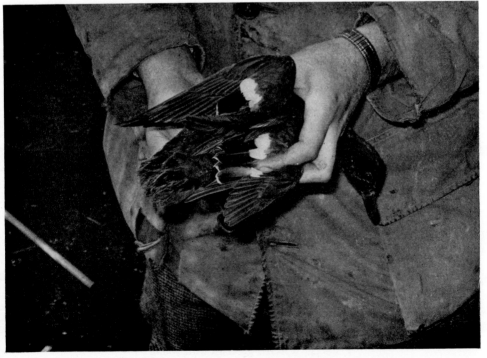

Plate 32. Teal ready for release to repeat the Netherby experiment

Plate 33. A WAGBI greylag on its nest

Plate 34. WAGBI greylags with young

hour before dusk and if the weather is rough enough to keep them down within shot, very large bats can be made under these conditions.

In the eastern half of Ireland, woodcock, though relatively more plentiful than in England, do not feature largely in a fowler's bag, unless one is lucky enough to come across large numbers on migration. In the west, around the shores of Lough Corrib and elsewhere, woodcock are found in considerable numbers from the beginning of December onwards and large bags are made. Understandably, the best of this shooting is carefully preserved.

Woodcock will be found in hazel plantations when the weather is mild, but under normal winter conditions show a preference for laurel and rhododendron. They leave their resting places by well-defined flight lines at dusk and one knows exactly where to go. On one marsh north of Dublin, where there is a pigeon flight as well, evening flights last for two hours, and one can come home with a mixed bag of pigeon, woodcock, snipe, mallard, teal, and possibly a hare or two as well, without having moved one's position.

The plaintive call of the curlew is a familiar sound all over Ireland in the summer, and large numbers of them remain on the inland marshes throughout the shooting season.

No apology is called for in mentioning hares in an article on wildfowling, first because the Irish hare is a distinct species, and therefore of interest to the visiting fowler-naturalist, and secondly because it is not possible to walk many bogs or marshes in Ireland without putting up a hare or two. The rule is that those who shoot them have to carry them, and it follows that owners of dogs inclined to run in are not popular on a snipe bog.

From the foregoing, it will be clear that the wildfowler in Ireland has very much more walking to do than his English counterpart. Waders will keep him dry, but those who choose to try them will wish that they were wearing almost anything else after an hour or so on a snipe bog. Usually it is possible to keep dry from the knee upwards, so that the best clothes are riding breeches with a change of shoes and stockings for the drive home. As a great deal of the shooting is at snipe, it is best to load with number 7 or 8 shot, and only to change to something heavier for evening flight—number 7 will, however, kill a goose as effectively as anything heavier, if it is within reasonable range, as it is likely to be, coming in at morning or evening flight.

CHAPTER 14

WILDFOWL CONSERVATION IN IRELAND

by Jeffery Harrison, M.A., M.B.O.U., F.Z.S.(Sc.)

Vice-Chairman and Hon. Scientific Adviser, Wildfowlers' Association of Great Britain and Ireland. Vice-Chairman, Wildfowl Conservation Committee, Nature Conservancy; British Representative, International Wildfowl Research Bureau; Council, The Wildfowl Trust.

IRELAND stands at the end of two main wildfowl "flyways", one from Greenland and Iceland, the other from the N.W. European mainland. It stands also on the brink of massive destruction of its wetland habitat, both by drainage and by pollution. Although much of the drainage is desirable for agriculture, a great deal more is indiscriminate and uneconomic, but if it continues as at present, then the next twenty years are likely to see the end of Ireland's heritage as a major European wildfowl resort. The situation can be seen therefore to have worsened very seriously since the previous chapter was written a mere eight years ago. In the North, there is now a ban on night shooting and on Sunday shooting.

As if this was not enough, Ireland is at present suffering from excessive shooting pressures, not only from her own countrymen, but far worse, by tourists, who are actively encouraged to visit the country for the shooting and are seldom satisfied with reasonable bags. In the winter of 1968–9 six visiting guns shot 900 snipe in a week in Co. Kerry. If this was an isolated incident, it might not perhaps be considered excessive at an average of twenty-one snipe per gun per day, but in fact the favoured areas are being shot day after day throughout the season, exploited by advertising to attract the tourists. Finally, Ireland, in the North and in the Republic is rapidly becoming "developed" industrially and for holiday resorts. It is the latter which threatens Akeragh Lough in Co. Kerry, one of the most important sites for gadwall and the best-known marsh in all Europe for American wading birds.

This gloomy picture is reflected in changes in the overall status of many of the main wildfowl species. Of the duck, mallard, teal, wigeon, scaup and common scoter show marked decreases, drainage being responsible for the first three coupled with excessive disturbance, while pollution of harbours and estuaries almost certainly accounts for the last two. Hooded crow predation is also an important factor in the decreases of breeding duck, particularly mallard.

It is the dabbling duck which are particularly affected by the drainage of the turloughs, a unique area of winter-flood fields, in Counties Galway and

Mayo. In all some 450,000 acres of prime habitat has been lost but great efforts have saved the last important turlough, Rahasane.

The drainage problems are aggravated by the fact that there are so many smallholders, farming fifty acres or less—and they can hardly be expected to appreciate their wetland "heritage" if it involves their farm being flooded for half the year.

The greylag goose has also decreased sharply. In 1946, over 6,000 were present on Wexford Slobs alone. In an aerial survey in January 1967, only 736 were found in the whole of Ireland, since when there has probably been a slight increase. A shift to winter quarters in Scotland probably accounts for this decrease. Small decreases have also occurred in the light-breasted brent goose and in the Greenland white-fronted goose. The situation is no better for snipe.

On the credit side, the gadwall, shoveler, tufted duck, shelduck, red-breasted merganser, mute and whooper swans are thought to be increasing but it is by no means proved that this is real rather than apparent.

Fortunately, all is by no means lost, for at well past the eleventh hour there has been a great awakening of interest in wetland conservation. In the Republic, this culminated in the formation of the Irish Wildfowl Committee in December 1965 and another big stride was taken when on 1st January, 1969, this organization merged with the Irish Society for the Protection of Birds and the Irish Ornithologists' Club to form the Irish Wildbird Conservancy. The Conservancy is concerned with the whole of Ireland and the Council consists of representatives from the North and the Republic, with Major R. F. Ruttledge as its first President.

The Conservancy liaises closely with the Department of Lands and with the Irish Game Protection Association, the National Association of Regional Game Councils and the National Sporting Association.

A number of vital projects were initiated by the Irish Wildfowl Committee and are now being continued by the Wildbird Conservancy. Wildfowl counts are being established, with winter surveys for particular species, such as brent, barnacle and greylag geese, Bewick's and whooper swans, which are particularly suitable for special studies.

In 1967, Ireland was covered for the first mid-winter Wildfowl Census organized throughout Europe by the IWRB. Unfortunately foot-and-mouth disease seriously upset the 1968 census, but without doubt wildfowl counts are becoming established and will ultimately come to form the basis for the proper conservation of wildfowl.

A wetland survey covering 118 areas was carried out in 1967 and a scheme drawn up which could form the basis for a chain of wildfowl refuges to be established in the future. The list is being continually revised to assess the importance of the areas in a European context and to keep abreast of changes in the habitat. An amended list will be published by the IWRB in due course.

It is most encouraging that there is excellent co-operation between Northern Ireland and the Republic over wildfowl matters and an annual All-Ireland Conference on Bird Conservation is held alternatively in north and south.

In Northern Ireland, the Ministry of Development is responsible for the establishment of statutory reserves and for the nomination of areas of scientific interest, for which it is advised by a Nature Reserves Committee. There is close liaison with the forestry, drainage and fisheries divisions, as there is in the Department of Lands, in the Republic.

Voluntary organizations are all most active in the North, notably the Royal Society for the Protection of Birds, the National Trust and wildfowling clubs affiliated to WAGBI, all of which co-operate closely with each other. The Ulster Game and Wildfowl Society and the Northern Ireland Game Trust are also becoming increasingly interested in wildfowl problems.

A number of important reserves have been established in Ireland in the past few years. A National Wildfowl Refuge has been established jointly by the Department of Lands and the IWC on Wexford North Slob, which holds up to 6,000 Greenland white-fronted geese, or two-thirds of the world population, together with large numbers of duck and waders. The initiative for this stemmed from the support given at the Second European Meeting on Wildfowl Conservation in Holland in 1966. A research programme into the ecology of the whitefronts is being carried out. A warden has been appointed for this refuge.

Another important IWC reserve, "Tern Island" in Wexford Harbour, serves as an important winter roost for these whitefronts, although its prime importance is for nesting terns. On the other side of the harbour, Rosslare Back Strand Reserve supports important populations of wigeon, some light-breasted brent and many waders.

The Strangford Lough Wildlife Scheme was brought into being through the enterprise of the National Trust (Northern Ireland Committee) with the full co-operation of the Strangford Lough Wildfowlers' Association in the main and also the Killyleagh, Crossgar and Comber Associations. The Lough provides winter quarters for up to 3,600 light-breasted brent (or half the Irish population), 14,000 wigeon and many other wildfowl and waders. Six wardened reserves have been established with observation posts and displays provided. In co-operation with the Mackie family, feral flocks of greylag and barnacle geese are being established. Steps are also being taken to control the spread of spartina grass, which threatens to choke the *zostera* beds. There is evidence that the limiting factor for brent, wild swans and wigeon on Strangford is *zostera* and when the beds are eaten, these species move elsewhere.

The Royal Society for the Protection of Birds has been able to establish two reserves on Lower Lough Erne, the site of the largest nesting colony of common scoters in Ireland. A research project on their breeding biology is under way and habitat management is planned.

The uninhabited Inishkea Islands, off Co. Mayo, are annually declared a non-shooting zone, as they support half the Irish population of barnacle geese. An area of shore-line, six miles long in the north-eastern part of Lough Neagh is being set aside as a reserve. The Lough holds a massive diving duck population, which is likely to be increasingly disturbed by the building of a new town in the immediate vicinity.

The North Bull Island within the Dublin city boundary must be the only tidal wetland reserve actually inside a capital city. Owned by the Corporation, it supports up to 400 light-breasted brent and large numbers of wigeon, teal, pintail and waders. This reserve is now seriously threatened, first by the Dublin Port and Docks Board, which intends to reclaim a large area of mud-flats between the harbour and the North Bull Wall and second, by the City Corporation, which proposes to reclaim the channel between North Bull Island and the mainland at Clontarf.

One of the most exciting research projects is that into mallard ecology being undertaken by Brian Stronach on the Lough Carra Wildfowl Refuge in Co. Mayo, which was officially opened by Mr. Micheál Ómoráin, who did so much for wildfowl conservation during his tenure as Minister of Lands.

This Lough holds the largest breeding concentration of mallard anywhere in Ireland, as well as sizeable numbers of other dabbling and diving duck. This whole population is being systematically studied including a detailed breeding survey. An intensive ringing programme is being carried out, using the WAGBI ringing organization. A long-term study into the effects of predation has already started. Intensive hooded crow control is already showing a marked increase in the breeding success of mallard. The Carra project will undoubtedly yield highly valuable results, but it is worrying that the proposed drainage of the Lough Mask watershed could very seriously affect this area, by lowering the water level in Lough Carra by three feet, which would destroy most of the habitat.

WAGBI clubs are very active in Northern Ireland. In all, there are sixteen affiliated clubs and a Northern Ireland representative has been appointed to the Management Committee.

The Strangford Lough WA which is co-operating so successfully with the National Trust was the first club to be awarded the Stanley Duncan Conservation Trophy, in 1969, by WAGBI. Their club house and conservation centre just outside Newtownards is decorated with wall charts of wildfowl and waders and wildfowl food plants by their Vice-President, the well-known bird artist, R. W. Milliken. This club again won the trophy in 1960.

Behind the headquarters is their rearing area, a high and a low-level lake joined by a stream, which supports a large stock of mallard, wigeon, pintail, pochard and tufted duck. Offspring are released on to their Kiltonga Reserve adjoining the main road to Belfast, which supports up to 800 teal and a flourish-ing flock of feral greylags among a number of other species of wildfowl. A lecture hall is also under construction.

The Larne Lough WA has also been able to establish a number of its own local reserves and is very active in crow control, as well as supporting the WAGBI duck-rearing scheme as do a number of other clubs in the North. The Killyleagh and Crossgar Clubs are also closely involved with the Strang-ford Lough Scheme and both have their own local reserve. The Victoria Gun Club, Lurgan, and the Derrytrasnar Gun Club each have an island reserve on Lough Neagh, while the Fermanagh Gun Club is very active in crow control on Lower Lough Erne, working in co-operation with the Royal Society for the Protection of Birds.

Mallard released in Northern Ireland have already yielded some interesting recoveries in N.W. Europe, but at present only very few have been released in the Republic as part of the WAGBI Scheme, mainly by the Lough Wildfowl Trust in Cork. More recently Brian Stronach has started two release trials, one near Dublin, the other in Co. Donegal, which should provide interesting comparisons.

WAGBI would welcome any co-operation with gun clubs in the Republic in projects of this kind and would gladly make its services and rings available, as it does in the Lough Carra project. Its title—the Wildfowlers' Association of Great Britain and Ireland—can hardly be said to be correct until we have built up the closest liaison possible.

It can be seen therefore that some progress has been made in wildfowl conservation in Ireland in the past two or three years, but the situation is still poised on a knife-edge. It is my firm impression from what I have seen on the spot that the situation will just be saved, but it will need the full support of every naturalist, every wildfowler and every government administrator to bring this about. Undoubtedly the formation of the Irish Wildbird Conservancy through the amalgamation of three other organizations was a great step forward. One is almost overwhelmed by the plethora of different organizations still trying to achieve much the same ends in many different ways and there is still room for a great deal of similar streamlining.

Time is no longer on Ireland's side as traditionally it always has been.

CHAPTER 15

REARING WILD DUCK

by Bill and Harry Mouland

Bill Mouland, Honorary Member, WAGBI. Harry Mouland, WAGBI Member.

EVERY worth-while sportsman puts back into his sport more than he takes out. The game shot has for centuries realized the importance of rearing. Unfortunately, this has not always been the case with the wildfowler. He has argued that his birds are truly wild and most originate in other countries. Why should he rear duck for release and probably never see them again? Of recent years there has been a change of thought and many wildfowlers and shoot-owners have come to the conclusion that conservation is a thoroughly good thing, but you must first have something to conserve. The answer is for every shooting man to rear a brood or two of mallard every year and then see how the duck population really can increase. It is doing well as it is, but with every shooting man playing his part, it could still be far better. These notes, therefore, are designed for the average wildfowler and rough-shooter, rather than the large-scale game farmer.

Nature provides the best rearer of all—the mother duck, but left to her own devices, she and her brood are at the mercy of predators, both fur and feathered, and the elements. We have a saying locally that once you find a duck's nest, you might just as well put your foot on it. That is to say, if you do not pick up the eggs, the crows or foxes will find them nine times out of ten. Also there is the weather to contend with. A cold wet spell at hatching and when the ducklings are small can easily mean no insect life, chilling, and a high mortality. It is not at all unusual to see large broods reduced to nil during a day or two of bad weather.

The most popular method of incubating the eggs is by setting them under hens or bantams. Hens have the advantage of covering more eggs—ten or twelve—but bantams are by far the safer brooders. If an equal number of bantams and hens can be set at the same time, the bantams are quite capable of brooding all the ducklings when hatched.

Testing for infertile eggs is best left for at least fourteen to twenty days. The infertile eggs will either be clear, as with a fresh egg, which can be detected by handling, or they will be rotten and slop about inside when given a short sharp shake. If the testing is left until just before the hen is returned to the nest, the bad eggs can also be detected by lightly pressing against the lips. An infertile egg will feel noticeably cooler. This art comes with practice and is best left if in doubt, as good eggs are often thrown out, even by experts. A rotten egg will float if tested in water with the chill off.

The sitting box, in which the hen is to be confined during brooding, should have adequate height and air holes to allow good ventilation. The holes should be no larger than half an inch as larger ones would let in too much light. Hens sit better in a subdued light. The box should have a solid door, hinged at the bottom and have no floor.

The dimensions of the sitting box are not less than 14″ × 14″ × 14″. More headroom can be given if large hens are to be used.

The nest should be made by cutting a sod of turf the size of the floor area and beating down the centre to form a hollow. On top of this place fresh soft

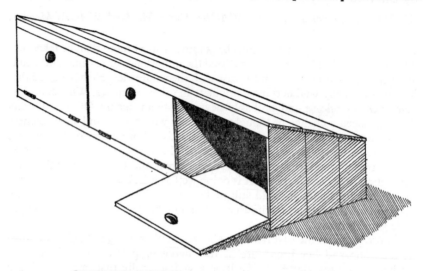

SITTING BOXES

Fig. 15.

hay to form a lining. The hen should first be set on dummy eggs for twenty-four hours to ensure she is sitting tight. If all is well the eggs to set should then be introduced. She should be left undisturbed for a further twenty-four hours before her first feed and water. The hen should always be lifted off the nest and the box closed up for thirty minutes while she feeds and drinks. It is an advantage to tether her by the leg or site the box in a small enclosure as she can be difficult to catch when putting back on the eggs. A kibbled maize wheat mixture fed once a day with grit *ad lib* is sufficient. The incubation period of a duck is twenty-eight to thirty days. If the eggs are fresh the ducklings should all be hatched by the twenty-ninth day. Remove the empty shells while hatching takes place, but do not remove the ducklings until they have all hatched, unless the hen becomes restless or fidgety. They should then be put on warm flannel in a basket near a fire or stove to keep warm. If this is not done an excited or clumsy hen can easily trample a whole brood.

Rearing the ducks can be very easy with bantams which are light and excellent mothers. If hens have to be used a strict watch should be kept on them for the first few days. If any ducklings are trampled, the hen should be taken away and the ducklings placed in a well-insulated coop or box at night or during cold days. We have found it is better to risk the chance of chills than the large feet of a clumsy hen.

Another preference of ours is for medium sized runs as against coops and small runs. That is to say a wire-netted run 8 ft. long by 3 ft. wide and 3 ft. high, with an open-fronted coop or box to provide shelter. Around the bottom edge of the run should be a 6" × ½" board to give shelter from cold winds. The top third of the run should be hinged to provide a large door for easy access. The shelter should be placed inside and the whole thing moved

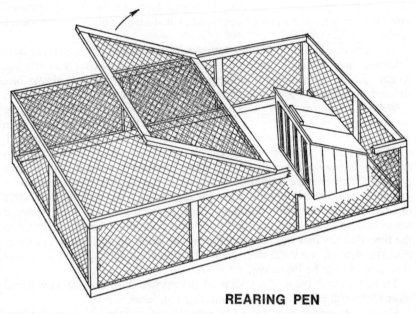

REARING PEN

Fig. 16.

regularly on to fresh grass as it will soon foul and get dirty. Most important of all, the young ducklings must not be allowed to get into any water. A font which just allows them to drink is ideal. A high-protein food is also necessary. It pays to feed the very best food for at least the first two weeks. Turkey starter crumbs or hard-boiled egg and bread, if you only have a few, is ideal. Never feed a wet mash as this will clog their bills and can eventually kill them.

Serious feather pecking is not a common fault of ducks as it is with poultry. No doubt the blunt bill and more kindly disposition has a lot to do with it. However, the feeding of wet mash has been known to cause ducklings to feather peck as the mash can get on the backs of the ducks and the others will try to peck at it. An obvious cure is to feed dry food, but if this does not stop it the birds should be given a larger run or their run moved on to fresh grass more often. Great care should be exercised in using aerosol sprays on the market which the makers claim will prevent feather pecking, as these can cause inhalation broncho-pneumonia and the death of the duckling.

We always put their food at one end and their water at the other end of the pen. This does seem to stop them making a mash of their own. After two weeks, the protein can be weakened gradually by adding a little middlings, barley meal, or even mixed corn; after about six weeks they will feed on practically any mixture. Many rearers have failed by neglecting to provide high-protein food and allowing their ducklings to paddle in their drinking water.

The birds should be fed twice a day and limited to what they can eat without waste, as rats attracted by uneaten food are a great nuisance and usually find young ducklings a better meal than the wasted food. An old pipe or upturned box containing rat poison should be situated at strategic points as a precaution against possible trouble.

The hen can be removed after four weeks and as soon as the ducks have feathered they should be marked either by tagging, or better still ringing. Much valuable information is being gained by the latter and it is always nice to know just where your birds seem to disappear to when the season starts.

WAGBI organize a very efficient duck-ringing scheme and provide the necessary rings and recovery results. Not only does this service help you as an individual, but also the sport as a whole benefits by the information gained.

The artificial incubation of duck eggs is quite successful, provided the eggs are fresh and one realizes that much more moisture is needed than for hen eggs. The temperature should be about $103\frac{1}{2}$ degrees with the thermometer just above the tops of the eggs. Turn the eggs twice a day and dip the fingers in luke-warm water while handling them. From the second week sprinkle warm water over the eggs once daily while turning. Turn the eggs right up to the time that the first egg pips and during the hatch-off sprinkle warm water over the floor of the incubator room. Ducklings do not come off as fast as chicks, so do not be impatient.

There are many types of brooders on the market. Two that we have found most successful are the infra-red lamp and the "electric hen".

The rearing-house floor should be covered with a four-inch layer of shavings, or rather less of sawdust or sand. The ducklings should be confined by boards or stiff cardboard close to the lamp or brooder. As they grow, this barrier can be opened out and eventually taken away.

The infra-red lamp is the cheapest method but tends to give a concentrated heat and care should be taken to ensure that the birds are not too hot or too cold. A good guide is to watch the birds; if they huddle under the lamp it should be lowered until they spread out evenly under it. Too hot and they will be around in a circle and the outside ones may chill.

The "electric hen" consists of a wooden tray on four adjustable legs. The floor of the tray has an electric heater wire through it, similar to the electric blanket principle. It takes very little electricity and is very simple. There is no need to worry about the temperature as the heat is evenly distributed over the area of the brooder and the ducklings snuggle under with their backs touching the soft warm blanket—like the underside of a tray.

Care must be taken when hardening off the ducklings. The heat can be turned off for a few hours after the first three weeks and then gradually the time increased until it is off altogether. One disadvantage of artificial brooding is that the ducks tend to get very tame and prefer to walk rather than fly. This can be prevented by putting them in runs as far away from people as possible.

It has been shown that hand-reared Mallard brought up away from water develop slightly larger legs than wild-bred birds (Harrison 1965). This is believed to be due to the added growth stimulus from the extra running on

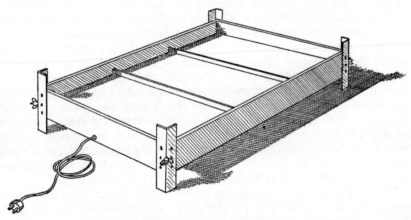

ELECTRIC HEN BROODER

Fig. 17.

dry land, rather than swimming, before they are released. Any birds showing any abnormalities, such as out-turned primaries, albinism, etc., should be ruthlessly culled.

If one is fortunate enough to have a pond or small lake large numbers of birds may be reared very simply. The system is to let the ducks do the incubating, then to pick up their broods at a day or two old. This is best done by either waiting until they are away from the water or driving them quietly off. Using a fisherman's landing net, catch up the duck as she fusses round to protect her brood. Never catch up the ducklings first, as it is then almost impossible to capture the mother once they have been caught. If two or even three broods are caught up at the same time, one duck will easily rear them all and this is the method we use most successfully. The duck is put in a rearing pen with her own and her adopted ducklings and the same procedure is followed as with a hen.

These principles can be applied to all the common British duck except the teal, which is a species which will not breed at all freely in captivity. Teal numbers are very variable in Britain, probably due to migratory shifts. WAGBI would like to be able to increase teal by every means possible. Since hand-rearing appears impracticable, an attempt is being made to repeat the famous experiment carried out by Sir Richard Graham at Netherby at the end of the nineteenth century (Blezard 1966).

Briefly, decoy-caught duck of various species were held flightless through the period of spring migration by having their primaries pulled from one wing, after which they were released on the Solway Moss. By the time that their new quills had grown, the birds had lost their migratory urge, settled down and nested most successfully. Species induced to nest in this way included teal, pintail, wigeon and gadwall.

In 1969, a total of twenty-one drake and eight duck teal which had been caught in WAGBI's decoy at Boarstall, were held captive in a special aviary, prior to having their primaries pulled on 9th March. They were then ringed and released on to a large area of reclaimed Kentish saltmarsh.

The aviary in which such birds are kept should be as large as possible, to enable the fully-winged birds to exercise by flying up and down. To prevent any damage that would result by the birds crashing into the aviary wire, sacks or better still hessian should be tied to the sides and top. A minimum size would be 40 ft long and 15 ft wide and 6 ft high. Also, we found during our first season that the floor of the aviary became very muddy and this tended to ball-up on the birds' feet. This was overcome by covering the floor with a 2-in. layer of sandy gravel. A second and important advantage of using the hessian is that the birds remain much quieter through not seeing outside activities so well, and soon become used to their confinement.

The preponderance of drakes is a typical if unfortunate feature of decoy-caught teal. Regrettably, the spring of 1969 was exceptionally late, so that by the time these birds were flying again in mid-April, some migrant teal were still present. It was thought that these would probably take some of the released birds back with them. This would seem to have happened, for one WAGBI ringed bird, B 015, a first-year female, was shot on 24th August 1969, in Randersfjord, Jylland, Denmark. Nevertheless four broods of young teal were found later in the area, including two, one with seven flying young the other with three or four, on the release marsh. Also, on 21st June a flock of ten drake teal moulting into eclipse was found on a neighbouring marsh, where the other two broods were located. There seems to be little doubt that these were WAGBI birds and it is hoped to continue with this experiment, which is still in its earliest stages.

REFERENCES

BLEZARD, E. (1965). "Duck rearing at Netherby", *WAGBI A.R.* 1965–6: 85–89.
HARRISON, J. G. (1965). "A comparison of weights and measurements of hand-reared and wild-bred Mallard", *WAGBI A.R.* 1964–5: 92–96.
MOULAND, W., MOULAND. H. and HARRISON, J. G. (1970) "The Netherby Experiment repeated with Teal" *WAGBI A.R.* 1969–70: 55

CHAPTER 16

RINGING A DUCK

by the late Major-General C. B. Wainwright, C.B.

Late President, Essex Joint Council of Wildfowling Associations; Member, Nature Conservancy, Wildfowl Conservation Committee; and Council, The Wildfowl Trust.

THE scheme for rearing and releasing ducks is perhaps the most valuable part of the wildfowler's excellent conservation programme. Unless these ducks are ringed before release it will not be possible to find out the true success of the scheme. However, a duck with a badly fitted ring means that the time, trouble and expense of rearing it will have been wasted.

A badly fitted ring will cause considerable suffering and make the bird useless for sport or as a possible breeder in the wild state, where it would have increased the number of ducks for another season. A badly fitted ring may injure the leg or get caught in vegetation, or, if it does not come off altogether, it may slip over the hind toe and deprive the bird of the full use of the leg.

To get the full value it is necessary to record the number of the ring and the date of release. All this takes time but, if time is pressing, I would most definitely state that it is better to ring half the number well and let the others go without a ring than to ring the whole lot badly.

With the experience gained by ringing over twenty-five thousand ducks and re-ringing several hundred of them when they have been recaught, up to nine years later, and their rings have started to wear, I have drawn up the following notes with the hope that they will help ringers to let their birds go and feel that their rings could not be faulted.

1. POINTS FOR PERFECT RINGING

(*a*) Ring as near a circle as you can get it.

(*b*) Ring should turn round on the leg.

(*c*) Ring should move up and down the tarsus, i.e. between hind toe and "knee".

(*d*) Ring not big enough to go over hind toe or over "knee".

(*e*) Ring not overlapped.

(*f*) Edges of ring tight together so that the thinnest blade of grass cannot get caught.

(*g*) No sharp edges to cut into leg.

2. GEAR REQUIRED

(*a*) Rings of the right size: 7 mm. diameter for teal and garganey; 9 mm. diameter for wigeon, shoveler, pintail, gadwall, tufted duck; 11 mm. diameter for mallard, pochard and shelduck. If the right size is used it will automatically stop you putting a ring on a duckling before its leg is big enough—because it will fall off. If you must mark ducklings before their legs have grown, use a Wing Tab (see fig. 19).

(*b*) The correct size of pliers for each ring size; they should have a round hole which fits the outside of the ring when the ring is closed (fig. 18).

(*c*) A strong wrist that can exert steady, controlled pressure.

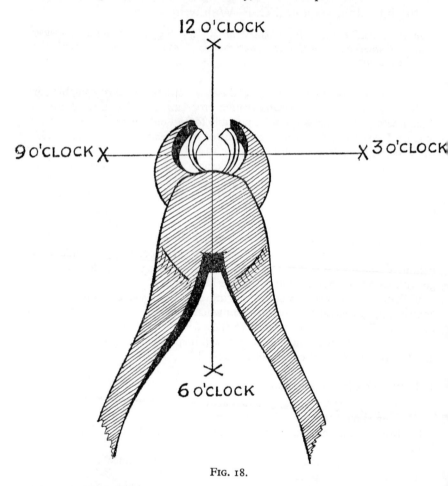

FIG. 18.

3. How to Achieve

(*a*) Load ring into pliers with opening of ring opposite opening of pliers, and leave on table or where it can be easily picked up.

(*b*) Hold the duck round the neck with your left hand back towards you on your thigh, wings either side of your leg. It is best to sit down with a sack or apron, if bird is not house-trained!

(c) Take hold of centre toe of duck's right foot between finger and thumb of left hand.

(d) Pick up pliers with ring inside with right hand and fit over leg.

(e) Press edges of ring together until they nearly meet.

(f) Release pressure on pliers and turn ring so that opening is about 3 o'clock (see fig. 18) and press edges together, taking care they do not overlap.

(g) Release pressure on pliers and turn ring so that join is about 7 o'clock.

(h) Use your strong wrist and edges should meet without a gap and ring should be a true circle. If edges do not meet try again at 8 o'clock.

(i) See that ring turns easily on leg and moves up and down. (If it does not you have used too small a ring and you have a difficult job (see section 5 below).)

(j) Put duck in a sack and do the next one. It is best at least two—I prefer five or six—to go together as a single one gets lost. (I learnt this to my cost as after ringing and letting go singly, I went flighting and shot one of my lost singletons.)

4. RELEASING

(a) Fliers. Take one big duck or two small ones in each hand—the more assistants the better—and on the word "Go" all throw the ducks together as high as you can. If their feathers are wet they will soon dry but if you had let them fly out of your hand they would probably crash. If very wet treat as (b).

(b) Non-fliers. Take a sack load and shake them all out together into some vegetation by the side of the water. If you have the mother, hold her until the ducklings start to move and although she will fly she will know where to come back and find them. Clear right away at once.

5. HOW TO REMOVE A BADLY-FITTED RING

(a) Get an assistant.

(b) Get two pairs of sharp-nosed pliers.

(c) Assistant holds the duck and the leg.

(d) Try to get a grip on each side of opening of ring with one pair of pliers on each side and prise open. This is a very ticklish job and is only necessary because of incompetence on the part of the original ringer. It does happen, however, and even after ringing over 25,000 ducks I still make mistakes.

Discard the ring, it will not go on nicely again.

6. WING TABS

If you want to mark a duckling with legs too thin to ring, use a wing tab (fig. 19) like those used by poultry farmers. Do not use one on a duckling less than seven to ten days old because the end of the wing (fig. 19) is liable to go through the bow. Put the pin of the bow through the loose skin. Push bow down so that pin goes into slot and clamp slot tight.

I always cut off the tab—by cutting through pin (fig. 19) if I catch the

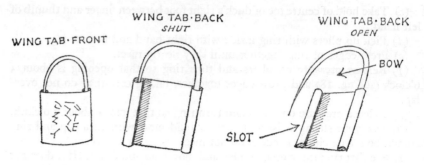

WING TAB·FRONT

WING TAB·BACK
SHUT

WING TAB·BACK
OPEN

BOW

SLOT

WING TAB IN
POSITION

LOOSE SKIN

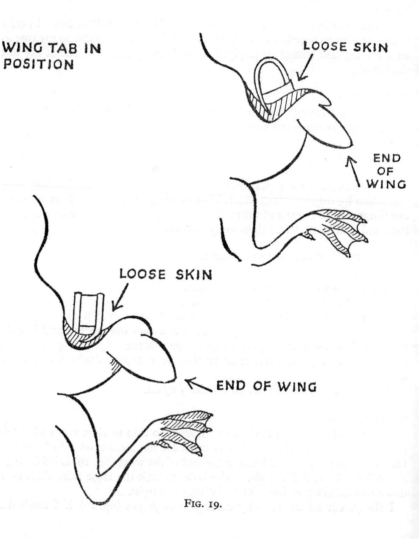

END
OF
WING

LOOSE SKIN

END OF WING

FIG. 19.

Plate 35. An area of sandy islands before planting

Plate 36. The same area three years later

Plate 37. Wildfowlers planting a reserve

Plate 38. A typical "loafing spot"

duckling later when it will take a ring. However, I have had several good returns of wing tabs alone from as far as Spain.

The diagram below shows the principle of the Abberton duck trap:

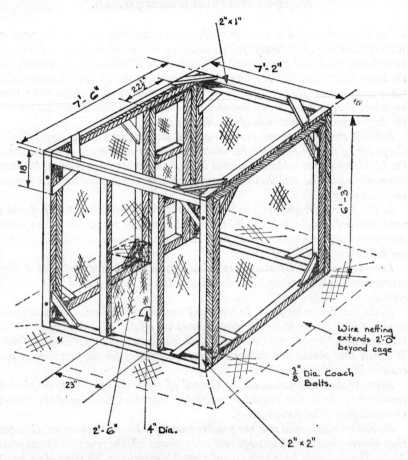

FIG. 20. *Design for a Duck Trap. The funnel is shown at the front centre, the door at the far left. Drawn by J. G. Tatham, Esq., from a design by Major-General C. B. Wainwright.*

Such cages of course cannot easily be moved, whereas those lacking wire-netting floors can quickly be moved to allow for big alterations in water levels.

The door, placed on the far end of the left side of the plan, is closed by bolts, one on each side, the inner one for use when the ringer is within catching the duck. A padlock may also be advisable.

G

EDITORS' POSTSCRIPT

Major-General Brian Wainwright, C.B.

Brian Wainwright died in October 1968, aged seventy-five, and with his passing, WAGBI lost one of its firmest friends and most influential supporters. He was a keen shooting man and President of the South Essex Wildfowlers' Association and the Essex Joint Council. For many years he served on the Wildfowl Conservation Committee of the Nature Conservancy and it was there, perhaps more than anywhere else, that his shrewd and sometimes outspoken comments earned for him the deep respect and gratitude of our Association.

Brian Wainwright started his distinguished service career in the Royal Flying Corps during the 1914–18 war, but entered the Royal Artillery soon after its end. On his retirement as a Major-General in 1948, he came to live close to Abberton Reservoir where he established a ringing station which was soon to become internationally famous.

In the April before he died, he ringed his 100,000th bird, almost half of which were wildfowl, caught in his well-known Abberton type traps. More than 9,000 duck recoveries have now resulted from his efforts, leading to a great increase in our knowledge of wildfowl biology.

Long before WAGBI started to release gadwall, he predicted that a high proportion would move overseas in winter. Events have proved him entirely correct.

In the year before his death, he successfully negotiated two outstanding achievements—for Abberton Reservoir was declared an official Bird Sanctuary and a lease was signed for Nacton Decoy in Suffolk to operate under the Wildfowl Trust. It is here that pintail and wigeon are now being ringed for the first time in this country in significant numbers.

Brian Wainwright served on the Council of the Wildfowl Trust, the ringing committee of the British Trust for Ornithology and was Chairman of the British Ornithologists' Club from 1962–5.

He always maintained that the poacher caused far less disturbance on Abberton than the trespassing bird-watcher and to be chased off the reservoir by the irate Major-General must have been an unforgettable experience. To those of us proud to call him friend, we shall always remember him as one of the kindest and most hospitable of people, bubbling over with enthusiasm and humour. He was a superb example of a dedicated amateur ornithologist, whose lasting achievements would do credit to the finest professional.

J.G.H.

CHAPTER 17

WAGBI DUCK TO SUPPLEMENT WILD POPULATIONS

by Jeffery Harrison, M.A., M.B.O.U., F.Z.S.(Sc.)

Vice-Chairman and Hon. Scientific Adviser, Wildfowlers' Association of Great Britain and Ireland; Vice-Chairman, Wildfowl Conservation Committee, Nature Conservancy; British Representative, International Wildfowl Research Bureau; Council, The Wildfowl Trust.

and John Wardell, M.B.O.U.

Chairman, Wildfowlers' Association of Great Britain and Ireland, 1967–70; Member, Wildfowl Conservation Committee, Nature Conservancy.

WAGBI's massive experimental release of hand-reared mallard to supplement the wild population started in 1954 with the liberation of the first 110 birds. By the end of 1968, this figure had risen to 108,626, all carrying WAGBI rings. The scheme was born out of the controversies over the *Protection of Birds Act 1954* and it was the first step in conservation to be taken by WAGBI. The basic idea was to encourage an interst in conservation in every wildfowler; to answer those critics who were constantly proclaiming that the wildfowler never attempted to replace any of his quarry and (possibly at that time last of all) to augment our native mallard population.

The scheme owed a great deal to the foresight of Ray Butt, a Fenland farmer and stauch WAGBI supporter, who has since been elevated to an Honorary Membership of the Association for his pioneering efforts and his perseverance, for in those days there were probably few, if any, naturalists who believed that achievements of any interest or practical value could possibly result from the scheme.

Such ringing results of hand-reared mallard as were available in this country at that time were hardly encouraging. These birds had been released on sporting estates where the land owners concerned not unnaturally looked for a direct recovery rate of up to 90 per cent as being a fair return for their money. In 1956, Hugh Boyd published his analysis of these early ringing experiments and having calculated that the mallard can maintain its numbers with a first-year mortality of 70 per cent he then found that the mortality of hand-reared birds was no less than 94 per cent.

Furthermore he reported that "British hand-reared mallard are extraordinarily sedentary. Forty-one of forty-six recoveries of hand-reared mallard marked at places within two miles of the coast were obtained where ringed. But 592 recoveries of hand-reared mallard released at places farther inland have included only two from the coast. The ringing stations involved have been spread over eleven counties, but none has been more than fifteen miles from the shore. Clearly, if wildfowlers are to benefit from the mallard they rear, the birds must be liberated very close to the place where it is intended that they should be shot."

It was in this rather depressing atmosphere that WAGBI embarked on its mallard release scheme. The first decision taken was to prove correct and vital. It was simply that so far as possible our birds should not be shot in their first year. Instead it was hoped to infiltrate them into the wild population and allow them to breed in the wild. In other words, the Association was not rearing directly for sport, but only indirectly, by increasing the wild population.

The idea quickly caught on and it was soon found that it was easy to encourage the wildfowler to rear a few mallard, often under a heater in his garden shed. The moment of conversion, so far as the wildfowler is concerned, comes, as in marriage, with the application of the ring! It is then that he realizes that his eight-week old "flapper" needs to be released in a place of safety, preferably a reserve well frequented by wild mallard, so that his bird can join them.

Logically, the conversion of the wildfowler into a wildfowler-conservationist follows and in human terms this has been the greatest achievement of the mallard-rearing scheme. The need for his club to manage a reserve, to improve it by planting suitable food and cover plants for his duck, leads to an appreciation of similar efforts by his local naturalists and so on up the scale to the chain of National Wildfowl Refuges established by the Nature Conservancy.

Similarly, the idea that some greedy flight-pond shooter might slaughter his duck in a most unsporting manner becomes abhorrent, as does the idea of shooting them when they are weak from hunger during prolonged spells of hard weather.

Let there be no misunderstanding therefore. Speaking conservationally, in human terms, the breakthrough in the wildfowler's education came from duck rearing. Even if the results from the ringing recoveries had only confirmed the early findings published by Hugh Boyd, this alone would have been well worth while. In fact the results have exceeded every expectation; the biological information now available has astonished us all—not only our early critics of those early days, but even the most optimistic of WAGBI supporters.

Release points must be carefully selected to provide as much natural duckling food as possible and adequate emergent shoreline vegetation for escape cover in which they can swim about freely. Ideally, these released duck may join broods of wild-bred duck, but in any case, they need to be large enough to care for themselves, which in practice means about seven weeks old, by which time the leg is large enough to carry the ring.

Hand-feeding after release must be minimal, otherwise the birds quickly become excessively tame. As Ray Butt wrote in 1956, "I am convinced that the only way [to prevent adult tameness] is for the birds to see humans as little as possible; the only person who should visit them regularly is the one who feeds them and he should frighten the life out of them every time he goes near them!"

The larger the release area and the more islands the better, so far as safety from predators is concerned. If pools smaller than half an acre are selected, these should if possible be fenced against ground predators. Excess food should never be left about for fear of attracting rats. With careful choice of release area the birds soon become acclimatized as there is no evidence of a high mortality after liberation.

In spite of the fact that the earlier ringing results had strongly discouraged the release of mallard at inland localities, WAGBI decided that this should be encouraged, if only because the mallard was, above all, the rough-shooter's duck and therefore it was correct to attempt to build up inland, as well as coastal populations. It is, perhaps, not inappropriate that the present long distance record recovery of a WAGBI mallard comes from an inland release point near Newmarket to finish its travels at Verkhayaya-Toyma in Russia, 1,800 miles east, just 300 miles short of the Asiatic border.

Such recoveries are exciting and a great stimulus in human terms, but the real purpose of ringing, of course, is to determine to what extent WAGBI mallard survive after release and how they infiltrate the wild population. Whereas the flight pond shooter may hope for a recovery rate of up to 90 per cent of the birds released, as we have seen the WAGBI policy of releasing on to reserves postulates a low return. Up to the end of the 1968 season, WAGBI recoveries stood at just under 7,500, amounting to some 7·6 per cent of all releases. Each season the rate has varied, the limits ranging between 6–9 per cent.

All recoveries have been analysed to determine the time interval since release; the distance from the release point and the method of recovery— shooting, found dead, killed, etc. The following figures, in which first year birds and adults have been differentiated, show the overall amount of movement, which is considerably more than the early ringing results suggested.

	1st Year	Adults
Local recoveries	88·5	78·7
Recoveries ten or more miles from release	10·5	14·4
Overseas recoveries	1·0	6·9
	100·0	100·0

The movement rate, like the recovery rate, has been found to vary season by season, and this can be shown to be related to the weather and harvesting conditions each autumn, which in turn effects the available food supply for mallard.

As one might expect, warm and dry conditions are associated with easy harvesting and early ploughing of the stubble. Under these conditions mallard tend to move away from their release areas in search of food and are at a greater risk of being shot. Conversely a wet autumn postulates a poor harvest, an abundant food supply for mallard and little tendency to wander in search of food. Thus, the autumns of 1961 and 1964, both drier than normal, resulted in first year recovery rates of 5·6 per cent and 4·1 per cent, and first year movement rates (more than ten miles from release point) of 16·8 per cent and 15·4 per cent respectively. For the wet autumns of 1960 and 1965, the recovery rates were 3·8 per cent and 3·8 per cent and the movement rates 6·4 per cent and 12·4 per cent.

As one might expect the movement away from the release areas is a gradual one, the August/September range having been calculated at 5–12 per cent, compared with 11–30 per cent in January/February.

In order to determine as precisely as possible the actual mortality occurring among WAGBI mallard, an assessment has been made using methods developed by Lack, Balham and Miers and others. This method makes the assumption that the sample taken, i.e. those rings recovered, mainly due to shooting, is relatively constant, and that the numbers reported annually from a given release year reasonably reflect the numbers that remain alive at that time and are therefore available to be recovered. Quite obviously shooting seasons vary, but by working on cumulative results these tend to average out.

TABLE I: MORTALITY RATE FOR WAGBI MALLARD

Year	Number released	Recoveries in years following release				
		One	Two	Three	Four	Five or more
1954	110	—	2	—	—	—
1955	403	11	1	—	—	—
1956	911	32	13	10	1	6
1957	1,311	48	24	5	3	7
1958	1,361	50	23	6	3	7
1959	3,413	199	52	29	13	13
1960	5,278	190	172	56	23	27
1961	7,268	398	110	46	16	17
1962	8,972	449	130	55	29	22
1963	10,219	463	125	58	30	23
1964	11,364	595	182	79	43	27
1965	13,328	677	182	112	59	
1966	12,891	827	364	80		
1967	14,959	432	142			
1968	16,838	593				
Total	108,626	4,964 of 108,626	1,522 of 91,788	536 of 76,829	220 of 63,938	149 of 50,610

	%	%	%	%	%	Total %
Rings recovered	4·6	1·7	0·7	0·3	0·3	7·6
Mortality	60·6	22·4	9·2	3·9	3·9	100·0
Cumulative Mortality	60·6	83·0	92·2	96·1	100·0	
Survivors	39·4	17·0	7·8	3·9		
Mortality rate p.a.	60·6	57·0	54·1	49.9		

There is little doubt that from a sample of 108,000 WAGBI releases and 7,400 recoveries, a reasonable assessment of the mortality actually occurring in the WAGBI population can be made.

Table I (Page 198), expresses deaths for each year as a percentage of the number of birds at risk—the survivors of previous years. This in turn enables us to calculate the mortality rate per cent per annum. Mortality rate has been defined as "the number dying in a given age interval divided by the number alive at the start of that interval". In the table it is arrived at by dividing the mortality percentage for the year by the survival percentage from the previous year.

TABLE IIA: OVERSEAS DISPERSALS
Release Areas

Country of recovery	N.W.	East Anglia Lincs.	S.E.	Midlands	N.E.	Scotland	West	South	Wales	Northern Ireland	Channel Isles	Total
Denmark	—	—	—	1	—	—	—	—	—	—	—	1
Germany	—	—	1	—	—	—	—	—	—	—	—	1
Holland	—	7	3	—	—	—	—	—	—	—	—	10
France	5	7	8	2	—	—	—	—	—	2	1	25
Eire	2	—	1	—	1	—	1	—	2	—	—	7
N. Ireland	1	—	—	—	—	—	—	—	—	—	—	1
Scotland	—	—	—	—	—	—	—	—	—	2	—	2
Isle of Man	1	—	—	—	—	—	—	—	—	—	—	1
Total	9	14	12	3	1	—	1	—	2	4	1	48
Rate per 1,000 releases	0.5	0.7	0.8	0.2	0.2	—	0.1	—	0.3	0.9	—	0.4

The mortality rates have been compared with published data for wild mallard stocks in Britain and elsewhere, which show a first-year range of 60–72 per cent and an adult range of 43–59 per cent. The low first year figure for WAGBI mallard is a deliberate result of our policy of releasing on to reserves which are not shot over, in order to increase the chances of survival over the first winter. Adult losses are within the range for wild stocks and the progressively lower figures for adults indicate that as WAGBI mallard gain experience, their chances of survival increase.

In the Mortality Table the mallard of five or more years old include sixty-seven recoveries of birds aged six to eleven years; clearly individual birds can survive for a very long time.

The question arises as to whether the mortality experienced by WAGBI mallard is such that they are able to maintain their numbers through annual productivity. A precise study of WAGBI mallard breeding in the wild has not been possible, but field work over a long period at the WAGBI-Wildfowl Trust Reserve and by certain clubs indicates results very similar to wild birds. In all, over 100 successful breeding pairs of hand-reared birds have been identified and recorded as yielding an average brood size of 7·4 juveniles per pair.

With first year mortality around 60 per cent, there will be approximately twenty breeding pairs available in the following spring and if these rear an average of five young, the original numbers will be restored. However, this is overstating the productivity required, as a proportion of each generation will survive to breed for several seasons and because of this, the assessment must be based on a weighted mean mortality rate covering the whole life span of each age group. For WAGBI birds this is 59·0 per cent. Balham and Miers have deduced a formula and have shown that for a population of 100 adults (50 pairs) the following relationship holds:

Young per pair required to maintain numbers $\left\{ \dfrac{\textit{Weighted mean mortality rate}}{50\,(1\text{ minus 1st yr. mortality rate})} \right.$

Applying this method to the WAGBI results, we arrive at a requirement of just under three juveniles per pair, which from the small amount of data available of actual breeding results in the wild, is believed to be well within their capacity, even allowing for the fact that not every pair will nest annually.

In analysing the movements of WAGBI hand-reared mallard, only those of

TABLE IIB: ABMIGRANTS

Country of recovery	N.W.	East Anglia Lincs.	S.E.	Midlands	N.E.	Scotland	West	South	Wales	Northern Ireland	Channel Isles	Total
Russia	—	5	—	1	1	—	—	—	—	—	—	7
Latvia	1	2	—	—	—	—	—	—	—	—	—	3
Poland	—	1	1	—	—	—	—	—	—	—	—	2
Rumania	—	—	1	—	—	—	—	—	—	—	—	1
Finland	—	5	—	—	1	—	—	—	—	—	—	6
Sweden	5	6	—	6	3	2	—	—	—	2	—	24
Norway	—	3	—	—	1	1	—	—	—	—	—	5
Denmark	10	8	1	2	1	3	1	—	—	—	—	26
Germany	4	4	1	1	4	—	1	1	1	1	—	18
Holland	5	15	14	4	4	—	1	1	—	—	—	44
Belgium	—	3	3	1	—	—	—	—	—	—	—	7
France	—	2	5	2	—	—	—	2	—	—	—	11
Eire	2	—	—	—	1	—	—	—	2	—	—	5
N. Ireland	2	—	1	—	—	1	1	—	—	—	—	5
Scotland	—	—	—	—	—	—	—	—	—	2	—	2
Isle of Man	1	—	—	—	—	—	—	—	—	—	—	1
Total	30	54	27	17	16	7	4	4	3	5	—	167
Rate per 1,000 releases	2·0	3·1	2·5	1·1	2·9	2·8	0·6	0·4	0·9	1·3	—	1·8
Overall rate per 1,000 releases Tables IIA & IIB	2·5	3·8	3·3	1·3	3·1	2·8	0·7	0·4	1·2	2·2	—	2·2

fifty miles and over have been included. These can be divided into five main categories:

(*a*) *Home dispersals*. (Fig. 21.) A dispersal flight has been defined by A. Hochbaum as an exploratory flight undertaken by a young bird in its first autumn and winter and made without the influence of migratory mallard. These flights are presumed to be of a random nature. This is confirmed by the 159 WAGBI home-dispersal recoveries set out in the form of an orientation chart, each recovery being plotted to the nearest $\frac{1}{16}$th of the compass bearing. In practice, all recoveries up to the end of February following release have been included as dispersals. There is a minimal bias between N.W. and N.N.W. with 18·2 per cent of recoveries (see also adult movements).

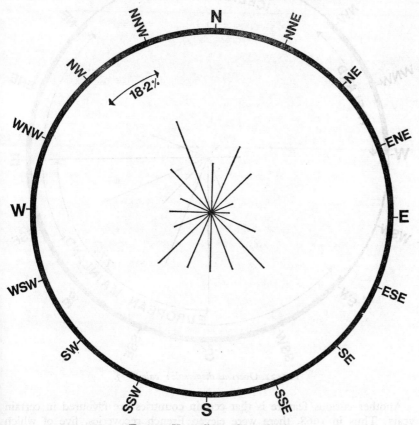

FIG. 21. *Home dispersals: scale 1/1.*

(*b*) *Overseas dispersals*. (Fig. 22; Table IIA.) This was the most unexpected feature to be revealed by the ringing of WAGBI mallard, for previously it was unknown for any young mallard to move overseas from this country in this way.

Table IIa lists the forty-eight overseas dispersals setting out release in relation to recovery areas. The remarkable orientation bias of these recoveries is shown on fig. 22, in which 77 per cent have moved between East and South, in complete contrast to the home dispersals on fig. 21. Overseas dispersals can obviously occur very soon after release. Two birds released by the South Lincolnshire WA on 12th May, 1961, were recovered in northern France on 14th July—the distressingly early opening day of the French wildfowling season.

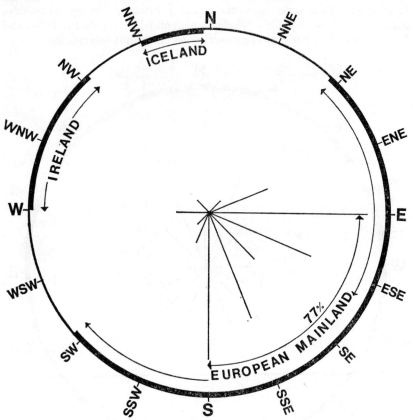

FIG. 22. *Overseas dispersals: scale* × *3.*

Another curious feature is that certain countries are favoured in certain years. Thus in 1968, there were eleven French recoveries, five of which originated in Lancashire, two in Norfolk and Kent and one in Essex and Lincolnshire. Six other French recoveries were reported in 1961, originating from Lincolnshire (4) Leicestershire (1) and Essex (1). In 1959, six recoveries came in from Holland, five from birds released in Lincolnshire and the other from Kent.

Possibly the weather may play an important role in determining these recoveries and certainly the autumn of 1968 was characterized by an exceptionally prevalent north-easterly wind, which might have led to a southward drift.

Undoubtedly some of these birds move abroad in company. The five Lancashire birds from France in 1968 were all released near Southport and both of the Norfolk birds were released at Ditchingham. Both of the Dutch recoveries (and the only German recovery) in 1967 originated from Tillingham, Essex, while the two French recoveries in 1966 were released at Killyleagh in Northern Ireland. Both were shot still in company at Abbeville on 25th December. The same fate befell two others released together at Ash, Kent, in June 1965 and shot in the Pas de Calais on 19th September.

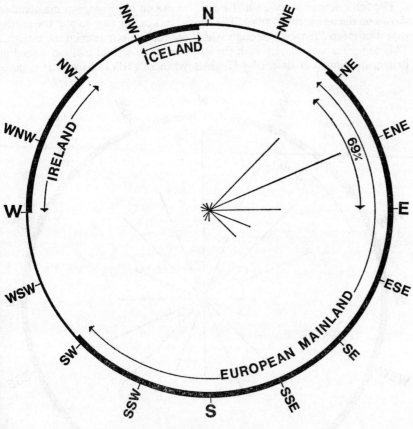

FIG. 23. *Abmigrants: scale* × ½.

(c) *Adult overseas dispersal.* This category had to be defined as the result of a most remarkable recovery, the chances of which must be infinitesimal. A duck mallard, WAGBI No. 32141 was known to have reared two broods successfully on Dr. C. K. Brown's land at Sandbach, Chesire in 1960 and

1961. On 28th July, 1961, it was last seen accompanying its well-grown brood. Only three days later, on 1st August, it was caught and released in a duck decoy in northern Holland, some 400 miles to the east. Possibly this was initiated by some underlying moult-migratory urge. Certainly there seems to be no reason to believe that it was influenced by any other migratory mallard, as in the next category.

(d) *Abmigrants*. (Table IIB and fig. 23.) The term abmigrant as used here is to denote an overseas recovery of a WAGBI hand-reared mallard after the end of the season following its release, the inference being that the majority have paired with wintering immigrant mallard from the European mainland and have returned with them to their country of origin.

The full range of WAGBI mallard recoveries on the European mainland is shown on the inside cover maps. The abmigrants can be seen to plot the north-west European "flyway" through which we receive our immigrant mallard. This compares very closely with the summer range of wild mallard ringed in Britain in winter, as shown by Hugh Boyd in an earlier chapter. It is clear

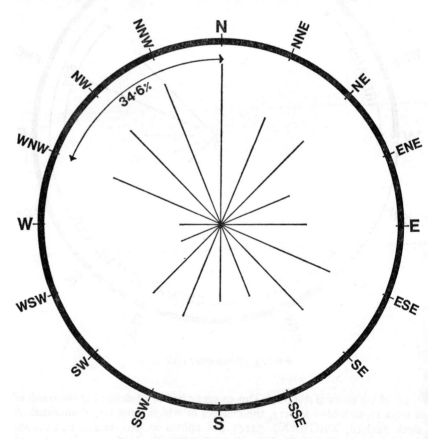

FIG. 24. *Adult home movements: scale × 2.*

that these WAGBI birds keep to the great north-west European plain and that the French central massif, the Alps and Carpathian mountain ranges form a barrier to south-east Europe. The one bird in south-east Europe, from Avrig on the Danube plain in Rumania, just north of the Bulgarian frontier, probably joined a Black Sea "flyway" from Russia, thus bypassing the Carpathians. It was released in Essex.

The two extensions into western France both owe their origin to the Arctic weather of 1963, but it is interesting to note that the first-year recoveries were the farthest south.

It is, of course, impossible to distinguish abmigrants from birds which may have left originally on overseas dispersal flights, but the remarkably different orientations as shown on figs. 22 and 23 must point to this being of little significance. On fig. 23 no less than 69 per cent are orientated between N.E. and E. The adult overseas recoveries from Ireland and the Isle of Man have been included in this category, although it is doubtful if they are true abmigrants.

There is a definite indication of a relationship between the release areas and the country of recovery. Thus, there is a preponderance of Danish recoveries from the north-west and of German recoveries from the north-west and north-east, while those from Holland and Belgium originate mainly from East Anglia and the south-east.

In Table IIB, abmigrant recoveries are expressed as a rate per 1,000 released. As expected, the highest rates are all from East Coast release areas. The low returns from the south and west reflect the relative lack of mallard

TABLE III: ORIENTATION DATA

Movement of 50 miles and over

Direction	Home Dispersals	Overseas Dispersals	Adult Overseas dispersals	Abmigrants	Adults in Britain
N.N.E.	14	—		3	10
N.E.	10	1		36	11
E.N.E.	4	4		54	7
E.	3	10		26	8
E.S.E.	8	7		17	11
S.E.	14	4		13	11
S.S.E.	11	7		2	7
S.	11	9		3	7
S.S.W.	11	2		—	9
S.W.	14	1		3	9
W.S.W.	7	—		2	4
W.	8	2	1	2	4
W.N.W.	6	—		2	11
N.W.	11	1		2	12
N.N.W.	18	—		2	14
N.	9	—		—	15
Total	159	48	1	167	150

movement through those areas, but in contrast, the comparatively high figure for the Midlands was quite unexpected.

There is a tendency for slightly more drakes than ducks to abmigrate. Thus of 75 sexed abmigrants, 57 per cent were drakes. This compares with 51 per cent drakes in a sample of 48,640 sexed at release between 1962–7, and 54·5 per cent drakes in 2,902 recoveries during the same period, showing a small bias towards drakes in the bag.

Hard Weather Dispersals   Jan.–Feb. 1963

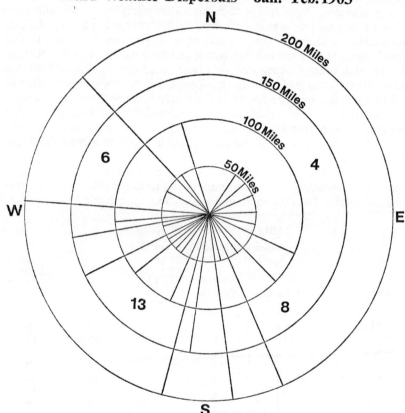

FIG. 25. *Hard weather dispersals Jan-Feb 1963.*

(*e*) *Adult movements in Britain.* The orientation chart (fig. 24) shows a slight bias between W.N.W. and N., with 34·6 per cent of recoveries. It is tempting to link this and the home dispersal findings with the inborn north-westerly "nonsense" orientation, which Dr. Geoffrey Matthews has demonstrated in several British populations on release, but he has also shown that this is lost after three or four miles flight. Nevertheless there are several inexplicable differences appearing in the orientation charts, which may become clearer in time.

Another encouraging feature about WAGBI mallard was their behaviour during the Arctic conditions which covered the British Isles from December 1962 to early March 1963. The combined rate for home and overseas dispersals of ten or more miles for January–February 1963 was 43·8 per cent compared with an average of only 18 per cent for January–February 1960–2.

Adult Hard Weather Movements Jan.-Feb.1963

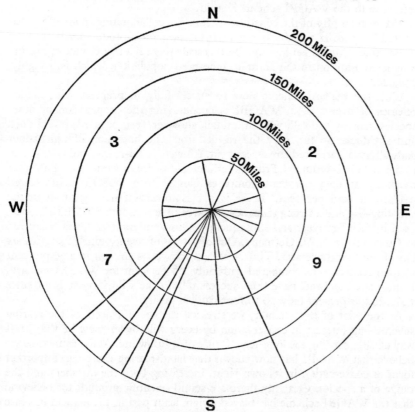

FIG. 26. *Adult hard weather movements Jan-Feb 1963*

Figs. 25 and 26 clearly demonstrate that there was a marked directional bias in first year birds between S.E. through W. to N.W., which in the adults was even more concentrated between S.E. and S.W. These results are in complete contrast to those illustrated in figs. 21 and 24 and clearly indicate that WAGBI mallard are capable of undertaking a weather migration, which must have contributed very materially to their survival. Included in this movement was the most southerly recovery of any mallard, wild or hand-reared, ringed in Britain; WAGBI No. 40432 released at Gumley, Leicester-shire and recovered at Rodez, Aveyron, France on 13th January 1963, 550 miles S.S.E.

Although shooting was stopped by WAGBI on a voluntary basis when the weather conditions became severe, the records of mallard found dead during the cold spell increased and recoveries in subsequent winters from this age group indicate that the mortality during this hard winter was somewhat higher than normal.

In conclusion, it is appropriate to quote from Dr. Geoffrey Matthew's lecture to the 5th Annual Game Seminar in Eire in February 1965, when in reference to the WAGBI scheme he said:

"More than fifty of the constituent clubs are collaborating in an effort that started by putting 100 ducks out in 1954; now their production is running nearer 10,000 ducks per annum. On this scale there is a real chance of making a national addition to the natural home-bred population, which is, roughly, 150,000."

With the mallard scheme now so successfully in progress with annual releases of over 15,000, WAGBI is encouraging the propagation of other species, namely gadwall, wigeon, pintail, shoveler, teal, pochard, tufted duck and shelduck. So far, only the results from the liberation of ninety-four gadwall have warranted any assessment. All were hand-reared and released on to the WAGBI-Wildfowl Trust experimental reserve in west Kent. First year mortality at 62·3 per cent compares closely with WAGBI hand-reared mallard at 60·6 per cent. There is a bias towards female gadwall in the shooting-bag and a strong tendency for birds to move southwards into France, both in their first year and subsequently. One abmigrant has been recovered at Cuxhaven in N.W. Germany. Out of a total of twenty-nine recoveries six have been found overseas. Thus, overseas recoveries amount to 20·6 per cent of total recoveries as compared with only 2·9 per cent for WAGBI mallard. Hand-reared gadwall have bred successfully in the wild in west Kent since 1967, but at present only up to four pairs annually.

At the start of this chapter, we stressed the social aspects of the rearing scheme—an interest in conservation by every wildfowler must be the surest way of safeguarding the long-term future of wildfowling. At the same time we believe that WAGBI has now shown that hand-rearing can be an important form of conservation in its own right, increasing both the numbers and the range of a species. Certainly there are sound scientific grounds for believing that the WAGBI scheme has played a significant part in the marked increase which has taken place in the British mallard population.

By ringing our birds, we add to the knowledge of the behaviour patterns of wildfowl, which in turn enables us to direct future conservation efforts to the best effect.

APPENDIX

Selected recoveries of WAGBI hand-reared duck other than mallard

Species	Release Data	Sex	Recovery Data
Gadwall	10.8.65 Sevenoaks, Kent	♂	15.10.65 La Rochelle, FRANCE
	18.8.66 Sevenoaks, Kent	♂	20.11.67 Dunkirk, FRANCE
	25.7.67 Sevenoaks, Kent	♂	25.10.67 Ault, FRANCE

Species	Release Data	Sex	Recovery Data
Gadwall	25.7.67 Sevenoaks, Kent	♂	4.12.67 Bretignolles-sur-Mer, FRANCE
	25.7.67 Sevenoaks, Kent	♀	14.7.68 Rue, FRANCE
	25.7.67 Sevenoaks, Kent	♀	15.8.68 Cuxhaven, GERMANY
	10.8.65 Sevenoaks, Kent	♂	7.11.65 Frome, Somerset
	18.8.66 Sevenoaks, Kent	♀	31.1.68 Amersham, Bucks.
	17.9.66 Sevenoaks, Kent	♂	1.1.67 Tollishunt D'Arcy, Essex
Pintail	–.7.66 Millom, Cumberland	?	–.1.67 Co. Galway, EIRE
	–.7.68 Millom, Cumberland	?	–.12.68 Slimbridge, Glos.
Wigeon	14.6.65 Holbeach, Lincs.	?	6.8.67 Worksop, Notts.
Shoveler	7.8.63 Spalding, Lincs.	♂	1.1.65 Penzance, Cornwall
Pochard	25.6.66 Sleaford, Lincs.	?	15.12.67 Sandringham, Norfolk
Tufted Duck	31.8.66 Stow-on-the-Wold, Glos.	♂	Autumn '67 Kaasa, FINLAND
	23.9.67 West Hampton, Worcs.	♂	14.10.69 Mellegard, DENMARK

REFERENCES

BALHAM, R. W. and MIERS, K. H. (1959). "Mortality and Survival of Grey Duck banded in New Zealand", *New Zealand Dept. of Int. Affairs, Publication No. 5.*

BOYD, H. (1956). "The use of hand-reared ducks for supplementing wild populations", *Wildfowl Trust, 8th A.R.*: 91–94.

BOYD, H. and HARRISON, J. G. (1962). "First autumn dispersal of hand-reared Mallard", *Wildfowl Trust, 13th A.R.*: 70–74.

HARRISON, J. G. and WARDELL, J. P. M. (1963). "Mortality and Survival of WAGBI hand-reared Mallard", *WAGBI A.R.*, 1962–3: 30–32.

HARRISON, J. G. and WARDELL, J. P. M. (1963). "WAGBI hand-reared Mallard in the cold spell of 1962–63", *Wildfowl Trust, 15th A.R.*: 33–37.

HARRISON, J. M., HARRISON, J. G., and HARRISON D. L. (1969). "Some preliminary results from the release of hand-reared Gadwall", *WAGBI A.R.*, 1968–9: 37–40.

HOCHBAUM, H. A. (1965). *Travels and Traditions of Waterfowl*, University of Minnesota.

MATTHEWS, G. V. T. (1961). " 'Nonsense' Orientation in the Mallard *Anas platyrhynchos* and its relation to experiments on bird navigation", *Ibis*, 103a: 211–30.

MATTHEWS, G. V. T. (1965). "Artificial propagation of Waterfowl", *WAGBI A.R.*, 1964–5: 73–75.

MATTHEWS, G. V. T. (1966). "Some parameters of 'nonsense' orientation in Mallard", *Wildfowl Trust, 18th A.R.*: 88–97.

REID, B. (1966). "Hand-reared Mallards in Southland", *New Zealand Dept. of Int. Affairs. Publication No. 86.*

WARDELL, J. P. M. (1967). "WAGBI hand-reared Mallard as abmigrants", *WAGBI A.R.*, 1966–7: 51–53.

CHAPTER 18

GOOSE CONSERVATION

by Jim Ellwood

Hon. Secretary, Goose Conservation Sub-Committee, WAGBI.

and John Ruxton

Chairman, Wildfowlers' Association of Great Britain and Ireland; Member, Wildfowl Conservation Committee, Nature Conservancy.

THE first major steps in wild goose conservation by wildfowlers were those taken by WAGBI in 1957. Prior to this, the Wildfowl Trust had undertaken the catching up of surplus Canada geese from private estates in England. The transporting of these birds has been largely the task of WAGBI. In 1957, however, the wildfowlers were asked to take over the complete operation.

The next few years were devoted to this redistribution and during this period the techniques of netting, transferring and releasing were evolved and improved upon. It quickly became obvious to those involved that there was a limit to the numbers of Canada geese which could successfully be redistributed.

The greylag goose now became the focus of the wildfowlers. Here was a wild goose which was native to the British Isles, in fact there were still a few hundred breeding pairs in Scotland. It had also been shown quite clearly by certain estate owners that provided suitable habitat was made available, it was quite possible to establish a feral flock.

WAGBI now commenced a rather more ambitious greylag scheme. This was an attempt to establish in new areas truly wild-breeding greylags, ranging over considerable distances and only returning to their release areas at infrequent intervals.

The netting of wild geese can be successfully carried out only by teams of experienced catchers. Late June or early July is the period, because the adults are flightless in full wing moult and the juveniles are still unable to fly.

It is impossible to be dogmatic about the technique of netting wild geese since this must vary according to the site. Basically the birds are driven from the water on to land and then herded towards a net previously erected at a suitable point.

A central catching pen is provided with a comparatively narrow entrance from which stretches a long guide net some sixty yards in length on both sides.

The netting must be four feet in height and sufficiently robust to withstand a large number of geese pressing against it. The whole driving operation is undertaken at a slow pace so as to minimize the alarm felt by the birds.

It is a fundamental error to permit any chasing or running down, if this involves more than a few seconds' time, otherwise exhaustion and subsequent death of the geese may well result. Juveniles particularly must not be over-heated in capturing them, to avoid the risk of pneumonia.

Any fairly large container type of vehicle can be used successfully for the transportation of wild geese, but the less enclosed the better. An open lorry or trailer with a net cover is well suited provided it is divided into a number of small compartments through which air can pass freely.

Segregation of adults and juveniles is important, as is isolation of any birds which in any way appear exhausted. An ample supply of dry litter on the floor of the containers is desirable. For travel by rail, a tea-chest with a hessian cover or netting top is excellent for two geese.

Experience has shown that the family unit is a vital part of the wild goose's make-up and great care must be taken to ensure that on release at their new home this balance is preserved. All release parties must have a few adults with each collection of goslings. The experienced older birds will greatly protect the juveniles during their settling-in period.

It should be noted that in the British Isles the capture of wild geese by methods similar to those described above is of course illegal, unless the persons concerned have previously been granted a formal licence to undertake this work by the Nature Conservancy.

It was in 1959 that WAGBI decided to extend its conservation activities to include the greylag goose, which was at that time restricted as a breeding species to small numbers in the Outer Hebrides and N.W. Scotland, but was formerly found breeding in much of Scotland, north and east England. In 1959 there were also a few feral flocks in Scotland and East Anglia.

The object with this species was to re-establish it as a wild breeding bird in some of its former haunts and elsewhere, where practicable. A small commit-tee, to be known as the Goose Conservation sub-Committee, was therefore formed by WAGBI to organize this project.

The initial problem was to find a source of greylag geese or goslings for introduction to suitable sites. One suggestion was that a number of wild greylags should be netted and placed in pens as breeding stock. However, this idea was abandoned on advice that it would probably be at least ten years before the captured migratory wild birds could be expected to breed.

The next idea was to obtain a supply of geese or goslings from one or more of the few feral flocks. In July 1959 a small catching team travelled to northern Scotland to catch some feral greylags, by the kind permission of the owner of a 63,000 acre estate, on which a flock had been established. This produced twenty-six, mostly young birds, which were left full-winged and released on three reserves, one in Lincolnshire and two in the southern Lake District. It was only possible to capture eleven birds on this estate in 1960, but a further seven goslings were donated by a Norfolk landowner, who was to contribute more to the scheme in the following years.

By 1963, a total of 171 birds had been captured as adults, or juveniles, from several feral flocks and transferred to twelve separate sites as far apart as Durham and Kent. However, by this time it was becoming increasingly difficult to catch birds from the two feral flocks in Scotland, on which our main supplies depended. It became all too obvious that the person who coined the phrase "a wild goose chase" had himself tried our tactics! The standard catching technique used by the team was the one described earlier for netting of wild geese. The flightless adults and juveniles had to be moved off large lochs towards the nets by a series of sweeps in boats. On the first occasion that this ploy was used on each particular flock, it was highly successful. On the second occasion, one year later, most of the flightless adults in the flock remembered the drill and refused to be herded, breaking back in the last few yards of the drive and diving under the boat, taking the goslings with them. The more one tried, the wilder they became. In each case, the third annual attempt was a non-starter for, as soon as the flightless adults heard the sound of the launching of the boat, they left the lochs and disappeared with all of the youngsters into the dense scrub, bracken and heather on the shores of the loch. On two occasions, the catching team would have returned from a long tiring journey, almost gooseless, had it not been for a canine member of the team which captured, unhurt, nineteen and twenty-five goslings respectively.

Since the continuing supply of goslings was essential for the success of our scheme and there were no more feral flocks at our disposal, a fresh approach had to be made to the problem. It was known to be an established fact that freshly laid goose eggs would not travel well, resulting in a poor hatch, with a proportion of deformed goslings. The Goose Conservation sub-Committee then decided to investigate the possibilities of moving partially incubated eggs long distances to the hatching point. This was first tried in 1964. Eggs were gathered, with the help of the headkeeper of a large estate in Scotland, the same gentleman who had laboured long and hard with the catching team the previous and other years. The eggs were kept warm by taking heated, insulated containers directly to the nests and keeping them warm throughout the long journey to the south Cumberland and Westmorland hatching and rearing points, where they were incubated, using both broodies and incubators. The result was an 87 per cent hatch, with almost the entire hatch reared. We were back in business. The resulting goslings were again distributed at six to seven weeks old to the various approved sites for release.

Each year, from 1965 to 1969, the WAGBI team collected partially incubated eggs from the same large feral flock in Scotland and brought them south for distribution to carefully selected sites for hatching, rearing, ringing and release. During this period, a number of goslings were also donated by kind owners of other feral flocks.

By the end of 1969, a total of 845 greylags, mostly juveniles, had been released into the wild through the efforts of WAGBI and a few affiliated Associations. It must be mentioned here that little could have been achieved without the co-operation of landowners, including the Forestry Commission and the National Trust, together with individual wildfowlers and the general public at large.

The first successful nesting of introduced greylags was on the WAGBI goose reserve on the Cumberland shore of the Duddon Estuary in 1961. In

1962, successful breeding was reported from reserves in Cumberland, Westmorland and Kent. At least three pairs nested for the first time and raised young in the wild, in the Lake District, in 1963. More successful breeding in the wild was reported from Kent and from several places in the Lake District in 1964. Twenty-two greylags left their wintering quarters at the South Cumberland Reserve in the spring of 1964. Sixty-four birds returned there in the following December. The Cumberland and Westmorland introductions prospered and by 1969 the greylag goose was again a soundly established breeding species in the English Lake District. Greylags were breeding in single pairs or small groups on many of the several hundred large and small waters of the Lakes area. The largest colony on the west side produced in excess of thirty nesting pairs. Eight nests, with a total of forty eggs, were present on a small half-acre island situated on a five-acre tarn. This flock now consists of more than 100 birds. During the winter of 1968, on one occasion, no less than 120 greylags were counted grazing on the saltmarshes that are part of this private estate. There are three main colonies in the northern lakes area with a combined total in excess of 200 birds. In the southern area of the Lake District, the combined wild stock, from introduced greylags is also in excess of 200 birds. In October 1969, 128 greylags flighted into the South Cumberland Reserve to feed at morning flight, where the first pair had nested in 1961.

By 1969, reports had also been received of greylags nesting in Cumberland, Lancashire, Westmorland and Yorkshire. Introduced greylags and their off-spring were also breeding in and around the WAGBI-Wildfowl Trust Reserve in Kent where fifty-seven were recorded in September and others, introduced by the Hull and East Riding Wildfowlers' Association, were nesting in the wild, with the land-owners' protection, in the East Riding of Yorkshire. With help and advice from WAGBI, the Strangford Lough Wildfowlers' Association has also assisted in re-establishing the greylag on Strangford Lough, Northern Ireland. Wildfowling clubs around the Lough have also agreed to shoot no greylags.

During the ten years that the WAGBI Goose Conservation team has been engaged on its reintroduction work, many lessons have been learned, some of them the hard way. Possibly the most important of these is that there are certain basic essentials necessary for the successful establishment of a nesting flock of truly wild greylags.

Several thousand acres of suitable terrain are required ideally, where the shooting of geese can be banned, completely, until breeding has taken place for several seasons, to allow the introduced birds to become soundly established. The area must contain some fairly large ponds, small tarns or a large lake with islands, where the birds can feel secure to nest and pass through the dangerous time when they are flightless from wing-moult. Whilst the banks or shores of any water should have a certain amount of cover, there must be a reasonable amount of open grass adjoining the water, where goslings can graze in safety until they are fledged. These basic essentials may be difficult to provide, but they are dictated by the geese. If greylags do not like the place where they are released, they will very quickly leave permanently. It is, therefore, a matter of common sense and simple economics, not to attempt introductions in situations where past experience has shown that the geese will not settle.

Predators have to be controlled in the introduction area. Fox predation can be a major problem. Not only do foxes take the sitting goose and the eggs, but unless the parents can get the goslings to water, soon after hatching, they will take the brood and possibly one or both of the parents, as they attempt to protect their offspring. Once the brood is on the water, they are reasonably safe from foxes, the parents bringing them ashore to graze and returning to the water, or an island to rest. This continues until the young are fledged. Another problem can be from large pike. We have seen a pike circling a young brood. The parent birds were swimming around the close-packed brood of four goslings, fiercely fending off each attack.

Crows frequently take the first egg laid in the nest, which is only rarely covered by the goose, causing the bird to desert the nest. There is a way of overcoming this problem if one can find the nest before the crow. When this happens, the first egg is substituted for a dummy attached to a short cord. If the crow then finds this and attempts to break it open, the egg may roll from the nest during the crow's efforts. The cord ensures that the dummy remains close enough to the nest for the goose to replace it. When the second egg is laid, the goose will cover the two with down and the dummy can then be safely replaced with the real egg.

The safest and most successful method of introduction is by the "release and feeding pen" system, as used on the WAGBI South Cumberland Reserve. For this method, the release pen must be sited close to or, better still, actually in the introduction area. The great advantage of this method over the "direct release into the wild" method being that the birds are hatched and reared in the pen, from which they are free to move out and find suitable breeding sites of their own, whilst using the security of the release pen for feeding and sanctuary until they do so.

The release pen in south Cumberland consists of $1\frac{1}{2}$ acres of wet land, flanked on one side by an oak wood. A triangular pond of just over half an acre was constructed in the pen by damming a depression and diverting a small stream as a feeder. The whole area was fenced with four-feet-high post and wire-netting fence, topped with a double strand electric fencing circuit, with fox flashers along the side near the wood. These electric wires along the top of the fence have proved to be the greatest possible deterrent to foxes, cats and dogs attempting to get over the fence. The release pen is situated in an area where no shooting is allowed. It is within one mile of the Duddon Estuary and saltmarshes over which the South Cumberland Wildfowlers' Association have held the sporting rights since 1952. Since the start of the greylag reintroductions, this Association, in common with the other Wildfowlers' Associations in the area, have banned the shooting of all species of wild geese, in order to give the introduced birds maximum protection. The pen is also within three miles, as the goose flies, from Coniston Lake. Many smaller tarns and large ponds are much nearer. From 1959 until 1965, goslings were hatched and reared in the pen, ringed when old enough and left full-winged. The pen is fed daily, throughout the year, with grain, the birds being free to come and go as they please.

From this site, birds have spread out to nest on various tarns, ponds and larger lakes, some near-by, others many miles distant. Some goslings have joined other flocks as they become established, but many return to the protection of the release pen to feed during the winter months. Each year, several pairs return to the pen with goslings hatched and reared in the wild in the Lake District. Our experience has been that, while the goslings hatched and reared at the release pen can, and often do, get very confiding, their offspring are not so confiding and birds of the second generation are completely wild and will not come near the pen when humans are around. They are, in fact, truly wild geese. Of the 128 greylags present in the autumn of 1969, only thirty-two birds had rings to indicate that they were introduced birds.

Similarly, in Kent, greylags on the WAGBI-Wildfowl Trust reserve have nested regularly on islands in a lake some miles away, but the parents have always brought their young back to winter on the reserve as soon as they can fly. A bigamous gander produced two broods here in 1967 and 1969.

With the success of the Lake District, Yorkshire and Kent colonization by greylags now reasonably assured, WAGBI intends to extend the scheme to other areas of the British Isles where experience indicates that success is practicable.

As yet, ringing results of WAGBI greylags have shown no traditional habits developing as Canada geese have done, in which birds from a population in N.E. England have been found to undertake a moult-migration to N.E. Scotland.

However, at least three greylags have "homed" from the Lake District to S.W. Scotland and another released in 1965 in the same area was shot in Co. Monaghan, Eire, in January 1966.

One WAGBI greylag, a juvenile captured at Loch Inch on 14th July, 1962, and released on the South Cumberland Reserve, was reported shot at Arnanes, Nesjapreppur, Iceland, on 20th April, 1967. This is the only known occasion on which one of the non-migratory British greylags has infiltrated the migratory Icelandic population.

In 1969, the WAGBI Goose Conservation sub-Committee extended their activities to include the breeding, rearing and release into the wild of barnacle, bean, European white-fronted and pink-footed geese. All of these species are now breeding in a WAGBI reserve and young of these birds have been ringed and released. Release areas are being carefully selected to infiltrate these species into the appropriate wild population.

CHAPTER 19

NATIONAL WILDFOWL REFUGES

by E. Max Nicholson, C.B.

Vice-President, Wildfowlers' Association of Great Britain and Ireland; Former Director-General, The Nature Conservancy; Past Vice-President, The Wildfowl Trust and the British Ornithologists' Union; Past Vice-Chairman, The British Ornithologists' Club.

To many people it is still a new and strange idea that wildfowlers and naturalists, including the keenest protectionists, belong not in opposite camps but on the same side. This outlook is especially odd because British sporting traditions, which have done so much to influence sportmanship all over the world, are deeply bound up with some of the highest ideals and many of the most practical techniques of conservation. Ever since the Middle Ages, game and particularly wild deer have been conserved in Royal Forests under strict laws and elaborate provisions for management in the interests of hunters. The abundant records make it clear how vigilantly not only the stocks of game but their habitats were conserved.

In contrast to a number of other countries in Europe and North America where game stocks have been depleted or wiped out because it was nobody's job to care for them, Great Britain has preserved a strong tradition through the successive generations of private landowners in favour of maintaining game habitats and conserving breeding stocks with the aid of a considerable force of gamekeepers, stalkers and other field staff.

The one great exception to this tradition has been on coastlines, estuaries and sheltered waters where growing fire power and mobility together with increased disturbance and loss of breeding and resting grounds have been making it more and more difficult to reconcile the old free-for-all approach with the maintenance of stocks and the enjoyment of the sport of wildfowling. In the absence of responsible guidance and forbearance, a relatively small number of unsportsmanlike shooters have demonstrated that they can make conditions unpleasant or at times even intolerable for others and can give rise to abuses which harm the good name of wildfowling and in turn, encourage extremist proposals for limiting shooting or stopping it altogether.

Although for a quarter of a century before the *Protection of Birds Act 1954* much valuable preliminary survey work and discussion had been going on with the support of both naturalists and wildfowlers, the discussions in Parliament and in the Press at the time of this Act revealed a horrifying state of ignorance, confusion, suspicion and emotion on which all of us must look back with shame. On the other hand, wildfowlers, naturalists and conservationists in Great Britain are entitled to feel pride in the record of the past fourteen years firmly suppressing the resentments and enmities which had inevitably been stirred up. Leading wildfowlers and leading naturalists got together in 1955 under the auspices of the Nature Conservancy to probe fearlessly and thoroughly into the causes of an almost intolerable situation.

Several points soon became clear. First, there could be no real progress while the elementary facts about wildfowl numbers and trends were in dispute and therefore it was necessary not only further to develop wildfowl counts and many other investigations but to place the responsible representatives of the wildfowlers in a position to criticize, participate in and vouch for the results, so that in due course it should become the exception rather than the rule for the facts about wildfowl in any area under discussion to be in dispute. Secondly, the somewhat conspiratorial atmosphere in which many wildfowlers felt that plots for closing areas to wildfowling were being hatched by various groups up and down the country should be replaced by open discussion of each project of mutual interest from its earliest stages. Thirdly, and following from this, wildfowlers like other sportsmen should accept the fundamental principle of conservation of habitats and stocks essential to the permanent welfare of their sport, while the protectionists on their side should accept the legitimacy of wildfowling when carried out in a sportsmanlike manner and in accordance with the law of the land and the principles of conservation. Fourthly, in order to replace vague and emotional generalities by a body of tested fact, large-scale practical experiments in selected areas should be initiated in order to demonstrate just how amicable and successful co-existence could be achieved between wildfowling and managements of wildfowl refuges.

The realization of these objectives bristled with difficulties, scientific and technical, administrative and legal, financial and above all, psychological. That they have been so triumphantly surmounted is due to a number of factors high among which comes the great good fortune that in the Wildfowl Trust, brilliantly guided by Peter Scott, and in WAGBI, wisely and courageously led by a group of men to whom all sportsmen and also all naturalists should be grateful, there were the necessary minimum size and quality of team to carry through keenly, practically and consecutively agreements and projects endorsed by the informal tea-parties which took place at the Nature Conservancy.

Although these tea-parties have been formalized since 1960 as the Wildfowl Conservation Committee with an official term of reference "to consider all matters affecting wildfowl, in particular the establishment of a national system of Wildfowl Refuges and to advise the Nature Conservancy accordingly", I hope I may be permitted to express a sense of nostalgia for what is now past. There seems something agreeably English in resorting to tea-parties to bring about, with complete success, a peaceful revolution through a meeting of minds when several eminent Committees and the combined efforts of both Houses of Parliament had failed to produce a workable means for naturalists and wildfowlers to get along together.

As the host at these parties I look back with pleasure not only on what they achieved but on the satisfaction of the gradual dawning on all of us that people whose personalities, views and activities had in imagination promised to be most uncongenial could discover not only a common interest but many grounds for mutual respect and friendship, without abandoning any of their loyalties.

Another thing that has been impressive is how devotedly and effectively wildfowlers work for what they believe in, and the inconveniences and sacrifices they are ready to accept with cheerfulness. If all the groups concerned in conservation pulled their weight as well as the wildfowlers, conservation would be very much more advanced than it yet is.

Following the transfer to the Wildfowl Trust of responsibility for the national wildfowl counts, means were found of bringing WAGBI into more intimate contact with them. Thanks to the energy of the National Organizer Mr. George Atkinson-Willes and his many collaborators, we are now in possession of a wealth of information which is constantly being added to and which greatly facilitates informed discussion and planning.

In the case of projects for sanctuaries, refuges and nature reserves, misunderstandings have occurred from time to time but, apart from the earliest ones, they have been of a local character and have been resolved without undue difficulty. It has also been generally accepted by responsible wildfowlers that the future of their sport demands conservation of habitats and stocks, and conversely by naturalists that wildfowling in itself is a legitimate activity which it is no part of the aims of conservationists to oppose in principle.

It seems worth dealing a little more fully with the fourth point since the large-scale practical experiments in selected areas have proved strikingly successful not only in obtaining practical knowledge of wildfowl conservation and refuge management, but also in enabling both wildfowlers and naturalists to reconsider preconceived views about the possibilities of reconciling bird protection with sport.

The first of these experiments was on the Humber, which many naturalists feared was in danger, some fifteen years ago, of becoming a "burnt out" estuary from which the regular wildfowl stocks would be permanently driven away by excessive disturbance, as had happened already in several other places.

Following a great deal of preparatory work by the wildfowlers' representatives, some leading local naturalists and the Nature Conservancy, a meeting was held on Saturday, 15th January, 1955, at the offices of the Humber Conservancy Board at which it was agreed to adopt as basic assumptions that the maintenance and, if possible, increase of stocks of wildfowl and waders of all kinds on the Humber are in the interests of all concerned and in the national interest; that any divergences between the various parties concerned should not prove an obstacle to a comprehensive agreed scheme meeting their various objects and needs on a basis of recognition of the existence of the different interests; that there must be provision for regular fact-finding discussion and reconciliation of difficulties; that in addition to control of numbers shot and methods of shooting there should be provision for discouraging disturbance and attracting wildfowl; that the Nature Conservancy should be responsible for securing legal sanction to any scheme which might be agreed. It was agreed that the primary question was the conservation of stocks of pink-footed geese and that adequate measures for this purpose would incidentally provide the necessary protection for other species.

After thorough discussion, it was agreed that steps should be taken to set up by Order under the *Protection of Birds Act 1954*, a Humber Wildfowl Refuge covering the tidal Humber below the line from Faxfleet Ness Beacon to Trent Falls and west of a line drawn from Brough Haven to Whitton Ness Beacon, excluding an area stretching 100 yards below the bank or any patches of shore vegetation growing outside it. A full-time warden would be provided during the shooting season by the Nature Conservancy and would act under the supervision of a local joint Committee consisting of two representatives each from the Hull and East Riding Wildfowlers' Association, the Holderness and Humber Wildfowlers' Association, the Lincolnshire Naturalists' Trust, the North Lincolnshire Wildfowlers' Club, the Yorkshire Naturalists' Trust and the Yorkshire Naturalists' Union.

The Press, which had previously been supplied with only an alarmist forecast, awaited a promised statement of the results of the meeting, and it was comic to observe their disappointment on being informed that unanimous agreement had been reached on proposals for the future conservation of wildfowl in the Humber area. They had counted confidently on something more newsworthy in the way of a public row.

A warden for the new Reserve was appointed in the autumn and was in attendance at a meeting of the Humber Wildfowl Refuge Committee in Hull on the 1st October, at which also it was reported that the Home Secretary was about to sign an Order under Section 3 of the *Protection of Birds Act, 1954*, prohibiting the killing or taking of any birds from 1st September to 20th February inclusive within the area covered by the Refuge. Mr. Trevor Field, J.P., of the Hull and East Riding Wildfowlers' Association, was elected Chairman and Mr. Frank Mason, Honorary Secretary. The Refuge, covering some 3,130 acres, thus came into operation under local control and although originally envisaged as an experiment, it proved so successful that by common consent it is being continued indefinitely.

With so many variables to be considered, it is never possible accurately to trace cause and effect in trends of numbers of protected species following the creation of a Refuge, but there is no question that the numbers and stability of wintering populations of wildfowl on the Humber since the Refuge began have proved satisfactory to all and that the fears previously felt of a catastrophic decline in wildfowl numbers or of an inacceptable interference with wildfowling have been entirely set at rest. Almost the only departure from the original plan has been a waiving of the originally agreed rotation of the chairmanship, which has with the approval of all continued to be discharged by Mr. Trevor Field. Several offenders against the Sanctuary Order have been successfully prosecuted, the police and the warden being assisted in their duties by local wildfowlers. Much valuable experience on refuge management has been gained and the success achieved on the Humber has had a profound influence throughout the country.

At Southport in Lancashire a public controversy between naturalists and wildfowlers over a previously existing local sanctuary led to discussions on a

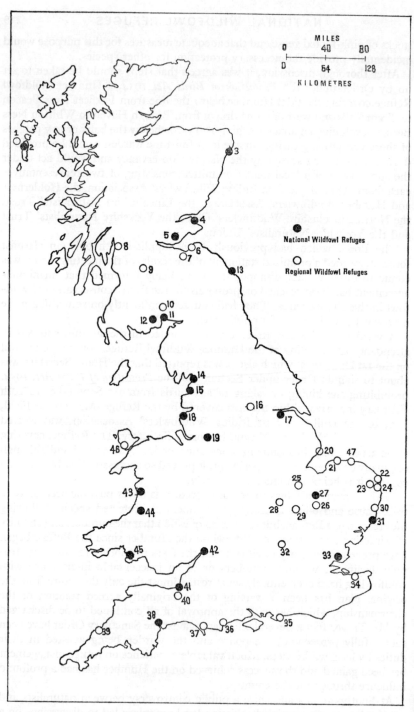

MILES

0   40   80

0   64   128

KILOMETRES

● National Wildfowl Refuges

○ Regional Wildfowl Refuges

FIG. 27.

KEY TO THE MAP OF WILDFOWL REFUGES

A. National Refuges in ENGAND AND WALES

Name	Status	Main Interest
33. Abberton Reservoir, Essex	Statutory Sanctuary	Teal, Mallard, Pochard
43. Borth Bog and Dovey Estuary, Cards.	National Nature Reserve	Greenland Whitefront, Duck
41. Bridgwater Bay, Som.	National Nature Reserve	Moulting Shelduck
44. Cors Tregaron, Cards.	National Nature Reserve	Greenland Whitefront
38. Exe Estuary, Devon	Statutory Sanctuary	Brent, Mallard, Merganser
17. Humber, Yorks and Lincs.	Statutory Sanctuary	Pinkfeet, Duck
14. Leighton Moss, Lancs.	RSPB Reserve	Duck
13. Lindisfarne, Northumberland	National Nature Reserve	Pale-bellied Brent, Whooper, Duck
27. Ouse Washes, Cambs.	RSPB, Wildfowl Trust and Naturalists' Trust Reserve	Duck, Bewick's
31. Orfordness-Havergate, Suffolk	National Nature Reserve	Duck
19. Rostherne Mere, Cheshire	National Nature Reserve	Duck
42. Slimbridge, Glos.	Wildfowl Trust Reserve	Whitefronts, Bewicks', Duck
18. Southport, Lancs.	Statutory Sanctuary	Pinkfeet
45. Whiteford—Burry Estuary, Glam.	National Nature Reserve	Pintail, Wigeon, Brent
15. Wyre—Lune, Lancs.	Statutory Sanctuary	Pinkfeet

B. Regional Refuges in ENGLAND AND WALES

Name	Status	Main Interest
25. Borough Fen Decoy, Northants.	Wildfowl Trust Reserve	Duck
24. Breydon Water, Norfolk	Local Nature Reserve	Russian Whitefront, Bewick's, Duck
36. Brownsea Island and Littlesea, Dorset	Statutory Sanctuary and National Nature Reserve	Dabbling Ducks
23. Bure Marshes, Norfolk	National Nature Reserve	Breeding Wildfowl
47. Cley Marshes, Norfolk	Naturalists' Trust Reserve	Breeding and wintering duck
40. Durleigh Reservoir, Som.	Statutory Sanctuary	Duck
16. Fairburn Ings, Yorks.	Local Nature Reserve	Duck
29. Grafham Water, Hunts. (part)	Naturalist's Trust Reserve	Duck
20. Gibraltar Point, Lincs.	Local Nature Reserve and Statutory Sanctuary	Pinkfeet, Duck
22. Hickling Broad, Norfolk	National Nature Reserve	Duck
30. Minsmere, Suffolk	RSPB Reserve	Duck
46. Newborough Warren, Anglesey	National Nature Reserve	Duck
35. Pagham Harbour, Sussex	Local Nature Reserve	Duck, Brent
28. Pitsford Reservoir, Northants.	Naturalists' Trust Reserve	Duck
37. Radipole Lake, Dorset	Statutory Sanctuary	Duck
21. Scolt Head, Norfolk	National Nature Reserve	Brent
34. Stodmarsh, Kent	National Nature Reserve	Duck
32. Tring Reservoirs, Herts.	National Nature Reserve	Duck
39. Walmesley Sanctuary, Cornwall	Statutory Sanctuary	Russian Whitefront, Duck
26. Wickden Sedge Fen, Cambs.	Statutory Sanctuary	Duck

A. National Refuges, SCOTLAND

Name	Status	Main Interest
11. Caerlaverock, Dumfries.	National Nature Reserve	Barnacle, Pinkfeet and Greylag
2. Loch Druidibeg, Inverness	National Nature Reserve	Greylag breeding area
5. Loch Leven, Kinross	National Nature Reserve	Pinkfeet, Greylag, Duck
3. Sands of Forvie, Aberdeenshire	National Nature Reserve	Eiders breeding
4. Tentsmuir Point, Fife.	National Nature Reserve	Pinkfeet, Eider
12. Threave Marshes, Kircudbright	National Trust Reserve	Bean, Greylag, Greenland Whitefront

B. Regional Refuges, SCOTLAND

Name	Status	Main Interest
6. Aberlady Bay, East Lothian	Local Nature Reserve	Pinkfeet
10. Castle and Hightae Lochs, Dumfries.	Local Nature Reserve	Greylag, Duck
7. Duddingston Loch, Midlothian	Royal Parks Sanctuary	Pochard
9. Hamilton Low Parks, Lanarks.	Statutory Sanctuary	Duck, Greylag, Whooper
8. Loch Lomond (Endrick Mouth), Stirling	National Nature Reserve	Greylag, Duck
1. Monach Isles, Inverness.	National Nature Reserve	Barnacle

national level and the making of agreed recommendations to the Home Secretary who, having consulted his Advisory Committee and given public notice of proposed changes, made a new Order from 1st June, 1956, covering an area of approximately 14,300 acres and giving full protection to the goose roost north-west of the Southport Pier. As this area is part of the foreshore of a major seaside resort, there is no control of access as there is on the Humber. Reports from WAGBI showed that the provisions of the Sanctuary Order were being violated and, at their request, the Nature Conservancy therefore assisted the preparation of a scheme, similar to that on the Humber, for ensuring the effectiveness of the Order.

Unfortunately, in the early days of the sanctuary the local police could not be persuaded to take an effective interest in enforcement. A Sanctuary Committee under the Chairmanship of Mr. R. Wagstaff, an eminent ornithologist and Keeper of Vertebrate Zoology at Liverpool Museum, came into existence in 1958 and undertook a publicity campaign as well as appointing a team of honorary wardens. Unfortunately, however, these efforts met with only limited success and it therefore proved necessary to appoint a full-time paid warden. While difficulties were to be expected in this highly populous and accessible area, it was disappointing that the local authorities should not have been able to be more helpful in enforcing the law of the land within the County Borough and that so much national effort and devoted work by volunteer naturalists and wildfowlers should have been required to achieve what should have been an elementary level of conservation. Undaunted by this initial local official indifference, the Sanctuary Committee pressed ahead with control based on education and co-operation between the warden and local wildfowlers and naturalists. Over the years, from 1960 onwards, the Sanctuary has become more and more effectively controlled until today the Southport area is the most important wintering ground in England for pink-footed geese.

While the Humber and Southport Refuges were covered by Statutory Orders under the *Protection of Birds Act, 1954*, a different approach was adopted at the Caerlaverock National Nature Reserve on the Solway in Dumfriesshire which was declared by the Nature Conservancy under the *National Parks and Access to the Countryside Act, 1949*. The Solway has long been one of Britain's most important and favoured wildfowling haunts, being visited by shooting men from almost every county in the country. During the war, the construction of a military road afforded an unwelcome degree of access and during the immediate post-war years a number of would-be wildfowlers, many of them quite inexperienced and unacquainted with sportsmanship, were proving too much for the birds and were incidentally ruining everyone's sport as well as causing great anxiety and trouble for the owner of the fringing land, the Duke of Norfolk. The area had been proposed on several grounds as a National Nature Reserve before the Conservancy came into existence and the Duke of Norfolk offered to sign a Nature Reserve Agreement in respect of the long tract of merse or saltings within his ownership.

At the same time, WAGBI had proposed the creation of a Refuge on

Humber lines to protect the roosting geese out on the mud of Blackshaw Bank and these various proposals were combined in a draft scheme for a Nature Reserve which was discussed nationally in 1954 and after considerable delays owing to a number of legal and other snags was laid before a meeting presided over by the Lord Lieutenant of Dumfriesshire in March 1957 at Dumfries. In addition to the Nature Conservancy and the County and Town Councils, WAGBI and the Cumberland and Dumfriesshire Wildfowlers' Association, the Dumfries Natural History and Antiquarian Society, Solway River Purification Board, the Net Salmon Fisheries District Board, the Haaf Net Fishers and other interests, including the Department of Agriculture for Scotland were represented.

The Conservancy explained that they had completed negotiations with the owners for a Reserve of some 6,200 acres, about 1,420 of which were merse, which included only a very small part of the public shooting available in the district. Part of the merse would be available for shooting by the owner and part in the centre by the courtesy of the owner would be open to shooting by the public on a permit system, while the eastern part would be a total sanctuary together with all the foreshore. By-laws would be made for the area. Considerable discussion followed and certain aspects of the scheme were strongly opposed. The Conservancy agreed to follow up the suggestions and criticisms made in direct talks with local wildfowlers and other interests. This was done at a further meeting in April at which it was finally agreed that a three-man panel consisting of a representative of the Nature Conservancy, a representative of WAGBI and the Duke of Norfolk's representative, should be set up to supervise the issue of permits and to watch the working of the scheme.

The Caerlaverock Reserve was declared accordingly and by-laws confirmed for it in 1957 and a resident warden was appointed. In 1959 his work was assisted by the provision of a strategically placed watchtower. In the first two wildfowling seasons, 1957–8 and 1958–9, over 850 applications for shooting permits were made by about 600 individual wildfowlers of whom about eighty were living close to the Reserve. Comments from permit holders were most favourable, and only a very few persons showed themselves unwilling to co-operate with the necessary regulations. During the first three seasons, permit holders killed each year an average of 275 geese, mostly greylag and pink-footed geese, on the permitted shooting area. There was, of course, no shooting of barnacle geese whose numbers have risen most satisfactorily while their feeding habits strongly suggest that they fully appreciate the freedom, provided by the sanctuary area of the Reserve, from disturbance not only by shooters but from over-zealous bird-watchers, who are equally finding that the warden is very quickly on their track if they inconsiderately invade the quiet which the geese need. In August 1960 the Northumberland and Durham Wildfowlers' Association drew the attention of the Nature Conservancy to the great increase in uncontrolled and often indiscriminate shooting in the Holy Island area and asked that consideration should be given to the establishment there of a Wildfowl Refuge. Early in 1961 and quite independently of the wildfowlers, a request was made by the local naturalists that, to offset the increasing disturbance to wildfowl and seabirds caused by irresponsible shooters, a Nature Reserve be set up which should include Holy Island, the neighbouring inshore flats and parts of the mainland shore.

Following discussions with the wildfowlers, naturalists and local land-owners, it was decided that the Nature Conservancy should combine these proposals by establishing a National Nature Reserve and National Wildfowl Refuge. The Reserve, named Lindisfarne, was declared in 1964. Its management programme provides for the traditional sport of wildfowling to continue over part of the area where shooting is controlled by a permit system. The remaining parts of the Reserve are sanctuary zones, where no shooting is allowed.

To advise the Nature Conservancy on matters relating to the conservation of wildfowl in the Reserve, a panel, representing the local wildfowlers, WAGBI, and the local naturalists, was set up, its first chairman being Mr. Frank Stabler, who had played such a large part in bringing about the creation of the Reserve. Following Mr. Stabler's death in 1967, he was succeeded by Mr. Robin Donally of the Nature Conservancy's staff, who has a considerable knowledge of wildfowling and who also had much to do with the negotiations leading up to the establishment of the Lindisfarne Reserve and Refuge.

In 1965, the Humber Wildfowl Refuge Committee, with the support of the local wildfowlers' associations and the Nature Conservancy, brought into being a shooting-by-permit scheme over an area on the north bank of the Humber, adjoining the Refuge, in order to provide additional protection to the main roosting ground. So successful has this proved, in regulating the wildfowling use of the area for the benefit of all concerned, that the scheme was extended in 1969. What was introduced on an experimental basis may become a permanent management feature of the Refuge.

It is on the basis of experience gained in these and in other Refuges established more recently that plans are now proceeding with much more confidence for the provision of a national system of wildfowl refuges, coupled in suitable cases with provision for controlled shooting areas, now that the soundness of this approach has been demonstrated and that the dangers of loss of habitat through disturbance and development must be clear to all. It is to be hoped that wildfowlers and naturalists in their common interests will lend wholehearted support to their own representatives and to the Nature Conservancy in following up, while there is still time, the promising start which has been made.

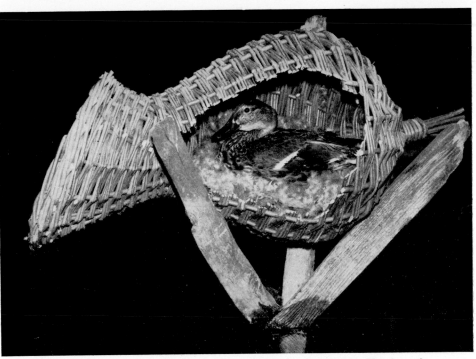

Plate 39. Duck nesting basket—bird mounted by Dr. James Harrison for exhibition purposes—with the side of the basket cut away

Plate 40. Mallard taken into captivity and rearing their own ducklings

Plate 41. Captive wild mink

Plate 42. Wild mink skins from animals trapped in Britain

CHAPTER 20

LOCAL RESERVES

by James Harrison, D.S.C., M.B.O.U., F.Z.S.(Sc.), M.R.C.S., L.R.C.P.

Vice-President, Wildfowlers' Association of Great Britain and Ireland. Past Vice-President, British Ornithologists Union and Past Chairman, British Ornithologists' Club.

and Jeffery Harrison, M.A., M.B.O.U., F.Z.S.(Sc.)

Vice-Chairman and Hon. Scientific Adviser, Wildfowlers' Association of Great Britain and Ireland. Vice-Chairman, Wildfowl Conservation Committee, Nature Conservancy; British Representative, International Wildfowl Research Bureau; Council, The Wildfowl Trust.

IT is WAGBI policy that each of its affiliated clubs should ultimately come to manage its own local reserve, on which to carry out a full programme of conservation. Clubs are also encouraged to co-operate with any other naturalist organization in similar enterprises.

Such reserves are unlikely to be large enough to support controlled wild-fowling, as on some of the much larger National Nature Reserves. A prime requirement therefore is freedom from disturbance and shelter from the elements. Access by the public needs to be controlled and these reserves are usually managed by a gentleman's agreement with the owner. They serve as an excellent public relations image and conducted parties should be encouraged and observation hides constructed where suitable. Size is not necessarily of great importance, whereas habitat is. An excellent example is the 1½-acre pool of WAGBI's decoy at Boarstall, which is beautifully secluded in the decoy wood and at times holds up to 500 duck.

WAGBI keeps a register of all local reserves, which records the essentials for a management plan—namely a description of the reserve and its wildfowl, also of any other birds of interest using the area. Details are included of habitat improvement, any wildfowl which may be released and of liaison with other interested organizations. For some of the bigger reserves, wardening and financial details are kept and progress reports issued.

The variety of places which can be managed as local reserves is far wider than may be realized. Gravel and clay pits, natural ponds and lakes, streams, rivers, bogs and saltings can all be utilized—even the moat of a ruined castle!

A local reserve must provide for the four main necessities of wildfowl if it is to play its full part in building up a large population of wildfowl in the vicinity. It must serve as a nesting and midsummer moulting area, as a winter roost and as a natural feeding area throughout the year.

H

It was to study these requirements that in 1956 we were granted management facilities on behalf of WAGBI for a working gravel-pit in West Kent. Three years later we were joined in this venture by the Wildfowl Trust and it is the lessons and achievements of this reserve which will be drawn on to illustrate the main principles of reserve management.

Dealing in turn with these four main necessities, all have their own special requirements. So far as nesting is concerned, it was Al Hochbaum at the Delta Waterfowl Station in Canada who first demonstrated that a pair of duck take up and defend a length of shore-line as a nesting territory. It follows that the longer the shore, the more pairs that water will hold. However, the size of the territory depends upon how far the duck can see. One pair will be content with a small but secluded bay, whereas the male will defend a much longer length of straight shore.

Thus several females may nest in close proximity in the same cover, which may be some way from the water. It is only when they return to their mates by the shore that their territorial requirements must be maintained.

From this, it follows that to increase the number of nesting pairs, a water should be either enlarged (which is often impossible in these over-populated islands, or brings in competition from water sports) or made as irregularly shaped as possible, by leaving (or creating) islands, spits and bays.

In deep water gravel-pits, leaving islands unexcavated can be highly expensive. On the experimental reserve, a natural island approximately 15 × 8 yards, is supported on an underwater cone of gravel valued at £800. On more recent shallow lakes, however, it has proved quite easy to use the topsoil to create a number of islands while the lakes were being excavated.

Ideally, islands should provide sloping banks to make it easy for fowl to walk up from the water. If shaped like a cross or a horseshoe, there is almost always a bay sheltered from the weather. Short, thick nesting cover should be provided by bramble or harsh rush, while on one side alder, birch or oak can be planted against the prevailing winds (and to provide food seeds). Islands of course are fox-proof in most cases.

Artificial raft islands can be anchored in deep water. On the experimental reserve these are of two types. The first consists of three float tanks welded together to form a 6 × 6 foot raft with about a foot of freeboard. A raised edge is formed by poles welded to the tanks to retain the top soil. The second consists of a float tank at each end with railway sleepers in between, all welded to a metal frame, forming a 6 × 12 foot raft. Such rafts will stand up to the worst winter storms. The float tanks are popular with nesting geese, while great crested grebes nest annually on the sleepers. In winter, they are frequently packed with day-roosting duck.

Another way of increasing the nesting potential is by the provision of spits. If these can be left by the drag line, when, for instance, a gravel-pit is being worked, so much the better. On the reserve this was not always possible, but some have been made by dumping top soil back into the water mechanically—a lengthy procedure.

Once made, a spit must be planted with trees and with a surrounding fringe

TABLE 1 ANNUAL WILDFOWL USAGE (IN WILDFOWL DAYS) OF THE WATER-AREA AT
SEVENOAKS, 1956-69

Year includes summer and following winter, e.g. 1956-7 refers to summer 1956 and winter 1956-57. Figures in parenthesis refer to birds seen flying over the Reserve and are not included in totals.

	56/57	57/58	58/59	59/60	60/61	61/62	62/63	63/64	64/65	65/66	66/67	67/68	68/69
Dabbling/Grazing Ducks													
Mallard	6,150	7,900	9,500	14,700	17,100	19,900	22,370	27,945	33,104	38,201	41,314	64,326	64,804
Teal	12	2	7	8	10	31	84	69	53	69	324	285	424
Garganey			1	1					1		3	1	3
Gadwall		3		20	2	25	77	6	101	497	491	1,165	1,557
Wigeon							6	5	4	41	11	10	80
Pintail							17	8	33	1		4	7
Shoveler		1	2				3	2	2	27	10	16	21
Shelduck		1			2	11				7	7	28	7
Total	6,162	7,907	9,510	14,729	17,114	19,967	22,557	28,035	33,298	38,843	42,160	65,835	66,903
Diving Duck													
Pochard		9	2	13	12	337	324	166	324	213	443	734	822
Tufted Duck		24	73	22	13	159	431	457	1,722	1,663	3,134	4,389	4,734
Goldeneye						7	11		20	1	3		6
Eider							6	6					
Common Scoter		1					10	1					
Red-breasted Merganser	1					109	178	4					1
Goosander					28	14	248	5	8	1		163	55
Smew											1		1
Total	1	34	75	35	53	626	1,208	639	2,074	1,878	3,581	5,286	5,619
Geese and Swans													
Whitefront							(295)			(100)	(45)		1
Eastern Greylag								78	118				2
Lesser Snow										36			
Barnacle								156					103
Russian Brent										1			
Mute	90	114			2	14	243	439	248	196	523	653	349
Whooper							73						
Bewick's							(7)						
Total	90	114			2	14	316	673	366	233	523	653	455
Grand Total	6,253	8,055	9,585	14,764	17,169	20,607	24,081	29,864	35,986	41,151	46,264	71,774	72,977

of pond sedge and hard rush, not only to provide food and cover, but also to prevent water erosion.

That all this works in practice is shown by the experimental reserve, where the numbers of nesting pairs of duck have increased from 10 pairs in 1962 to 79 pairs in 1969—to become the most concentrated nesting area in Kent. (See Table III.) It must be stressed however, that this reserve is a completely natural one. Some clubs are managing what might be termed a "duck factory", using large numbers of wickerwork baskets or other artificial nesting sites positioned round a small pool, which has to be heavily fed. Such a reserve must, of course, be adequately guarded and the young ultimately infiltrated into the wild population, for it is impossible to provide enough natural food.

A good reserve should always act as a daytime roost for all the duck which may spread out at night over many miles of country to satisfy their differing food requirements. For this, a reserve will prove more attractive the larger it is, provided that the water is adequately sheltered. For resting, both duck and geese like to be able to swim ashore, to bath and preen in shallows and to sleep on mud and sandbanks or rest on such places in shelter from rough weather.

A reserve must always therefore cater for these "loafing spots", by providing suitable banks on which the growth of vegetation should be controlled if necessary. Polythene sheets, buried a few inches below the surface will effectively prevent any growth.

The choice of moulting areas for adult drakes in midsummer seems to depend very largely on the provision of these "loafing spots", where they like to congregate at the start of the body moult. Later, when flightless from wing moult, they require adequate shore-line cover in which to lurk. The moult period of females in late summer is more spread out, so that they do not flock, but tend to remain hidden in thick cover.

It is often important to consider the requirements for grazing species when flightless, such as geese and wigeon. These need to be able to walk ashore to grass, which must adjoin the water, so that they can return at once if attacked by a predator, such as a fox.

The management of a working gravel- or clay-pit has one great advantage over a mature water, for there is the opportunity to create new habitat by planting without having to carry out preliminary clearance. Another physical requirement is for varying depths of water to give the maximum range of habitat for planting with emergent and submergent food plants and to cater for both dabbling and diving duck.

A zone of shallows round any deep water not only greatly increases its safety, but also allows it to be planted with food and cover plants. Such shore-line cover is an important factor in duckling survival, providing shelter in rough weather, cover from predators and it attracts many insects to provide a vital duckling food.

A separate chapter details a wide range of wildfowl foods. On the experimental reserve, the main food preferences were assessed by analysing the stomach contents of locally-shot duck from 1956 to 1960. In the following nine years, 7,675 trees and 4,816 other plants were established. Included in these totals was as wide a range of food plants as possible, including 3,945 alder, 2,080 bur-reed, 1,825 silver birch, 1,778 reed-grass, 480 sea club rush, 360 pond sedge, 226 bramble, etc.

Other plants have been established to diversify the habitat with the object of increasing a wide range of other birds. This applies particularly to such species as willows, hawthorn, mountain ash and other berry-bearing trees and shrubs.

The reserve is visited daily by one of those involved in its management, so that it has been possible to produce a figure for the annual wildfowl usage. This is a wildfowl/day cumulative total for each year and each species. In the first few years, some mallard were released to encourage a lead to the water. More recently, a number of gadwall have been liberated and greylag geese have also been established. Both the latter are now breeding successfully.

Table I gives the wildfowl/day totals for the first thirteen years of the reserve and clearly demonstrates the success of its management plan. The results are in marked contrast to the findings on new reservoirs where the population rises to a peak after the first two or three years and then falls to level out some way below this initial peak. Management on the experimental reserve has ensured an annual rise for each of the thirteen years to date. It will be noted that Canada and greylag geese are excluded from this table, as being introduced species unlikely to be affected by any planting activities.

It is also of the greatest interest to note how the overall breeding bird population has built up as the result of the creation of new habitat. Here an annual census has been carried out each spring from 1964. The basic unit for this survey has been the territorial singing male, the pair, or any positive evidence of nesting. The overall increase has been remarkable, particularly in the way that the newly created habitat has been populated. A decrease in the total population in 1969 was almost entirely due to the heavy mortality suffered by the sand martin colony, presumed to have resulted from a severe depression over the Mediterranean at the time of their spring migration.

Table II lists these results, which provide positive evidence of the great benefit that can result to all birds from wildfowl reserve management. If any evidence was needed to prove to naturalists the value of co-operating with wildfowlers, this is it.

It must, of course, be remembered that all successful local reserves form a reservoir from which wildfowl spread out to stock other suitable waters over a large area. During the past eight years, the WAGBI-Wildfowl Trust Experimental Reserve has produced 1,393 young duck which have been reared in the wild and have reached the flying stage. Details are given in Table III.

The cost of a reserve such as this has worked out at approximately £600 a year from 1957 to 1968 inclusive. This has been shared almost equally between the gravel-pit company (Kent Sand and Ballast Co., Ltd. and later Redland Quarries, Ltd.) and the wildfowler-naturalists. In cash terms of course, much of the cost, as for instance with planting, has been paid for in "work done". Nevertheless, it is most important to appreciate the finances involved, in view of the widespread ideas that wildfowlers and naturalists are seldom prepared

TABLE II: THE BREEDING BIRD CENSUS – ESTIMATED PAIRS, 1964–9
Figures in brackets = Pairs in New Habitat 1965–9

	1964	1965	(1965)	1966	(1966)	1967	(1967)	1968	(1968)	1969	(1969)
Great Crested Grebe	2	2	(2)	6	(6)	8	(8)	8	(8)	8	(8)
Mallard	27	28	(28)	44	(44)	57	(57)	65	(65)	70	(70)
Gadwall	—	—	—	—	—	2	(2)	3	(3)	3	(3)
Tufted Duck	—	—	—	5	(5)	5	(5)	6	(6)	5	(5)
Greylag Goose	—	—	—	—	—	—	—	3	(3)	4	(4)
Canada Goose	6	6	(6)	3	(3)	2	(2)	4	(4)	6	(6)
Kestrel	—	—	—	1	—	1	—	2	(1)	1	—
Partridge	—	1									
Red-Legged Partridge				1		1		1	(1)	2	
Pheasant	2	2	(1)	2	(1)	1	—	5	(1)	3	(1)
Coot	—	1	(1)	1	(1)	7	(7)	12	(12)	13	(13)
Moorhen	3	6	(6)	9	(6)	18	(16)	17	(13)	16	(13)
Little Ringed Plover	1	1	(1)	1	(1)	1	(1)	2	(2)	3	(3)
Snipe										1	
Stock Dove	—	—	—	1	—	—	—	1	—	1	—
Wood Pigeon	2	2	—	5	—	3	—	6	(1)	12	(6)
Turtle Dove	3	3	—	5	(1)	4	—	3	(1)	7	(2)
Tawny Owl						1		1			
Little Owl								3			
Kingfisher		1	(1)	1	(1)			1	(1)	2	(1)
Cuckoo								1		2	(1)
Green Woodpecker		1		1						1	
Great Spotted Woodpecker	1			1							
Lesser Spotted Woodpecker										1	
Skylark	2	5	(1)	7	(3)	5	(2)	6	(2)	8	(4)
Swallow								1	(1)	1	(1)
Sand Martin	90	185	(185)	320	(320)	467	(467)	772	(772)	406	(406)
Carrion Crow	—	1	—	2	—	2	—	2	—	6	—
Magpie	1	1	—	2	(1)	2	(1)	3	(1)	1	—
Jay	1	1	—	2	(1)	1	—	2	(1)	2	(1)
Great Tit	3	10	(3)	12	(4)	15	(4)	20	(6)	11	(4)
Blue Tit	9	18	(4)	32	(8)	31	(12)	28	(8)	27	(9)
Coal Tit	—	—	—	1	—	1	..	—	—	1	—
Willow Tit								1		2	
Long Tailed Tit				1				2		1	
Tree Creeper	1	1	—	2	—	2	—	4	—	5	—
Wren	8	9	(3)	13	(3)	18	(3)	23	(5)	31	(5)
Dunnock	10	16	(6)	21	(11)	18	(9)	33	(19)	34	(18)
Mistle Thrush	1	3	—	2	(1)	3	(2)	3	(1)	4	(2)
Song Thrush	12	16	(8)	25	(10)	20	(8)	16	(5)	22	(9)
Blackbird	18	28	(15)	45	(19)	45	(21)	46	(23)	58	(25)
Nightingale	—	—	—	1	—	—	—	—	—	—	—
Robin	9	15	(4)	18	(7)	21	(5)	20	(8)	30	(8)
Grasshopper Warbler				2	(1)						
Sedge Warbler				1	(1)			1			
Blackcap	6	5	(1)	5	—	2	(1)	10	(2)	5	(2)
Lesser Whitethroat	3	—	—	3	(1)	—	—	1	—	2	—
Whitethroat	7	10	(4)	13	(8)	13	(3)	20	(8)	9	(7)
Garden Warbler	1	—	—	1	—	1	(1)	1	—	1	—
Willow Warbler	4	7	(3)	7	(5)	6	(3)	13	(7)	17	(7)
Chiff-Chaff	1	2	—	4	—	3	—	4	—	4	(4)
Spotted Flycatcher	2	—	—	1	(1)	1	(1)	2	(1)	2	(2)
Pied Wagtail	3	4	(3)	3	(2)	5	(4)	3	(3)	6	(6)
Starling	9	18	(4)	24	(6)	25	(8)	31	(9)	35	(13)
Greenfinch	1	2	—	3	(2)	8	(2)	9	(1)	13	(2)
Linnet	1	3	(1)	11	(6)	5	(3)	6	(4)	11	(9)
Bullfinch	1	2	(2)	5	(3)	3	(2)	3	(2)	7	(5)
Chaffinch	10	9	(2)	15	(4)	17	(4)	16	(2)	15	—
Lesser Redpoll										2	(2)
Goldfinch	4	3	(3)	8	(4)	7	(3)	8	(5)	10	(8)
Yellow Bunting	1	2	—	1	—	2	—	1	—	1	—
Reed Bunting	5	7	(4)	7	(5)	6	(3)	9	(5)	17	(14)
House Sparrow	10	20	(9)	21	(14)	24	(11)	28	(15)	36	(19)
Tree Sparrow	3	4	—	11	(3)	8	(1)	8	(1)	10	(1)
Total Pairs	284	461	(311)	738	(523)	895	(682)	1,300	(1,039)	1,069	(729)
Total Species	40	41	(28)	52	(38)	44	(34)	55	(41)	57	(41)
Percentage of total in new habitat		67·5		70·9		76·1		79·7		68·2	

TABLE III: DUCK BREEDING RESULTS 1962–69

	1962 Mallard	1963 Mallard	1964 Mallard	1965 Mallard	1966 Mallard	1966 Tufted duck	1967 Mallard
Estimated number of pairs	10	26	38	42	47	5	57
Number of broods	8	16	27	28	44	5	51
Number of mature young	34	81	128	112	250	5	314
Average per pair	3·4	3·1	3·3	2·7	5·3	1·0	5·5

	1967 Tufted duck	1967 Gadwall	1968 Mallard	1968 Tufted duck	1968 Gadwall	1969 Mallard	1969 Tufted duck	1969 Gadwall
Estimated number of pairs	5	2	65	6	1	70	6	3
Number of broods	2	2	34	3	1	72	6	2
Number of mature young	9	17	145	5	6	254	26	7
Average per pair	1·8	8·5	2·2	0·8	6·0	3·6	4·3	2·3

to pay anything towards the costs of the privileges they enjoy. These are as shown par the experimental reserve (see Costing Table overleaf).

Some of these items, such as the cost of the scientist working on food analysis and the part salary of a full-time worker have been incurred in establishing a show-piece experimental reserve. Other local reserves can be managed at far less cost now that the basic principles have been established and evaluated. It is on this that WAGBI intends to build up its network of local reserves.

One aspect of the creation of new wetland habitat not mentioned so far is the use of small explosive charges to produce flooded potholes. This is described in detail in the Eley Game Advisory Station's Annual Review 1968/69. In expert hands and in areas with a high water table there are undoubtedly many advantages to be gained by such work, but no one should attempt it without the advice of a real expert.

COSTING 1957–69

	Gravel-Pit Co.	Wildfowler/ Naturalist
Tree planting at 8d. per tree	£83	£304
Other plants at 8d. per plant	—	177
Research analysis of wildfowl foods (1957–64 part salary)	—	2,500
Excavating shallow pools at £1 10s. per hour	27	—
Spit Construction at £5 10s. per hour	557	—
Raft Construction	200	—
Raft Maintenance	50	—
Leaving Natural Island	800	—
One third salary of full-time worker (1960–69)	2,050	—
Mileage at 2,500/year	—	321
Rearing Mallard and Gadwall	—	448
Establishing Greylag Geese	—	40
Establishing Bean Geese	—	18
Ringing	—	50
Notice Board	10	—
Flood Clearance (1968) at £5 per hour	—	30
Maps	5	—
Boat and upkeep	—	120
	£3,782	£4,008

REFERENCES

Summaries of the year on the WAGBI-Wildfowl Trust Experimental Reserve are published in each WAGBI Annual Report.
The following papers give detailed accounts of various aspects of the reserve:

HARRISON, J. M. and HARRISON, J. G. (1965). "The Management of a gravel-pit wildfowl reserve", Trans. Vth Congress Int. Union of Game Biol. 323-31.
HARRISON, J. M., HARRISON, J. G. and MEIKLE, A. (1965). "The establishment of a winter wildfowl population on a local reserve", WAGBI A.R. 1964-5: 76–88.
HARRISON, J. M., HARRISON, J. G., MEIKLE, A., OLNEY, P. J. and POLLARD, D. (1967). "The WAGBI-Wildfowl Trust Experimental Reserve—the first eleven years", Wildfowl Trust 18th A.R.: 43–63.
HARRISON, J. G. and MEIKLE, A. (1968). "An assessment of the efficiency of the WAGBI-Wildfowl Trust Reserve", WAGBI A.R. 1967-8: 44–51.
HARRISON, J. M. and HARRISON, J. G. (1969). "The value of wildfowl reserve management for other birds", WAGBI A.R. 1968-9: 34–37.
HARRISON, J. M., HARRISON, J. G. and HARRISON, D. L. (1969). "Some preliminary results from the release of hand-reared Gadwall", WAGBI A.R. 1968-9: 37–40.
HARRISON, J. G. (1970 in press). "Creating a Wetland Habitat", Bird Study.

CHAPTER 21

MANAGEMENT OF RESERVES BY WAGBI AND ITS CLUBS

by Barry Bailey, B.A.

Development Officer, formerly Assistant Director, Wildfowlers' Association of Great Britain and Ireland. Hon. Secretary, Frodsham and District Wildfowlers' Club.

IN the immediate post-war period as conditions slowly returned to normal and interest in recreational activities increased, so wildfowling became a reality once more. At this time the average wildfowler was interested only in shooting, and the meaning of the word conservation was either suspect or virtually unknown. How different is the situation today (December 1969), when the majority of WAGBI'S 228 affiliated clubs each contribute in some way towards a comprehensive conservation policy. The interest shown in conservation work, and the satisfaction obtained by those participating, is one of the most gratifying trends of the post-war period. It is also one of the most important and vital factors relating to the future of wildfowl and this fact has not been overlooked by all who recognize and appreciate the work of the Association.

The different unshot reserves managed by wildfowling clubs can be classified into three distinct types: the "duck factory", the educational reserve and the established refuge area. It should also be appreciated that most clubs lease their own shooting rights and these areas, in which there is controlled shooting, also serve as partial reserve areas which can be declared non-shooting areas in times of severe weather and in which the habitat can be managed.

The "duck factory" reserve involves the use of massed artificial nesting sites, baskets, rafts, etc. Among the outstanding examples is the 8-acre reserve at Glenvale Lodge, Newtownards, Northern Ireland, under the control of the Strangford Lough W.A. Large numbers of wildfowl are reared each year on this small mill dam reserve—mallard principally, but latterly the trend has been towards other species.

In order to start a "duck factory" reserve, the first requisite is a suitable site; the next most important need is for an enthusiastic band of volunteers to prepare the site. WAGBI clubs all have their teams of volunteers, and indeed membership of some clubs can only be retained by active participation in conservation work. An example of this is well illustrated by the Carmarthenshire WA which has an area of fresh marsh leased from a number of farmers. Club membership is divided, so many members per farm according to size, each unit being responsible for the rearing, ringing and releasing on to unshot waters of as many wildfowl as possible, as well as improving the habitat of the area as a whole. This system results in a healthy spirit of competition between each unit.

In the smaller and more concentrated area of a "duck factory", stock birds are kept for breeding purposes and the eggs are collected up when laying commences and hatched in incubators. The ducklings are then reared under brooders. Broody hens, once popular for rearing, are no longer easy to obtain because of modern poultry husbandry. When reared, these ducks are then released on to larger reserves in the area where they receive complete protection and then in time infiltrate the wild population.

Educational reserves are usually to be found in public parks, in towns and cities, and are the result of co-operation between local clubs and local or municipal authorities. On a larger scale, St. James's Park, London, and the grounds of the Wildfowl Trust at Slimbridge could be quoted as prime examples, the latter being a world-famous show place. Excellent examples of our own, on a smaller scale, can be seen at Wensum Park, Norwich, where a collection of wildfowl has been provided by the Norwich and District WA and is of great interest to members of the public. There are many other examples, such as twenty-five acres of natural park lakes at Ipswich, under the care of the Anglian WA and GC, also the West Park at Wolverhampton, whence a tufted duck reared, ringed and released there by members of the North Worcestershire Roughshooting and Wildfowling Club, has been recovered in Denmark. An interesting recent addition is the half-acre lake at Langstone, Hornchurch, established by the South Essex WA in memory of their late President, Major-General Brian Wainright, C.B.

These small educational reserves are important in exhibiting different species of wildfowl, particularly to the younger generation, as well as promoting the image of WAGBI in the field of conservation. Breeding is frequently effected, particularly if good nesting cover is available or introduced, or if nesting baskets are provided. However, care must be taken to ensure that the stock does not become inbred, which results in an increasingly albinistic mallard stock (Harrison, 1962). Lack of attention in this respect can all too often be seen in public parks which possess stocks of wildfowl not subject to a controlled breeding policy.

Further examples of educational reserves can be seen in the Grizedale Forest area of the Lake District where many species of wildfowl have been introduced through co-operation with the Forestry Commission.

At the Haws reserve at Millom, the WAGBI greylag goose scheme was started. This 100-acre reserve contains a $1\frac{1}{2}$-acre enclosed field including a half-acre pond and owned by Captain V. Craven-Hodgson, F.R.G.S. In time greylag goslings reared at the Haws reserve were introduced into carefully selected areas of the forest through co-operation with Head Forester Mr. W. Grant. Today several species of wildfowl can be observed by the many visitors to the area, in addition to the greylag geese which are now common to the whole of the Lake District throughout the year as a result of the scheme. Barnacle, white-fronted and pink-footed geese are all breeding in this reserve; bean geese have recently been added and pintail also nest.

At the 35-acre Kiltonga Reserve at Newtownards, owned by Mrs. S. M.

Wright and Newtownards Borough Council and managed by Strangford Lough WA as their release area, several species of geese can be seen as well as large numbers of duck—the whole area of the reserve being visible from the road—a fact which is appreciated by many members of the public, who may see up to 500 teal in the air.

Established Refuge areas are of great importance to wildfowl. The interest in wild life today is such that many reserve areas are zealously guarded by Naturalist Trusts and ornithological societies, the majority of which are only too pleased to co-operate with wildfowling clubs, whose conservation activities are widely admired.

An outstanding reserve, well-known to many, is the Experimental Reserve at Sevenoaks, Kent, now owned by the Redland Group of Companies Limited, and which is a joint WAGBI-Wildfowl Trust venture. This reserve, consisting of 90 acres of water in 200 acres, was established in 1956 and has been the subject of many interesting articles during the years of its development. Today introduced greylag geese and gadwall, as well as many other species of wildfowl are soundly established. The whole area, still under development, is a model example illustrating the wildfowl food plants of all species, nesting cover and trees, all of which attract wildfowl throughout the year as well by providing food and nesting cover, open water and nesting places. The Kent Wildfowlers' Association, in conjunction with the Kent Ornithological Society, control the 350-acre reserve of Westbere, near Canterbury. Here a management plan is under way which will cover all interests including sailing and angling.

In 1963, the South Essex WA purchased the 478-acre Bridgemarsh Island on the Crouch Estuary for £2,200, and set aside 100 acres as a reserve, with controlled shooting over the remainder.

In Scotland, the Achray Forest Reserve in the Trossachs, Perthshire, attracts a wide variety of wildfowl in winter. Owned by the Forestry Commission and under the supervision of WAGBI, this 100-acre area of river and shallow inlets provides winter habitat for mallard, teal, pochard, tufted duck, pintail and wigeon, as well as whooper swans and greylag geese. Near by, Loch Venachar also contributes to the success of this reserve in providing day-time roosts as well as food and nesting cover on the banks. There are many examples of local reserves under the combined control of wildfowling clubs and naturalist societies throughout the country, some of the better-known examples of which are the Foxcote Reservoir at Maids Moreton, Bucks, under the charge of the Berkshire, Buckinghamshire and Oxfordshire Naturalists' Trust. This 100-acre reservoir, constructed in 1951, holds up to 3,000 wildfowl in winter. The Lydd Beach Gravel Pit in Kent is yet another example, owned by the Amalgamated Roadstone Co., and under the control of the RSPB, assisted by the Lydd WA; 2,400 mallard were present here in December 1969. This reserve is fully documented in our Annual Reports.

The total area of local reserves managed by WAGBI clubs, together with those jointly managed in conjunction with other bodies (e.g. RSPB, Wildfowl Trust, Forestry Commission, Naturalist Trusts, etc.) totalled 4,300 acres in 1967. In January 1970, the acreage was 20,160. As previously stated, the controlled shooting areas leased by clubs must also be considered. These areas, totalling 332,199 acres, in which restricted shooting is permitted, are also carefully studied with regard to their wildfowl populations. Not included in this total are a further fifty-eight miles of foreshore. Disturbance is kept to a reasonable level, always within the limits which wildfowl can stand. In 1970, designated European Conservation Year, one of the Association's main contributions is the restoration of the Decoy at Boarstall, near Brill, Bucks. This, known as the WAGBI Conservation Centre, is being improved by the erection of an Exhibition Hall which will contain details of the WAGBI work, in addition to other relevant displays. The decoy, now restored and being worked, together with the near-by pens of wildfowl and wildfowl food plants, will be open to the public and a nature trail provided. In December 1968, the decoy pool held 500 duck.

If conservation as practised by WAGBI clubs, often in co-operation with other organizations, continue to thrive, we believe that the outlook for wildfowl in the future, despite the increase of industrial and urban areas, gives reason for optimism.

REFERENCE

HARRISON, JAMES M. (1962). "Some effects of in-breeding on wildfowl", *WAGBI A.R.*, 1961–2: 41–44.

CHAPTER 22

NATIONAL WILDFOWL COUNTS

by George L. Atkinson-Willes

Life Member, WAGBI; Member, Wildfowl Conservation Committee, Nature Conservancy; Chairman, Duck Working Group, International Wildfowl Research Bureau; Organizer, National Wildfowl Counts.

THE National Wildfowl Count scheme has been in operation for just over twenty-one years. During this time about 75,000 records have been received from more than 2,000 places scattered over the length and breadth of Britain. With an average of four or five species to each return, the data now available amount to upwards of a third of a million entries. The investigation can thus be regarded as one of the most intensive and sustained efforts in the history of British ornithology, and as such deserves the attention of every wildfowler.

The purpose of the counts is to provide the essential information on which to base a sound policy of wildfowl conservation. The main aim is to discover whether there is any change in the numbers of ducks, geese and swans wintering in Britain, and to determine which species, if any, stand in special need of care and attention. The records are also used to assess the relative importance of the various wildfowl resorts, and to pinpoint those which are of particular value to one or more species. In both these studies the emphasis is on the common species, in which the wildfowler is most interested.

Before the scheme started most of the information on wildfowl was founded on opinion rather than fact; one person would recall the vast hordes he had seen in his youth and lament their passing, whilst another would argue that the present situation was better than ever before. Only on rare occasions could either viewpoint be substantiated by records made at the time. Even then the opinions were often parochial, and ignored what might be happening elsewhere. Now, with regular reports coming in from all parts of the country, a wealth of detail is being placed on permanent record, and, for the first time, the national situation can be viewed as a whole.

The design of the investigation is governed by a number of important factors. Firstly it has to deal with twenty or more species, all highly migratory, and all with their own variations in behaviour and distribution. There is also the likelihood that the winter population of some species comprises a different set of birds to those appearing in autumn and spring. The counts must therefore be made on as wide a scale as possible, and must be repeated on a number of occasions each winter. Moreover the dates on which the counts are made must be synchronized throughout the country, to avoid any chance of the same flocks being recorded twice. The dates selected are the Sundays nearest to the fifteenth of each month, starting in September and continuing until

March. The counts on these occasions are not intended to be a complete census of every duck in the kingdom; all that is required is an adequate sample of the main concentrations. This is sufficient to give a reliable indication of the trends in population, provided that the same places are covered regularly each month.

Although these various factors dictate the general policy, the running of the counts is left very largely to the discretion of the organizers in each county. By decentralizing in this manner full use is made of local experience, and the scheme can be more readily adapted to meet special conditions. Amongst other things, the organizers are responsible for selecting a team of reliable observers, and for deciding which places ought to be covered, tasks which are better done on the spot than from a central headquarters.

The accuracy of the counts has been tested in a number of ways, and although there are many possible sources of error, the results are believed to be reliable. An obvious query is whether the observers are capable of rendering an accurate account of what they see. On most waters in Britain this is not a serious problem, because the number of ducks is usually small enough to permit a count and recount of individual birds. It is only when the flocks are unusually large or restive that recourse must be made to estimates, with their much greater element of doubt. To test their accuracy in this respect, various groups of counters were asked to make a quick estimate of the numbers of geese appearing on a series of photographs (Matthews, 1960). Some of the attempts were far from correct; it was found, however, that when all the various under- and over-estimates were set against each other, the errors cancelled out, leaving a net discrepancy of only 10 per cent. Thus, with several hundred observers, the counts can be expected to provide quite accurate results.

Another possibility is that a count on a set day each month may not give a true indication of the numbers of birds which are normally present. To test this, daily counts were made on one water over a period of three years. The counts on the set dates were then compared with the averages of those made during the fortnight before and after. This showed that although the former were sometimes unrepresentative, the plus and minus variations again tended to cancel out; thus, a long run of monthly counts is likely to give a very fair indication of the average numbers present on any given water. If a group of waters is being covered, the monthly totals will be even more representative. It seems therefore that the present system provides the best compromise between accuracy and economy of effort. To show any marked improvement the counts would have to be made at weekly intervals, and even that would not be perfect.

Tests have also been made to discover whether the accuracy of the counts is likely to be affected by factors, such as the phase of the moon, and the time of day. In each case the results were negative; nor were any other unsuspected sources of error brought to light. The raw data can thus be accepted with some confidence, provided always that the sample under consideration is sufficiently large.

The collection of information is, of course, only the first stage; before any interpretation can be made the raw data have to be condensed into a more manageable form. The first major analysis was published in 1963 (Atkinson-Willes, 1963) and comprised a detailed study of the numbers of wildfowl recorded in each district of England, Scotland and Wales. In areas for which no counts were available, use was made of general reports, supplied in many cases by the local wildfowl clubs. Before publication the text was checked by WAGBI, and the final version represents an agreed statement of the situation in Britain during the 1950s and early 1960s.

The data are also being used to keep a running check on any changes which may be occurring in the British winter population. After each count a brief report is compiled, comparing the records for the current month with those in previous years. These reports are based on the counts from a selected sample of about one hundred and twenty places, and are normally available within three weeks of the count being made. At the end of each winter the monthly results are combined to give a single index of abundance for each of six common species. These annual indices take into account any variations which may have occurred during the course of the seven months, and allow the season to be reviewed as a whole. In some years, for instance, there may be more birds than usual in autumn, but fewer later on, whilst in others the reverse is true; a good season has high numbers throughout. Some examples of the results are contained in figs. 28–32. In each case the season of 1959/60 has been used as a base-line, and by definition has an index of 100. The results for the other seasons show the percentage increase or decrease compared with that particular season. To give some idea of the number of ducks involved, the monthly counts for 1959/60 reached a peak of about 40,000 mallard, 30,000 teal, 50,000 wigeon, 6,000 tufted duck and 5,000 pochard.

The interpretation of the diagrams is for the most part straightforward. Mallard, pochard and tufted ducks have all shown a marked increase during the past twenty years, although the numbers have sometimes fluctuated from season to season. Wigeon have also shown wide fluctuations, but over the period as a whole have maintained the same general level. There is perhaps some indication here of a six- or seven-year cycle of up and down, but the period is still too short to be certain. Teal are at present standing at about the same level as they were twenty years ago, but the picture is confused by the seasons of great abundance which occurred around the early 1960s. These influxes were a direct result of the drainage by the Dutch of a new polder in the south-east corner of the Ijsselmeer. Reclamation began there in 1954 with the closing of the dyke, and by 1958 the water level had been reduced to a depth of a few inches over an area of 125,000 acres. In October of that year it was thought that upwards of a million ducks, mostly mallard and teal, were concentrated in the area. By the autumn of 1959 much of the shallow water had been removed, and three-quarters of the migrants arriving there were forced to move on in search of alternative feeding grounds; hence the very large numbers which flooded into southern England. In the autumn of 1960 the counts in Britain were relatively low, due possibly to the unusual amount of flood-water, but in 1961 and again in 1962 much larger numbers than usual were present in October and November—the beginning, it seemed, of a

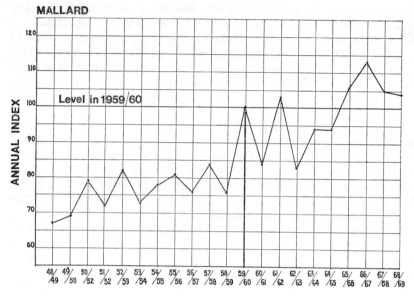

FIG. 28.

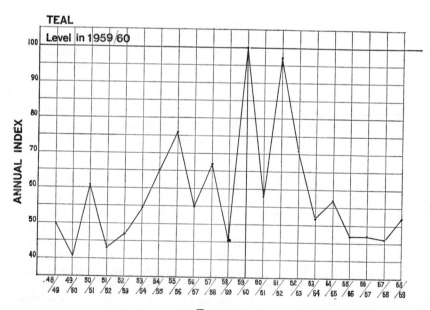

FIG. 29.

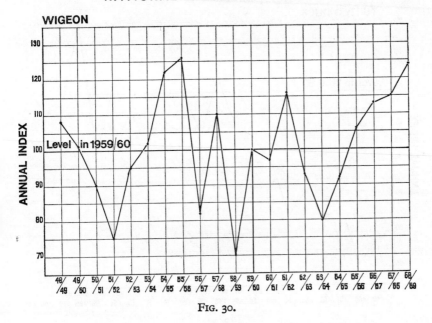

FIG. 30.

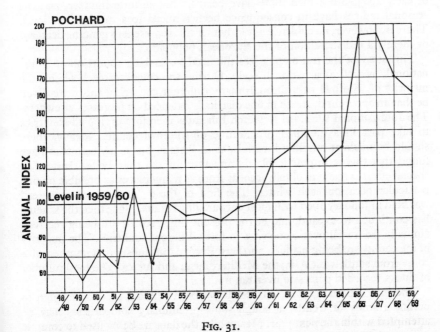

FIG. 31.

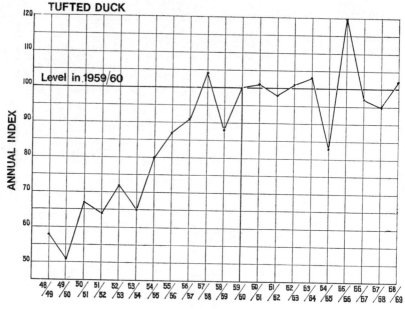

FIG. 32.

new tradition. If this in fact existed, it was totally disrupted by the cold winter of early 1963. Since then there have been no big autumn influxes, and the seasonal indices have in consequence been reduced to a much lower level. There is, however, no evidence as to whether this represents a genuine decrease or merely a redistribution of the European population.

This story of the teal emphasizes the need for making counts on an international, as well as a national, scale. During the course of each season the majority of wildfowl pass through many different countries, and it may well be that an apparent decrease in one district is balanced by increases elsewhere. The International Wildfowl Research Bureau is therefore urging all countries to take part in a modified programme of wildfowl counts. Ideally, these should be made at monthly intervals, as in Britain, but many countries have found that this is impracticable, at any rate for the time being. Instead, a special effort is made to obtain records from as many places as possible on one particular occasion each winter. The first of these "mid-winter censuses" was held in January 1967 with most encouraging results. Since then the scheme has continued to expand, and at the present time records are being received annually from well over 6,000 sites in forty different countries. The majority of the counts are being made in northern Europe, but substantial numbers also come from south-west Asia, the Mediterranean and Africa. The total number of ducks recorded comes to over ten million.

The international censuses have not yet been running for long enough to permit a study of trends, although some preliminary comparisons may be attempted within the next year. Meanwhile, the data are being used to compile

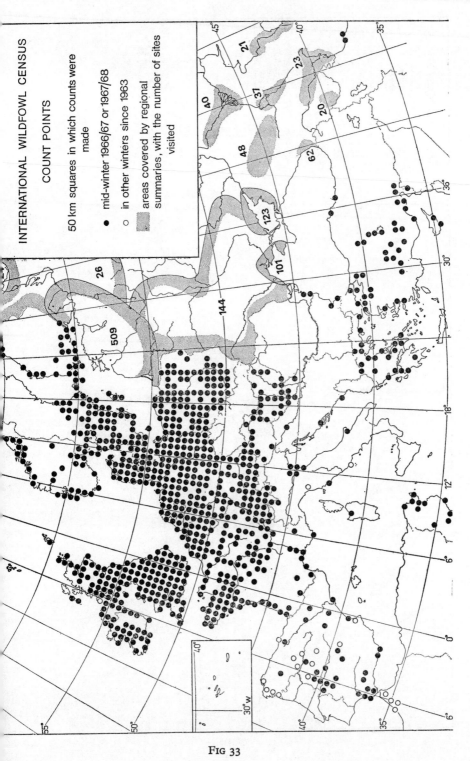

INTERNATIONAL WILDFOWL CENSUS
COUNT POINTS

50 km squares in which counts were made

● mid-winter 1966/67 or 1967/68
○ in other winters since 1963
▒ areas covered by regional summaries, with the number of sites visited

FIG 33

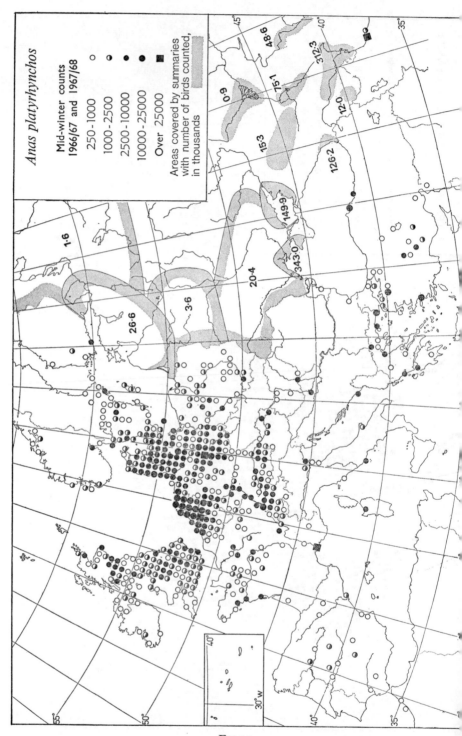

Anas platyrhynchos

Mid-winter counts
1966/67 and 1967/68

○ 250 - 1000
◑ 1000 - 2500
● 2500 - 10000
⬤ 10000 - 25000
■ Over 25000

▨ Areas covered by summaries
with number of birds counted,
in thousands

Fig 34

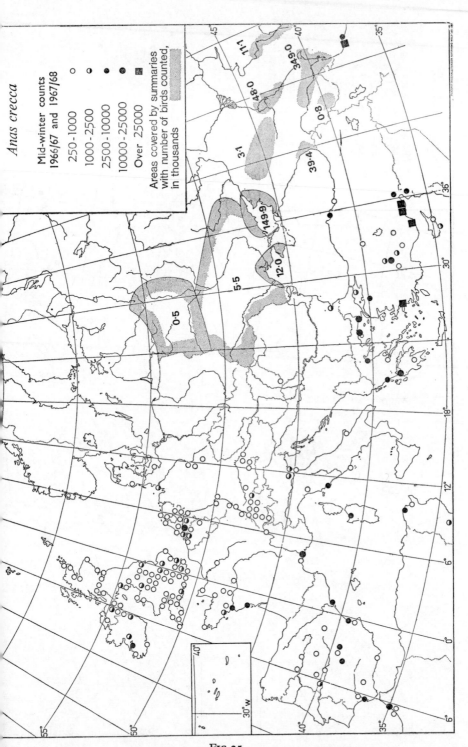

Anas crecca

Mid-winter counts
1966/67 and 1967/68

○ 250-1000
◑ 1000-2500
● 2500-10000
⬤ 10000-25000
▣ Over 25000

Areas covered by summaries
with number of birds counted,
in thousands

Fig 35

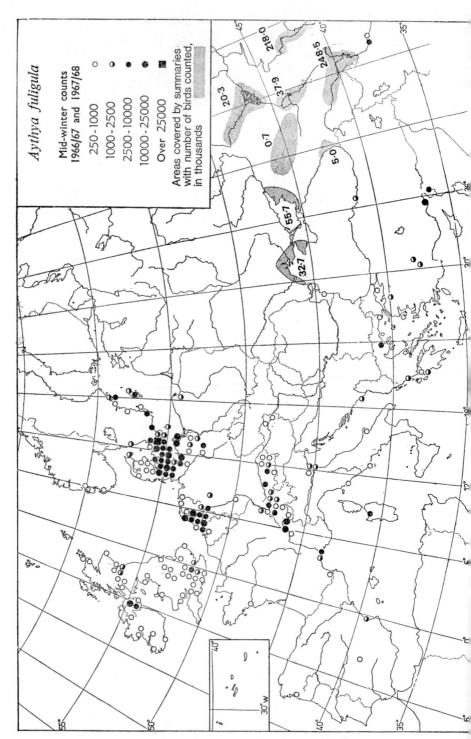

Aythya fuligula

Mid-winter counts
1966/67 and 1967/68

○ 250 - 1000
◐ 1000 - 2500
● 2500 - 10000
● 10000 - 25000
■ Over 25000

Areas covered by summaries
with number of birds counted,
in thousands

FIG 36

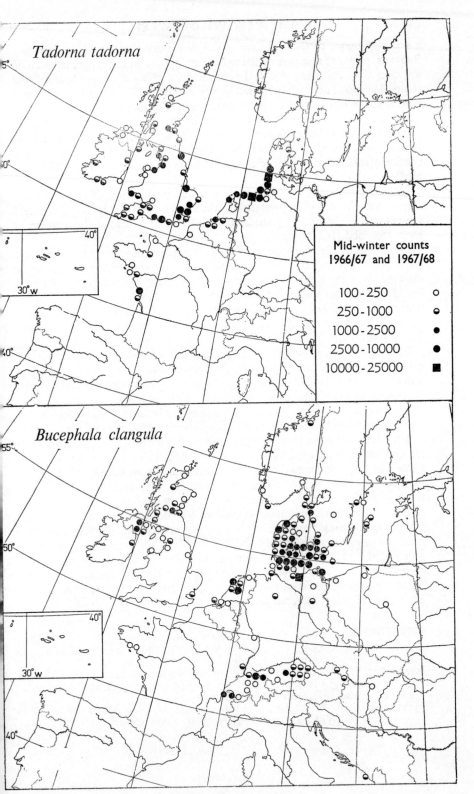

Tadorna tadorna

Bucephala clangula

Mid-winter counts
1966/67 and 1967/68

100 - 250	○
250 - 1000	◐
1000 - 2500	●
2500 - 10000	●
10000 - 25000	■

FIG 37

a series of maps, to show the numerical distribution of the various species. Some examples of these are contained in figs. 33–37. The mapping is based on a system of 50 km. grid squares, the records for each square being consolidated to provide a total for each species. The size of the total is indicated by a symbol placed in the centre of the square concerned. The location of the squares in which counts have been made is shown in fig. 33. This should be read in conjunction with the species maps in order to avoid misleading impressions; in many areas, particularly in southern Europe, the paucity of symbols on the species maps is due to lack of records, and not necessarily to an absence of birds.

The data from the U.S.S.R. were received in the form of regional summaries, and cannot yet be presented in the same detail. The regions concerned are shown on the maps by shading, with figures to indicate the number of birds recorded (Isakov 1968).

Despite their obvious incompleteness, the maps indicate quite clearly the important areas towards which the main effort of conservation ought to be directed. In some cases the population within these districts is evenly distributed over a large number of sites, which in itself provides some measure of protection; in others, the birds are concentrated into relatively small areas, many of which are highly vulnerable to drainage, disturbance and pollution. These focal points deserve special consideration as potential reserves.

The present maps refer only to January; at other times of the year the distribution will, of course, be quite different, and in due course further maps will have to be compiled to show the situation in spring, summer and autumn. A start has already been made towards this, with the introduction in 1969 of a second census during November. A study of the breeding populations is also being undertaken in a number of countries, including Britain and the U.S.S.R.

The aim of all these studies is to ensure that the limited resources available for conservation are used to best effect. In the first instance it is essential to know which species stand most in need of care; one must then decide how best to afford the necessary measures of protection. This applies particularly in the case of reserves, which are expensive items to establish and maintain, and which are also bound to impose restrictions on wildfowlers and other interests. Their creation must therefore be justified from every point of view; hence the need for solid facts. In Britain the Wildfowl Counts have already provided much of the basic information, but the situation is changing both here and abroad, and a constant watch must be kept for the first inkling of decline. Timely action can then be taken to safeguard the stocks of wildfowl for the enjoyment of future generations.

REFERFENCES

ATKINSON-WILLES, G. L. (Ed.), 1963. *Wildfowl in Great Britain*. Monographs of the Nature Conservancy, London.
ISAKOV, YU. A., 1968. (Results of the midwinter waterfowl census in the U.S.S.R. in January 1967.) Booklet of the Moscow Association, Biological Section, 4: 92–114. (In Russian with English summary.)
MATTHEWS, G. V. T. (1960). "An examination of basic data from wildfowl counts", *Proc. XII Int. Orn. Cong. Helsinki*, 1958: 483–91.

CHAPTER 23

THE STATUS OF WILD GEESE IN BRITAIN AND IRELAND

by Malcolm Ogilvie

Scientific Staff, The Wildfowl Trust. Member, Goose Working Group, International Wildfowl Research Bureau.

THE distribution of the eight kinds of wild geese that winter in Britain is known in some detail. In every case the number of haunts is limited, usually by their particular requirements for feeding and, more especially roosting. The use of haunts is strongly traditional so that changes tend to occur rather slowly, except where the habitat is drastically and rapidly altered. With this knowledge it has proved possible to carry out complete censuses of most of the populations of goose species in recent years, and to census some of them at least annually.

Five breeding populations of geese winter exclusively within the British Isles. These are: the Greenland whitefront; the pinkfoot (breeding in Greenland and Iceland); the greylag (from Iceland); the barnacle goose (from Greenland); and the light-bellied brent (from northern Greenland). Although there are some advantages in having the whole population within our country, censuses being easier to organize for one thing, it does lay an added responsibility on our shoulders, as the conservation and well-being of the population is ours and ours alone.

The populations of geese which winter in the British Isles and elsewhere can be divided into those of which a significant proportion of the total stock winter here, a half or more, and those of which a rather smaller or irregular proportion do so. In the first category is the barnacle goose again (this time from Spitzbergen) and the dark-bellied brent (from the Soviet Union). In the second category are placed the European whitefront (from the Soviet Union), the light-bellied brent (from Spitzbergen) and the bean goose (probably from Scandinavia or the Soviet Union).

The present numbers of these populations wintering in the British Isles will be given below in detail, together with a summary of changes over the past twenty years. In addition two resident populations of geese, the Canada and the greylag, will be dealt with briefly.

BEAN GOOSE, *Anser fabalis*

This is the least common of the wintering geese in Britain. Formerly much more numerous and widespread it is now to be found regularly at only two haunts and total numbers barely reach two hundred. The exact status of the bean goose in past years is obscure, largely because of the confusion in distinguishing it from the pinkfoot and other grey geese. However it was clearly quite common in northern England and Scotland at the turn of the century, since when there has been a steady decline. The reasons for this are not definitely known though it is reported that some former breeding areas in Scandinavia, whence it is assumed though not proved that our birds come, are now deserted.

Regular counts are available for most years since the war from the two remaining regular haunts. These are in Kirkcudbrightshire and Norfolk. At the former site a peak of about 200 was reached most winters until 1955–6. Since then there has been a drop to under 100, with a short-lived recovery in the hard winters of 1961–2 and 1962–3. The numbers in Norfolk have always been subject to more fluctuations, with years when apparently none appeared and peaks of about 150. Here, too, there has been a recent decline with the peak not reaching fifty in most years. There are a few additional sites in Britain where small numbers of bean geese appear irregularly. Up to twenty-five appeared for a few years in Dunbartonshire in the early 1960s but hardly any since, and there are infrequent records of a flock in Aberdeenshire.

Thus the total numbers in Britain continue to fall slowly and it may only be a matter of time before regular wintering ceases. From a total of 400–500 after the war, numbers have fallen to 150–200 in the last few years.

PINK-FOOTED GOOSE. *Anser brachyrhynchus*

The whole breeding population of Iceland and East Greenland winters within Scotland and England and in each November since 1960 it has proved possible to carry out a fairly complete census of its numbers. Sufficient counts and estimates exist for earlier years to enable a reasonably reliable figure to be arrived at for each winter since 1950. These totals are given in Table I.

TABLE I: NUMBERS OF PINK-FOOTED GEESE IN THE BRITISH
ISLES, 1950–1 TO 1969–70

Figures since 1960–1 are from the annual November censuses

1950–1	30,000	1957–8	36,500	1954–5	65,500
1951–2	34,000	1958–9	54,000	1965–6	69,000
1952–3	35,500	1959–60	54,000	1966–7	76,500
1953–4	32,500	1960–1	57,500	1967–8	65,500
1954–5	37,000	1961–2	59,000	1968–9	65,000
1955–6	42,000	1962–3	56,000	1969–70	74,000
1956–7	49,500	1963–4	57,000		

With minor fluctuations the rate of increase from 30,000 in 1950–1 to the peak of 76,500 in 1966–7 has been remarkably steady. So much so that it has proved possible to forecast future trends in numbers, despite the complication of the drop in 1967–8 and 1968–9. If the increase continues at the same rate, and the latest census, that of November 1969, puts it back on course, there could be as many as 90,000 pinkfeet by 1975. However there are two factors which make it unlikely that this total will ever be reached. We know rather little concerning the causes but they are none the less interesting. It has been noted from regular counts of the proportion of young birds in the wintering flocks and of the average family size that both have been falling slowly over the years so that the effective fertility has not kept pace with the rise in population. In other words the non-breeding fraction of the population is getting ever larger. If this state of affairs continues then there must be a drop in numbers. A more serious and tangible threat comes from a well-advanced plan to flood the principal breeding grounds for the species, the Thjorsaver oasis in central Iceland, as part of a hydro-electric project. It is probable that about half of all the breeding pairs nest in the oasis and the flooding would totally deprive them of the habitat. It is not thought that there is sufficient room elsewhere for them all to find new breeding places.

Although there has been a large increase in numbers it has been accompanied by a retraction in range, which is much less satisfactory. Haunts in England are now used much less than they were even fifteen years ago and the process is continuing. The birds are now remaining in larger numbers and for much longer than formerly in the traditional Scottish haunts, particularly the central lowlands of Perthshire, and in the Lothians. Here there has been a great increase in the growing of barley and potatoes, and the pinkfeet, when they arrive in the autumn, feed first on the barley stubbles and then on the harvested potato fields. The greatly increased supplies of these two preferred foods encourages the geese to use these areas much more instead of moving south. This is a rather unsatisfactory situation from every point of view, be it that of the shooter, the conservationist, or someone who just wants to be able to see large numbers of wild geese.

EUROPEAN WHITE-FRONTED GOOSE, *Anser albifrons albifrons*

The geese of this species which winter in Britain, mainly in southern England and Wales, form part of a much larger population which also winters in Germany, the Netherlands and Belgium. The breeding grounds are in the Soviet arctic, particularly Kolguev and south Novaya Zemlya islands and on the adjoining mainland. Britain is thus at the far end of the migration route and conditions farther east can affect the numbers of birds coming here each winter.

There are nine haunts in Britain where over 100 whitefronts regularly winter, together with another twenty places where birds sometimes appear. A number of haunts have been lost in the last twenty years through drainage or disturbance, a process which is unhappily continuing. However the numbers do not appear to have suffered, as shown in Table II. Regular censuses are held most winters and very frequent counts at most of the major haunts. From these figures a maximum total has been calculated for each winter and these are set out in the Table.

There is some tendency for hard winters (1946–7, 1955–6, 1962–3) to produce higher numbers with conditions in Belgium and Holland having the most effect. The very high peak in 1967–8 was directly due to the foot-and-mouth outbreak in Britain which effectively cut down disturbance at all the haunts in the country by restricting human interference, be it by birdwatchers, wildfowlers, or just the farm workers.

TABLE II: MAXIMUM NUMBERS OF EUROPEAN WHITE-FRONTED
GEESE PRESENT IN BRITAIN, 1946-7 TO 1968-9

1946-7	10,500	1954-5	8,600	1962-3	9,800
1947-8	6,600	1955-6	8,400	1963-4	7,400
1948-9	8,400	1956-7	5,600	1964-5	6,000
1949-50	7,400	1957-8	8,400	1965-6	8,400
1950-1	8,900	1958-9	8,000	1966-7	7,300
1951-2	6,300	1959-60	8,400	1967-8	12,000
1952-3	10,000	1960-1	6,800	1968-9	11,200
1953-4	9,000	1961-2	8,600		

The figures show no trend, which is perhaps surprising when related to the changes that have occurred on the continent in the last fifteen years. In the mid-1950s the total numbers wintering in Holland, the headquarters of the population, were between 30,000 and 40,000. This total has increased since to a peak of about 70,000 by 1964. It is thought more probable that there has been a redistribution of geese than an overall increase, but the change is none the less striking and yet not reflected at all in Britain. It may well be that the British haunts are already holding about their maximum though some changes that have occurred in recent years, with numbers declining at some places and building up at others, suggest that careful management might increase the total substantially.

GREENLAND WHITE-FRONTED GOOSE, *Anser albifrons flavirostris*

This is the one species of goose wintering in the British Isles which has never been accurately censused. The total population is thought to amount to 13,000-15,000 but this figure is built up from counts at different places in different years, and there is no way of showing whether any changes have taken place in total numbers. The species breeds in West Greenland and winters in western Scotland, including the islands, and in Ireland. There are three major wintering localities, on the Wexford Slobs where about 7,000 winter, on the island of Islay, Argyllshire, where there have been recent counts of about 2,500, and in Kirkcudbrightshire where there are another 1,000. Apart from these there are at least another twenty to thirty sites in Ireland where small flocks occur and nearly as many in Scotland plus a few in Wales. Several of these are on inaccessible islands and in remote places so that a simultaneous census has never been practicable.

GREYLAG GOOSE, *Anser anser*

Britain has two populations of greylag geese. There is a small resident stock breeding in the Outer Hebrides and in the north-west of Scotland, and there is the very much larger wintering population which comprises the whole of the Iceland breeding stock. In addition there are numerous feral flocks established in the last forty years by landowners and wildfowlers.

The native population is thought to number between 1,000 and 2,000 birds. The largest numbers are found on South Uist where up to seventy pairs breed on Loch Druidibeg. A moulting flock of up to 300 also gathers here in summer, dispersing through the islands for the remainder of the year. The total numbers of the population have probably not changed much in the last twenty years.

The Iceland population of greylags has been censused in Britain at the same time as the pink-footed geese, in each November since 1960. These figures are set out in Table III together with totals for earlier years compiled from less complete records.

TABLE III. NUMBERS OF GREYLAG GEESE IN THE BRITISH ISLES, 1952–3 TO 1969–70

Figures since 1960–1 are from annual November censuses

1952–3	25,000	1958–9	20,000	1964–5	43,000
1953–4	29,000	1959–60	20,000	1965–6	45,000
1954–5	25,000	1960–1	30,000	1966–7	60,000
1955–6	21,000	1961–2	36,000	1967–8	53,000
1956–7	24,000	1962–3	38,000	1968–9	61,000
1957–8	21,000	1963–4	34,000	1969–70	62,000

For the first nine years shown there was no definable trend, but in the last ten there has been a very marked increase, which may now have levelled out. There is a parallel here with the pinkfoot, not only in the increase but also in the retraction of range which has accompanied it. Greylags are now quite uncommon in Ireland and north England where once there were regular wintering flocks. Instead haunts in Scotland are carrying many more than formerly and again this is largely due to the great increase in the two staple foods, barley and potatoes.

BARNACLE GOOSE, *Branta leucopsis*

Greenland population

The entire breeding population of barnacle geese from East Greenland winters in western Scotland and western Ireland, principally on islands. The only practical way of censusing them is by aerial survey as many of their haunts are uninhabited and inaccessible. Despite the fairly high cost this has been done five times in the last twelve years and the results are set out in Table IV.

TABLE IV: NUMBERS OF BARNACLE GEESE IN BRITAIN, 1957–66

Region	1957	1959	1961	1962	1966
Scotland, except Islay	4,400	3,200	4,300	4,800	6,700
Islay, Argyllshire	3,000	2,800	5,500	4,800	8,500
Ireland	4,400	2,800	4,100	4,400	4,800
Total	11,800	8,800	13,900	14,000	20,000

The initial reaction to the Table is that there has been a considerable increase in numbers, but that this has taken place only in the Scottish half of the range and not at all in Ireland. Islay is given a separate line in the Table not only because it is far and away the most important locality but also because although there has not been a complete census since 1966, regular counts have been made of the numbers wintering there. In November 1966 there were again 8,500 on Islay and in February 1967 this had risen to 10,500. The next autumn there was a massive count of 16,500 in November, but this undoubtedly included many birds which were soon to pass on to other haunts and the count in February 1968 was similar to the previous year at 10,800. In the winter 1968–9 there were three counts, in November, January and February. All three totalled between 12,300 and 13,300. This represents a greatly increased total wintering on the island. Unfortunately in the absence of counts from the rest of the wintering range it is not possible to say whether Islay now holds a much greater proportion of the total, which seems probable, or whether the whole population has risen to the same degree.

Spitzbergen population

It has been shown by ringing that the barnacle geese that winter on the Solway are drawn solely from the breeding population of Spitzbergen and that there is no mixing of these birds with the East Greenland stock, even though the headquarters of the latter, Islay, is a bare hundred miles away. The numbers of barnacle geese on the Solway have increased gratifyingly from a very low level just after the war, being greatly helped by the declaration of a National Nature Reserve covering their main locality in 1957. They had been much more numerous before the war but were severely reduced in numbers by gross disturbance. Very regular counts are made of the numbers wintering on the Solway and the annual maxima are given in Table V.

TABLE V: MAXIMUM COUNTS OF BARNACLE GEESE ON THE SOLWAY, 1946–7 TO 1968–9

1946–7	400	1955–6	500	1962–3	3,000
1949–50	700	1956–7	1,000	1963–4	4,250
1950–1	420	1957–8	1,150	1964–5	3,300
1951–2	600	1958–9	1,300	1965–6	3,700
1952–3	720	1959–60	1,650	1966–7	3,000
1953–4	1,000	1960–1	2,500	1967–8	2,700
1954–5	1,500	1961–2	2,800	1968–9	2,200

It was formerly believed that the numbers wintering on the Solway represented the whole of the Svalbard population but in recent years there has been sufficient evidence from the counts to know that some at least, possibly as many as 1,000, spend most or all of some winters in southern Norway, which lies on their migration route. For example, in both 1963–4 and 1964–5 the peak counts were made in March and both were nearly 1,000 birds greater than any count earlier in the winter, while in 1965–6 the peak count of 3,700 was made in November, and later counts never got above 3,000. Because a large number of the birds have been ringed, some with colour rings, any other wintering haunt in the British Isles would have been discovered by now.

DARK-BELLIED BRENT GOOSE, *Branta bernicla bernicla*

Dark-bellied brent geese from the Soviet arctic winter on the east and south coasts of England, and on the coasts of Holland and France. The species was undoubtedly much more numerous in the past, suffering severely in the 1930s when disease wiped out much of its main food plant *Zostera*. Regular censuses have been held in Britain since 1954 and the results are set out in Table VI.

TABLE VI: NUMBERS OF DARK-BELLIED BRENT GEESE IN BRITAIN, 1954–5 TO 1968–9

1954–5	10,800	1959–60	8,300	1964–5	10,000
1955–6	10,000	1960–1	14,800	1965–6	14,000
1956–7	8,500	1961–2	13,900	1966–7	15,600
1957–8	10,600	1962–3	15,000	1967–8	16,000
1958–9	12,200	1963–4	11,500	1968–9	13,700

There has been an unmistakable increase over the period covered by the censuses, though with marked fluctuations which are the result of great variations in breeding success from year to year.

The numbers in Britain amount to a half or rather more of the total population, with France holding the bulk of the remainder. The coast of Essex provides wintering sites for up to two-thirds of the British total and it is here that the latest conservation battle is now being fought, over the proposal to site the Third London Airport at Foulness, on the prime brent haunt in the country, and indeed in Europe.

LIGHT-BELLIED BRENT GOOSE, *Branta bernicla hrota*

Greenland population

The whole of the northern Greenland population of light-bellied brent apparently winters within the British Isles, almost all in Ireland. There they have only been counted thoroughly in 1960 and 1961 and in each winter since 1965. The figures are set out in Table VII.

There has been an obvious decrease from the first two censuses since when numbers have been fairly stable. There has also appeared the very curious and yet constant drop through each winter. No satisfactory explanation of this has yet been forthcoming. The drop seems greater than expected winter losses, no one has located the birds elsewhere in Britain or in Europe, and in each succeeding winter the Irish counters have endeavoured increasingly to cover every possible locality they might be in. It remains a bit of a mystery. A very few birds of this stock appear on the west coast of Wales and Scotland each winter, but the numbers rarely top 100 all told.

TABLE VII: NUMBERS OF LIGHT-BELLIED BRENT WINTERING
IN IRELAND, 1960 TO 1968–9

	November	February/March
1960–1	12,000	no count
1961–2	12,000	no count
1965–6	7,300	5,500
1966–7	8,000	6,200
1967–8	8,300	7,500
1968–9	7,800	6,000

Spitzbergen population

Flocks of several hundred light-bellied brent geese appear each winter at Lindisfarne, on the Northumberland coast. The birds form part of the Spitzbergen population of this species whose main wintering grounds are in Denmark. The total population is small, less than 3,000, and the numbers in Britain are entirely dependent on the weather conditions in Denmark. Some years only 500 appear, in 1962–3 as many as 2,000 were reported.

CANADA GOOSE, *Branta canadensis*

This species was introduced from North America two or three hundred years ago and put down on park lakes and other private waters as an ornamental and sporting bird. It gradually spread to other waters but it was not until this century that numbers started to increase greatly. Soon after the war there were sufficient in some areas to lead to complaints of damage from farmers, and first the Wildfowl Trust and then the Wildfowlers' Association undertook to remove birds from places where there were too many and to distribute them to landowners and wildfowling clubs who wanted to establish flocks. The first census of the Canada geese was in 1953 when the total lay between 3,000 and 4,000. It was not until 1967 that another census was attempted, when the total was found to have risen to about 10,500.

Undoubtedly the redistribution had helped the species enormously, by putting birds down on waters where they were encouraged to breed and relieving the pressure in the localities from which the birds were taken so that numbers increased again there. Coupled with this has been the great increase in artificial waters in Britain, especially gravel-pits, which form excellent breeding places for the geese.

Canada geese are pretty well distributed throughout England, but there are few in Wales and only a few hundred in Scotland. Some of the more populous areas are the Thames valley, the west Midlands and Yorkshire. Non-breeding birds from the latter area now undertake a moult migration each summer to the Beauly Firth. This behaviour apparently began just after the war, when less than fifty birds were involved. In the last few years over 300 birds have been making the journey.

Recent extensive ringing has shown that apart from this one migration the geese are fairly sedentary, rarely wandering far, and hardly ever mixing with

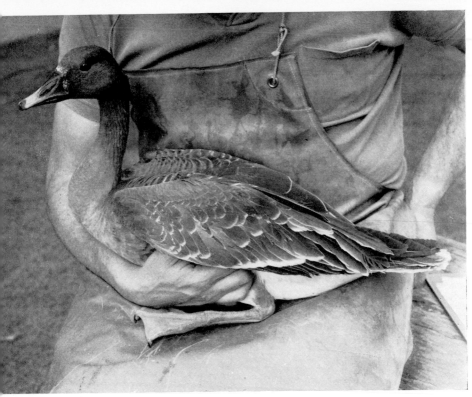

Plate 43. Young bean goose ready for ringing and release

Plate 44. Greylags bean and whitefronts taking off

Plate 45. September mallard flighting to stubbles

Plate 46. Mallard on ice

geese from other areas. This makes for easier control, something which is certainly necessary in some areas. Shooting is the most satisfactory method, though there are flocks which rarely present a sporting shot, merely walking from roosting lake to feeding field and back again. If the geese can be proved to have caused damage, rather more drastic steps can be taken under the existing law, including the culling of them outside the shooting season.

Conclusion

The present overall status of wild geese in the British Isles must be judged as being generally very healthy. Taking the average counts for the last few winters there are at peak about 200,000 geese present. Not only are numbers high for a comparatively small country but the variety is also great, with nine species or sub-species represented and altogether twelve different populations. Several of these have shown very satisfactory increases over the last twenty years even though there has been an accompanying retraction in range for some. Only the bean goose has steadily declined and perhaps it is surprising that the remaining few have hung on so long.

The increasing pressures on goose habitat will inevitably make themselves felt and we may have to face severe losses in the future which will of course have their effect on goose numbers. Some species are known to be adaptable to change, and can be assumed to have an assured future, but the specialists among the geese, those with a restricted diet or preferred habitat, will be the ones to suffer. The past twenty years have produced an encouraging picture. It is now up to all of us to see that the next twenty are equally good for the geese.

CHAPTER 24

CONSERVATION AND BIRD PROTECTION

Part One by Philip Brown

WAGBI Management Committee member; Editor "Shooting Times"; formerly Secretary, The Royal Society for the Protection of Birds.

Part Two by Peter Conder

WAGBI Member. Director, The Royal Society for the Protection of Birds; Member, Wildfowl Conservation Committee, Nature Conservancy.

PART I

CONSERVATION means, quite simply, preservation. Wildfowling involves the killing of duck and geese. Superficially, therefore, the two do not seem to be compatible. But any superficial consideration, like superficial knowledge, is of little value and can be highly dangerous.

Conservation, when applied to wild life, also involves killing. It is often customary to refer to this as culling, but that is only killing under another name. Wildfowling is simply one method of taking a cull from a number of agreed species whose status will not be in any way affected in the process. As a sport, it is merely a form of culling which is rather more difficult than most, demanding physical stamina, an ability to shoot and, for any sort of success, a considerable knowledge of the quarry. It provides pleasure, healthy physical recreation and food for the pot.

Every living creature demands two basic needs: a place where it can reproduce its kind in due season and a sufficiency of food, not only for itself and its offspring in the breeding season, but throughout the year. Without interference—often gross interference—by man, there would always be a sufficiency of breeding habitats. However, there would certainly not always be a sufficiency of food. Almost every animal (man himself is a striking example) produces far more offspring than is necessary merely to maintain its population. Nature is the biggest and most efficient culler (or killer) of all. By our own standards the survival rate of many animals is appallingly low. Starvation and disease, storm and predators all take their toll as they did long before man strode late on to the evolutionary scene to exploit almost every natural resource for his own selfish ends.

It is untrue to say, even today, that every wildfowler is a conservationist, though the majority of true wildfowlers certainly are. Not all of those who pursue duck and geese with a shotgun are wildfowlers anyway. Some of them, unfortunately, are little better than inexperienced louts who have acquired a gun and want to shoot something. Their gun-handling is rudimentary. They feature in the newspapers as a result of poaching other people's pheasants or because they were caught trespassing and shooting on a marsh where they had no right to be. Most of them appear to know nothing about close seasons and some would be unable to distinguish between a pintail and a pheasant.

Judging by the aforesaid newspaper reports, a good percentage of these highly undesirable gentlemen are foreigners who have settled, permanently or temporarily, in this country. They probably know nothing of our sporting traditions. If, as is quite likely, they come from some of the countries bordering upon the Mediterranean Sea, where almost anything that flies may be commonly regarded as fair game at any season, their behaviour may be understandable if inexcusable. It is these people, minority though they may be, who hit the headlines and do untold damage to the reputation of one of our most honourable field sports.

There is no doubt in my mind that the Wildfowlers' Association of Great Britain and Ireland, better known today by its simple initials as WAGBI, has played a leading role in upholding the best traditions of the sport and in leading it triumphantly forward into the 1970s. Founded as long ago as 1908, the Association has gained enormously in membership and strength over the past fifteen years, ably supported by more than 225 clubs all over the British Isles and even abroad.

If the future of wildfowl in this country is by no means assured, the prospects have surely become rosier. There is a greater degree of accord between wildfowlers and naturalists than ever before. After all, many wild-fowlers are good naturalists and vice-versa. It is also as well to bear in mind that a great deal of WAGBI's work in the field of conservation has been of inestimable benefit to many other birds and animals apart from wildfowl. On the other side of the coin any intelligent wildfowler will surely appreciate that the welfare of his quarry (and therefore the future of his sport) has been greatly aided and abetted by conservation bodies such as the Royal Society for the Protection of Birds, the Wildfowl Trust and the Nature Conservancy.

With a rising population we are inevitably suffering in this country from a shortage of land. More and more of the countryside is despoiled (as country-side, anyway) by new building estates. Land vanishes under huge artificial reservoirs and this is likely to be a continuing process. Motorways, however necessary they may be, mop up thousands of acres of good agricultural land. These and other factors have helped to make land more valuable to the nation than it has ever been before. It has also made it much more difficult to preserve wild places, especially wetlands where duck can breed and feed and find safety from their natural enemies.

This situation can be paralleled in many other countries and as most of our duck and geese are migratory, the problem of reserves and refuges is an international one. However, thanks largely to the more energetic wildfowling clubs and to regional bodies like the network of Naturalists' Trusts (most of which maintain a close liaison with WAGBI clubs) small reserves are being established all over the country, many of which are true refuges, where shoot-ing is forbidden. These reserves aid all wild life and they are often used for releasing duck reared under the now long-established and successful scheme initiated by WAGBI, on the good principle that a fowler ought to try to put back what he takes out. Where there are enough volunteers who are really prepared to bend their backs in sheer hard labour for a cause in which they believe, such reserves can soon become of real importance. Anybody who doubts this statement has only to visit the astonishing WAGBI-Wildfowl Trust Reserve at Sevenoaks.

Much as I should like to think otherwise, I do not believe that the conservation of wild life and wild and lovely places is going to be easier in the years ahead. We suffer increasingly from over-urbanization and super-suburbia, so that the rift between town and country is likely to grow wider. For the average townsman the country is unlikely to be much more than a summer playground, at any rate in the foreseeable future and he is more likely to be excited by the idea of a barrage over the Solway than worried about the future of the geese which he has never seen nor is ever likely to see.

The wildfowler, of course, is at present in the pillory, along with all other field-sportsmen, to those who oppose any form of killing for sport. This, the so-called "anti" movement is not novel, but it is dangerous, both to sport and to the conservation of wild life, because it springs largely from urban-dwellers most of whom, inevitably, know nothing of the facts and can only believe what they are told.

Fortunately, for anyone with a modicum of spunk, life is only dull and boring when it is easy. There is a challenge in the years ahead for all who enjoy fowling and love wildfowl and the lonely, wild places in which most of them can be found. If you know your wildfowlers then you can be sure that the challenge will be taken up with vigour and resolution, led by WAGBI, a body which has already done so much for fowl and fowling that it regularly comes in for doses of robust criticism which is the hall-mark of real success.

P.B.

Part II

Bird Protection is only a part of the very much wider field of Nature Conservation, and if one uses the word in its strict sense, protection is largely a negative or defensive part of nature conservation. As Miss Phyllis Barclay-Smith said in her essay on the subject in the *New Dictionary of Birds* it is the legal protection of wild birds against excessive human predation or cruelty. So far as one can trace, people began to protect birds in earlier times for the same sort of reasons that they protect them now: one of the earliest recorded bird protectors was St. Cuthbert, an early Northumbrian Saint, who obviously liked birds for their own sakes and wished to see them live unmolested. On the other hand it was the sportsman who originated legal protection: the first measures were introduced in the Middle Ages to protect the heron which was one of the main quarry species of falconers. This piece of legislation was really designed to protect "property" for a certain group of individuals. The first bird protection act as we understand bird protection legislation today was the Act for the Preservation of Sea Birds of 1869 which was designed to protect the seabirds of Bempton cliffs from the sportsmen of the day who sailed their boats below the towering cliffs of Bempton and shot at the seabirds as they circled above their heads, no doubt in some disarray. Since those days both types of legislation have developed: the game acts protect game for the landowner as his personal property; and the bird protection acts protect wild birds as the property of the nation.

But legislation is only a basis. The current *Protection of Birds Acts 1954 and 1967* are or should be as much as anything a code of behaviour and a guide to the spirit in which we should consider birds. Nature conservation means the wise use of nature and its natural resources. This implies, among other things, that nature or rather the surplus of nature can and, in some cases, should be cropped at the appropriate time of the year in such a way that sufficient of this harvest is left to reproduce itself in the following year. This is where the bird protector meets the wildfowler.

It has often been said to me that the bird watcher and the wildfowler are "on the same side". In many situations it is true but there are some fundamental differences and I think that better understanding is achieved by spotlighting these differences than by hiding or pretending that there are none. At least in this way one knows the other person's thoughts and may understand what he is getting at even though one cannot agree with him.

My predecessor who wrote the article under a similar title in the first edition of *The New Wildfowler* decided that he was not going to discuss ethics of wildfowlers. I decided that in a personal capacity I could hardly write this article and avoid what I consider to be the motives behind wildfowling and bird-watching. These are the points where the bird-watcher and the wild-fowler disagree or at least do not see eye to eye.

The fundamental difference, it appears to me, between a bird-watcher and a wildfowler, when both are in full cry, is that when a mallard comes into range the bird-watcher with his binoculars looks at it, admires its plumage and tries to understand its behaviour, whereas the wildfowler shoots it and enjoys its flesh. Whilst most bird-watchers appreciate the logic of shooting for the pot, and the legality of the operation, few like to see a bird, which they admire as a living, beautiful creature, and whose behaviour they think they understand, shot—even legally.

At this point I feel I must mention one other question which I am frequently asked by people: "Is it civilized to feel pleasure in taking life?" I have myself thought around this question to see how it affects the wildfowler and I suggest that the wildfowler, or the rough-shooter after rabbits, pigeons and so on, is perfectly justified in "shooting for the pot". (Of course, rabbits and pigeons are serious pests and it may well be that shooting will prove to be the most economic method of controlling the pigeon.) I do not see why it is not logical and ethically correct to hunt one's own meat and natural food—unless someone is going to say that *homo sapiens* should be vegetarian, which he never has been. If meat is man's natural food and an individual is entitled to obtain his own, is he not therefore allowed some pleasure at success in his hunting? It would be somewhat unrealistic to suggest that one should go about this with an attitude of grim determination. The question is an awkward but a legitimate one and I think the wildfowler and the rough-shooter can answer honestly that he is shooting for his own pot, and pleasure comes with success. It would be more difficult for the person who is behind a butt shooting at driven birds to be able generally to give the same sort of answer. The pleasure seems chiefly to be in the accuracy of the shot rather than in the hunting.

But there are an enormous number of spheres in which bird-watcher and wildfowler can and must see eye to eye. So far I have taken only one characteristic of a wildfowler into consideration in order to highlight, for the purposes of discussion, an essential difference from the bird-watcher. If we come to the similarities: the first and most obvious is a liking for wild, wet and open places. Then we have an interest in birds, particularly wildfowl of course, but extending to many of the waders and well beyond that. These similarities are important because they do lead on to the field which is wide open for further co-operation—I say "further" because there has already been a remarkable degree of co-operation in all kinds of conservation projects but there is room for more.

There is little need nowadays, I hope, to emphasize how the British countryside is changing and how the wilder parts of Britain are gradually being whittled away. In addition, those parts which are left are becoming contaminated by man's effluent in one form or another: an insidiously creeping disease of the environment. All too often pollution is not spotted until a disaster is upon us. The Irish Sea bird disaster of 1969 brought home to a wide public the possible dangers from chemical effluents. In this case polychlorinated biphenyls (PCBs) had been detected in birds' bodies a year or two before by the Nature Conservancy but what effect this had on seabirds was not known. When some bodies of birds found dead in the Irish Sea were analysed, fairly large quantities of PCBs were found. Whilst proof was lacking that PCBs caused the deaths of birds, suspicion was focused on these persistent compounds and the public at large realized again how effluents of one sort or another might well be seeping at present undetected into the environment in such quantities that ultimately they could cause a problem.

In my view the most important task before us is to secure permanently as much land of conservation interest as possible. Preferably this land needs to be purchased or given rather than rented. Purchase by a non-statutory body does not necessarily safeguard the land against the compulsory powers of government departments or local authorities but if the voluntary body is big enough it can raise an enormous storm if there should be attempts to take that land away by compulsory means. In spite of purchases or nature reserves agreements by the Nature Conservancy, the County Naturalists' Trusts, the National Trust and other voluntary bodies such as RSPB and WAGBI the amount of land which is in one way or another safeguarded for conservation is pitifully small and I feel strongly that any organization concerned with our countryside must use all its energy to beg or buy land to ensure that we keep it for those who, with the same interests, follow after us.

Many generations before us have felt the biting, cheek-reddening winds on the east coast, or walked along river banks, through wet meadows in the warm spring air, smelt the scent of flowers, listened to the calls and wingbeats of the lapwing, the drumming of the snipe and the skylark's song. All of us have been moved. Some can express themselves better than others and this is reflected by poets, painters and writers. This countryside is our heritage. They have enjoyed it, we enjoy it, now what?

I have heard it said by some naturalist and wildfowling organizations that they have not enough money to buy land. Of course no organization has money at the start but it does not get any more by saying that and never trying. Most successful clubs have small beginnings—even the RSPB. I can pick out two recent examples of organizations that wanted land and had faith in their ability to buy land and raise the money. First, the Cambridgeshire and Isle of Ely Naturalists' Trust (CAMBIENT) virtually began its existence by buying in faith Hayley Wood and raising the £5,000 and additional money for management afterwards. It has followed this policy of sticking its neck out courageously. Since then, because it has accomplished something, it has always succeeded in attracting support, which enables it to buy still more scientifically valuable land.

My second example is also taken from Cambridgeshire, the county in which I live. The Fenland Wildfowlers' Association, which is, I would think it fair to say, a comparatively small club, has raised money to buy land in the Ouse Washes in Cambridgeshire and is now part of a conservation group which consists of representatives of CAMBIENT, RSPB and the Wildfowl Trust, all of whom own land in this most important area. The Fenland wildfowlers have started something and I feel from personal experience that once they know that they can do it they will expand rapidly.

I have mentioned the Fenland wildfowlers but there are of course a number of other clubs which have also taken the plunge and have purchased or leased land for nature reserves. I expect that the wildfowl refuge which is best known is the Sevenoaks gravel-pits which have been developed so energetically by Jeffery Harrison and his colleagues and which are now an important refuge and breeding location for wildfowl. Then there is the Foxcote Reservoir reserve which wildfowlers are managing, helped by the Berks, Bucks and Oxfordshire Naturalists Trust. Elsewhere in this book there are lists of other reserves managed by wildfowling clubs. Nevertheless I feel that still more land must be bought because it is by owning the land that one has the best chance of safeguarding it for wildfowl.

I know that many clubs are involved in the duck-rearing scheme. I have already got into trouble with some wildfowlers for saying that I think that preserving land is of far greater importance and, since I am a guest on these pages, it is with very bad taste (for which I apologize in advance) that I say again that I wish that the money which is put into the duck-rearing scheme could go into land purchases and consequent management to ensure optimum breeding conditions.

Buying land is vital. The longer one leaves it the more expensive land may well become. The longer you leave it the more apathetic you will become. I have dealt with this subject at some length because I believe it to be of prime importance and because I think that some wildfowlers, whilst professing to be conservationists, are lagging behind the voluntary nature conservation movement in foresight and . . . courage?

I would now like to say something about another sphere where wildfowlers and bird-watchers work as one, and that is in the field of gaining facts about the numbers of our birds.

As the various IWRB conferences have emphasized, wetlands are amongst the most threatened habitats in Europe. This was particularly emphasized at the MAR conference, which was held in 1963 at Les Saintes Maries de la Mer in the south of France, in a number of resolutions to governments and the International Union for the Conservation of Nature amongst others. To impress upon these authorities (some of whom may wish to use the wetland areas for other purposes) that these areas are important, we badly need facts.

In the old days before the arrival of modern monitoring methods, coal miners used to carry canaries into the mines to detect coaldamp. Birds are still one method of detecting pollution in the environment but our scientific methods of monitoring the rise and fall of bird populations still have to be refined, so that an accurate assessment can be made of the changes before one even starts to disentangle the causes of these variations. I will give only two recent cases where wildfowlers and wildfowling clubs co-operated closely with bird clubs to provide facts in official assessments of the importance of certain areas. The first of the investigations in which wildfowlers and conservationists are involved is the Morecambe Bay barrage study. This study is aimed at discovering the feasibility of constructing a barrage across Morecambe Bay with the primary aim of impounding fresh water and, where feasible, at the same time creating polders for agriculture and providing a shorter road across the bay. The Water Resources Board arranged for the National Environment Resources Council to take responsibility for a thorough ecological survey of all the possible effects of the barrage on the natural environments. The ornithological aspect was the direct responsibility of the Nature Conservancy but they arranged with the RSPB local warden, and the contacts which he had established in the area, to be responsible for collecting information about birds and their distribution in the Bay. It was here that members of four local wildfowling clubs were able to help by providing past records of figures of ducks and waders as well as information about their usual roosting places and feeding grounds.

The other recent case where wildfowlers have been able to provide useful figures was for the Foulness site inquiry in stage two of the Roskill Commission search for a site for London's Third Airport.

Many wildfowlers help with the monthly wildfowl counts organized by the Wildfowl Trust, but I wonder how many wildfowlers keep diaries or note the numbers of wildfowl and waders which they see in the waters they visit whilst wildfowling or walking. If the records are kept accurately they can often be of immense importance on all sorts of unexpected occasions. Neither of the wildfowling clubs at Morecambe and Foulness had any idea when they started that the records they were collecting would be useful in two of the biggest and widest-ranging ecological studies that have been made in this country.

The Irish Sea seabird disaster is an indication of the value of having a network of observers who regularly visit areas—in this case, the coastline—and report on dead birds found. For years the RSPB ran a survey of oiled birds but then with the advent of the Seabird Group, and following the Torrey Canyon disaster, the network was widened and a number of wild-fowling clubs, whose members count over estuaries and shorelines, also took part in the scheme. It was this network of observers who first realized the immensity of the disaster in the Irish Sea and were able to report the facts to the Nature Conservancy which set in train the investigations necessary to sort out the causes of the deaths of the seabirds. This network can never really be too big and wildfowlers have an enormous opportunity to assist in the monitoring of what is happening to the environment. More help is needed by the RSPB from those who regularly haunt coast and estuaries and who are prepared to record what they see.

I began by spotlighting differences between bird-watchers and wildfowlers. In the middle I, who live in a glass house, threw a stone or two. Now at the end we are together with an interest in birds and a love for the countryside. Looking to the future, we must act now to ensure that this countryside is a worthy heritage for our successors.

P.C.

CHAPTER 25

INTERNATIONAL CO-OPERATION IN THE CONSERVATION OF WILDFOWL AND WETLANDS

by Geoffrey Matthews

WAGBI Member. Director of Research, The Wildfowl Trust; Director, International Wildfowl Research Bureau; Member, Wildfowl Conservation Committee, Nature Conservancy; Professorial Fellow, University College, Cardiff.

INTRODUCTION

FOUR-FIFTHS of the ducks and all bar 5 per cent of the geese which winter in the British Isles come from overseas. Wildfowlers are thus largely dependent for their quarry on events taking place on distant breeding grounds and in the countries through which the birds migrate. While much effort can be put in Britain into habitat conservation and improvement, and into artificial propagation, this will not suffice to maintain British sport if the situation deteriorates in other countries. To paraphrase Pitt the Younger, Britain cannot save herself by her exertions though she may save Europe by her example. And not only Europe; the wildfowl populations of north-west Europe are linked with a complex of populations breeding across north Asia and with flyways extending southwards into the Mediterranean, the equatorial regions of Africa, southern Asia, and even the Pacific coasts of North America. Developments in the vast expanses of the Soviet Union may affect any or all of them.

It is therefore of paramount importance that those concerned with the conservation, and exploitation, of wildfowl in Britain should know what is going on elsewhere. They should also be in a position to bring pressure to bear where necessary and be prepared to exert moderation in their own exploitation if required to do so for the benefit of the common stock.

THE IWRB'S ORGANIZATION

Britain can be proud of the fact that, in the Old World, she has played a lead in getting accepted the concept of international responsibility for the conservation of wildfowl. A start was made before the Second World War and the initiative was taken up again immediately afterwards. After several permutations in the bodies concerned, the International Wildfowl Research Bureau emerged in 1954. Its headquarters were then at the British Museum of Natural History, London, with Dr. Edward Hindle, F.R.S. as Honorary Director. In 1962 Dr. Luc Hoffmann took over the reins, with headquarters at his Station Biologique de la Tour du Valat in the Camargue, southern France. After a further seven years, during which it increased greatly in stature and

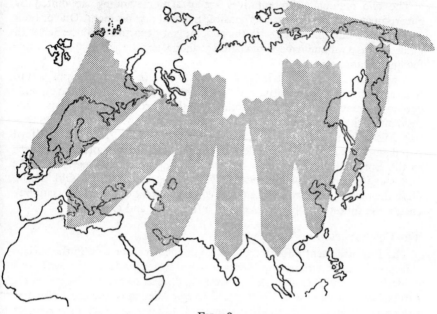

FIG. 38.

activity, the Bureau moved again, to Slimbridge. Here it is housed and serviced by the Wildfowl Trust, but remains a completely independent organization.

The multilingual headquarters staff comprises only an Administrator (Mr. E. Carp) and a secretary. The bulk of the Bureau's work is carried out on a voluntary basis. However it is under the leadership of professional research workers based in different countries and using such time and facilities as their national institutes can set aside for international matters. In addition many of the countries subscribe towards the upkeep of the headquarters staff and the administrative costs. Private donations and grants from the World Wildlife Fund are the Bureau's other main sources of income.

The IWRB maintains a scrupulous independence from any sort of political affiliation. Any country with wildfowl and wetlands within its borders is welcome to join in the work of the Bureau and to take part in guiding its activities by nominating official representatives to the Executive Board. At present the following twenty-four countries are so represented:

Austria	Greece	Portugal
Belgium	Hungary	Rumania
Bulgaria	Iran	Spain
Czechoslovakia	Ireland	Sweden
Denmark	Italy	Switzerland
East Germany	Netherlands	U.K.
Finland	Norway	U.S.S.R.
France	Poland	West Germany

The two national representatives are of senior standing, appointed by government agencies or other responsible national organizations. One or both should be closely connected with the government department concerned with nature Conservation, have a biological training and be acceptable to wildfowling organizations.

A number of other countries in Asia and Africa are not yet in a position to nominate official representatives. Here the Bureau itself appoints correspondents to maintain the essential liaison. Often these are Europeans temporarily resident in the country concerned. In quite another category come countries like Australia, Canada, New Zealand and the U.S.A. Here the wildfowl populations are largely independent of the Eurasian stock of primary concern to the Bureau. Moreover their conservation and research programmes are long-standing and of a sophistication yet to be achieved in the Old World. Here the need is not for organizational co-ordination but for an association to ensure the fullest possible exchange of information and expertise.

THE CONSERVATION OF WETLANDS

The Bureau is kept informed of developments, good or bad, in the various countries by their national representatives and correspondents. It is with their guidance that the Bureau offers advice to and seeks to exert pressure on the national agencies concerned with conservation. Wetlands, the areas of marsh and shallow water, are particularly vulnerable to rapid destruction by modern techniques of drainage and empoundment, and to degradation and pollution incidental to technological advances. Since wetlands are essential to the wellbeing of wildfowl, the IWRB has, from its start, been intimately concerned with Project MAR, an international effort directed to their conservation, so named because the word for marsh begins with those three letters in many languages.

It was quickly realized that there was a dearth of basic information about the location, present condition and relative importance of wetlands in many countries. Project MAR, working through national contacts, set about providing it. First a massive documentation on the techniques of wetland conservation was prepared. Next an annotated list of more than two hundred wetlands of international importance was drawn up for Europe and North Africa. This authoritative document, by affording an acknowledged status to the wetlands therein, has already provided invaluable support to the efforts aimed at averting many drainage and reclamation schemes. It is continually being up-dated on file and has been extended to cover Asiatic waters and those in equatorial Africa. In addition, the Bureau has compiled and distributed the details of existing wildfowl reserves in Europe, North Africa and western Asia. Such compilations are essential planning documents in the international context. At the national level they are equally necessary, but also the work of preparation often indicates where gaps in both knowledge and conservation measures lie.

Britain may be considered an "advanced" country where conservation is concerned. But even so the idea that "wetlands are not wastelands" is only just beginning to impinge on the public consciousness. It is still difficult to convince the government agencies, the engineers, the agriculturists, that marshes are not merely places to dump waste, to build factories and airfields, to convert to marginal farm land. As often happens in life, the value of something is only realized when it is nearly too late, when scarcity makes the need to save it glaringly obvious. Our colonial forebears over the hundred years' past heedlessly slaughtered the great herds of mammals in Africa. Now we have the temerity to demand that native governments behave with restraint and foresight. Similarly the great wetlands in north-western Europe have been destroyed and it is on the countries in the south and east that the international community must rely if sizeable wetlands and myriads of wildfowl are to be left to our descendants.

In an endeavour to help in putting across the message that the conservation of wetlands is a moral, aesthetic, scientific and economic necessity, Project MAR also produced an attractively illustrated booklet called *Liquid Assets* in the English version, *Ressources Méconnues* in the French. Italian and German language editions are in preparation. The booklet was widely distributed, particularly within those agencies most likely to be destructive of wetlands.

Liquid Assets also sought to demonstrate the ways in which various recreational activities—fishing, boating, water-skiing, bird-watching, shooting can be organized so that they do not clash and do not eradicate wildfowl from a district. Such sharing of the common resource, the wetland, is now gradually becoming an accepted policy in government planning in some countries, but by no means in all.

To encourage this development, the Bureau has been concerned over the past few years in the evolution of a Wetlands Convention to be signed by governments. There is no need to describe in detail the manœuvres that have gone into the preparation of a text that is likely to be acceptable to sufficient governments to make it effective. However, the end does now appear to be in sight. The aim of the Convention is not to bind governments to rigid undertakings enforced by sanctions. These do not work. Instead the governments are encouraged to make a public statement that they recognize certain wetlands within their borders to be of international importance. Equally publically they are then required to pledge themselves to conserve such wetlands to the best of their ability. At the very least such a Convention will bring wetlands and their conservation to the notice of governmental planners. It may do much more.

THE IWRB RESEARCH GROUPS

One of the bedrock principles of the IWRB is that its advice on conservation matters should be based on adequate and scientifically determined facts. The headquarters does not carry out the research itself, but seeks to co-ordinate the researches being carried out at national level and to encourage the starting of other necessary research programmes. The national representatives keep themselves informed on research activities as well as conservation matters, but they are not necessarily concerned with the organization of the former. This is done through a series of Research Groups, each concerned with a different aspect of wildfowl conservation. Each has a Co-ordinator, highly experienced in that particular field. He gathers together a team of similar specialists, one in each country, who in turn organize their compatriots. In this way those workers with common interests are brought together and, in particular, younger workers are enabled to participate in the Bureau's activities.

The first group to be established was the *Goose Research Group* (Co-ordinator, Professor M. F. Mörzer Bruijns, the Netherlands). In some ways the work of this group is relatively easy because many races of geese are restricted to north-west Europe where there are plenty of experienced ob-servers. Moreover, geese tend to congregate in relatively few places, making it possible to get near-complete censuses. By the same token, of course, they are particularly vulnerable to changes in the wetland situation. The Group has now documented all the major goose wintering haunts throughout Europe.

Britain is fortunate in that most of its wintering geese come direct from three sparsely-settled countries, Greenland, Iceland and Spitzbergen, where they are little exploited. The breeding grounds too were, until recently, largely free from disturbance and destruction. The survival of flourishing populations of these geese was thus largely in British hands. As long as Britain provided sufficient wintering grounds and shooting was held to a reasonable level, the birds' future was assured. Now modern technology is reaching into and threatening the arctic. The main pink-footed goose breeding area in central Iceland, for instance, is threatened with drowning as a result of a new hydro-electric scheme. Maybe this can be mitigated by careful planning, but such intrusions will become more and more the pattern of the future. Politically speaking, however, it is much easier to effect some compromise when only two countries are concerned, one providing the wintering grounds, the other the breeding areas.

This is not the case in two other important races of geese, the Russian whitefronts and the dark-bellied brents. Both breed in the northern coastal tundra of Siberia, where they are no longer slaughtered by Samoyedes when flightless in wing moult. For the moment, too, their breeding habitat is relatively secure. This is not so on the wintering grounds. The whitefronts fan down to a wide arc from Iraq to Britain. They prefer wet grassland, and over much of their range such habitat is fast disappearing, and with it the geese. To some extent they have shifted to other areas, particularly in the little known countries of south-east Europe and Asia Minor. But the outlook is not encouraging as the drainage programmes there accelerate. Britain can now have little direct influence on the outcome since the 10,000 or so that winter in England are only about 1 per cent of the total Eurasian population.

The position is quite the reverse with regard to the dark-bellied brent, for Britain winters more than half the population, even though this is small, around 25,000 to 30,000. In the early fifties there was great controversy, at times virulent, concerning the measures needed to conserve these geese. This was largely due to the lack of precise information about its status. The IWRB has been assiduous in ensuring that this is now continuously monitored. In the event the brent was afforded full protection in Britain and France, the main wintering areas, and in nearly all the countries through which it passes, back to the Soviet Union. Yet the total numbers have increased but slowly.

Studies over the past fifteen years have shown why. In seven years there was an almost complete lack of young birds in the wintering flocks. This is now known to be a phenomenon common to other birds breeding in the high arctic latitudes. The summer season, between ice-melt and the first snows, is so short that the birds must arrive back ready to lay. If snow cover remains unusually late they cannot nest and the eggs are reabsorbed internally. Similarly any subsequent check imposed by bad weather may set the growing young back sufficiently to prevent them migrating in time to escape the onset of the cold. Such wildfowl, which do not produce a regular annual crop of "harvestable" young surplus to the requirements of maintaining the population, are basically not suitable quarry species. Most informed and thoughtful wildfowlers now accept this proposition. Additionally, there are worrying signs that the brent population has reached a ceiling, imposed almost certainly by the increasing shortage of winter habitat. They are an unusually specialized goose, restricted in winter to feeding on the plants *Zostera* and *Enteromorpha* growing on estuarine mudflats. These are rapidly becoming one of the rarest forms of wetlands in north-west Europe, being most vulnerable to the technological threats enumerated earlier. At the time of writing there is a proposal to establish the Third London Airport off Foulness, Essex. If this goes through, the winter quarters of a fifth of the total dark-bellied brent goose population will be destroyed. And it is doubtful if they can be accommodated elsewhere.

The second IWRB group to be formed was the *Duck Research Group* (Co-ordinator, Mr. G. L. Atkinson-Willes, United Kingdom). Because of the greater dispersion of duck populations, complete species censuses are virtually impossible. Instead, the effort has been concentrated on making representative sample counts, so that population trends may be measured with confidence. Again Britain has led the way in this field; the first monthly counts began in 1938 and were restarted immediately after the war. Since 1952 they have been in the capable hands of George Atkinson-Willes who describes them in detail in Chapter 22. Since trends in the British sample could well be produced, or obscured, by geographical shifts in duck populations elsewhere in Europe, international co-ordination of counts over a wide area was obviously desirable. This has now been achieved, and is also described in the same chapter. As many duck migrations have a strong east/west directional component the success of the international duck counts emphasizes the way in which, more and more, the conservation of migratory birds is being lifted clear of political considerations.

The existence of a *Wader Research Group* (Co-ordinator Mr. F. Spitz, France) of the IWRB may surprise some, used to considering wildfowl as comprising duck, geese and swans. The Bureau took waders under its wing because they share habitats with wildfowl proper and many of the conservation problems were the same. In many ways the wader situation paralleled that of the ducks just after the war, there were very few numerical data and it was not at all clear which species were in need of further protective measures. The small size, dense flocking and high mobility of many waders makes censusing or sample counting a difficult operation. However, there is growing appreciation that the shooting of small waders, such as dunlin, is neither rewarding nor very sporting, and other countries are following the British lead in removing them from the shooting list. However there is much headway to be made in those countries where the shooting of similarly-sized finches and thrushes is still applauded. There is more reasonable controversy over the question of the larger waders such as the plovers. The Americans and Canadians decades ago decided that no "shore-bird", let alone the "peeps", could withstand shooting of modern intensity, and protected the lot. But it is preferable that the Old World should be in the possession of its own facts rather than blindly follow the example of the New.

Again and again, the emphasis must be laid on the collection and careful interpretation of facts. Shooting regulations should be based on biological realities not on personal prejudices or national self-interests. In recognition of this the IWRB has set up a *Hunting Rationalization Research Group* (Co-ordinator Dr. T. Lampio, Finland). Already, by 1966, the Bureau had published a compilation of information on shooting seasons and other methods of restricting the kill of wildfowl. The new Group will extend and complete this work. It will then formulate proposals for the international rationalization of such regulations, on the basis of the numbers, rates of reproduction, migration routes and concentrations of the different species. This is something of a tall order, but, in truth, therein lies the hope of the survival of worth-while wildfowling, let alone wildfowl.

The proposals will, of course, have to be discussed and argued with the wildfowlers themselves; at the national level by organizations like WAGBI, at the international level by the Conseil International de la Chasse (CIC). This organization (President, Dr. I. G. van Maasdijk) at one time had a rather unfortunate reputation for exclusiveness and inertia. It is now broad-based and active, and closely associated with the workings of our Research Group. Such collaboration is vital, for it is far more effective if wildfowlers themselves propose necessary restrictions to the legislature rather than have abolitionists put forward blanket proposals.

The need for new controls on wildfowling varies in the different flyways. It is generally accepted that present-day stocks cannot stand the depletion of mass-destruction for market selling. Yet market-hunting continues in Africa, Asia and southern Europe; and although the commercial exploitation of geese is now banned in Britain, thanks to a campaign initiated by WAGBI, no such restriction yet applies there to duck. In the affluent countries arguments based on protein shortages cannot carry weight and the exclusion of market-hunting is really a question of moral leadership.

For the moment the wildfowl counts and censuses indicate that most of the populations in the north-west European flyway, of which Britain is a part, are holding their own. This is in part due to the generally advanced state of conservation practices in the countries concerned; in part it is due to the fortunate circumstance that the northern countries producing the wildfowl exploit them relatively little. But the situation can change rapidly if the shooting pressure increases as more people become more affluent and more mobile. An American, coming from a State in which the duck-shooting season is barely a month and the daily bag limit is three birds, regards the British

♂ Winter

♂ Summer LONG-TAILED DUCK ♀ Winter

♂ HARLEQUIN ♀

♂ SURF SCOTER ♀

♂ VELVET SCOTER ♀

♂ COMMON SCOTER ♀

♂ EIDER ♀

♂ KING EIDER ♂ STELLER'S EIDER

SEA DUCKS

LONG-TAILED DUCK
Male in summer:
Needle tail, white
face-patch.
Male in winter:
Needle tail, pied
pattern.
Female: Dark wings,
white face, dark
cheek-mark.

HARLEQUIN
Male: Dark; rusty
flanks, harlequin
pattern.
Female: Dark; face
spots, small bill.

SURF SCOTER
Male: Black body,
white head-patches.
Female: Light face
spots, no white on
wing.

VELVET SCOTER
Male: Black body,
white wing-patch.
Female: Light face
spots, white wing-
patch.

COMMON SCOTER
Male: Plumage all
black, yellow spot
on bill.
Female: Dark body,
light cheek, dark
crown.

EIDER
Male: White above,
black below.
Female: Brown,
heavily barred.

KING EIDER
Male: Whitish fore-
parts, black back,
orange shield.
Female: See below.

STELLER'S EIDER
Male: White head,
chestnut under-
parts, black spot.
Female: See below.
FEMALE EIDERS can
be told by their bills;
long and sloping in
the Eider, with a
long lobe extending
to the forehead;
stubbier in the King
Eider, with less
lobing; no obvious
lobes in the Steller's.

MERGANSERS, SHELD-DUCKS AND "STIFF-TAIL"

RED-BREASTED MERGANSER

Male : White collar, wispy crest.
Female : Crested head, *blended* throat and neck.

GOOSANDER

Male : Long white body, dark head.
Female : Crested; *sharply defined* throat and neck.

SMEW

Male : White, marked with black; white crest.
Female : Chocolate cap, white cheeks, thin dark bill.

SHELD-DUCK

Rusty belt encircling fore-parts, red bill. Male has knob on bill; female is without knob.

RUDDY SHELD-DUCK

Orange-brown body, pale head. Male with narrow black neck-ring; female without.

WHITE-HEADED DUCK

Male : Dark body, white head, blue bill (in summer).
Female : Light cheek crossed by dark line.

♂ RED-BREASTED MERGANSER ♀

♂ GOOSANDER ♀

♂ SMEW ♀

♂ SHELD-DUCK ♀

♂ RUDDY SHELD-DUCK ♀

♂ Summer WHITE-HEADED DUCK ♀

The Mallard Flight   *(From a painting by Peter Scott)*

Greylag Geese Taking Off

situation as enviably liberal. But the logic is inescapable, the more people exploiting a stock of wildfowl, the smaller must be the individual share if the stock is not to decline.

This, unfortunately, is just what appears to be happening to the populations composing the flyways from the Soviet Union through south and east Europe to Africa, and those southward to Asia. The breeding areas for these lie in more thickly populated parts of the Soviet Union and the wildfowl are thoroughly exploited before leaving her borders. Thereafter they are attacked almost without control. It is small wonder that the Soviet researchers are expressing alarm and advocating their own restrictive measures. These can be quite effective because of the enormous territories under Soviet control, but basically the solution will only be found by international agreement.

The Hunting Rationalisation Research Group will thus have its hands pretty full. Being the part of the IWRB organization most intimate with the wildfowlers and their organizations, this Group will also seek to stimulate research based on the activities of the wildfowlers themselves. Once again Britain has given the lead in such activities as the collection of wildfowl guts for analysis of food items and/or parasites; in the collection of wings for the analysis of age and sex ratios in the kill. But unlike, for instance, their Danish opposite numbers, the British wildfowlers have been very reticent regarding the size of their bags.

A very important contribution wildfowlers can make is meticulously to return any rings they find on birds they shoot. The information to be gained from ringing permeates all the population research on wildfowl, their numbers, mortality and movements. In general the capture of ducks and geese require massive trapping installations, expensive projectile nets or elaborate and costly expeditions to high-arctic breeding sites. Wildfowl ringing is thus associated with the efforts of rather few national research institutes. A special Research Group of the IWRB has not therefore been needed to co-ordinate ringing analyses. A number of continent-wide studies have been made, a particularly elaborate one being that for the garganey. The main requirement for international co-ordination has been with regard the methods of recording and reporting details of ringing and recoveries of ringed birds. This has been achieved for European bird-ringing as a whole by an association of the national ringing institutes known as Euring (Chairman Mr. R. D. Etchecopar, France). With uniform coding agreed, the way is now open to speedier analyses of ringing data by the use of up-to-date computer techniques.

Even if the international community knew all about the size, distribution and movements of its wildfowl stocks and agreed upon their rational utilization, it would avail little if the wetlands disappeared. The Bureau's efforts to prevent this have already been described. But it would be starry-eyed to imagine that further losses of wetlands will not occur. We are faced therefore with the necessity of making better use of those wetlands which remain if wildfowl stocks are not to decrease. Moreover, wetland habitat is one of the most unstable of ecological types, rapidly evolving to a drier scrub-dominated situation if left to its own devices. The answer to both these problems is the development of ecological researches that will give us the knowledge necessary for the management of wetlands to keep them in prime condition for wildfowl. To encourage such research and to bring together such knowledge as is already available, the IWRB has set up the *Habitat Management Research Group* (Co-ordinator Dr. J. Szijj, West Germany). Since such research requires specialist biological disciplines, the Group is seeking to encourage Universities to make studies of direct application to wetland management. A handbook on existing techniques is in process of preparation; or rather a series of handbooks, for the problems differ widely in the different types of wetlands. To deal with this the Group has formed Branches, such as those concerned with the special problems of the Mediterranean estuaries (Dr. L. Hoffmann, France) and with the area of the Danube basin and its saline lakes (Dr. A. Festetics, Austria).

REGIONAL WILDFOWL SURVEYS

The Research Groups have largely confined their activities to Europe. This is because only there, in the Old World, are sufficient specialists, amateur as well as professional, available to carry out such detailed researches. In Africa and Asia, where conservation is most urgently needed and efforts can be particularly effective, work must necessarily be at a more superficial level. The aim has been to mobilize such specialists as there are to provide the basic information on the distribution of wildfowl and of wetlands. They also seek to arouse interest in and action on the problems of research and conservation throughout a wide region.

In Africa there has long been an effective Southern African Survey (Co-ordinator, Professor J. M. Winterbottom, S. Africa) and more recently there has come into being the West African Survey (Co-ordinator, Mr. F. Roux, France). The other areas of Africa have yet to be covered in this way. In Asia there is the flourishing South West Asia Survey (Co-ordinator, Mr. C. D. W. Savage, Pakistan) covering India, Ceylon and Afghanistan as well as Pakistan. Recently formed is the Central Asia Survey (Co-ordinator, Dr. V. E. Flint, U.S.S.R.) covering the Asiatic part of the Soviet Union west of the Yenesi River, Western Mongolia, Iran, Iraq and Arabia. The Soviet Union east of the Yenesi, Eastern Mongolia, Korea and Japan are covered by the North East Asia Survey (Co-ordinator, Dr. A. A. Kishchinsky, U.S.S.R.). China, as in many other respects, remains an enigma.

INTERNATIONAL MEETINGS

While much co-ordination can be achieved through correspondence, through special publications and through the periodical Bulletin issued by the Bureau, actual meeting of the people involved are essential. The Executive Board, comprising Co-ordinators, national Delegates and representatives of associated international organizations, such as CIC, meets once a year, usually in a different country each time. Besides discussing the Bureau's business, such meetings help to stimulate conservation activities in the host country, for research associates there are also invited.

At longer intervals the Bureau is concerned with other organizations in convening wider ranging conferences at which all aspects of wildfowl and wetland conservation can be discussed and at which Governments can be represented at high level. These have taken place at Stes Maries-de-la-Mer, France, in 1962; at St. Andrews, Scotland, in 1963; at Jablonna, Poland, in 1965; at Noordwijk, the Netherlands, in 1966; at Ankara, Turkey, in 1967; at Leningrad, U.S.S.R. in 1968. The next large international conference is scheduled to take place in Babolsar, Iran, in 1971. Besides the possibilities these conferences provide for influencing governmental opinion, their published Proceedings bring to the attention of a wide audience the current position, and problems, in wildfowl research and conservation in Europe, Asia and Africa.

PUBLICATIONS

Past issues of the IWRB Bulletins and of research papers prepared under its aegis are available from Headquarters at the flat rate of 5/- per publication. Future issues of Bulletins will be sent to organizations or individuals subscribing a minimum of £1 per annum to Bureau funds. (IWRB a/c, Lloyds Bank, Dursley, Gloucestershire, England.) The following publications are also available:

Project MAR. The Conservation and management of temperate marshes, bogs and other wetlands. Ed. L. Hoffmann, I.U.C.N. Pub. N.S. 2, pp. 475 (42/-).

Project MAR. List of European and North African wetlands of International Importance. Ed. P. J. Olney. I.U.C.N. Pub. N.S. 5, pp. 102 (22/-).

Liquid Assets. Ed. G. L. Atkinson-Willes. Many illustrations. pp. 15 (5/-).

Proceedings of the First European Meeting on Wildfowl Conservation, St. Andrews, Scotland. pp. 289 (28/-).

Proceedings of the Second European Meeting on Wildfowl Conservation, Noordwijk, The Netherlands. pp. 225 (46/-).

Proceedings of the Meeting on International Co-operation in Wildfowl Research, Jablonna, Warsaw. pp. 356 (20/-).

Proceedings of a Technical Meeting on Wetland Conservation, Ankara. I.U.C.N. Pub. N.S. 12. pp. 273 (22/-).

Legislative and Administrative Measures for Wildfowl Conservation in Europe and North Africa. Looseleaf format (roneo-ed) (42/-).

Wildfowl Refuges in Europe, North Africa and the Middle East. Volume I. Volume II. Looseleaf format (roneo-ed) (42/-).

CHAPTER 26

THE NORTH-AMERICAN WILDFOWL SITUATION

by Jeffery Harrison

Vice Chairman and Hon. Scientific Adviser, Wildfowlers' Association of Great Britain and Ireland. Vice-Chairman, Wildfowl Conservation Committee, Nature Conservancy; British Representative, International Wildfowl Research Bureau; Council, The Wildfowl Trust.

THIS chapter could equally appropriately have been entitled "How North America has Saved its Wildfowl". It is hardly surprising that those who concern themselves with the future well-being of European wildfowl should look across the Atlantic at times, both with admiration and envy, to the tremendous achievements of the North-American wildfowl conservation movement.

The problems in North America are very different from those in Europe, as Walter Crissey pointed out at the first European Meeting on Wildfowl Conservation. The breeding grounds of this great migratory population of wildfowl are in the north, covering most of Canada (except the mountainous west) and Alaska. Within this wide area, far and away the most important concentrations of nesting duck are to be found in the famous prairie and parkland pothole region, within the Provinces of Alberta, Saskatchewan and Manitoba in Canada, and the States of North and South Dakota and Minnesota in the United States.

This is an area of rich agricultural land, including most of the wheat-growing areas of Canada. It is also an area of low rainfall and is subject to cycles of wet and dry conditions, leading at times to severe droughts, when many of the potholes dry out completely and become useless for breeding. In 1955 and 1956, during a very wet period there were some six million potholes in the prairie province alone, but by 1961 at the height of the severe drought which began in 1957, the potholes had decreased to a mere half million in these regions. Opportunity was taken at this time by many farmers to reclaim the land permanently for agriculture. Fortunately we are now entering the next wet cycle.

There is no doubt that it is the pothole region which, when conditions are right, produces the bulk of the North American migratory duck population. If this region were ever to be destroyed, then the ducks will go too. Fortunately the appropriate authorities in both the United States and Canada are well aware of this and are taking steps to preserve this unique and invaluable habitat.

Ringing has shown that in times of drought many of the duck which normally nest in the potholes move farther north on spring migration, but when they are forced to do this, production rates have been found to be lower than usual.

Strangely enough it is this cycle of wet and dry years which renews the fertility of the potholes, returning them to the ideal condition for nesting habitat, so that the North-American duck population would seem to be always liable to alternating cycles of abundance and scarcity. This is something for which, so far as we know at present, we have no equivalent in Europe, although looking at the population trends of wigeon and teal, it is possible that we may eventually find some similarity, but certainly not on the scale of the North-American fluctuations. As such, this has provided a great stimulus for research and conservation. Thanks to this, the population was nursed through the severe drought of the early 1960s.

Three facts stand out to someone from Europe looking at the North-American wildfowl picture for the first time. First, there is the high degree of international co-operation between the three countries concerned, the United States, Canada and Mexico. It is nice to think that Great Britain was concerned in the first treaty, which was signed between ourselves and the U.S.A. in 1916 for the protection of migratory birds moving between Canada and the U.S.A. A second treaty between the U.S.A. and Mexico was duly ratified in 1937, thus bringing the most southerly of the wildfowl winter quarters under the same jurisdiction. This kind of politics makes sense.

These treaties obliged the three nations to give up spring shooting of migratory birds and provided the legal basis to regulate the shooting season.

This brings us to the second fact and that is the widespread acceptance through North America of the idea of harvesting a crop of wildfowl. The whole wildfowl population is managed by means of shooting regulations and habitat manipulation. In this respect, so far as Europe is concerned, the American viewpoint is probably closest to that of the Russians.

Finally, there are about two million people in the United States who shoot duck. They are prepared to spend a lot of money and to accept severe restrictions for the privilege of so doing, but at least they have the satisfaction of knowing that a good proportion of their money is ploughed back into wildfowl conservation.

Dealing first with the shooting regulations, these vary from year to year and are worked out by biologists working for the U.S. Fish and Wildlife Service and the Canadian Fish and Wildlife Service, both of which are financed by their respective governments.

Walter Crissey, at the First European Meeting on Wildfowl Conservation, gave an excellent account of the working of the Fish and Wildlife Service and with Gus Swanson went on to give a concise account of the wildfowl shooting regulations in the U.S.A., which must have come as a surprise to many an English wildfowler with his season of almost six months, his moonlight flighting and his unrestricted bags of duck or geese.

The Fish and Wildlife Service carries out five major data-collecting programmes annually. The first of these is a winter survey to assess the distribution of the population and population trends. This takes place in late December and early January, and involves the use of some 150 aeroplanes. This is equivalent to the mid-January European and Western Asiatic Wildfowl Census, the first of which was carried out in 1967, when over two million duck and swans were counted outside Russia.

The second programme is a survey of the breeding grounds. This is done by flying aerial transects over the breeding grounds, the specially trained crews covering about 80,000 miles of transect at an altitude of about 100 feet.

These routes are covered twice, first in late May to assess the number of breeding pairs and again in July to assess the production of young. In addition to the aerial surveys, certain areas are intensively studied from the ground. In this way the varying proportions of the different species seen from the air can be calculated in relation to changing ground cover, water levels, etc.

The third survey is that of the wildfowl killed by shooting. This consists of a questionnaire sent through the post to a random sample of some 50,000 shooters. From the answers, techniques have been developed for calculating the annual kill, allowing for the strong tendency of those responding to the questionnaire to exaggerate somewhat!

The fourth survey is based on a duck wing and goose tail analysis. The Americans pioneered this technique to assess the annual production of young wildfowl—a technique with which we are now experimenting in Great Britain. A sample of hunters in the U.S.A. who reported taking one or more duck in the previous season receives an appropriate number of envelopes for mailing one wing from each duck shot during the following season. A sample of upwards of 90,000 duck wings is received for identification, sexing and ageing and in this way a valuable check is obtained for the survey estimates obtained in the previous summer.

Work is now going on with goose tails, collected in the same way. It would seem that the ageing of Canada geese from tail feathers is far from easy, which is similar to our findings on tail feathers of both greylag and pink-footed geese.

The final data-collecting programme is from ringing (banding). At the time of the First European Meeting in 1963, a total of three million wildfowl had been ringed in North America, to give half a million recoveries. About 300,000 wildfowl are now being ringed each year, resulting in about 40,000 recoveries—a formidable achievement. Unlike Europe, the majority of the birds are ringed on the breeding grounds, which gives vital information as to which harvest areas are likely to be affected by changes found on the breeding survey.

Extensive ringing is also carried out on concentrations of moulting adults and flightless young in late summer. This yields details of population structure which are different from the figures produced by the wing survey. When these figures are compared with the ringing results, it is possible to calculate with some accuracy the size of the total population before the start of the open season and the proportion of young for that year.

With these basic figures available year by year it has become possible to predict population trends and the correct bag limits with considerable accuracy. For duck, the appropriate regulations are announced prior to the opening of the season. For geese the necessary regulations are altered the year after the population change occurred, for these are based only on a winter survey and figures for the age and sex ratios of the kill.

American figures have proved beyond doubt that by altering the shooting regulations, it is possible to control the proportion of the population which is harvested. The main objective to be achieved from the shooting regulations is to hold the breeding population between acceptable high and low extremes. The low figure is determined by the minimum number of pairs required to lead to a very rapid recovery under optimum water conditions on the nesting grounds.

At the other extreme, in peak years, it is an established fact that there is a surplus of birds over and above the carrying capacity of the breeding grounds in the following year. In other words, in North America it is conditions on the breeding grounds which control the population level. It is during the wet years of the weather cycle therefore that the season and bag limits can be increased to maintain the population just within the carrying capacity of the breeding grounds.

Obviously this varies from species to species, as the nesting requirements for dabbling duck and diving duck are often different and there are specific differences within these two broad groups. The ideal management therefore may call for different season and bag limits from species to species and this calls for accurate field identification on the part of the shooters.

As a result of ringing, it has become clear that there are four great migrational routes for wildfowl moving south to their winter quarters in the United States and northern South America. These have been defined as the famous "flyways"—the Atlantic Flyway, the Mississippi Flyway, the Central Flyway and the Pacific Flyway. While biologically they are not quite so well defined as the uninitiated might think, a clear-cut division between them enables the population to be divided into four administrative units. Shooting pressure is not the same in all four flyways. Wildfowl production may also vary in any one year within this great area. It is therefore highly desirable that the management control of each flyway should be independent of the others.

Administrative meetings of "Flyway Councils" are held twice a year. Each council consists of administrative and technical members of both U.S., Federal and State wildlife agencies, Canadian Federal and Provincial representatives also attend, though they naturally take only a limited part in framing the proposals on the regulations to be made in the U.S.A. (The Councils do not recommend regulations for Canada.) The length of the season and the bag limits are set at a summer meeting, using the breeding data that are available by mid-July. The season opens progressively as the migratory wave moves southwards, varying from State to State. The length of the season is limited to $3\frac{1}{2}$ months in any State, between 1st September and 1st March, each State deciding its own dates. The Federal Governments decide how long a season shall be permitted and this has been as short as twenty-five and as long as ninety-five days in recent years.

There may be completely closed seasons in some years for low population species and this may at times only apply in certain areas. In the United States bag limits are set, ranging in geese from one to five and for game ducks from two to seven. Possession limits are usually twice the bag limit. Occasionally, seasonal quotas are used. There is a total ban on the sale of wildfowl. Canadian regulations are similar, although allowing rather larger bags in the Yukon and North-West Territories.

All rifles are prohibited and no shotgun larger than a 10-bore is allowed and none may be used which is capable of firing more than three cartridges without reloading. It is forbidden to feed flight ponds, to use live decoys and electric callers. There must be no shooting from mechanically propelled boats and fowl at rest on open water must not be disturbed. Finally shooting is only allowed from half an hour before sunrise until sunset.

Before anyone in the U.S.A. can shoot wildfowl a Federal "Duck Stamp" has to be bought and at present costs $3 (£1), also a State small game licence (about the same price for residents; £5 for visitors). Failure to possess a "Duck Stamp" renders the shooter liable to a fine of up to £175 and/or six months' imprisonment. The entire proceeds of the "Duck Stamp" are used for conservation work—and with over 1½ million people buying one each season this is a significant sum—Oh that we could have something similar in Great Britain! Most hunters then join a Rod and Gun Club, which can prove very expensive—but many provide excellent private shooting. One rather interesting development in 1967 was that the Mouse Lake Gun Club, Portland, Oregon, applied for formal affiliation to WAGBI—a much-appreciated gesture of friendship.

In 1966, for the first time, Canadian waterfowl hunters were also required to obtain a $2 Canadian Migratory Game Bird Hunting Permit as well as a Provincial Licence. The proceeds from these permits are also applied to conservation.

It is quite obvious that the North-American wildfowl population will always be subjected to fluctuations as conditions vary, particularly water levels on the breeding grounds. In the spring of 1962 the duck population was as low as it was considered it should ever be allowed to go. Severe regulations in 1963 were designed to halt any further decline—and they succeeded, to be followed fortunately by the onset of the next wet cycle.

The great safeguard for the future must be to conserve and restore suitable wetlands. This was recognized as long ago as 1934 when the President of the United States, Franklin D. Roosevelt, set up a "President's Committee on Wildlife Restoration" under Thomas Beck. This Committee reported "There is incontrovertible evidence of a critical and continuing decline in our wildlife resources—especially migratory waterfowl due to the destruction and neglect of vast, natural breeding and nesting areas by drainage, encroachment of agriculture and the random efforts of our disordered progress towards an undefined goal."

At that time the Federal Government already owned fifty-five wildlife reservations potentially suitable for migratory birds, covering five million acres. This included Pelican Island Refuge in Florida—the very first refuge—which was established in 1903 through an order of President Theodore Roosevelt. In 1924, $1½ million were authorized to establish the Upper Mississippi

Refuge. In 1926, the Bear River Migratory Bird Refuge was established at a cost of $\frac{1}{3}$ million. As a result of the Beck Report, Henry Wallace, Secretary of Agriculture announced that the Government had allocated a further $8\frac{1}{2}$ million for wetland preservation.

By 1963, the United States had established 220 wildfowl refuges covering just over $2\frac{1}{2}$ million acres of wetland. In addition, 66,000 acres of potholes had been acquired. Further refuges have been established by the States. By 1961, these already covered $4\frac{1}{2}$ million acres, aided by financial help from Congress, through the *Pittman-Robertson Act 1937*. Canada, too, has made a great contribution to this North-American network of refuges.

Almost all refuges are actively managed, particularly with regard to the control of water levels. Many of them have been made self-supporting through farming and forestry, but the primary goal is always the needs of wildfowl. An annual budget of no less than half a million dollars is shared between three goose refuges in southern Illinois. There is no doubt that the refuge system has been tremendously successful—so much so, that this has brought its own problems. It has been found possible to alter the migration routes of some species through a well-planned "route" of refuges. This particularly applies to Canada geese. When this happens, the concentrations of fowl may build up to astonishing proportions and result in severe crop damage. In many cases allowance is made for this by farming for wildfowl on the refuge through extensive food planting. Although controlled shooting is also allowed on many refuges, some not only attract great numbers of birds, but also great numbers of shooters, who ring the refuge and this has occasionally resulted in a gross overkill.

There is some evidence that the refuge programme has encouraged birds to stay too far north in areas which can become unsuitable in severe weather. In Missouri, where the State agencies aim to re-establish enough native ducks to make local hunters independent of the uncertain supplies of migrant duck from the north, tens of thousands of mallard are now being released annually. Large numbers of Canada geese are also being redistributed.

No account of the refuge system would be complete without an account of the part played by those who shoot. As in WAGBI, so in the American duck clubs, many are carrying out their own marsh management and have established private reserves—approximately 6,000 clubs manage 3 million acres of wetland and have 130,000 acres of reserves.

Another remarkable act of conservation was the establishment of "Ducks Unlimited"—an organization formed in 1937 by duck shooters to raise money to be spent on restoring the wildfowl breeding grounds in Canada. It is utterly unselfish, for not only is money raised in the United States to be spent in Canada, but very often those subscribing the money know full well that it will not even be spent to the benefit of their own particular "Flyway".

As pointed out in Anglia Television's *Survival* programme covering "Ducks Unlimited", this is probably the biggest piece of private enterprise wildfowl conservation that the world has ever seen. Since its formation "Ducks Unlimited" has spent well over $10 million. They have built 800 dams, some of them major engineering projects; they have dug a network of canals and put in sluices to bring water back to land that had become completely barren. Over 750 new lakes and swamps have been formed. The shore-line of these equals the entire coastline of the United States.

One of the things which staggered John Anderton, WAGBI's Director, on his 1966 visit to the United States was a DU fund-raising dinner in New York at which nearly £20,000 was contributed in the one evening. Such figures are indeed impressive, as is the whole of the North American wildfowl conservation movement.

In 1969, Lorne Cameron, newly elected President of "Ducks Unlimited" (Canada) announced that "to ensure the population of ducks required by 1980 will require a minimum of another $4\frac{1}{2}$ million acres of dependable wetlands over and above the 2 million now DU controlled". This was the fantastic target presented at the directors' annual meeting in March. Forty new developments were then approved at a cost of $1\frac{1}{2}$ million. The necessary funds will be provided by United States sportsmen.

Can the North-American wildfowl population be preserved for the future? I believe that it can, for in North America far more than in Europe, hunters, naturalists and the general public have come to appreciate the full value of wetlands—and that is why each and every one of us can play our part in the proper conservation of our wildfowl and our wildlife. Therein lies the great hope for the future.

CHAPTER 27

CONTROL OF PREDATORS

by Charles Swan

Duck Conservation Sub-Committee, WAGBI; Experimental Officer, Ministry of Agriculture and Fisheries.

ONE part of wildfowl conservation is the hand-rearing and subsequent release of duck and geese which implies the control of predators or other adverse factors in the environment. Much has been written about the "balance of nature" and we shall not expound the theories here, other than to say that a high concentration of a prey species will attract predators that must be kept to an acceptable minimum or the results of our efforts will be nullified.

The theory of predator—prey relationships implies a *steady* population and as Harrison has pointed out in the section of "A Wealth of Wildfowl" dealing with this topic, if one wishes to increase a population of wildfowl, it may be necessary to tilt the scales somewhat in their favour. This involves some degree of predator control.

The most vulnerable period is from nesting time until the young are strong on the wing and a great deal can be done to protect the birds during this vital time.

Recent legislation has greatly affected the forms of control that can be used and the species that may be killed. It is therefore the responsibility of all shooting men to be fully conversant with the law in this respect. Briefly the main points are these:

(*a*) Poisons are illegal except for rats, mice and moles.

(*b*) Only the birds in Schedule II of the *Protection of Birds Acts 1954–1967* (which now excludes all hawks, falcons and owls) may be taken throughout the year by *authorized* persons.

(*c*) No spring traps may be used for birds.

(*d*) The only spring traps that may be used against mammals are the Juby, Imbra, Fenn, Fuller, Sawyer and Lloyd and these must not be used other than in an approved manner.

No matter what control method is used, it will only succeed if executed with efficiency. Slap-dash operations will only be a waste of time and money and will have a limited effect on predator numbers, e.g. misuse of poison for rats, so that the animal takes a sub-lethal dose, will make the rat "bait shy" in the future, and malfunctioning traps that spring but fail to catch, will only serve to make the animal more cautious, just two examples of bad workmanship that will increase difficulties.

Although trapping is one of the most effective means of reducing predators, it is the most neglected. Traps work twenty-four hours a day every day of the year and if correctly sited and used will account for more enemies of wildfowl than any other control method, with the exception of poisons on high concentrations of rats.

Traps must be adjusted to function correctly before being used in the field. It is a common error to expect new traps direct from suppliers to be ready for use. Traps that have been mishandled in transit will need readjustment before use and the careful application of a file or pliers will often make the difference between real success and complete failure. The practice of making traps "tittle" or hair-triggered in every instance is also an error, they should be made and adjusted to stand the best chance of catching a specific animal. Tunnel traps set to catch rats and stoats should not be sprung too often by fieldmice and voles. The only predator for which a trap should be set very lightly is the weasel.

The components of most traps are of steel and they will quickly rust and fail to work in damp conditions. Therefore they should be regularly sprung and reset. Should lubrication be necessary, the use of animal fat, instead of mineral oils or grease, will reduce unwelcome scent on the trap.

The siting of traps is important and the careful placing of each trap so that it is firm in position, and pegged down, is essential. The treadle should be level with the ground when set. Where there is loose rubble a *little* moss or dry grass placed under the plate will prevent any stones or twigs rolling under and preventing the treadle being depressed.

Most animals do not appear to be trap-shy but individuals within a species can be wary of traps. This may be due to a previous near-miss which may make the animal extremely cautious for some time. It is, therefore, advisable to disguise and camouflage traps at all times, especially if there is the slightest risk of interference from members of the general public near to a right-of-way, ride or footpath.

In hard weather traps must be set in dry sites or they will be frozen solid if covered with moist material. In permanent tunnels, either natural or artificial, the conditions are usually dry enough to prevent traps freezing during frost. Slight snowfall can assist the trapper as the tracks of the species present will be clearly visible. Full advantage should be taken of this opportunity before a thaw distorts and obliterates the tell-tale marks.

The Imbra and Juby traps were primarily designed as rabbit traps and if used for this purpose must be set below ground. These traps are also useful against other mammals but may be used above ground if set in natural or artificial tunnels. Hollow logs and tree trunks, overhangs or banks, drains, culverts, piles of logs, stone walls, sheds and other outbuildings, stacks, etc., may all provide good natural trapping sites and if there is a need for a tunnel to be built in a favourable site, it is easily constructed if materials such as bricks and stones, logs, turves, drainage tiles and slates are to hand.

As a last resort portable tunnels, can be easily made of wooden boards to exactly the size required. A "split" tunnel that is made in two sections, to allow the arms of the trap jaws to close in a slot between the two sections and so keep the height of the tunnel to a minimum, is the most economical and effective way to build artificial tunnels for the Imbra and Juby traps.

The Fenn, Sawyer and Lloyd traps may also be used against rats and mice only in the open on their runs. It is therefore necessary, for most of our trapping, to use these traps in tunnels also. Fortunately these traps are less bulky than the Imbra and Juby and can frequently be sited in positions unsuitable for the larger traps. If artificial tunnels are made they should be no larger than is absolutely necessary, as with all tunnel trapping the animal must be guided as directly and as low over the trap as possible. All approved traps are designed to give a high percentage of kills to strikes when used correctly, this is the purpose of a "humane" trap.

The Fuller trap is a squirrel trap and is built as a box to provide its own "tunnel". There is a small entrance hole at one end of the box inside of which is a bait tray that acts as a trigger when depressed. The bait recommended for squirrels is whole maize but as this will also attract pheasants it is necessary to provide additional protection in the form of a short tunnel made of wire mesh running up to the entrance of the trap. This should be firmly pegged in position.

There are no restrictions on the use of mole traps, but moles scarcely concern wildfowl, except when their runs give access to the occasional weasel, which may prove harmful to young ducklings.

We are also unrestricted in the use of cage traps to catch Schedule II birds and mammals, alive and uninjured. Cage traps are often superior to spring traps when large concentrations of predators have to be controlled, particularly when multi-catch traps are suitable for species such as rooks, jackdaws, rats and squirrels.

There are numerous designs of large cage traps for rooks and jackdaws usually constructed so that they are easy to dismantle and re-erect. Cage dimensions average 6 ft. to 10 ft. long by 6 ft. wide by 4 ft. 6 in. to 6 ft. in height and may have ground entrances in the shape of funnels or a roof entrance of a letter-box shape. Some tops are fitted with sheep netting, cone-shaped wire mesh or a ladder-like grill made of timber. All have various advantages according to design but generally it is unwise to have roof entrances for jackdaws as these birds seem to have an uncanny ability to find exits that are the least bit accessible in the top of the cage.

The best method of using these traps is to site the trap on a regular flight line or in the vicinity of the area where the birds are feeding, such as rearing fields, free-range chicken fields, or near feeding troughs or ricks, taking care to protect the cage from damage by domestic stock. The trap should be erected minus the roof section and baited with bread, cereals, eggs, etc., until the birds are seen to be using the cage. The roof is then placed in position. The trap should catch well in the first day after it has been set. If some decoys from the first catch are left in the trap (with food and water) for the second and perhaps third day, more rooks and jackdaws may be caught. If, however, the catch falls to very few birds it is best to revert immediately to a prebaiting period again until more birds are using the cage, and then reset. It is far more profitable to have a few catches of fairly large numbers of birds at, say, weekly intervals, than to catch only two or three birds at a time each day. Cage traps of this type are most successful in the late spring anp early summer and are least successful in the autumn when the living is good on stubble and acorns.

When the traps are baited it is a good practice to cut a perch or two to fit across the inside of the trap away from entrances. A stout stick about 1½ ins. in diameter, with short 3 in. to 4 in. pieces of twigs left along its length when trimming the side shoots off, provides the ideal perch. Slices of bread and other bait can then be threaded on the twigs which will be visible for good distances, but if all the bait is placed on the floor of the cage it may be obscure.

There is also a net trap that folds over when the treadle is stuck, designed to catch the larger birds, but unfortunately it is only a single-catch trap and although it will catch corvids, the careful camouflage that is necessary makes setting a laborious business for usually poor results.

The types of cage traps that may be used for mammals are so numerous that it would be impossible to list them all in this short chapter. Many are listed in manufacturers' catalogues together with instructions for their use. Among the most useful of these traps are the Legg squirrel traps, double-ended wire cage traps of various sizes and the M.A.F.F. trap, designed mainly for mink, but useful also for rats, stoats, squirrels, hedgehogs, etc.

The main points that must be considered when using cage traps are these. The trap must be constructed of the most robust material possible within reasonable limits, the action must be crisp and positive, the doors should be locked when the trap is sprung so that should a larger animal be tempted to try to get at the trapped animal by overturning the trap the door will not re-open, and all mechanisms, should if possible, be inside the trap to make it easy to camouflage. If the mechanism is on the outside of the trap it will become obstructed by twigs and other material used to cover the trap and so make the trap malfunction.

Box traps are usually of a design that entails the tugging of the bait to release a trap-door after the animal has entered the trap, or long narrow boxes with false bottoms that operate like a see-saw. In the latter instance the trap has a transparent (either glass or plastic) end that gives the animal the impression that it can go right through the trap, but when it passes the point of balance in the centre of the floor of the trap, the floor tilts and closes the entrance. These traps are particularly good in sites such as stone walls and in hedges with exposed roots of larger trees.

We will not go into the highly skilled use of dead-fall traps, benders and similar devices, since this would call for very detailed explanations. Any trapper interested but not familiar with these techniques should seek a demonstration from someone who is practised in their use. He will almost certainly be of the older generation.

The decision to bait or not to bait traps will depend on the type of site chosen and the species that we hope to catch. Some form of bait will be necessary for bird traps and mammals such as squirrels, rats and hedgehogs, but it is not essential to bait traps set for mustelids (mink, stoats and weasels) if we use tunnel traps. Cage traps for these species should be baited. It is also best to place baits in holes that have been specially dug in river banks to conceal a spring trap set to catch mink.

Baits that are chosen because they are the normal food or prey of the species that we wish to catch are usually attractive or at least do not deter the animal. We should, however, be cautious of some other methods of enticing animals into traps, especially the use of scent from animals of the same species as those that we intend to catch. It is well known that individuals of many species hold territories and that others have a system of dominant and subordinate individuals within a group. These animals mark out their territory or hold their position partly by the use of scent from glands or urine. It is therefore possible that by artificially contaminating a trap with the scent of a previously killed dominant animal, the trap could be made repellent to the others of the same species that we wish to attract. The only apparently safe use of this form of enticement is the use of female scent to catch males at the breeding season and it is doubtful if even this is as successful as we are led to believe.

The only predator that we need consider when using snares is the fox, and then with due consideration for local hunting interests. For all other species there are more economical methods. The main points to consider when snaring foxes are these. Ensure that the materal used is adequate for the job and that the snare is made with some form of swivel to avoid the wire twisting and kinking, and make certain that the snare is anchored securely to a post, sapling, fence, log or peg that, although it may "give", will not break or be dragged more than a few feet. Make sure when inspecting snares that you are equipped to kill the captured fox quickly and humanely.

When trapping it is vitally necessary to visit all traps and snares at least once a day, preferably twice. For snares, soon after dawn is the best time. With bird traps visits at dusk prevent birds being left in the trap overnight. With all traps, inspection about two hours after dawn is the ideal time, for many predators are very active until well after daylight and a high percentage of captures occur at this time. On a number of occasions mink traps inspected at dawn and found empty have caught animals by mid-morning.

A trapped animal, caught alive, that has to be killed, must be dispatched as humanely as possible. Usually any mammal caught in a spring trap and still alive can be killed by a sharp blow on the back of the head with a stout stick, but animals caught in cages can often prove more difficult. Trappers should always be prepared for emergencies and should carry either a ·410 or ·22, alternatively a large polythene bag, some cotton wool and carbon tetrachloride. If the cage trap with its occupant is sealed in the polythene bag together with a swab of cotton wool soaked in carbon tetrachloride, the animal will be quickly and humanely killed and can then be easily removed from the trap.

The skilful and intelligent use of the shotgun and ·22 rifle will often be found the most effective means of controlling certain predators. Foxes can be shot at drives and the carrion crow and magpie can be accounted for by the use of the shotgun when trapping is unsuccessful.

The ·22 is frequently used on fledgeling rooks or "branchers", from early May for a week or two, but if this form of control is undertaken only birds perched clear of the nest should be shot, so that any wounded birds will then fall to the ground where they can be quickly killed instead of tumbling into the nest to die a lingering death.

The crow is a difficult bird to trap. The practice of shooting at the nest site or by using a decoy and hide on a flight line is likely to be more successful. The method of putting a crow off its nest by two persons, leaving one in hiding near the nest to shoot the bird on its return, is a well-known device, but the use of a decoy, in a fairly clear area on the flight line soon after dawn is perhaps the more profitable, for a well concealed patient gun will have a better chance of killing more than one crow in this way. Crow calls can be most effective, particularly in fog. Crows may also be shot when coming in to roost and there are records of many birds being accounted for at communal winter roosts, especially in the north. Magpies will also come to decoys and to crow calls.

The most neglected predator of all is the brown rat. This is all the more astonishing since it causes more damage than any other animal. It eats eggs, kills young and sometimes adult birds, eats and contaminates food, gnaws and damages pens and other equipment, disturbs breeding stock and carries disease, in many forms, to infect both stock and humans. The rearer is often complacent about an infestation of rats yet spends many hours and cash on the control of other species.

Poisoning is by far the most economical way to deal with this pest, both in time and money. Gassing, both of foxes and rats is best left to experts. Cymag is too dangerous in inexperienced hands. It is illegal to gas badgers. A good advisory leaflet on poisoning on this subject is available at any of the Ministry of Agriculture's Divisional Offices. If it is possible to visit the site daily, then Warfarin poison should be used. If we are unable to make daily visits, an acute poison (probably zinc phosphide) should be used. The reason for this is that Warfarin has a cumulative effect over several days and baits must therefore be topped up to permit rats to feed at will for a period of time, whereas with acute poisons the rat must take a lethal dose before it begins to feel any ill effects. Rats associate discomfort with something they have eaten and if they take a sub-lethal dose and recover from the poison it may be a long time before they will accept another poison bait.

With acute poisons the site should be pre-baited with the unpoisoned bait only. When rats are seen to be feeding well on the bait base, the poison should be added which should then be readily taken.

Baiting points should be chosen so that rats can get at the bait easily but it should be inaccessible to other animals, places like the inside of unused drainage tiles, tunnels made with timber, slates or bricks, in rat holes, etc., taking care not to disturb the area too much until after the treatment, when tidying up and the collection and destruction of surplus bait should take place. In certain circumstances it is a good policy to establish permanent baiting sites in an area to kill rats as they move in.

Some predators are not necessarily a pest to other countryside interests. Many predators are useful to farmers and foresters, thus careful control as opposed to indiscriminate killing will determine the true conservationist. Our outlook must never be so narrow as to overlook the fact that our diminishing countryside has to be shared with an increasing number of other interests.

For this reason we should always consider means of protecting our stock birds by adequate proofing. Good fences and pens, initially costly items, may turn out to be the cheapest and least troublesome method of predator control, for if we can rear our birds to a stage past the main period of vulnerability the need to kill predators can be reduced to a minimum.

Of course, good proofing can rarely be the complete answer, for even if we ensure that predators cannot actually gain access to our birds they may well cause considerable losses by just harassing penned birds. This applies equally well to birds that are released. Initially they must be kept quiet so that any eventual dispersal is of their own will. Birds that have been dependent on humans for food and protection from hatching, need time to acquire the ability to find food and become wary of enemies.

Let us consider the winged enemies of wildfowl. As mentioned previously, all the owls, hawks and falcons are protected by the *Protection of Birds Act 1954*, many of them by special penalties. This leaves the corvids in Schedule II and the greater and lesser black-backed gulls and the herring gull. These may be taken by authorized persons, that is, the owner, occupier or persons authorized by the owner or occupier, such as the shooting tenant of the land on which the birds are taken. The Act also defines methods that may not be used to take wild birds.

The crow is probably the worst feathered enemy of wildfowl and the most difficult to control. Its food varies from cereals and animal foods, the carcases of dead animals and other cadavers, the eggs and young of birds, young and adult small mammals, to crustaceans from the shore-line and pickings from rubbish dumps. Early duck nests with a limited cover of vegetation are very prone to attack from crows and for this reason we should carry out control measures as early in the New Year as possible. The crows killed at this time are potential parents and should be removed from the nesting site before they have the chance to multiply. The opportunity to reduce the crow population at any time of year should not be missed, but the early spring is the time for real effort. Shooting at roosts, at the nest site or over a decoy is the best method of control, but if trapping is attempted very careful siting of traps, either cage or net, using egg or carrion bait will be necessary to outwit this the most cautious of birds.

We may look upon the magpie and jackdaw as smaller editions of the crow so far as damage is concerned, but we will need to treat them separately when we decide our tactics to reduce their numbers.

The jackdaw, a stealer of eggs and killer of young birds, usually because of its numbers, is no less a pest than the magpie. If a ground-nesting bird is once disturbed by jackdaws there is little hope for her clutch or brood, for while she is doing her best to defend against one intruder another will be robbing her of her young or eggs.

Many advocate the large cone trap for taking jackdaws but experiments with a variety of cage traps has proven the 6 ft. cube-shaped trap made of $1\frac{1}{2}$-in. wire mesh with a plain but portable top and tunnel-shaped ground entrances reducing from about 1 ft. 6 ins. high by 1 ft. 6 ins wide, to not more than 5 ins. high by 4 ins. wide on the inside, to be the most efficient and escape-proof design. A door on one side just large enough for the trapper to enter should

K

open inwards and have a fastening on both sides. If the trapper prefers a trap with a roof-entrance the "ladder letter-box" type is the most efficient but none of the roof entrance type traps are as secure for jackdaws as the correct size ground entrances.

The gun will not be so useful for jackdaws. Some may be shot when they begin to nest in hollow trees or in crevices or rabbit holes on cliffs, but after one or two visits they become "educated" and will be off before it is possible to get within gunshot. The time spent waiting in a hide at these sites does not justify the results obtained.

Too many rooks can also be a problem for although less predatory than the crow they can still account for many marshland nests and young birds. This bird is perhaps more of an opportunist than a deliberate searcher for nests, for it seems that only when its numbers are high and there is insufficient cereal, animal food, insects and other natural food does it become a predator harmful to ground-nesting birds.

There can be no doubt that damage caused by rooks can be considerable and the increase, in many parts of the country, of smaller but more numerous rookeries, often in places inaccessible to the keeper because of the proximity of houses, is reducing the amount of control possible by the use of the gun at "branchers" and making the use of cage traps more essential.

The traps should be used in the same way as for jackdaws but with slightly larger entrances. Rooks will also enter roof entrances more readily than jackdaws and are less likely to escape by this exit. However, frequently mixed flocks of rooks and jackdaws are caught and most game rearers would prefer to catch and retain as many jackdaws as possible even if this meant fewer rooks being caught.

The black-backed gulls and the herring gull will only be a pest in certain inland localities and on the coast. There is no doubt that duck nests and up to half-grown ducklings fall to these gulls, mainly in estuary areas. Of the Schedule II birds that prey on wildfowl, these gulls can lead to the greatest chance of violation of the 1954 Act. Although coastal fowlers have greater opportunities to shoot these species, they may not qualify as "authorized" persons. If the fowler is on land where he has shooting rights all will be well but, if he should be on "free" land—an area where he and others go unrestricted—without direct permission of the owner, he will not be "authorized" and therefore liable to prosecution.

These gulls have caused considerable concern to some local authorities at refuse tips. The tips, normally covered with a few inches of soil as tipping progresses, have been raked over by gulls and corvids to expose the refuse. Cage traps similar to the rook and jackdaw traps have been used with success at these sites.

Always keep on good terms with your neighbour, though his pets can often cause a good deal of trouble. A cat, apart from the actual killing that it can do will often disturb and harass your birds. The domestic cat gone feral must be discouraged and it is fortunate that it is comparatively easy to cage trap. It will readily fall for a fish or offal bait and the trap need only be sited near to a track or ride.

Some advocate the use of cats to control rats. If a rat population around buildings is low a cat or two may keep it this way, but cats will do little to reduce a heavy infestation of rats and we should use poisoning and trapping to control their numbers. These rats are only part of the problem, for it is often the colonies in the banks and ditches away from buildings that cause the rearer the most concern. We cannot proof wild stock against this pest and in this situation poisoning and gassing become essential.

A line of tunnel traps around the perimeter of our rearing area, and at strategic positions inside, will be our best defence against stoats, although the recent use of cage traps for mink has shown that stoats are readily caught in this way much more easily than was previously suspected. Stoats will be attracted by any of the baits used for mink including fish and, almost certainly, more weasels would be caught in this manner but for the fact that the $1'' \times 1''$ mesh normally used for mink cages is too large to hold a small male or a female weasel.

Whether or not hedgehogs deliberately set out to take eggs, there is no doubt that they do, and the use of cage or tunnel traps baited with carrion type baits or bread will usually prove effective. At night a walk round the area with a torch can be well worth while for the hedgehog is anything but silent in its wanderings and can often be heard scuffling among the leaves and vegetation making sufficient noise for an animal many times its size.

The grey squirrel is a nuisance to most country interests, but hardly concerns the wildfowler. It is easily trapped in both cage and tunnel traps. Although there are many baits suitable for squirrels, the most convenient and one of the most effective is whole maize. The squirrel will eat a great variety of cereals, nuts, seeds, fruit, bulbs, eggs and small young birds but it is selective and will only eat the best of the food available.

Care must be exercised when using grain or other baits attractive to birds, to ensure that trap entrances are too small to permit these birds to enter. Normally a grille of hazel sticks will serve this purpose.

A number of our common mammals have been introduced from overseas. The most recent species to be added to this list is the mink. This versatile predator could become a serious threat to much of our wildlife. It is difficult to get precise figures on its density and spread, but it is reasonable to assume that it will exist in every county within the next few years, for it is already known to be present in at least sixty-nine counties in England, Scotland and Wales.

There are authentic records of mink killing almost every species of mammal, with the exception of other mustelidae, up to the size of and including rabbits. The records also show predation of domestic poultry, ornamental and other wildfowl, racing pigeons, pheasants and fish up to 4 lb. in weight. Reptiles are also taken. Those who have seen the remains of animals at a mink nest will need no further evidence of the wide range of food acceptable to mink. As mink kill far in excess of their food requirements there should be no need to emphasize the need for stringent control.

Cage trapping is the most effective way of taking mink and although captures will be fewer in the first quarter of each year, than at any other time, the animals caught will be potential breeders and would probably be feeding a litter of young by midsummer. In the autumn they will disperse and although trapping results will rise dramatically, the chances of catching complete litters will diminish as the year progresses. Tunnel trapping is effective especially on the odd occasion when trap-shy individuals are encountered. The Imbra and Juby traps will serve best in this situation as they are much more likely to kill than the other, lighter, spring traps.

If a mink is known to be present in a hole in a tree or river bank it can be "squeaked out" and shot in the same manner as used for stoats. The law requires occupiers of land to report the presence of mink on their land to the Ministry of Agriculture.

Some fish must be considered to rank as major predators of duck. Although large pike can take an occasional full-grown duck as large as a mallard, it is the smaller pike in the 2–6 lb. range which may take significant numbers of young ducklings when they are feeding in the shallows. This particularly applies to young diving duck.

It must never be forgotten that there is also some balance between predators. Foxes and stoats for instance may be taking significant numbers of rats and one must always therefore endeavour to take a balanced view in deciding what control measures are necessary.

There seems to be more mystery and myth about pest control methods than almost any other rural pursuit. Men who have a lifelong experience will argue their different techniques, but often get similar results in the field. The one myth above all others that should be dispelled is that only those who have had their "know-how" handed down through generations have any hope of real skill. The use of plain common sense applied to certain basic principles will enable anyone to start on the work with modest results. Experience will bring a skill and finesse that will enable the trapper to perform with humane efficiency, which should be the real aim of everyone.

CHAPTER 28

WILDFOWL IN CAPTIVITY

by Edmund Gleadow, M.B.

British Avicultural Society.

MANY wildfowlers, either as individuals or through local reserves run by their clubs, are becoming interested in rearing various species of wildfowl in captivity. Wild duck, even pinioned birds brought back from the marsh, make most handsome pets and give endless pleasure to those who never before may have been able to observe them in living detail, as well as bringing surprises in a deeper understanding of their voices, habits and behaviour; even in their plumage changes they will present details which many a fowler has never had a chance to observe. Eventually, some, properly ringed, may be allowed to go free-winged, initially on to reserves. It should be noted here that hand-reared birds will breed much sooner than wild-caught ones, which may take five or more years to settle down, although apparently quite tame.

Anyone with a small pond and a little surround may keep a duck. It is only in the breeding season that the instinct to roam occurs and it is at this time that birds which may have been living behind wire-netting only thirty inches high, will start looking for holes and trying to climb. Collectors living in the country, of course, will have to take suitable precautions against losses from vermin, particularly foxes.

This, then, is a brief account of some British species which are of particular interest to the wildfowler, either in the strictly ornamental sense or as part of his conservation programme. Those most handsome of duck, the teal, are particularly suitable for the back-garden collector, as it is only when they are kept in really constant proximity to man that these birds become properly tame. There are households where teal will walk up with the other duck to the garden door, and indeed would enter the house were that allowed.

Teal have a reputation as escapers, but in captivity most birds soon become very reluctant to leave the quarters which they know so well, even for the pleasures of the adjoining stretch of river. The duck love to make themselves neat nests in the long grass but unless already very tame will prove shy sitters and apt to desert before completing a full clutch. They sit only twenty-one days and produce about the smallest of our ducklings. The supposed difficulties in rearing them chiefly relate to giving them small enough food often enough, and most important of all a small foster-mother. They will usually rear extremely tame and only develop their characteristic wildness when contact with man becomes infrequent. The young are easily sexed in first feather by the relatively brighter speculum of the drake, and the duck is usually obliging enough to quack.

The garganey is our only other duck of comparable size: more confiding than the teal, it makes an admirable foil with the delicate tones of the feathers. The eggs are probably a little larger than the teal and the duck certainly shows a great deal more determination—she may even let you stand on her tail before she will leave the nest. By size the duckling may be confused with the teal, although there is less contrast between the upper and lower parts, and only the two black spots behind the legs are really well marked. The ducklings are very easily separated by the eye-line, double in the garganey with the lower line very strong and complete, the bill end turned up and the ear end turned down like a very thin S on its side. The worst drawback to this species is the extraordinary long time which the male spends in the eclipse; commonly they are not in full plumage until the New Year, and first-year birds often not until February.

The mallard is not only one of the most striking and beautiful of our duck, but also the easiest to tame and to rear, though it has earned itself exclusion from many a collection of ornamental waterfowl by its pushing behaviour and rather coarse habits. The gadwall relies upon a more subdued grace for its appearance, but is enough of a mallard not to let this quieter dress influence its behaviour too much, and in fact during the spring the drakes are apt to make a nuisance of themselves to all around. The duck lays well, fertility is high and hatchability good, so this species might well be the subject of a mass-rearing effort by any wildfowling club which could spare the time and space to house a few stock pairs. The ducklings, in fawn and creamy yellow, do almost as well as mallard and rear very tame.

A white egg similar to the gadwall's but perhaps a little smaller and more pointed at both ends belongs to the wigeon. This is a favourite species, starting with the duckling whose peculiarly attractive reddish tint is a promise of the really beautiful female and eclipse plumage; whilst the drake, in addition to enlisting admiration for the variety of colouring in its courting dress, is so free with the use of his call that he will help you to pass the night hours should they be waking, in addition to greeting you at morn and upon your coming home in the evening.

Pintail are quiet birds, for the drake is very sparing with his whistle, and although the duck has quite a lot to say she is easily mistaken for other birds in the collection. The eggs seem rather too small for the bird and are a dark olive in colour, providing the most attractive blue-grey ducklings that crouch low with outstretched neck when alarmed, and for the best part of the first week will spend much of their time underneath the hen unless the weather is hot. This tendency to be out of sight leads the owner to make sure that they are all right and of course the more one makes sure, the less all right they are likely to be.

Shoveler must be placed in a class of their own, not only because they offer a unique appearance and a striking beauty, but also as they are traditionally hard to raise and to keep. Most people regard a freshly-running stream as the ideal for keeping duck, but the shoveler, on account of its specialized method of feeding, is more likely to do well on waters where the less active elements of aquatic life can congregate undisturbed. Certainly they can be kept in good health on artificial foods, but they will have to become used to a special diet to ensure the proper intake of proteins and vitamins. It is quite possible and practical to raise the ducklings entirely on artificial foods, but where supplements are relied on, it is essential to provide these in proper quantities or a poor bird will be the result. This is because bird and owner have taken diametrically opposite views. The owner considers the proprietary food as the main course with the chopped worm and small helping of duckweed as delicacies intended to make up for any possible deficiencies—the bird on the other hand regards the chopped worms as a delight, is prepared to make do with the duckweed as a main course, and will only have the proprietary food from sheer hunger. The legend of difficulty is not without foundation.

All these birds, examples of the dabbling duck, that feed by tipping up in shallow water, thrive in captivity and apart from protection against cats, require little beyond natural shelter, a handful of corn and some chopped greenstuff. Some of the species, particularly wigeon, are capable of selecting their own green food or of shortening the lawn, but those less inclined to graze will need their salads prepared if they are to thrive.

One of the easiest birds to rear is the shelduck and one of the most delightful ducklings, snow white with black markings. Their natural friendliness and sturdiness make the task of the foster-parent simple—that a lot of rather undersized specimens are produced is probably due to dietary failure, particularly when the birds are feathering. Very large numbers of eggs and young are credited to the shelduck, but in practice the owner is hardly likely to be inconvenienced, large numbers of eggs in any species are likely to be the product of more than one bird, while with shelduck the large number of young are only found late in rearing when several families amalgamate under one mother. The eggs and ducklings are large enough to be left in the charge of an ordinary hen, and the adults will do well on a diet of corn and grazing, despite their reputation as foreshore carnivores.

In contrast to the shelduck, the red-crested pochard is much more difficult to rear. Although this is a shallow diving duck that normally lives upon weeds and the small animals therein, it seems unable to maintain itself on the convenient diet of corn and grass, while the young are prone to develop leg troubles unless fortified by vitamins. Compared with the calm and stately progress of the adults, the ducklings prove unexpectedly active and nervous, but if they are doing well their weight will prevent them from overdoing the exercise. In the event of weak legs developing, the duckling may be dosed with exactly the same vitamin drops that you would give to the baby, but more rarely.

The common pochard presents a strange contrast in habit to its American cousin the redhead which it resembles so closely in appearance, as in captivity it seems to be a much more shy breeder with considerably lower fertility. The egg, too, is radically different from the redhead or the red-crested, being very much larger, longer and darker, while one considers the duck rather the smallest of the three. The ducklings are charming fellows which do well if allowed to probe and prod about in a flash of shallow water on grassland. They present no particular difficulty in rearing on artificial foods, but being true diving duck with their legs set rather far back are not suited to much exercise on land and will fatten unduly unless swimming is provided.

Tufted duck are one of the best stayers for those who like to keep their birds full-winged, while their very tidy appearance and habit of continual diving make them most attractive to watch. As with the common pochard, the egg seems relatively large and as the duckling is completely dark it cannot be confused with any other British species. They are notably confident and inquisitive young, which thrive on simple rearing methods, but very much enjoy titbits in the shape of fragments of fish, tiny minnows or maggots; from their earliest days, if there is something to seek under the water, the ducklings will dive for it in exactly the same manner as the parents; a minnow rather too large for them will be harassed round their pool in a most comical manner.

The scaup is really a sea-duck which is going to do best with natural additions to its captivity diet, drawn from the items which it would normally obtain in the wild—for this bird, small shellfish. As mentioned earlier the problem lies in getting the bird to live on a man-made diet and make up its deficiencies with items drawn from the wild. It is true that hand-reared examples of this species have been kept for two years at a time on a goldfish pond of the smallest size, but like the shoveler they require a good deal of animal life in the water to do well. The ducklings offer a very superficial resemblance to the red-crested pochard, but the bill is heavier, the legs even farther back, the colour a plain brown and the temperament in the early stages far more confident.

Wild birds are notoriously shy breeders in captivity because they cannot obtain their accustomed range and seclusion. Prenuptial flight is no longer possible and the close proximity of other idle, inquisitive, and even lecherous birds will interfere with the whole mating ritual. Birds bred in captivity will often overcome these difficulties only to find that they cannot rear their young owing to interference by their neighbours and it is for this reason that the use of a bantam foster-mother is so often necessary. Those wildfowlers who already possess a drake and now wish to see their own ducklings swimming on the pond would be well advised to obtain a hand-reared duck from one of the ornamental waterfowl farms.

The day that success is at last achieved and the first duckling hatched, the proud owner's excitement may run wild and his temptation too: temptation to ruin the whole affair by interfering. Given average conditions of moisture, the duck is going to achieve a hatch most efficiently without our help, and in the ensuing few days it is essential that she shall have the chance to brood her ducklings and take them feeding without disturbance. Once she feels insecure she will be always on the move and can lose a whole brood from fatigue or cold in less than twenty-four hours.

The rearing of ducklings is a much simpler matter than many of the books would lead us to anticipate. The ideal conditions for rearing young are the same throughout the warm-blooded creation, namely reasonable heat, reasonable cleanliness and plenty of good food. It is unlikely that we can influence the true mother beyond teaching her to come to a suitable spot for feeding and accustoming her in advance to the food which is going to be provided for the ducklings. Where the foster-mother used for the parent bird is really tame it is easy to provide shelter from both the wind and the rain and indeed to add one of the many forms of artificial heat should that seem necessary.

Once the duck is confined in her range, then cleanliness becomes very important and the young must not be given the opportunity of working over fouled ground. As to food, the old books are full of recipes for mash and for exotic titbits—in practice any of the modern proprietary starter preparations will provide the necessary ration. It is important to remember that the duckling's natural day is from dawn till dusk and that if the day is shortened by its being kept shut up in a coop until release is convenient, then growth must suffer. Even this quiescent period of night lasts only so long as the need is felt for the mother's warmth.

Like most wild things that have a predator in mind, duck sleep only in snatches, and do not often do that for more than a couple of hours at a time. They may not feed very seriously after dark, but even in conditions of hard frost may be found taking a bath at two o'clock in the morning, or perhaps just changing their ground. The parents can be trained to live like domestic fowl, even to walking into their shed to be shut up at night, but if they are to be a credit to you the young must be treated in the same way as nature had in mind.

CHAPTER 29

THE DISEASES OF WILDFOWL

by Arthur Jennings, M.A., M.V.Sc., M.R.C.V.S.

Lecturer in Animal Pathology, University of Cambridge.

FREE-LIVING duck and geese are not always in the state of good health which one might expect; indeed, like all living creatures, they are subject to many forms of sickness and disease. Whilst it is true that obviously sick birds are not often seen by the wildfowler, a detailed post-mortem examination of a good day's bag will sometimes show some evidence of disease in one or more birds. Sometimes, albeit rarely, outbreaks of disease occur and then attention is focused on such conditions.

Although wildfowl are susceptible to a great many diseases, it is reassuring to the fowler to know that the vast majority of such diseases are specific for birds and even if, by chance, a diseased bird were eaten the chances of man being infected from wildfowl diseases are very remote.

The diseases of any of the free-living birds are of interest for several reasons. First, such conditions form part of the natural regulating mechanisms of bird population; secondly, many bird diseases are transmissible to domestic birds and animals and, less often, to man himself, so that it is probable that certain birds are concerned in the epidemiology, or spread, of some of the infectious diseases.

From the viewpoint of the wildfowler, diseases are important since epidemics may reduce his bag and, because sick birds are weakly fliers and flight badly, his sport is reduced. Finally, there are the intangible, but nevertheless important aesthetic losses which result from bird diseases.

Although we all know roughly what is meant by disease, it is a most difficult condition to define in a precise way. Possibly one of the shortest and yet most comprehensive definitions is that "disease is the opposite of health" and any disturbance in the finely adjusted balance which we call health may lead to disease. The effect upon the bird of this abnormal state may be to produce obvious clinical signs such as the inability to fly, or violent bouts of diarrhoea, or wasting of the muscles, or sometimes rapid breathing, and so forth. These signs are usually the result of certain structural changes which occur within the body of the bird and such changes may be visible to the unaided eye or they may require the use of a microscope to be detected. These structural changes in the tissues are called lesions and they act as signposts to a pathologist and indicate to him the location and nature of the disease processes present in the body.

Many agents can produce disease; some causes of disease are living creatures such as various parasitic worms, certain bacteria and viruses, whereas other causes are chemical poisons such as lead. Bacteria are tiny organisms of various shapes and sizes found everywhere in nature; the majority of them are harmless but some produce diseases and these are called pathogens.

The pathogenic viruses are much smaller than bacteria and require special methods to detect them since they cannot be seen with ordinary high-power microscopes. Moulds or fungi also cause disease and one of them, *Aspergillus*, is an important pathogen of British wildfowl.

Parasites of various kinds, the tapeworms, the flukes, the round worms, and the one-cell protozoa are all common causes of sickness and sometimes death of birds. The flukes and tapeworms are flattened creatures; the former are usually leafshaped whereas the tapeworms consist of a head and many segments. The nematodes or round worms are long slender cylindrical worms tapered at each end and the thorny-headed worms, so common in many kinds of duck, are large white worms with a retractile proboscis armed with recurved hooks.

Outbreaks of infectious disease are not common in British wildfowl and when they do occur they are not of the magnitude seen in other countries. For example, a bacterial disease, botulism, has on occasion killed millions of American waterfowl, but for several reasons such widespread devastation is unlikely to occur in Britain. Several infectious conditions occur here in sporadic fashion and a brief description of some of them follows.

TUBERCULOSIS

Although there are few records of tuberculosis in wildfowl, some observers consider that the disease is not an uncommon one. There are no characteristic signs of the disease in life; affected birds are usually thin and the natural "bloom" of the feathers is lost. Drakes may appear drab and lifeless, the moult may be incomplete and the flightless period prolonged. Weakness is very noticeable in the late stages of the disease and affected birds are poor fliers. The vent feathers are usually stained indicating bouts of diarrhoea.

The infection gets into the body *via* the digestive tract and the lesions, or tubercules, are found particularly in the liver, spleen and intestines. These organs contain yellowish white masses usually with a marbled appearances due to the presence of concentric rings in their structure. The disease in birds is due to a different type of tuberculosis organism than that which causes disease in man and has been recorded in Britain in a shelduck, pochard and several wigeon.

PSEUDO-TUBERCULOSIS

A disease which resembles tuberculosis but due to a different organism, *Pasteurella pseudotuberculosis*, is common in wild birds and mammals in Britain. In ducks and geese the disease is often an acute one and birds which have been seen alive with this disease have had ruffled feathers, general drowsiness, a foetid diarrhoea and were unable to fly. The changes or lesions are most marked in the liver and spleen, these organs being covered with small or large yellowish white foci.

DUCK CHOLERA

Duck cholera is an acute disease caused by *Pasteurella aviseptica*. Fortunately, in Britain only sporadic cases have so far been encountered. Death takes place quickly after infection; birds may be found dead from this disease with their heads up in a natural position. The carcases appear to have almost black skins because of the acute congestion of the subcutaneous blood vessels. Small haemorrhages throughout the body are a feature of duck cholera.

SALMONELLOSIS

Salmonella infections or paratyphoid are sometimes seen in free-living waterfowl, but the disease is more serious in domestic birds and in waterfowl collections. Two peak periods of mortality appear in ducklings and goslings; the first is seen three to five days after hatching with a second peak about three weeks later. Great thirst, diarrhoea, and convulsions are prominent signs of the disease. The lesions take the form of yellowish grey nodules in the lungs and liver.

ASPERGILLOSIS

A fairly common fungal infection of wildfowl is that due to *Aspergillus fumigatus*. In one survey some 7 per cent of pink-footed geese were shown to be carrying the spores of this organism (Beer 1957). The mould is commonly found in certain soils, and heaps of decaying vegetable matter are sometimes heavily contaminated with the spores of this fungus. Goslings may be affected soon after hatching or the infections may be picked up later in life. Acute and chronic forms of the disease occur. The lesions are found in the lungs and air sacs and may be typical mould growths or small nodular lesions. Sick birds often show respiratory distress and have drab plumage.

LEAD POISONING

The swallowing of lead pellets causes lead poisoning in waterfowl. It has been estimated (Olney 1960) that 60–80 per cent of adult mallard with one ingested pellet will succumb if they are feeding on a diet of wild seeds. The availability of lead-shot pellets to wildfowl in a particular water is determined according to Olney by (1) the shooting intensity and number of shot deposited on the bottom; (2) the nature of the bottom material; (3) the size of the shot pellets involved. The signs of lead poisoning include lethargy, bright green droppings, a prominent keel bone, and "wing drop". The striking postmortem feature is extreme emaciation with great reduction in the flight muscles. There are other, less constant, changes in the body.

PARASITIC DISEASES

All wildfowl harbour parasites of one kind or another. Birds act as hosts to an infinite variety of living creatures and some idea of the numbers and types of parasites may be gained from a fascinating and erudite book—*Fleas, Flukes and Cuckoos*, by Miriam Rothschild and Theresa Clay.

In general the bird and its parasites reach a state of equilibrium, but if the balance between the two is upset then sickness and death may follow. Many of the parasites can be detected with the unaided eye and they are often present in very large numbers. Generally parasitic disease occurs sporadically, but sometimes many deaths occur at one time. Most parasites require an intermediate host to complete their life cycle; such secondary hosts are often small crustaceans, earthworms or molluscs, sometimes slugs and snails and, for some parasites, mosquitoes and other insects are needed to complete the cycle of infection.

Whenever there is a build-up in bird population numbers, especially with gregarious species, there is then the serious danger of "overstocking" and consequent outbreaks of parasitic disease. Such outbreaks sometimes occur in swans from tapeworm disease or from certain fluke infections.

Other outbreaks of disease have been caused by thorny-headed worms in eider duck and a nematode worm, *Acuaria*, is a common cause of death in ducklings of many species. In geese two pathogenic parasites often occur together and may cause heavy losses; these are the gizzard worm (*Amidostomum anseris*) and the coccidium that lives in the kidneys (*Eimeria truncata*). Pink-footed goslings in Iceland are not infrequently affected with these parasites and most adult geese of any species may be shown to harbour some of these parasites.

REFERENCES

BEER, J. V. (1957). *IXth Ann. Rept. Wildfowl Trust, 58–65.*
OLNEY, P. J. S. (1960). *XIth Ann. Rept. Wildfowl Trust, 123–35.*
ROTHSCHILD, MIRIAM, and CLAY, THERESA (1952). *Fleas, Flukes and Cuckoos.* Collins, London.

CHAPTER 30

WILDFOWL TAXIDERMY

by James Harrison, D.S.C., M.B.O.U., F.Z.S.(Sci.), M.R.C.S., L.R.C.P

Vice-President, Wildfowlers' Association of Great Britain and Ireland. Past Vice-President, British Ornithologists' Union and Past Chairman, British Ornithologists' Club.

TAXIDERMY is an art with many branches, but here I confine myself to wildfowl. In principle, the technique described will serve for all classes of birds, both with regard to skinning and the subsequent setting up. To be a good taxidermist it is essential to know birds well, both in the field and in the laboratory. In other words, one should be an observant field naturalist and to fulfil the second requirement one must know basically the surface anatomy of birds, though of course much of this is hidden under the covering of feathers. For this reason the handling of and familiarity with a plucked table bird are strongly recommended. This will demonstrate the relative positions of the limb segments and the various positions they can assume, and also the shift of the centre of gravity with the changing positions in flying, walking and at rest. It will also be appreciated what extreme mobility the head and neck of any bird is capable of and the position of the head on the neck in a bird at rest.

Next, learn to draw simple line diagrams of the bird's head, neck and body, and super-impose on the sketch limb segments at rest and in motion, in every conceivable position. This is not a waste of time, and if properly explored much of very practical value will be mastered.

As a preliminary, it is important to take proper care of the specimen as soon as it has been shot. Mud should be washed off. Bill and nostrils should be plugged with wool, shot holes similarly dealt with, and every care to prevent soiling by extravasation of body fluids. The bird should be wrapped in clean paper and carefully placed in the game bag. A specimen should not reach the bench covered in mud and blood. Taxidermists are only human after all and inclined to indulge in explosive expletives under such circumstances!

Proceed as follows: lay the specimen on a sheet of clean paper on its back. Separate the feathers, and with a sharp scalpel make a mid-line cut extending from the mid-point of the keel of the sternum to the vent (A–B fig. 39). This incision when over the abdomen should not open the abdominal cavity, but only the skin. Now separate the skin edges and proceed to free the skin on both sides of the breast and flanks, using plenty of hardwood sawdust to absorb fat and to keep the feathers clean. This will expose the knee-joints. These are to be thoroughly freed and cut through with strong scissors. Working your way downwards, you will presently come to the root of the tail. This in its turn must be thoroughly exposed and divided with scissors. Care is needed, for if

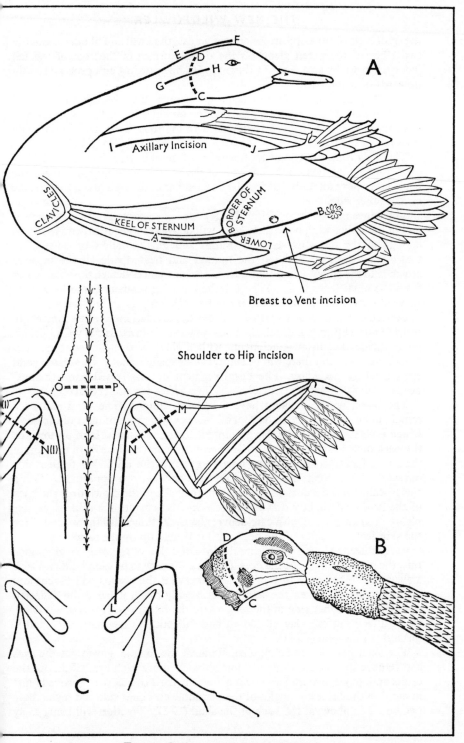

FIG. 39. *Surface anatomy and incisions.*

the quill ends of the tail feathers are cut across, they will all fall out! Clean the two lobes of the preen gland off the dorsal surface of the root of the tail (coccyx), keep the area clean by dusting with fine sawdust and proceed to skin upwards over the back.

The shoulder-joints will be awkward, but press them back with one hand until you have been able to expose one for dividing by cutting with scissors close up to the joint (M–N). Next deal with the root of the neck in the same way and so on across to the other wing shoulder (O–P), (M(1)N(1)).

The body is now out; powder the inside of the skin very liberally with sawdust. Now by traction on the cut ends of the knee, invert the skin as far as the heel and remove all flesh, leaving the cleaned bone (tibio-tarsus). Do the same on the other side.

The wings must next be skinned; they are not so easy. Traction on the cut end of the upper wing bone (humerus) will deliver this segment, and in many, enough of the forewing segment (radius and ulna) to allow of satisfactory treatment. Clean all flesh off the humeri and next divide all the muscles attached to the elbow-joint, but under no circumstances detach the secondaries from the ulna. If, as in some species, the forewing segment is too long to be skinned completely from within, it can be dealt with by an incision along the underside of the limb as required. Powder the divided muscle attachments to provide non-slip grip and pull the mass downwards towards the wrist. At this point divide the distal attachments with a sharp scalpel, or scissors. Any remaining flesh, and there will be some, can be easily removed by scraping and cutting where necessary. The distal segment or suppressed hand (manus) needs an incision on the underside to allow access for preservative.

The body, wings and legs have now been skinned. The head and neck remain to be done. Traction on root of the neck will produce most of the neck, which is then divided with sharp-pointed, strong scissors as high up towards the back of the skull as possible. Be careful to remove all fat from the skin of the neck. Paint on preservative now and return the neck skin feather side outwards again. Next, lay the head on the bench, crown uppermost. With a sharp scalpel make a dorsal incision from the back of the crown over the back of the head and slightly down the neck (E–F). Separate the skin edges, use plenty of sawdust, and with care deliver the neck stump into the wound. Free the skin from the sides of the head until it is held up by the ears.

Care is needed here to extricate the infolded skin of the ears. Having done this, the next check will be the eyes. Great care is now to be exercised, and with a sharp blade cut close to the eyeball, otherwise the eyelids will be cut and difficulties result. When the skin is successfully freed, it has to be deflected right down on either side to the area where the bill arises. If this is not done, the feathers will one day all loosen and fall out. An alternative method is through an incision (G–H).

The skull has now to be cleaned. Remove the tongue, gouge out the eyes and remove the two nasal glands, one situated above each eye. Clean out the orbits and, to remove the brain, cut across the hard palate, then vertically just internal to the posterior angles of the mandible on either side and make these two cuts join above at the back of the skull (C–D). Traction will bring away

Plate 47. Rats are serious predators. Common tern killed and dragged under sea wall stones by rats

Plate 48. Osprey—all hawks are protected

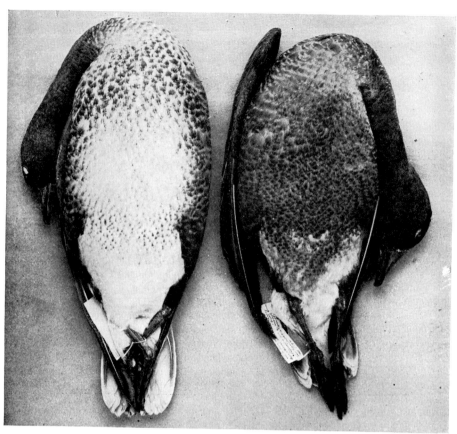

Plate 49. Goose skins for study (*left*) Siberian (*right*) Greenland whitefronts—both young

Plate 50. Mounted teal showing method of binding

Plate 51. Lough Akeragh—a threatened Irish wetland

Plate 52. A raft ready for its soil cover

Plate 53. Sir Ralph Payne-Gallwey, first president of the Wildfowlers'
Association, in his gunroom

Plate. 54 Shooter's shed

this triangular block of tissues. The brain matter can now be removed. Note, the jaw articulations must not be disturbed, but the flesh has to be cleaned off.

Some may prefer to approach the preservation of the head and neck from above; this is done by making the incision E–F (or G–H, fig. 39) and by dissection cleaning and defining the root of the neck, dividing all the structures thus exposed as well as the cervical spine, as close to the base of the skull as possible. Fill the area with fine hardwood sawdust and then by traction on the other end of the neck, pull this out.

One warning; where a wounded duck has been dispatched by wringing its neck, there will be much extravasated blood; this can be very troublesome. Save yourself as much trouble as possible in such cases by using the sawdust very freely; however, a wash and clean up is almost inevitable. The skull can now be cleaned and the work proceeded with as already described.

The cleaned head has now to be treated with preservative, then filled with finely chopped tow and returned within the skin.

Finally, to complete the act of skinning, the interior of the skin has to be throughly degreased. This may be a really arduous procedure and take perhaps two hours according to the amount of fat deposition and the size of the subject. It must never be neglected, and all fat and tags must be cleaned off. This is done with a large full-bodied scalpel and dusting with fine hardwood sawdust repeatedly during the process. Any tears or holes should be repaired as they appear, but make as few as you can.

Having done this, it is best next to do any necessary cleaning, using cold water and dabbing with absorbent cotton wool and dusting with heavy magnesium carbonate powder. Use this liberally to act as an absorbent of dirt and moisture. It may be necessary to repeat this a number of times. Use a soft brush to remove the powder, but only when the powder has absorbed all moisture and dirt, and after a preliminary shake off. This process is then to be repeated as often as necessary, using benzine or carbon tetrachloride, as these will also remove fat absorbed in the feathers. Do not work in a closed atmosphere as both substances are dangerous, particularly the latter.

When satisfied that the specimen is clean outside and inside, the skin surface has to be liberally treated with the preservative selected. When doing this, the feathers must be protected against further wetting and soiling. To preserve the scaly part of the leg (tarsus) pierce the ball of the foot with a suitable tool (a skewer) and paint this with preservative, working it up and down the leg (really foot!) a time or two to distribute the preservative fluid amongst the tendons.

It has been noted that most duck require the external incision through which to skin the head; there are, however, some exceptions, notably the saw-bills. There are a few passerine birds which have to be treated like duck, also some heavily crested non-anatidine species. These we need not specify in this article. There are two other incisions, which can be used, first a lateral incision under the wing (I–J); the same joints have to be exposed and divided as in the previous method and this approach has both advantages and drawbacks. It is not recommended to the beginner. The other is made from internal to the root of the shoulder blade to just short of the hip-joint (K–L). This gives an admirable exposure of the shoulder-joints and root of the neck. It can be recommended when a certain degree of proficiency has been attained. Setting a specimen up from these latter incisions is not made any easier, in fact difficulties are rather more, but they are the best for preparing skins for scientific study.

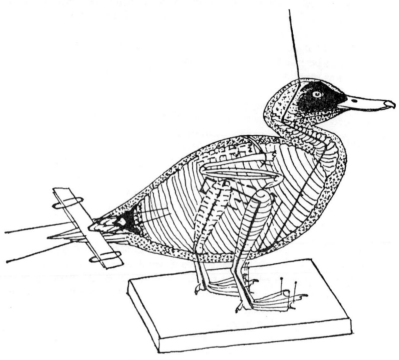

FIG. 40. *Wiring to a mannequin.*
Dark shading : pipeclay.
Light shading : chopped tow.

There are various methods of mounting birds; some are basically faulty, and the only method which, in my opinion, is satisfactory, is that which uses a firmly reproduced mannequin of the body and neck of the specimen being preserved (fig. 40). Various substances have been used for this purpose, amongst them peat, cork, wood-wool and tow. It is my practice to use a combination of the last two. In principle a hard core is made, through which, by transfixion and bolting back, the head and neck, wing and leg wires are secured to give stability and enable different life-like postures to be reproduced. The mannequin, when using wood-wool and tow, is made by compression in the hands and binding with good quality thread, gradually building the body up from the hard core, first, of course, using the former until as close a replica to the body removed is achieved—and the nearer the better—then giving it a covering of best quality surgical tow.

Depressions have to be produced by sewing through and through with thread on a packer's needle. The mannequin must be solid and of the exact size of the removed carcass. Any interstices it is desired to fill out can be suitably padded with finely chopped tow, e.g. at the root of the tail, the flanks, etc. This is, of course, particularly necessary in the cavities of the skull, in the cheeks, between the lower mandibles and in the throat and at the base of the skull and root of the neck. This substance, if properly chopped (this is done with scissors), will not form lumps and is readily moulded when the specimen is receiving its final touches. A taxidermist should have sensitive fingers, for there is much moulding and modelling involved in reproducing faithfully animal form and character.

The neck is usually made of tow and this must be of the correct length and thickness; it must also be of sufficient firmness to support the head. Its actual making is done by twisting the tow spirally, always in the same direction, binding with thread, retwisting in the same direction with more tow and rebinding until the correct dimensions have been achieved. It may with advantage fluff out at the base where it is to be attached to the artificial body.

We now have the skin ready, the mannequin body and neck prepared, and the next step is to select suitable gauge galvanized iron wire for the head and neck, wings and legs, and for securing the tail in position. The leg wires will need to be of stouter gauge than the rest, and the rule is stouter rather than less stout, but not so stout that they will damage the tarsi while being inserted. Having cut the wires of sufficient lengths for their various purposes, proceed

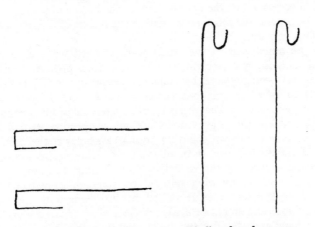

FIG. 41. *Wing staples.*   *Binding thread supports.*

to sharpen them, using an appropriate file and a hand-vice to hold the wire securely. The head and neck wire has to be sharpened at both ends, the tail and leg wires at one end only, the wing wires (wing staples) at both ends, two being cut for each wing (fig. 41). Usually three files should suffice, one coarse, one medium and one fine cut.

The next step is to pass the head and neck wire up the centre of the artificial neck, but do not push the sharpened end right through. Then paint the artificial neck with preservative and insinuate it up the skin of the neck. When the end is visible at the base of the skull, the point of the wire can be pushed through and can be made to pierce the vault of the skull. It can then be made to pierce the skin also, or what is rather more difficult, doubled back and bolted in under the vault of the skull. The first course is also the easier for subsequent control. The head, particularly at the base of the skull, has to be nicely filled with chopped tow and can then be sewn up neatly. The glass eyes can be inserted now, or later if desired.

With the skin lying on its back, the two humeri have to be securely tied together at that distance apart at which they were in life. The body and neck are now to be wired together; the root of the neck must again be at its correct position on the mannequin, as in life. Bolt back the sharpened wire into the artificial body and make it a firm attachment by sewing with thread if necessary. The leg wires can now be passed up the tarsi, the fleshy part between the knee and the heel being reproduced by winding tow round the bone and wire and binding on firmly with thread.

The mannequin can now be fully inserted into the skin. Pass the two tail wires through the tail stump and push them on into the mannequin, first, if deemed necessary, filling the base of the tail with chopped tow; or pipe clay.

The leg wires have now to be made to transfix the artificial body. Be sure they are not made to do this too far back, otherwise the centre of gravity will be lost and your specimen will present a ridiculous spectacle. Push the wire on until it comes out on the opposite side of the body and bolt it back securely. Do the same with the second leg. Review the matter of filling once more and, if satisfied, sew up.

It is presumed that, if the wings were skinned without recourse to an external incision, the forearm segment has been preserved and the flesh removed has been replaced by sufficient chopped tow. If, however, it was necessary to use an external cut, preserve this segment, fill with tow and sew the skin edges together. The bird is approximately shaped by bending the head and neck and legs into a provisional preliminary posture. It will look awful!

Now prepare the rough stand by boring two holes at the correct distance apart and put the leg wires through and bend them over to secure. Stand the bird up and proceed to the modelling and shaping. Position the two wings correctly and secure by wing staples, two for each wing being usually required. View from every angle and go on improving until you have got the best result you can; do not be easily satisfied. The specimen should now have solidity, shape and stability and be at least a semblance of the bird in life. Much patience and perseverance will yet be needed to finalize your work. A taxidermist should be a perfectionist, at any rate by intent.

The webs of the feet can be kept spread by securing with fine entomological pins. Some binding may be required with fine cotton to keep feathers in proper position, and constant control during the drying stage should be exercised until quite dry. Binding wires inserted into the back facilitate this (fig. 36). Notes should be made of the colours of the soft parts when the bird is quite fresh; these have to be faithfully reproduced in oil paints later, but do not use too much varnish. Needless to say, the specimen should be meticulously clean. To safeguard the tail feathers from distorting, secure them between two card strips fastened by the ordinary wire paper-clips.

Do not attempt other than simple positions until experienced. Flying birds, and birds with wings extended, need special wing wiring technique, and wing posturing for various flying attitudes is far from easy. Very large subjects need to have the body built up on a properly cut centre board, and the leg irons secured by staples and screws to correctly placed wooden blocks. Such specimens demand ripe experience.

The mounting of heads and necks of wildfowl on suitably cut shields finds favour with some and the technique involved is embodied, of course, in the directions for mounting already outlined.

A word must be said about the preparations of skins for research; this is an important branch of the work. Proceed as for skinning a specimen for mounting. The writer has a great preference for the incision from the shoulder joint to knee, which when sewn up is hidden beneath the long scapulars. It lends itself to enlargement upwards or downwards as required. The method of sewing up has already been given.

As in mounting, defatting must be thorough and the whole skin well painted with the preservative.

Next construct an artificial neck as already described. This should be the length and thickness of the natural neck. At its lower end, however, the tow may be allowed to fan out with advantage. Now take a length of suitable gauge galvanized iron wire; it should be about one and three-quarters the length of the bird, sharpen both ends. About half-way down make a series of close loops as shown. Push the point of the wire upwards through the artificial neck but do not yet push it right through. Now insinuate the artificial neck up the skin of the neck until the end is felt to impinge on the back of the skull. The wire is now to be pushed on through the top of the artificial neck and on through the vault of the skull. At this stage tie the upper end of the farther wing bone securely with suitable string leaving two long ends protruding into the wound. Now cushion off the wire by laying tow in the cavity. Having done this and, of course, filled the wings where flesh has been removed, also twist tow round the leg bones to fill the space adequately. Next grasp the lower end of the wire and push the point through the root of the tail, then with a pair of pliers grasp the end of the wire beyond the tail feathers and exert steady traction until the

close loops are half opened up: /\/\   this open series of loops

has to lie snugly flat on the back filling and will keep the head steady while the specimen dries.

All that is now needed is to complete the filling of the skin. This must be done with due regard and care—do not over nor under fill. Finally tie wing bone to wing bone at the correct distance and sew up neatly. The tarsi are to be preserved; pass a stout needle or other tool up through the ball of the foot bearing the preservative several times to distribute it liberally amongst the tendons, and paint the under surface of the paddles with preservative.

Positioning for drying is very important and can best be seen from the accompanying illustrations. It is good practice to put one wing under the flank feathers, the other over, so that on one side the former can be studied and on the other the wing speculum.

The writer prefers the tarsi crossed and the feet approximated and tied sole to sole with the toes straight: this arrangement greatly facilitates routine measuring. The skin having been positioned by manipulation is to be maintained by strips of open-wove bandage until quite dry, regular control being needed.

Since available space is often a matter of consideration, large skins such as swans and geese are often made up with the heads and necks turned back along one side of the body. Such specimens are aesthetically satisfying and as scientific material equally adequate. In such large subjects some of the tendons of the legs should be withdrawn through a small incision into the ball of the foot during preservation.

Meticulous attention is to be given to the eyes; these should be neatly set and filled with clean wadding. The mandibles are to be properly and naturally closed. Not only do these measures add to the beauty of the preparation but, more important, during systematic examination the measurements can be accurately taken.

A word about sexing and labelling. All specimens must have a neat tag label attached to the legs. On the front should be the name of the bird and its sex, if this has been confirmed anatomically, ♂ indicates the male and ♀ the female. If the sex cannot be confirmed it is best to write "? sex". The date obtained and locality should also be on the front. On the reverse side note the colour of the eyes and soft parts and any other interesting data.

To sex a bird anatomically, open the body along the whole length of the left side. This is because the ovary in most birds is a single organ situated above the kidneys on the left-hand side; a few species have paired ovaries. In the case of males the right-hand gonad can easily be identified by gently displacing the intestines so as to expose the whole of the gonad-bearing area at the upper ends of the kidneys. It is a good plan, when this is possible, to make a sketch of the gonad size; when too large give approximate size in centimetres.

Space precludes the description of ancillary work involved in taxidermy, for example the preparation of ground-work, cases, backgrounds, etc. Taxidermy for domestic decoration is now fortunately no longer in vogue, and the art now serves only museums and science. A living is now no longer to be made by a professional bird taxidermist outside an educational institution.

Collections of birds require special accommodation, occupy much space, and need careful, constant maintenance. If a collector of trophies tires of his dilettante hobby, the fruits of his labours will be found unsaleable and even hard to give away! Sobering thoughts!

The foregoing directions represent only the basic techniques involved. However, a paint-box and brushes never were responsible for the production of an artist—the same is true of tools and a taxidermist, who is strictly an artist in every sense of the word.

A collection of birds badly executed, housed under the wrong conditions, neglected in so far as proper care and attention is concerned, ravaged by moth and beetles, faded beyond recognition, is nothing but an exhibition of criminal folly, and as such should not be condoned.

There should be a plan and a purpose in such effort and not merely the selfish desire to possess rarities, an outlook and practice which is now, by common consent, rightly condemned. There is nevertheless still a need and a scope for the taxidermist, both professional and amateur, for he is the recorder in kind of the many interesting and beautiful forms of birdlife—and what could be more beautiful than wildfowl—but this is to be regarded as a privilege and a responsibility and one not to be lightly undertaken.

APPENDIX

Tools required : Scalpels of various sizes and a large fairly full-bladed knife for skinning large subjects: scissors of various sizes, a pair of good secateurs for going through joints will save the scissors from undue wear. Assorted needles, from small to coarse. Files of different cuts, coarse and fine. A hand-vice for holding wire whilst sharpening. Pliers of different kinds. Stilettos and one or two electrician's screw-drivers, which when sharpened at the tip are ideal for piercing the legs with. Brushes small and large for use with a liquid preservative. Very soft full-headed brushes for use on the plumage, and as a luxury an electric hairdryer.

Preservatives : The choice of a preservative is important and carries with it some equally important responsibilities. First it must indeed be a really effective preservative and, although many substances have been used for the purpose of preserving taxidermic subjects, the only one which has proved its worth is arsenic.

Arsenic is of course a deadly poison, unless used with strict precautions, dangerous to both the user and others. It has been employed in various forms—dry, as powder, and in the form of an arsenical soap, paste or solution. Dry arsenic is to be condemned as highly dangerous; I regard arsenic soaps and paste as undesirable and give preference to arsenical solutions. Such can be obtained commercially, an excellent preparation being made by the Atlas Preservative Co. of Erith, Kent. For most birds a suitable dilution is Atlas Preservative 1 part, spirit industrial meth. 1 part, water to 10 parts. For larger subjects a stronger solution up to $33\frac{1}{3}$ per cent can be used. Such arsenical solutions should be kept under lock and key and any vessels containing such solutions should be marked conspicuously "POISON" and it is an advantage when in foreign lands to have the usual and very appropriate danger sign of the skull and cross bones as a warning.

Avoid alum in preserving bird skins; it is too hardening. Wash the hands after using arsenic, clean the nails scrupulously and do not have any arsenic pot or arsenic-treated subject anywhere near food or drink. You are responsible for its safe keeping and any tragedy due to neglect is yours and yours only. Note: Non-poisonous preservatives are obtainable from naturalists' stores, but are not as effective.

Substances required: Tow, best surgical; wool, good quality absorbent; wood-wool, fine; fine hardwood sawdust; pipe clay, especially useful for filling skull cavities, etc., in large subjects; cotton, various strengths; thread, various strengths; galvanized iron wire, various gauges; adhesives—carpenter's glue, plastic wood, etc.; oil paints, brushes; copal varnish; carbon tetrachloride (never to be used in enclosed spaces nor near any fire nor open heating element); benzine (highly inflammable); detergents; arsenic preservative; heavy magnesium carbonate powder; glass eyes (obtainable from naturalists' stores), various sizes (a) uncoloured, (b) a variety of stock colours—hazel, red, yellow, green, blue, etc.; and finally an inexhaustible supply of patience and perseverance!

CHAPTER 31

WILDFOWL COOKERY

by Pamela Harrison, M.B., B.S.

Honorary Photographer and Life Member, WAGBI.

IT requires some ingenuity on the part of the housewife to produce a really appetizing dish from wildfowl, but with a little trouble the results can be amazingly good. Much depends on the variety, the age of the bird and time of the year. In general all surface-feeding duck are good to eat with the exception of some shoveler whose diet contains a high animal content. Undoubtedly the most delicious is the young corn-fed mallard in autumn. Diving duck are less palatable but pochard and tufted duck can be excellent. Goldeneye and sea duck with a high percentage of shellfish in their diet are not recommended. Of the geese the Canada and the grey geese feed by grazing or on corn or potatoes and are therefore good to eat, but the occasional bird can reach a considerable age and be dishearteningly tough despite the best efforts.

The length of time that a duck or goose should hang is, of course, largely dependent on the taste of the person eating it; on an average three or four days hanging outside in a game larder is sufficient, but in thundery weather decomposition is hastened and this may be too long. Conversely in hard weather a bird may require ten days before it is palatable and a tough greylag even longer. A Canada goose ringed as an adult four years before it was shot was perfectly tender after sixteen days hanging in November. An old bird will take longer than a youngster and birds that have been shot in the tail and lower abdomen a shorter time than usual. Birds should be hung in the feather and before being drawn. However, many birds I receive have had their stomachs removed for analysis of contents and I find that the absence of their alimentary tract makes no difference to taste or tenderness. Ducks must be protected from flies while hanging—the feathers are a deterrent, but if it is not possible to hang birds in a proper outdoor game larder of perforated zinc, sprinkling with pepper is some protection.

I usually hang wildfowl by the neck but there is a strong case for hanging wet and muddy birds by one leg, thereby enabling the air to get to the body more easily.

Plucking is relatively simple in ducks compared with geese; a sharp tug with the thumb and index finger against the direction of the feathers removes them easily. The terminal part of the wing I usually remove with scissors and thereby dispense with plucking the primaries. After plucking, the duck should be singed; the oil gland in the tails is removed by some and then the bird is drawn. With wildfowl I remove heart, lungs and windpipe, kidneys and liver as well as intestine (if this has not already been removed). I know some people prefer to draw a bird as soon as possible after it is shot and I think there is much to be said in favour of this method, particularly when the bird is shot in the tail or is of the grazing species such as wigeon. The duck is then wiped both inside and out with a cloth wrung out in very hot water—this will improve the appearance of the skin too.

Ducks that are to be deep-frozen are hung, plucked and dressed in this way and then placed in polythene bags singly and labelled. It is very difficult to tell the different ducks apart or even from another species in their frozen state. It is as well to add the date—twelve months in the freezer is just about the maximum time before the birds become too desiccated. Deep-freezing duck is of great value when one has a surfeit, but on the whole I think duck are best eaten during the winter—after a few months without wildfowl on the menu the September corn-fed mallard can be really appreciated.

Wild duck is always supposed to have a fishy flavour and although I am assured that the ducks normally eaten do not consume fish, there are occasions when precautions must be taken to remove whatever the flavour is, be it fish or only very strong salting. Wigeon, particularly in hard weather, are offenders in this way, as are curlew almost always, with a diet rich in crabs. This can be done either by soaking the bird in brine for twelve hours, or immersing it in salt water and bringing to the boil allowing it to simmer ten minutes before pouring away the liquid and then cooking normally.

In mild cases stuffing the duck with an onion may be enough, and another method most useful with curlew involves removing the skin, which holds much of the smell.

Wildfowl are traditionally served underdone—many books mention half an hour in a hot oven as sufficient for a mallard, but on the whole most people prefer a tender well-cooked duck and I allow about an hour at 400° or Regulo 6 for a large duck. Teal, of course, take a proportionately shorter time to roast and when cooking mallard and teal together I add the teal about half an hour after starting to cook. Wild geese usually weigh five or more pounds and I allow about 2½ hours for them.

Canada geese are now more numerous and therefore more likely to present the cook with a challenge. Nothing can be tougher or drier than a real old gander and as there is no fool-proof method of telling whether your bird is reasonably young or ancient I seldom risk a straight roast. Instead I prefer to stuff the bird, wrap it in foil and cook very slowly—for up to six hours. When using this method I prepare an extra quantity of rich gravy and immediately after the meal stir into it any meat left on the carcase—this makes an excellent stew for reheating. There are times when the thought of plucking one of these big birds is too much and time too short, and when this occasion arises I have cut off the breast and leg muscles after partly skinning the bird. Treating the flesh as hare makes a different dish and one that can be left to cook itself.

Wildfowl may be cooked in an open roasting pan covered with larded paper or fat bacon and require frequent basting. It is as well to start with the breasts down and turn the ducks over for the last twenty minutes or so. Before serving, ducks and geese should be "frothed" which gives them an additional crispness. To do this, sprinkle the breast with flour and salt and baste, immediately returning to the oven for a further ten minutes to brown. Much time can be saved by avoiding basting—this is possible if the duck is cooked in a roaster with a close fitting lid or wrapped in aluminium foil. But in both cases the duck must be exposed for the frothing. Ducks are roasted in butter or dripping, but it is as well to reserve the dripping afterwards only for duck. They can also be delicious when cooked on a spit. They are best done at a high temperature and must be basted frequently but take longer to roast by this method.

Wild duck is usually served with watercress and accompanied by an orange salad (the recipe for which will be found below), but there are alternatives which make a change. It may be served with apple sauce—in cases of emergency a well-known brand of strained apples prepared for babies is very useful. In Holland we have eaten mallard served with cranberries which was unexpected, different and delicious. A Sauce Bigarade is not as difficult as it sounds and always repays the effort, while a glass of cooking port added to the gravy is well worth while anyway. Occasionally I serve spiced oranges, particularly with cold duck, or fried orange rings can be served hot. Wild duck are not usually stuffed other than with the bird's liver, a knob of butter and perhaps an onion. Pickling onions are very useful for teal. But a goose or large mallard can be made most appetizing by filling the cavity with sliced raw apple and half a dozen soaked prunes. Sage and onion stuffing is another standby. An unusual recipe which I found in an old book combined artichokes with mallard—by mistake I used parsnips the first time and it was excellent.

Roast wild duck with braised celery is exceptionally good and for a change I can recommend serving your pintail, the "sea pheasant", with bread sauce, fried crumbs and red-currant jelly.

Teal can be split in half, seasoned, buttered and grilled and are delicious when treated in this way. Curlew can be cooked under the grill too, although in this case I skin the breast of a curlew, fillet off the flesh and pressure-cook the fillets (20 minutes at 15 lbs.) before grilling them covered with flank bacon and accompanied by fried onions, mushrooms and tomatoes.

Almost the best way, however, of treating curlew is to curry it. After pressure-cooking the fillets as above, make a good curry sauce, making certain that the curry powder is adequately cooked and serve with rice.

It is possible to use wild duck in the first course too in the form of Wild Duck Pâté—this is a useful way of using up an extra bird.

Snipe and small waders are popular for breakfast served on fried bread. They are cooked under the grill. Some people do not draw these small birds; the snipe should not have its head removed either, but they should be skinned and the beak passed through the legs and body to act as a skewer.

Larger waders such as woodcock, grey and golden plover I usually roast; these birds are well provided with fat and a nice crisp skin can be produced. Very occasionally if a bird comes my way after being skinned, I wrap the whole thing in a piece of fatty membrane obtainable from the butcher and known as a "caul"—this is most successful and makes a beautifully crisp skin.

RECIPES

PÂTÉ

Cold meat cut from one or two duck. The same weight of ox liver, fat flank bacon, liver sausage. One small onion. One clove of garlic crushed with salt.

Mince all ingredients twice and place in a basin in the pressure-cooker; $\frac{1}{2}$ pint water in the pressure-cooker is sufficient. Cook contents of the basin for 10 minutes at 15 lbs. per sq. in. Cool under cold tap and either re-mince or pass through the liquidizer. In the latter case a little extra fluid may be required and that in the bottom of the pressure-cooker may be used.

Press the pâté into earthenware pots and when cold seal with melted fresh butter. I deep-freeze this pâté and find it a most useful standby.

CURRY SAUCE FOR CURLEW

1. 1 tabsp. dripping.
2. $\frac{1}{2}$ lb. peeled and sliced onion.
3. Juice of half a lemon.
4. $\frac{3}{4}$ tabsp. curry powder.
5. 1 oz. ground rice.
6. 1 tabsp. Green Label chutney.
7. 1 tabsp. jam.
8. 1 apple, chopped.
9. 1 tabsp. desiccated coconut.
10. 1 teasp. allspice.
11. 1 tabsp. sliced ripe tomato.

Fry onions in dripping until soft. Add curry powder and ground rice and fry for a few minutes. Remove from heat and add 6, 7, 8, 9, 10 and 11 and about $\frac{3}{4}$ pint of water. Bring to boil—simmer for 1 hour. Press sauce through a fine sieve, add a little lemon juice.

SPICED ORANGES

12 oranges.
1 lb. sugar.
1 pkt. pickling spice.
$1\frac{1}{4}$ pts. vinegar.

Slice oranges lengthwise and then crosswise into $\frac{1}{4}$-in. thick pieces. Pressure-cook 10 minutes at 15 lbs. in $\frac{1}{2}$ pt. water: Meanwhile boil vinegar with the spice and leave for 2 hours. Strain. Bring to boil with the sugar and add the rings a few at a time. Cook gently until the rings clarify. Place in warm jars. Reduce vinegar until it begins to thicken and cover slices. Top and leave for 3 months.

FRIED ORANGES

Slice the oranges as above. Fry in butter, dusting with castor sugar until brown.

ORANGE SALAD

Slice oranges and arrange in a flat dish. Cover with a French dressing.

SAUCE BIGARADE

1. onion.
2. 1 nut butter.
3. Wineglass red wine.
4. 1 orange rind and juice.
5. 1 teasp. red-currant jelly.
6. Good gravy.

Soften chopped onion in the butter—add 3, 4, 5, and then mix with ½ pint of good gravy. Bring slowly to the boil.

MALLARD WITH ARTICHOKES

1 mallard, 2 lb. ground artichokes. Dash pepper, 1 tabsp. butter, 1 saltspoon salt, 1 tabsp. chopped shallots and parsley.

Season duck as for roasting. Scrape artichokes thoroughly and leave whole. Put butter into covered roaster—brown duck. Grate artichokes and add with salt, pepper, parsley and shallots. Stir over slow heat and then into slow oven until duck is tender and artichokes are very soft and brownish in colour. This takes about an hour. Remove and quarter duck and serve on bed of ground artichokes.

DUCKS AU MADÈRE

4 small or 2 big duck.
5 drops Tabasco.
½ lb. butter.

1 teasp. Worcestershire sauce.
2 cups sweet wine.

Brown ducks in hot butter. Add sauce and wine, salt to taste. Let the wine cook out of the ducks or until it cooks down into the gravy and serve with the ducks.

SALMIS DE CANARD SAUVAGE

From French section of *Recipes of All Nations* by Countess Morphy. This dish is of very ancient origin and the recipe she gives is the traditional one. In some parts of France, red wine is used instead of white.

Ingredients: 1 or 2 wild duck, 1 gill of white wine, 1 gill of Sauce Espagnole (see following recipe), 3 or 4 shallots, ¼ lb. mushrooms, a few truffles (optional), 1 liqueur glass of brandy, 1 bay leaf, a sprig of thyme, salt and pepper.

Method: Roast the birds and while they are being roasted, put the chopped shallots, the herbs, etc., in a small saucepan with the white wine, and simmer gently till reduced to about one third. When the birds are nearly done, carve them carefully, removing all flesh from carcase. Place the pieces of duck in a saucepan with the brandy and set alight. When the brandy is burnt out add a little Espagnole sauce, cover with a lid and keep warm. Chop up the bones or pound them in a mortar and add to the wine and shallots, mixing well. Add the remaining Espagnole sauce, stir well and simmer gently and skim carefully. Cook for about 20 minutes. Five minutes before serving, strain half the sauce over the pieces of duck and place the saucepan over a slow fire, but on no account should the sauce be allowed to boil. Remove the remainder of the sauce from the fire, add a few small pieces of butter, not quite 1 oz. altogether, and strain over the birds. Garnish with the cooked mushrooms, a few sliced truffles, and *croûtons* of fried bread.

LA SAUCE ESPAGNOLE

Ingredients: To make about 1 quart of sauce—¼ lb. of butter, 4 ozs. carrots, ¼ lb. onions, ¼ lb. lean gammon, a few parsley stalks, a sprig of thyme, a small bayleaf, 2 ozs. flour, 1 gill of white wine, 3 tablespoonfuls of tomato purée, 2 ozs. mushroom peelings, 2 tablespoons Madeira, $1\frac{1}{2}$ quarts good stock.

Method : Cut the vegetables in dice, put the butter in a saucepan and when melted add the vegetables. Simmer gently till the veg. are slightly coloured, then add the flour, mix well with a wooden spoon and simmer gently till the flour begins to brown. Then add very gradually the white wine and the stock. Bring to the boil, add the mushrooms and the tomato purée and simmer very gently for 1 hour, skimming carefully as the scum rises. Now strain into another saucepan through a sieve, replace on the fire, bring to the boil and again skim most carefully, as the sauce should be entirely free from grease. When finished, the sauce should be reduced to 1 quart. Remove from the fire, add the Madeira and strain once more. This sauce will keep for several days in a cool place and can be used as required for many dishes.

After reading through a number of cookery books on this subject I am amazed at the inaccuracies. One book recommends brent geese and another insists ruffs and reeves should be eaten in May. It seems both books were published with no regard for the Wild Birds Protection Acts.

Soften chopped onion in the butter—add 3, 4, 5, and then mix with $\frac{1}{2}$ pint of good gravy. Bring slowly to the boil.

MALLARD WITH ARTICHOKES

1 mallard, 2 lb. ground artichokes. Dash pepper, 1 tabsp. butter, 1 saltspoon salt, 1 tabsp. chopped shallots and parsley.

Season duck as for roasting. Scrape artichokes thoroughly and leave whole. Put butter into covered roaster—brown duck. Grate artichokes and add with salt, pepper, parsley and shallots. Stir over slow heat and then into slow oven until duck is tender and artichokes are very soft and brownish in colour. This takes about an hour. Remove and quarter duck and serve on bed of ground artichokes.

DUCKS AU MADÈRE

4 small or 2 big duck.   1 teasp. Worcestershire sauce.
5 drops Tabasco.   2 cups sweet wine.
$\frac{1}{2}$ lb. butter.

Brown ducks in hot butter. Add sauce and wine, salt to taste. Let the wine cook out of the ducks or until it cooks down into the gravy and serve with the ducks.

SALMIS DE CANARD SAUVAGE

From French section of *Recipes of All Nations* by Countess Morphy. This dish is of very ancient origin and the recipe she gives is the traditional one. In some parts of France, red wine is used instead of white.

Ingredients: 1 or 2 wild duck, 1 gill of white wine, 1 gill of Sauce Espagnole (see following recipe), 3 or 4 shallots, $\frac{1}{4}$ lb. mushrooms, a few truffles (optional), 1 liqueur glass of brandy, 1 bay leaf, a sprig of thyme, salt and pepper.

Method: Roast the birds and while they are being roasted, put the chopped shallots, the herbs, etc., in a small saucepan with the white wine, and simmer gently till reduced to about one third. When the birds are nearly done, carve them carefully, removing all flesh from carcase. Place the pieces of duck in a saucepan with the brandy and set alight. When the brandy is burnt out add a little Espagnole sauce, cover with a lid and keep warm. Chop up the bones or pound them in a mortar and add to the wine and shallots, mixing well. Add the remaining Espagnole sauce, stir well and simmer gently and skim carefully. Cook for about 20 minutes. Five minutes before serving, strain half the sauce over the pieces of duck and place the saucepan over a slow fire, but on no account should the sauce be allowed to boil. Remove the remainder of the sauce from the fire, add a few small pieces of butter, not quite 1 oz. altogether, and strain over the birds. Garnish with the cooked mushrooms, a few sliced truffles, and *croûtons* of fried bread.

LA SAUCE ESPAGNOLE

Ingredients: To make about 1 quart of sauce—$\frac{1}{4}$ lb. of butter, 4 ozs. carrots, $\frac{1}{4}$ lb. onions, $\frac{1}{4}$ lb. lean gammon, a few parsley stalks, a sprig of thyme, a small bayleaf, 2 ozs. flour, 1 gill of white wine, 3 tablespoonfuls of tomato purée, 2 ozs. mushroom peelings, 2 tablespoons Madeira, 1½ quarts good stock.

Method : Cut the vegetables in dice, put the butter in a saucepan and when melted add the vegetables. Simmer gently till the veg. are slightly coloured, then add the flour, mix well with a wooden spoon and simmer gently till the flour begins to brown. Then add very gradually the white wine and the stock. Bring to the boil, add the mushrooms and the tomato purée and simmer very gently for 1 hour, skimming carefully as the scum rises. Now strain into another saucepan through a sieve, replace on the fire, bring to the boil and again skim most carefully, as the sauce should be entirely free from grease. When finished, the sauce should be reduced to 1 quart. Remove from the fire, add the Madeira and strain once more. This sauce will keep for several days in a cool place and can be used as required for many dishes.

After reading through a number of cookery books on this subject I am amazed at the inaccuracies. One book recommends brent geese and another insists ruffs and reeves should be eaten in May. It seems both books were published with no regard for the Wild Birds Protection Acts.

CHAPTER 32

FAMOUS WILDFOWLERS OF THE PAST

by The Late Henry James, M.D.

Late WAGBI Committee Member and Chairman, Frodsham and District Wildfowlers' Club.

> *This is the place. Stand still, my steed.*
> *Let me review the scene,*
> *And summon from the shadowy Past*
> *The forms that once have been.*
> —LONGFELLOW.

COLONEL PETER HAWKER

WHILE it might be questioned that Hawker was the first to "discover" wildfowling as a sport, there is no doubt that he was the first to write a comprehensive treatise on the subject. His *Instructions to Young Sportsmen* and his "Diaries" are to be found wherever English is spoken and constitute a "monument more enduring than bronze". Born on 24th December, 1786, he was gazetted Cornet of the 1st Royal Dragoons in 1801. Six years later he fought under Wellington in the Peninsular War, and at the battle of Talavera received a severe wound of the thigh which troubled him all his life, and as early as 1813 put an end to his active career in the army. Instead of soldiering in the Low Countries and being present at Wellington's final victory at Waterloo in 1815, we find him almost every day of the season and many nights as well, engaged in his beloved wildfowling and game shooting.

From the age of sixteen he kept a diary and recorded almost everything that happened to him, not only shooting, angling, matters of health, travel and visits to gunsmiths, but even music of which he was a skilled exponent. This record he kept in detailed manner for fifty years—almost to the day of his death on 4th August, 1853.

Sir Ralph Payne-Gallwey writing in *Instructions to Young Sportsmen* many years later stated, "It is a book which for terseness, accuracy and original information is without an equal." This is a rather singular comment for, as will be seen later, Payne-Gallwey himself in editing the Hawker "Diaries" in 1893 is shown to be anything but accurate, if not indeed, misleading. Whether this was intentional or not, we can only surmise—if intentional, the reason must always remain obscure. However this may be, a false impression of Hawker was created which portrayed him, in the words of a modern wildfowling author as a "butcher and nothing else". This latter writer adds that at times Hawker's Diary is "quite sickening". However, it is pleasant to record that this acidulous impression did not last, for five years later this same sportsman described Hawker as "so lovable, so English, so Pickwickian".

Eric Parker in his edition of the Hawker "Diaries" (1931) which was based on the original typescript shows that unfavourable conclusions regarding Hawker are extravagant and unjust.

Hawker lived in the days of the muzzle-loader—flintlock and percussion. It is interesting to note that it was in 1853, the year of his death, that the first breech-loader, the Lefaucheux pinfire gun was put on the English market. Hawker never tired of experiments in the manufacture of guns and punts, and on days when he could not go shooting owing to his thigh wound, he was querulous and unhappy. He writes that when "almost fainting" and as "nervous as a cat" he would still go out and in spite of his physical suffering handle his gun effectively. On another occasion he records that "though half dead I never made more extraordinary shots". He cared little what the weather was like. Apparently gales had no terror for him—he describes some of them as Siberian!

One entry in his diary reads: "Confined to my bedroom and for the greater part of the time to my bed, in spite of cupping poultices, fomentations, colchicum and calomel." Another: "Weathercock with head where tail ought to be; dark, damp, rotten, cut-throat-looking weather . . . doctors galloping in every direction; an armistice from guns and shooting; the poor punters driven to oyster dredging, eel picking, day labour or beggary; not even the pop-off of a Milford snob to be heard in that unrivalled garrison of tit shooters."

Hawker was a keen student of the science of shooting and ballistics—slow to adopt a new device till he had thoroughly weighed up its worth. As a marksman he was supreme. One must remember the handicaps under which he shot. His guns were heavy and long barelled, and he had to reload from the muzzle after each shot. To these must be added the suffering from his wound which was liable to constantly recurring discharges of pus. Throughout his writings, his advice to the shooting novice is clear, crisp and concise. If, as Eric Parker remarks, the word breech-loader is substituted for muzzle-loader, it would do for the modern shooter all that it did for our forefathers one hundred years ago.

Eleven editions of the *Instructions* were published, the first in 1814, the tenth and eleventh, after his death, by his son. The ninth and best edition was published in 1853 shortly before his death. It is the "Diaries", however, which have the greater interest for the majority of wildfowlers. Let us here consider briefly their history.

A certain amount of mystery attaches to their survival. They remained unread and unknown for forty years after Hawker's death. In 1893 Sir R. Payne-Gallwey was asked, apparently by the Hawker family, to write an Introductory Notice of the author and edit extracts from the original volumes. There were in all thirty-four of these! When published it was assumed that the Payne-Gallwey edition was a digest of the recordings of Hawker himself, and that the numbers of wildfowl and game killed were actually shot by Hawker to his own gun; indeed on reading the text it is impossible to arrive at any other conclusion.

It should be remembered that Hawker's original records were never in-

Plate 55. Stanley Duncan

Plate 56. Wild-shot intersex mallard (*left*) and teal

Plate 57. Three wigeon and a shoveler drake

Plate 58. A pair of gadwall—the drake leading

Plate 59. Wigeon flighting

tended for publication. The Payne-Gallwey edition consisted of two handsome volumes which soon went out of print. Eric Parker relates that even after the First World War he had difficulty in finding a copy. He thought it lamentable that such a wealth of shooting lore should remain more or less a closed book to the modern shooting man. He recounts further how that when he had read them, he was at a loss to solve the mystery of why a man so "genial and high spirited" as Hawker should always prefer to go shooting alone and shun the company of his friends, not even taking with him his henchmen or his game-keepers. If for no other reason the size and weight of his bags would seem to demand an attendant. His wound, too, which caused him such physical suffering would almost necessitate a companion.

Eric Parker determined to search for anyone who might be able to clear up this obscurity and eventually discovered a great-grandson— Mr. Peter Ryves Hawker, then living in France. This Mr. Hawker when he returned to England found amongst his possessions portraits, books, various papers dealing with his great-grandfather and unexpectedly the typescript copy of the "Diaries" from which Sir R. Payne-Gallwey had worked, together with proofs from printers. Eric Parker then goes on to say that here was the answer to a riddle that had puzzled him ever since he first read the Payne-Gallwey volumes published in 1893. He discovered that for some unaccountable reason Payne-Gallwey had not only omitted to a great extent the names of the Colonel's shooting companions, including the second Mrs. Hawker, but ascribed to Hawker alone the total head of wildfowl or game killed. He gives numerous instances in the Diaries of where this occurred.

To quote an example, Sir R. Payne-Gallwey (1893) records Hawker's entry in his diary for 7th September, 1850 as follows: "My bag was 12 partridges and 2 hares. Scent worse than ever but no reason to complain as I killed all that it was possible to kill and took the lead of other parties."

Eric Parker (1931) records Hawker's entry *for the same date*: "Sent Charles Heath to scour Bullingham again but did not follow him till the afternoon. My bag was 12 partridges and 2 hares—*his 10 birds*. Scent worse than ever, but no reason to complain as *we* killed all that it was possible to kill and took the lead of other parties." This is one of scores of occasions where Payne-Gallwey fails to make it clear that Heath, Hawker's banking friend was present although, in this instance, he does not credit Heath's birds to Hawker's gun.

Let it be remembered that both these commentators took their information from the same source. Thus it is not surprising that some who have read only the account given by Payne-Gallwey have concluded that Hawker was an egotist and boasted of his own accomplishments. Through his researches Eric Parker has produced evidence to dispel this unsavoury impression.

In 1943 he further discovered that the original "Diaries", which for long were supposed lost, had like so many of our treasures, found their way to the United States. J. C. Gow relates that the late David Wagstaff, a noted American collector of sporting works, bought them from a London bookseller and presented them in 1945 to the library of Yale University. It is interesting to speculate how they came into the bookseller's hands!

L

CHARLES ST. JOHN

Charles St. John, a name inseparably connected with that entrancing record of natural history—*Wild Sports and Natural History of the Highlands*—was born at Chailey in Sussex on 3rd December, 1809. He was grandson of the second Viscount Bolingbroke. A schoolfellow described him as having from early days a zoological "bump". At his boarding school he at various times kept squirrels, guinea-pigs or rabbits and was never without livestock of some kind. He was in due course appointed to a clerkship in the Treasury, but this sort of life had no appeal to him and after a few years he settled down at Rosehall in Sutherland in a house left him by his cousin, the late Lord Bolingbroke. He lived here a more or less secluded life, and could indulge to his heart's content in shooting and fishing. Impecunious, he married at an early age a woman of fortune, and so was enabled to live the life of a sportsman and naturalist in the Highlands.

Morayshire was soon to claim him and, surrounded by mountain sport and a game country, the sea and numerous lochs, he spent a great part of his active life. After a time a neighbour of similar tastes who had spent much time in his company, and noted his keen sporting outlook and quality of accurate observation induced him to write short essays on mixed sport and natural history. At first St. John ridiculed the suggestion and did not think he could write anything which people would want to read. However, during the following winter he agreed to try his hand.

The friend who occasionally wrote articles for *The Edinburgh Quarterly Review* was short of "copy", and with his consent embodied some of St. John's material. Thus was born a story of world-wide fame—"The Muckle Hart of Benmore". The editor of the journal was delighted with it and wrote in such a complimentary strain that it served as seasoning for the shooting lunch which St. John and his friend Jeans shared next day amongst the whins! Jeans relates that St. John rejoiced greatly in the first money he had ever made by his own exertions, for of course they shared the proceeds. On his next visit to London the series of chapters were sold to John Murray who published them as *Wild Sports and Natural History of the Highlands*. I wonder if there is any shooting man who has not read this fascinating volume!

After a few years (1849) St. John moved his household to Elgin and here in the three following years he reached the summit of his sport and literary pursuits. Every walk furnished instances to record in his diary of nature study. His boys, when school permitted, were his constant companions, and both inherited his flair for drawing, sketching and water-colour painting of birds and fishes. Although leading a healthy and temperate life, when on his way out to shoot in December 1853, he was struck down by cerebral haemorrhage and became paralysed down his left side. He never recovered the use of his limbs but he rallied sufficiently to allow his moving to Brighton and later Southampton.

Until the last he hoped to return to his native heath and the scenes of his early sport, but this was not to be. He died at Woolston near Southampton on

12th July, 1856. He had asked to have the skull of Leo, his favourite retriever, placed within his coffin and this was done. Like many who have been devoted to animals, he was a most lovable man of broad views—an outstanding naturalist, a meticulous observer, and one who never recorded a fact of which he was not absolutely sure. St. John has been severely criticized over the matter of the osprey—that he had a part in the destruction of this great predator cannot be denied. He was a man of strong likes and dislikes, and with strange contradictions. The odd thing is that St. John realized the importance of its preservation, and yet, when opportunity presented, this side of his nature seemed to desert him and he put forward plausible reasons for its destruction. He had said that he knew no reason why the "poor osprey should be persecuted as it is quite harmless and lives wholly on fish", but later excused his shooting it by enlarging on the price put on its skin and the commercial interest that was involved.

Strangely enough, whilst vowing vengeance on the hooded crow, St. John speaks in glowing terms of the great black-headed gull—surely one of the worst predators we have? He stated that the "hoodie" was the only bird against whom he waged an unpitying warfare. Many regard *A Tour of Sutherland* as St. John's greatest literary work. It is noted for the recording of many interesting observations of natural history.

COLONEL CHAMPION RUSSELL

Colonel Russell was one of the greatest of the wildfowlers of the nineteenth century. An Essex man, he was a keen naturalist, especially where wildfowl were concerned, and all his life devoted much time to the welfare of birds and animals. It is strange that, like Marryat in the fly-fishing world, he left no personal record of his interests in this direction—no papers, not even notes of ornithological interest with the exception of some letters to *The Times* and the *Field*.

In his day, making a collection of rare birds was a popular hobby, and he had visited both Africa and America on this quest. Counties and County Boroughs still made their own close seasons and he took a leading part in having the close time for Essex altered. The commonest species of wild geese frequenting the estuary of the Essex Blackwater and adjacent coasts was the brent, and in hard winters enormous numbers would congregate on that coast. Fishermen-fowlers were heard to remark: "There are acres of them." Punt-gunning was a very popular pastime and would frequently account for huge bags. It is recorded that on an occasion in the winter of 1860 when "punting" with thirty other gunners, all firing together at an arranged signal, Colonel Russell killed 704 geese besides a large number of cripples which escaped and afterwards fell a prey to beachcombers and gulls. At these times he would be the "Admiral" of this creeping flotilla. This is usually regarded as the British punt-gunning record.

Christy, writing in 1890, records that even in Russell's day it was commonly said that the brent geese were not so plentiful as they used to be. This remark repeated *ad nauseam* in immediate post-war years no doubt accounted to a large extent for brent being placed on the protected list in 1954. It should be remembered that brent are essentially sea geese, and that in many instances whilst the coastal areas may appear deserted, large numbers have been identified some miles from land. Col. Russell remarked that brent geese used sometimes to remain all the winter without coming within sight of land. He also stated that he never saw a brent goose asleep—day and night they were always alert whether near the coast or far out at sea. He was a noted wildfowl shot, and had one of the biggest guns used on the Essex coast. It is said that in forty-five years of sport, he lost only one season when absent in America. Versatile in the extreme, he was a skilled photographer, yachtsman and chemist.

Col. Russell was also an excellent taxidermist, had punts built to his own design and to the poor homeless vagabond was kindly and generous almost to a fault. With his wide experience, it is much to be regretted that he left no records of ornithological interest. He died in 1887, in his sixty-seventh year.

SNOWDEN SLIGHTS

Snowden Slights, who was called the "last of the Yorkshire wildfowlers", lived at East Cottingwith in the Derwent Valley. He left no notes, and so it fell to one of his friends to tell us most of what we know about him. Second son of John Slights who taught the village school, Snowden first saw the light in July 1830, and from about the age of nine years accompanied his father when he went punt-gunning. He started work as a basket maker. This precarious calling showed poor returns, and when winter came he spent every available hour in the pursuit of wildfowl to help his livelihood.

For a time the years were ones of struggle. A planting of osiers which he had scraped up his savings to purchase was destroyed by floods, and he was thrown back more than ever on wildfowling to obtain a living. However, as the years passed, his reputation as a man of high principles was established. When he landed on hard times, the local landowners gave him facilities which helped him to weather the difficult years. A man of few words, benign and generous, he was a most astute observer, and there was little in the habits of wildfowl with which he was not familiar. Added to this was an iron constitution and first-rate skill as a weather prophet. Nature was kind to him, and even when in the "sere and yellow", and the years had shrunk his figure, his back was still straight, his mind alert and his eyes were bright.

Towards the end he was heard to remark that a professional fowler's life though full of hardships was also full of charm. Sometimes after a fruitless expedition he would come home, his clothes frozen on him and feeling half dead, he would have to be assisted to the fire and thawed out. Then after something to sustain the inner man he would turn in and sleep the clock round.

Owing to its formation the Derwent Valley was subject to floods and, the river having a long tidal course, both factors contributed to form an isolated area at East Cottingwith which is flat and offered sanctuary to duck and waders arriving from the coast. Snowden Slights was primarily and outstandingly a punt-gunner; flighting had little or no appeal for him, and it was seldom that he engaged in it. He always maintained that one shot at flight did more to unsettle the fowl than half a dozen from a punt. Others have suggested that the reason for this may be that duck have settled down before a punt-gun is fired at them, whereas at flight they are *en route* to their destination and their senses are strained in watchfulness.

Snowden Slights used to say: "I like the sport but I don't shoot for sport as much as for a living." His favourite shot with the punt-gun was at the duck on the ice at a range of thirty-five to forty yards—next to this a shot at similar range as they were rising from the water. Notwithstanding his fondness for punting he was a keen lover of guns of all types and was an accomplished shot with a shoulder gun.

His cottage was a veritable armoury and as long as he could scrape the necessary funds together he was constantly buying or exchanging fowling pieces. These varied from one weighing 140 lbs. used solely for punt-gunning, down to a little double fourteen-bore muzzle-loader which was his favourite fowling-piece. Snowden collected in all twenty-eight guns, and it is said that they occupied a part of his heart comparable with that of his children. Some of them eventually came to rest in the museum at York—amongst the number an old blunderbuss short-barrelled and bell-mouthed, which had been used for coach protection.

HENRY COLEMAN FOLKARD

Henry Coleman Folkard, barrister-at-law, was responsible in 1859 for a bulky volume entitled *The Wildfowler*. In the preface he gives his reasons for launching this treatise on the public and takes pains to show that it is not inconsistent with the dignity of a lawyer to follow a sport like wildfowling and to write about it! In the introduction to the fourth edition published thirty-eight years later (1897) he exhibits a querulous outlook, firstly complaining that though he was the sole inventor of this title another purloined it and for several years wrote a series of articles to the *Field* and other newspapers under the same title, and secondly, after pointing out that works on wildfowling were scarce and that Hawker's *Instructions to Young Sportsmen* was almost the only one, he attacks Hawker, declaring that he cannot be relied upon, and that many of his views are erroneous.

Strangely enough he states that Hawker's work was first published in 1824, whereas the first edition saw the light exactly ten years previously. The above series of articles were republished later by the *Field* in a volume entitled *Modern Wildfowling* (1880) by "Wildfowler". This was the *nom de plume* of Lewis Clement, founder and first editor of the *Shooting Times*.

The book is a charming account of the sport, full of common sense and excellent precepts. It has now become extremely scarce. That Folkard did not agree with the theories advanced in these articles is evidenced by the fact that he described them as impracticable. After discussing why comparatively few took up wildfowling as a distinct branch of sport, he came to the conclusion that it was "because it was in reality so little understood". Most amusingly he adds: "In this impression I am borne out by the opinion of Colonel Hawker who says that 'many of the greatest field sportsmen know no more about wildfowl shooting than children'". It will thus be seen that the kindly qualities which we associate with many sportsmen could hardly be attributed to Folkard. He was cantankerous and had an acidulous tongue, or perhaps I should say pen!

As an author and authority on wildfowling he had no small opinion of his own qualifications. He even criticized Daniel's *Rural Sports*, saying that the few intelligible remarks are so cramped and inaccurate that they tend rather to mislead than to instruct the inquirer! It may, however, be said that, although at times responsible for erratic statements, he was an astute observer and recorded many facts not mentioned by other writers.

He was one of the first to emphasize that non-diving and therefore non-fish-feeding waterfowl cannot have a fishy flavour. He also dwelt on the risks attaching to a fall on soft and deep mud if unaccompanied, pointing out that "the only practicable method of getting up from a fall on the ooze is by rolling over on the back so as to draw the arms out of the mud and then by placing one foot with the mud pattern firmly and flatly on the ooze, at the same time pressing both hands on the knee of the leg so raised and giving a cautious but determined spring and so bringing himself on to his legs again." He naïvely adds: "Care should be taken not to fall!"

Other examples of his potted wisdom include: "When away from the mainland don't go far from your punt and never lose sight of it in foggy weather."

"Brent geese when on the wing are known by their black-looking bodies and white rumps." A mere glance through the pages of Folkard's work quickly emphasizes that he was first and foremost a punt-gunner. That he was given to erratic statement will also be noted.

In the company of great wildfowlers of the past where are we to place Folkard? It is difficult to escape the conclusion that though he gave a very comprehensive account of wildfowling in many parts of the world, much of the subject matter is academic and seems to lack the personal touch. One searches almost in vain for an instance where he is quoted by later writers on the sport—in fact I can call to mind only one who acknowledged him in this way, and, oddly enough, this was Lewis Clement, whom he attacked.

SIR RALPH PAYNE-GALLWEY, BART.

In the annals of British sport there are not many wildfowlers with a reputation which could be compared with that of Sir Ralph Payne-Gallwey. As an all-round shooting man he had few equals, and was the foremost authority on gunning punts and their design. His specifications for the building of these craft are still widely followed.

Born in 1848 this "Eccentric Irish Genius", as he has been called, was a sportsman of many parts. A large photograph taken at his home, Thirkleby Park in Yorkshire, shows him in his gunroom surrounded by the implements of his sport. The photograph is autographed by him, and on the reverse he explains the reason why it was taken. (Plate 53.)

Payne-Gallwey was the author of several works—his first and most famous being *The Fowler in Ireland* written in 1882 when he was thirty-four. This is an exhaustive treatise on wildfowling, packed with instructive fowling episodes. It has now become scarce. His *Letters to Young Shooters* in 3 volumes (1890–1896) deals with shooting in its several branches, the third volume being given entirely to wildfowling. In this series he left us a wealth of shooting doctrine, a treasure in itself, and without which no shooting library would be complete.

As an exponent of the art of shooting Payne-Gallwey had few, if any, equals. One often hears eminent shooting men say, "I cannot explain exactly what I do, or how I do it." In contrast, Payne-Gallwey's instructions are clear and comprehensive and leave the reader in no doubt as to the methods he employed.

Payne-Gallwey's *Book of Duck Decoys* appeared in 1886, and about the same time he collaborated with the late Lord Walsingham in the well-known "Badminton" volumes on shooting. His place in the art of shooting and ballistics is exemplified in a work of outstanding merit—*High Pheasants in Theory and Practice* (1913)—the last of his researches to be given to his fellow sportsmen and one which leaves no doubt of his immense experience of shooting and the zeal with which he carried out his ballistic experiments.

I have referred elsewhere to Payne-Gallwey's editing of the "Hawker Diaries". He died at Thirkleby Park, Yorkshire, at the age of sixty-eight.

ABEL CHAPMAN

To students of big-game hunting, shooting, wildfowling and natural history, a glamour still hangs about the name of Abel Chapman. One of the greatest sportsmen of all time, it is recorded that every moment of his leisure he spent in shooting, fishing and the study of wild nature.

A north countryman, he was born at Silkworth Hall, Co. Durham, in 1851, and was the eldest of six sons. From early childhood Chapman was keen to learn. It is said that at ten years old he was an industrious student of the classics and showed a strong bent for natural history. At fourteen he went to Rugby where he formed a lifelong friendship with F. C. Selous. Here his love of the classics was further developed, and even to the end of his life he liked to quote passages from Greek and Latin literature and discuss them with his friends. After leaving Rugby he entered the business of his father—a brewer and wine importer in Sunderland. Shortly afterwards he made journeys to Spain, Portugal and Southern France primarily concerned with the business, but also including sporting interludes of shooting and collecting birds and beasts in the places he visited.

It must not be thought that he was merely a collector of specimens. Shooting was a fetish with him from the first. As soon as he could carry a gun it became almost an object of worship and by means of it he was able to further his study of wild life. He shot his first grouse on 12th August, 1866, when less than fifteen years old. At twenty-one he accounted for his first big game, a wild boar in Sierra de Ronda, Spain.

In his *Wild Spain*, written in collaboration with Walter J. Buck (1893), considered by many to be Chapman's greatest work, he gives an amusing account of the arrival of his gunning punt in Spain and states how the Spanish Customs were as much concerned as if a hostile fleet had appeared off Malaga! They had never seen or heard of anything like it before! Chapman was the first ornithologist to locate the breeding grounds of the flamingo in the marismas of Guadalquivir; in South Africa he was responsible for the founding of the Sabi Game Reserve, now known as the Kruger National Park.

Chapman was known for never making a statement unless he had absolute proof of its truth. His huge collection of trophies he bequeathed to the Hancock Museum in Newcastle upon Tyne.

Always an enthusiastic student of the natural history of the Border Country, he made a permanent home for himself on the North Tyne in 1898. It could scarcely be said that Chapman settled down here, but the quiet and secluded house at Houxty was his home for the remainder of his life.

Chapman was one who took a serious view of life, and maintained a strict self-discipline throughout his long years of activity. Like Oliver Cromwell, he was "thorough" in everything he undertook, a doughty fighter, and one who delighted in argument—but a staunch and loyal friend. Sensitive and tender-hearted, and like some who have spent much of their lives in the wild places of the earth, he was of a shy and retiring nature.

Abel Chapman was unmarried. He died on 23rd January, 1929, a great sportsman and naturalist of the old school—perhaps one of the greatest.

JOHN GUILLE MILLAIS

In the days before films were discovered and photography was in its infancy, the institutes of sport and kindred pursuits were conveyed to many from the brush of the great painters of the Victorian Era—Sir Edwin Landseer and Sir John Everett Millais. Both were accomplished sportsmen, but whilst Landseer was an incomparable animal painter, Millais was a far greater sportsman—angler, game shooter and deerstalker—but even he was surpassed in this respect by his son, John G. Millais, who was in turn soldier, sailor, a British Consul, artist, zoologist, author and landscape gardener.

This versatile Scot had a philosophy all his own and lived it to the full. "If variety is the spice of life, and a living can be made, give me the open spaces. It is far better than grinding all one's days at an office stool to amass wealth which once gained cannot always be enjoyed. The great thing in life is to live." Here we have in his own words the principles which underlay the life of one of the greatest big-game hunters, wildfowlers and naturalists of all time. Calm, collected and determined, he seems to have held fast to this doctrine all his life. That he had most indulgent parents even in early youth is obvious.

Born in 1865, he became a collector of British birds at nine years old and began to procure these with a catapult. At ten years he met with an accident when using an old 12-bore muzzle-loader. He was firing at an oystercatcher in the river Tay, when the nipple was blown out and cut his cheek. Soon afterwards he was presented by his father with a 20-bore fully choked, with which he shot the greater part of his collection in the estuaries of the Eden and Tay.

Between the years 1880 and 1890 he made many visits to the Orkneys, at that time shooting grounds little known to the public, and at twenty-two he had already killed a pair or two of almost all the birds resident in summer in the British Islands.

Millais soon became a brilliant shot. In 1885 his old flat-coated retriever "Jet" pointed in some bracken. Up got a brace of woodcock which he shot with a right and left. Hardly had he reloaded when another brace rose and he got both. Just as he was reloading and commenting to the keeper on his luck, a fifth bird rose which he killed with a long shot.

About 1886 he began to illustrate books and from then onwards his interests in this direction increased. He got opportunities to develop as an artist and naturalist—callings which he afterwards so greatly adorned. His father wished him to enter the army and after a crammer course in London, to the surprise of his tutor, he qualified in the preliminary examination and was commissioned in the Seaforth Highlanders. He was fortunate in having an indulgent Colonel where sport was concerned and leave was readily granted.

Previous to this, at the age of eleven he went to Marlborough, where a fellow pupil gave him special tuition in the art of catapulting and its ballistics! Commenting on his four years there he relates: "I worked so hard to improve my shooting—being perfectly absorbed in the hunting and preservation of my specimens—that I soon surpassed my master and became the leader of a gang of what my tutors described as undisciplined young reprobates." He naïvely adds, "I was the only boy who ever went through Marlborough and was birched by the headmaster four times (all for catapulting) without being expelled!"

He served five years in the Seaforths during which period he published the well-known *Game Birds and Shooting Sketches*. However, he soon began to realize that a military life was not his métier. He became restless and had set his heart on Africa.

If Millais could be with us today, forty years later, his confidence in the trusteeship of the white man would sustain a severe shock! He makes the interesting comment that "Like my friend, F. C. Selous, the book that first influenced me was Baldwin's *African Hunting*", adding that this volume used to be read to him and his brother on Sunday afternoons at Queen's Gate, when they would sit entranced and listen to adventurers in Africa.

Strangely enough, though a man of sanguine temperament, Millais had in common with Selous and Neumann a sense of the supernatural, as may be seen from reading his *Newfoundland and its Untrodden Ways*.

One of Millais's best-known works and one of much charm is his *Wildfowler in Scotland* (1900). This details many of his early wildfowling experiences and has now become scarce. Much wildfowling lore can be gleaned from its pages and it embodies the conclusions of one who weighed his words carefully.

He writes: "It is commonly accepted that big-game hunting, especially the chase of the lion, buffalo and elephant, is the most dangerous of all forms of sport. Personally I am inclined to doubt it, and should say that wildfowling in a punt in the northern firths is almost equally, if not quite, as easy a method of losing one's life. English and Irish waters are comparatively safe, but in the northern fifths the wildfowler will often be caught in sudden squalls when off poling ground and then nothing but skill and luck can save him. Never venture off poling ground in a punt in Scotland when the wind is in the south and be slow to do so if it is in the north. The game is not worth the candle, even though the firth may for the moment be as still as glass, and a big tempting pack may be floating down with the tide. . . . In a few seconds the placid waters may be lashed into a seething sheet of foam. As in big-game hunting rashness is the ever-present danger, and if pluck overrides judgement there is sometimes no second chance." If proof of this is needed, a walk through the cemetery in Nairobi will be convincing!

In wild-goose shooting Millais was an advocate of heavy bores and recorded many exciting occasions with his favourite 8-bore. It is interesting in this connexion to remember that there are about as many pellets of No. 2 shot in an 8-bore $3\frac{1}{2}$-inch case as there are No. 6 shot pellets in a 12-bore case, with the additional advantage that a pellet of No. 2 is far more likely to stop a goose. Thus wounding is much less likely to occur here than in countries like America where 8-bores are prohibited.

STANLEY DUNCAN, F.Z.S., 1878–1954

Son of an engineer, wildfowler and naturalist, not surprisingly Stanley Duncan followed these occupations. Further advances in these fields and for himself an international reputation as an authority in his subjects, were due solely to his conscientious sincerity in everything he did.

At the age of sixteen he began contributing to the *Shooting Times* and other sporting magazines and papers, thereby making friends throughout the British Isles who supported him when, with his personal friends, he founded the Wildfowlers' Association of Great Britain and Ireland in 1908.

WAGBI had Stanley Duncan as its secretary for over forty years and throughout the two World Wars. He was helped by his executive committees with clerical assistance firstly from a Mr Dunderdale, then in turn from four daughters of an original member and, for some time, his eldest son Cyril.

Realizing that wildfowling problems were a national matter, he dealt with any trouble by correspondence with the appropriate authority wherever and whenever it arose.

Although an engineer, he spent most of his spare time wildfowling, or attending meetings in the interests of WAGBI. Being descended from the Downeys, the Victorian Royal Photographers, he was able to illustrate *The Complete Wildfowler*, his classic book written jointly with Guy Thorne, and other writings with his own paintings, drawings and photographs.

He made, or modified, most of his punt-guns, having made two single guns from Sir Ralph Payne-Gallwey's double breech-loading punt-gun, and he designed no less than ten duck punts. He even began a motorized submersible one which he never completed. His last punt, a large double boat to carry the now famous two-inch-bore gun which he made, was eventually sold to James Robertson Justice, who entertained the Duke of Edinburgh to a morning's punt-gun shooting.

In the middle 1920s he rented two acres of land near Hull, employed a man full-time, made his own incubators and brooders and, with the help of his three sons and their friends, built pens for his hand-reared wild geese and duck. He experimented in rearing partridge, and pheasant, releasing the birds on to the 500-acre shoot that he shared with his friend, Trevor Field. The shoot was ideally situated, adjoining the Upper Humber just below the confluence of the Trent and Ouse. These waters are now The Humber Wildfowl Refuge.

In 1923, along with many other famous names, Stanley Duncan started "The Sports Protection Association", later taken under the wing of Nicholas Everett's "Field Sports and Game Guild" from which evolved "The British Field Sports Society" as we know it today.

Stanley Duncan broadcast five times on his subject of wildfowling, giving, without artificial aids, the bird calls used to bring his quarry within range, a gift that made him and his brother Norman famous. He tested prototype sporting guns, for firms such as B.S.A., and for many years ran the "Information Bureau" for the *Shooting Times*, a magazine to which he contributed regularly for sixty years. He bred, and trained many retrievers, some of which he exported to America, kept a loft of top-strain homing pigeons, started a successful gunsmith business for his sons and founded, with Trevor Field, "The Hull Gun Club" with one of the first skeet layouts outside London. He was also an able taxidermist.

As age took its toll, he relinquished his secretaryship of WAGBI, having made a brave effort to take over and re-establish for the Association defunct duck decoys at Ashby Golf Course, near Scunthorpe, and another near Selby, for the catching and ringing of wildfowl. The task proved too much for him, but until his death he attended the meetings concerning the Wild Birds Protection Bill as the representative for WAGBI, his brainchild.

A BIBLIOGRAPHY OF WILDFOWL
AND WILDFOWLING

ALPHERAKY, SERGIUS
  The Geese of Europe and Asia   1905
ARNOLD, RICHARD
  The Shoreshooter   1953
  The Shoreshooter's Handbook   1955
ATKINSON-WILLES, G. (Ed.)
  Wildfowl in Great Britain   1963

BARCLAY-SMITH, PHYLLIS
  A Book of Ducks   1951
BARBER, JOEL
  Wildfowl Decoys U.S.A.   1934
BARSKE, P. (ed.)
  The Black Duck: Evaluation, Management and Research   1969
BATTEN, H. MORTIMER
  Woodlore for Young Sportsmen   1922
  ((Wildfowling in Norfolk)
"B.B."
  The Sportsman's Bedside Book   1937
  The Countryman's Bedside Book   1941
  Sky Gipsy   1942
  The Idle Countryman   1943
  The Wayfaring Tree   1945
  Letters from Compton Deverill   1950
  Tides Ending   1953
  Dark Estuary   1953
BENSUSAN, S. L.
  A Countryside Chronicle   1907
BOLSTER, R. C.
  Driven Duck   No date
BOOTH, E. T.
  *Rough Notes on the Birds Observed during twenty-five years shooting
  and collecting in the British Islands*, 3 vols.   1881–87
BRADFORD, CHARLES
  The Wildfowlers   1901
BRATBY, M.
  Grey Goose   1939
BROWN, P.
  Birds in the Balance   1965
BRUETTE, WILLIAM
  American Duck Goose and Brant Shooting   1938
BUXTON, A.
  The King in his Country   1955

CADMAN, ARTHUR
  Tales of a Wildfowler   1957
  Goose Shooting   1963
  Shouldergunning for Duck   1963
CHAPMAN, ABEL
  Bird Life of the Borders   1889
  Wild Spain   1893
  The Art of Wildfowling   1896
  Wild Norway   1897
  Unexplored Spain   1910
  The Borders and Beyond   1924
  Retrospect   1928
  Memories of Fourscore Years Less Two   1930
CLEMENT, LEWIS
  Modern Wildfowling   1880
COLES, C.
  Game Conservation in a Changing Countryside   1968
COLQUHOUN, JOHN
  The Moor and the Loch: Wildfowl Shooting in the Highlands.   1840
CONWAY, JAMES
  Recollections of Sport: Wildfowl Shooting   1902
CORNISH, C. J.
  Nights with an Old Gunner   1897
  Wild England of Today   1895
COWARD, T. A.
  The Fauna of Cheshire and Liverpool Bay   1910
  (*The Dee as a Wildfowl Resort* by J. A. DOCKRAY)
CRAWFORD, J. H.
  The Wild Life of Scotland   1896
COY KENDALL, ROLF W.
  Wildfowling at a Glance   1967

DANIEL, REV. W. B.
  "Rural Sports", Vol. 3. *Wildfowling*   1801
DALGETY, G. T.
  Wildfowling (Sportsman's Library)   1937
DAWSON, MAJOR K.
  Letters to Young Sportsmen   1920
  Marsh and Mudflat   1931
DAY, J. WENTWORTH
  The Modern Fowler   1934
  Sporting Adventure   1934
  Sport in Egypt   1938
  Harvest Adventure   1946
  Wild Wings and Some Footsteps   1948
  Coastal Adventure   1949
  Marshland Adventure   1950
  Broadland Adventure   1951
  A History of the Fens   1954
DAVIES, G. CHRISTOPHER
  Peter Penniless   1884

DELACOUR, J.
The Waterfowl of the World — 1959–64

DE SCHNEIDAUER, T. R.
Cygnes et Oies Sauvages — 1961

DIXON, CHARLES
The Game Birds and Wildfowl of the British Islands — 1893

DOBIE, W. G. M.
Winter and Rough Weather — 1938

DROUGHT, J. B.
Green Memory — 1937
Successful Shooting — 1948
A Sportsman looks at Eire — No date

DUNCAN, STANLEY, and THORNE, GUY
The Complete Wildfowler — 1911 and 1950

DUNSANY, LORD
My Ireland — 1937

DUTT, W. A.
The Norfolk Broads — 1903
Wild Life in East Anglia — 1908

EDINBURGH, H.R.H. THE DUKE OF,
Birds from the Britannia — 1966

EINARSEN, ARTHUR S.
Black Brant—Sea Goose of the Pacific — 1966

ELLIOTT, DANIEL G.
Wildfowl in North America — 1898

EMERSON, P. H.
Wild Life on a Tidal Water — 1890

ENNION, E. A. R.
Adventurers' Fen — 1949

EVERITT, NICHOLAS
Broadland Sport — 1902

FALLON, W. J.
Practical Wildfowling — 1907

FARRINGTON, S. K. Junior
The Ducks Come Back — 1947
(The Story of "Ducks Unlimited")

FINLAY, E.
Down the Creek — 1968

FITZGERALD, GERALD
Pot Luck — 1938

FOLKARD, H. C.
The Wildfowler — 1859

FREUCHEN, PAD SALAMONSEN, F.
The Arctic Year — 1958

FRITH, H. J.
Waterfowl in Australia — 1967

FUR, FEATHER AND FIN SERIES
Wildfowl — 1905

GRIMBLE, AUGUSTUS
  Shooting and Salmon Fishing   1892
GRINNEL, GEORGE B.
  American Duck Shooting   1901

HAMILTON, C. W.
  Shooting Over Decoys, U.S.A.   1923
HAMILTON, COL. J. P.
  Reminiscences of an Old Sportsman   1860
  (Wild geese and wild duck in Ireland, Wales and Canada)
HANSON, H.
  The Giant Canada Goose   1965
HARRISON, JAMES M.
  Bird Taxidermy   1964
  Bristow and The Hastings Rarities Affair   1968
HARRISON, JEFFERY G.
  Estuary Saga   1952
  Pastures New   1954
  A Wealth of Wildfowl   1967
HARTLEY, GILFRID W.
  Wild Sport with Gun, Rifle and Salmon Rod   1903
  Wild Sport and Some Stories   1912
HARTING, JAMES E.
  Hints on Shore Shooting   1871
HAWKER, COL. PETER
  Instructions to Young Sportsmen   1814
  Diary of Col. Peter Hawker, 2 vols. with introduction by Sir R. Payne-
  Gallwey   1893
  Col. Hawker's Shooting Diaries, 1 vol. edited by Eric Parker   1931
HAYNES, WM. BARBER
  Ducks and Duck Shooting   1924
HAZELTON, WM. C.
  Wildfowling Tales   1921
HINE, R. L. and SCHOENFELD, CLAY
  Canada Goose Management   1968
HAILNER, VAN CAMPEN
  A Book on Duck Shooting   1943
HIGSON, DANIEL
  Seafowl Shooting Sketches   1909
HOFFMAN, L. (Ed.)
  Proc. of the Mar Conference   1963
HOLLAND, RAY P.
  Shotgunning in the Lowlands   1945
HORSLEY, TERENCE
  Sporting Pageant   1947
HOCHBAUM, A. L.
  The Canvas back on a Prairie Marsh   1944
  Travels and Traditions of Waterfowl   1955
HUTCHINSON, HORACE
  Shooting, 2 vols.   1903

JANES, EDWARD C.
  Hunting Ducks and Geese   1954
JOHNSGARD, PAUL
  Waterfowl: their biology and natural history   1967
  Waterfowl Behaviour   1968
JOHNSON, A. A. and PAYN, W. H.
  Ornamental Waterfowl   1968
JORDAN, DENHAM
  Annals of a Fishing Village   1891
  Among Wild Birds and their Haunts   1892
  With the Woodlanders and By the Tide   1893
  Woodland Moor and Stream   1896
  In the Green Leaf and the Sere   1896
  Wildfowl and Seafowl of Great Britain   1895
  Drift from Longshore   1898
  (All these works were edited ostensibly by "A Son of the Marshes",
  the *nom de plume* of Denham Jordan)

KEITH, E. C.
  Gun for Company   1937
  A Countryman's Creed   1938
KIRKMAN, F. B.
  British Sporting Birds   1936
KNOX, A. E.
  Game Birds and Wildfowl   1850

LACY, CAPT.
  The Modern Shooter   1842
LEFFINGWELL, WM. B.
  Wildfowl Shooting   1888
  Shooting on Upland Marsh and Stream   1888
LENNOX, LORD WM.
  Recreations of Sportsmen   1862
  (Including Wildfowling in Canada)
LINDUSKA, J. P. and NELSON, A. L. (Eds.)
  Waterfowl Tomorrow   1964
LLOYD, L. L.
  Game Birds and Wildfowl of Sweden and Norway   1866
LONG, WM. J.
  Whose Home is the Wilderness   1907
LYNN-ALLEN
  Rough Shoot   1942

MACQUARRIE, G.
  Stories of the Old Duck Hunters   1968
MACKENTY, J. G.
  Duck Hunting   1953
MACPHERSON, REV. H. A.
  A History of Fowling   1897
"MARKSMAN"
  The Dead Shot   1864

MAYER, ALFRED M.
  Sport with Gun and Rod   1883
  (Wild-goose and wild-duck shooting in Minnesota)
MAXWELL, W. H.
  Wildsports of the West of Ireland, 2 vols.   1832
  Wanderings in the Highlands and Islands, 2 vols.   1844
MCLEAN, C.
MILES, H. D.
  British Field Sports, 2 vols.   1860–70
  (Wildfowling: Shore and Pung-gunning)
MILLAIS, JOHN G.
  The Wildfowler in Scotland   1901
  Natural History of British Surface-Feeding Ducks   1902
  British Diving Ducks, 2 vols.   1913
  Wanderings and Memories   1919
MINER, J.
  Jack Miner and the Birds   1923
MORRIS, BEVERLEY R.
  British Game Birds and Wildfowl   1850

NICHOLS, J. C. M.
  Birds of Marsh and Mere   1926
  Shooting Ways and Shooting Days   No date
  Shooting by Moor Field and Shore   1929
  Wildfowling   1950
NYE, R. SCUDDER
  Scientific Duck Shooting   1895

OATES, W. COAPE
  Wild Ducks   1905
  (On the *jheels* of the North West Provinces)
OLNEY, P.
  *List of European and North African Wetlands of International
  Importance*   1965

PARKER, ERIC
  Shooting Days   1932
PATTEN, C. J.
  The Aquatic Birds of Great Britain and Ireland   1906
PATTERSON, ARTHUR H. ("John Knowlittle")
  Notes of an East Coast Naturalist   1904
  Nature in Eastern Norfolk   1905
  Wild Life on a Norfolk Estuary   1906
  Man and Nature in Tidal Waters   1909
  Wildfowlers and Poachers   1929
  In Norfolk Bird Haunts   1930
  Through Broadland by Sail and Motor   1930
  The Cruise of the "Walrus" on the Broads   No date
PAYNE-GALLWEY, SIR R.
  The Fowler in Ireland   1882
  The Book of Duck Decoys   1886
  Shooting, 2 vols. Badminton Library   1886

PAYNE–GALLWEY, Sir R. (Jointly with Lord Walsingham)
  Letters to Young Shooters, 3 vols.   1890, 1892, 1896
PEEL, C. V. A.
  Wild Sport in the Outer Hebrides   1901
PERRY, RICHARD
  At the Turn of the Tide   1938
PITMAN, IAN
  And Clouds Flying   1947
POWELL, BILL
  My Wild Goose Chase   1954
  The Grey Geese Call   1956
PRICHARD, H. HESKETH
  Sport in Wildest Britain   1921

QUEENY, E. M.
  Prairie Wings   1947

READY, OLIVER G.
  Life and Sport on the Norfolk Broads   1910
  Re-published in 1967 under the title "Countrymen on the Broads."
REYNARDSON, C. T. S. BIRCH
  Sport and Anecdotes of Bygone Days   1887
RICHARDS, COOMBE
  Wild Goose Chase   1948
RIPLEY, D. A.
  A Paddling of Ducks   1959
ROBERTS, E. L.
  Happy Countryman   1956
ROBINSON, BEVERLEY W.
  With Shot Gun and Rifle in N. America   1924
ROSS, ROBERT ERSKINE
  Wings over the Marshes   1948
SALISBURY, HOWARD M.
  Duck Guns, Shooting and Decoying   1947
SALVERDA, Z. (Ed.)
  Proc. of the Second European Meeting on Wildfowl Conservation   1966

SAVORY, ALAN
  Norfolk Fowler   1953
  Lazy Rivers   1955
SCOTT, PETER
  Morning Flight   1935
  Wild Chorus   1936
  Wildfowl of the British Isles   1957
  A Coloured Key to the Wildfowl of the World   1957
  Wildfowl and Esquimos   1953
  The Eye of the Wind   1961
SCOTT, PETER and FISHER, JAMES
  A Thousand Geese   1953
SCOTT, WM. HENRY
  British Field Sports   1820

SEDGWICK, NOEL M.
The Young Shot — 1940
By Covert Field and Marsh — 1946
A Shooting Man's Year — 1948
The Gun on Saltings and Stubble — 1949
Wildfowling and Rough Shooting — 1950
With Dog and Gun — 1951
Shooting Round the Year — 1952
Shooting Wildfowl and Game — 1953
Wader Shooting — 1963
SEIGNE, J. W.
Irish Bogs — 1928
SHACKLETON, K.
Tidelines — 1951
SHAND, ALEX INNES
Shooting (Hadden Hall Library) — 1902
Mountain Stream and Cover — 1897
SHARP, H.
Practical Wildfowling — 1891
SHEPHARD, MICHAEL
Come Wildfowling — 1953
SHARP, HENRY
The Gun Afield and Afloat — 1904
Practical Wildfowling — 1895
Modern Sporting Gunnery — 1906
SMITH, SYDNEY H.
Snowden Slights: Wildfowler — 1913
"SNAPSHOT" Wildfowler (Lewis Clement)
Shooting and Fishing Trips — 1876
(Thames, Medway, Blackwater, Chichester Harbour)
SOUTHGATE and POLLARD
Wildfowl and Waders — 1928
SQUIRE, L.
Wildfowling with a Camera — 1938
ST. JOHN, CHARLES
Wild Sport and Natural History of the Highlands — 1845
A Tour in Sutherland, 2 vols. — 1849
Natural History and Sport in Moray — 1863
STEARNS, PRIDE J.
Duck Stamps — 1967
"STONEHENGE"
British Rural Sports — 1855
Guns and Shooting — 1858, 1859
STOKES, TED
A Sailors Guide to Ocean Birds (Atlantic & Mediterranean) — 1963
SWIFT, J. (Ed.)
Proc. of the First European Meeting on Wildfowl Conservation — 1963

TAVERNER, J. H.
Wildfowl in Hampshire — 1962
TEMPLEWOOD, VISCOUNT
The Unbroken Thread — 1949

TENNYSON, JULIAN
Rough Shooting 1938
THOMAS, B.
The Shooter's Guide 1824
THORBURN, A.
Gamebirds and Wildfowl of Great Britain and Ireland 1923
THORNHILL, R. B.
The Shooting Directory 1804
THORNEYCROFT, NIGEL
Fowler's Moon 1955
TOZER, BASIL
Practical Hints on Shooting 1887
(Wildfowl and Trap Shooting)
TRYON, ALMER and MONAHAN, HUGH
The Wildfowler's Year 1952
TICEHURST, NORMAN F.
The Mute Swan in England 1957

WALSH, ROY E.
Gunning the Chesapeake 1960
Sanctuary Pond 1963
WHITAKER, PETER H.
Approach to Shooting 1954
WHITTAKER, J. RANDALL
Scribblings of a Hedge Row Naturalist 1904
(Contains most interesting Duck Flighting time table)
British Duck Decoys of Today 1918
Wildfowl Trust Annual Reports 1950–69
"WILDFOWLER" (Lewis Clement)
Modern Wildfowling 1880
WILLOCK, COLIN
The Gun-Punt Adventure 1958
The Bedside Wildfowler 1961
Duck Shooting 1962
Kenzie 1962
WINNALL, R. N.
Shore Shooting 1948
WHEELWRIGHT, HORACE WILLIAM (The Old Bushman)
Sporting Sketches 1866

YEATES, G. K. and WINNALL, R. N.
Rough Shooting 1941

INDEX

INDEX

Footnote : Additional information referring to **Chapter 17 WAGBI Duck to Supplement Wild Populations.**

PINTAIL RECOVERY

Details have been received while this book was actually in the press of a drake Pintail released by the Heart of England W.A. on July 13th, 1967 at Frampton-upon-Severn, Gloucestershire and recovered on November 29th, 1969 at Canakkale, Turkey—the first recovery of a WAGBI hand-reared duck in Asia.

RELEASE AREAS OF WAGBI MALLARD

(showing percentages of total released)

SCOTLAND 2·6

N W

N. IRELAND